LABOR'S GREAT WAR

The University of North Carolina Press / Chapel Hill and London

LABOR'S GREAT WAR

The Struggle

for Industrial

Democracy and

the Origins of

Modern American

Labor Relations,

1912–1921

Joseph A. McCartin

© 1997 The University
of North Carolina Press
All rights reserved
Manufactured in the
United States of America
The paper in this book
meets the guidelines for
permanence and durability
of the Committee on
Production Guidelines for
Book Longevity of the
Council on Library Resources.
Library of Congress Catalog-
ing-in-Publication Data
McCartin, Joseph A.
Labor's great war: the
struggle for industrial
democracy and the origins
of modern American labor
relations, 1912–1921 / Joseph
A. McCartin.
p. cm.
Includes bibliographical
references (p.) and index.
ISBN 0-8078-2372-4 (cloth:
alk. paper). —ISBN 0-8078-
4679-1 (pbk.: alk. paper)
1. Labor movement—
United States—History—
20th century. 2. Industrial
relations—United States—
History—20th century.
3. Trade-unions—United
States—History—20th
century. 4. Reconstruction
(1914–1939)—United States.
I. Title.
HD8072.M189 1997
331'.01'120973—DC21
97-9364
                        CIP

01 00 99 98 97
5 4 3 2 1

For my parents, with love and gratitude

CONTENTS

ILLUSTRATIONS & TABLES

ACKNOWLEDGMENTS

The real joy of writing this book was that it introduced me to scores of generous people and encouraged me to lean on faithful friends, colleagues, teachers, and family members without whose encouragement it never would have been written. Their help made the experience not only bearable but deeply enriching as well. So I take pleasure in offering them my thanks.

First, I would like to acknowledge several institutions. A President's Summer Fellowship and an incentive grant from the State University of New York at Geneseo helped fund some of the research for this project. So did grants from the American Philosophical Society, the Fund for Research on Dispute Resolution, and the Bureau of Labor and Management Relations and Cooperative Programs of the U.S. Department of Labor. The Hagley Museum and Library, the Herbert C. Hoover Presidential Library Association, and the Rockefeller Archives Center provided grants for visits to their collections. But, above all, I am grateful to the National Endowment for the Humanities. Its support was indispensable to the research and writing of this book.

From beginning to end, the preparation of this manuscript has been made easier by the professionalism of others. Numerous dedicated archivists helped me navigate through the research that informs this study. Of them, I would like to single out Pete Hoefer of the George Meany Memorial Archives and the capable staff of the National Archives in Washington, D.C., including Bill Creech, Tab Lewis, and especially Jim Cassedy. Jim expertly guided me through the records of the National War Labor Board, helped me find photographs for this book, and tirelessly answered my countless queries. The staff of the University of North Carolina Press has been most gracious, and they have made the task of bringing this book to print easier than I could have imagined. I especially thank executive editor Lew Bateman, his assistant Mary Laur, copyeditor Nancy J. Malone, and editor Pamela Upton for their help.

As I prepared this book over the years, a number of scholars generously shared their comments with me about portions of it that they read or heard in the form of conference papers, talks, draft chapters, or articles. For their insights, I thank Eric Arnesen, Ray Boryczka, John Bracey, David Brody, David Brundage, Cecelia Bucki, Willy Forbath, Pete Forcey, Alan Frank, Larry Gerber, Gary Gerstle, Julie Greene, Maurine Greenwald, Howell John Harris, Victoria Hattam, Thomas Kessner, Daniel Letwin, Nelson Lichtenstein, David Montgomery, Wendy Mink, Mary Nolan, Elisabeth Israels Perry, my longtime friend Doug Reynolds, Stanley Shapiro, Kitty Sklar, Judith Stein, and Shelton Stromquist. Several scholars deserve special mention. Alice Kessler-Harris helped me to see where I was going with this project before I myself knew it, and she encouraged me at an early stage to strive for my own scholarly voice. David Montgomery showed me great kindness as I formulated a thesis that challenged his own work in some respects. Michael Kazin urged me to think about the big picture as I made my final revisions of this book. Eric Arnesen and Dan Letwin helped me hone my understanding of labor history in the South. Dana Frank offered welcome support over the years. And Julie Greene compared notes with me about our mutual interests in Progressive-era labor and politics. My colleagues and students at the University of Rhode Island and the State University of New York at Geneseo also aided me in various important ways. I especially thank C. R. Bailey, Chen Jian, David Tamarin, and Bob Weisbord. The support of all these people taught me what it means to be part of a scholarly "community."

I also offer heartfelt thanks to those who read through the penultimate version of this manuscript and offered valuable advice. I am especially indebted to Robert Zieger for his close and searching reading of my work. He helped me refine my argument, encouraged me to be more direct in my prose, and brought several important citations to my attention. His help was crucial and made the final product a better book. Similarly, my dear friend Colin J. Davis took time from the completion of his own book to read my manuscript thoroughly and to suggest some important clarifications. His generosity was inspirational.

Two other individuals read my manuscript more than once—and after watching its author wrestle with it for years. Without their help, this book would never have been. In many ways the seed for this project was planted in an undergraduate paper that I wrote for Nick Salvatore many years ago. At that time, I came to admire the passion for history that Nick brought to the classroom, to his students' work, and to his own writing. His example first led me to consider graduate school. Without his warm encouragement, sound advice, and friendship, I'm not sure that I would have finished this book. Finally, my graduate adviser, Melvyn Dubofsky, nurtured this project since I first began it as a dissertation under his direction. Mel expressed faith in me as I worked on it over the years, offered critical help at every stage, and provided his own fine example of disciplined scholarship as a guide for me. I am most fortunate to have studied under such an exemplary mentor.

Nor would this book have been possible without the help of family and friends. Doug Ambrose, Ken Millen-Penn, Ben McTernan, Jennifer Miller, and Thom Wermuth read parts of this work, talked with me about it, or simply stood by me when I struggled with it. My aunt Dorothy did not live to see this book, but she never doubted that I would finish it and so helped me to believe the same. My siblings—Anne, Marybeth, Michael, Jude, and Jim—my aunt Alice, and my extended family of in-laws offered love and support. But I will never be able to thank adequately those to whom I dedicate this book, my parents, Marybeth and Joe McCartin. My mother, who read my undergraduate papers when I brought them home each summer, was my first real scholarly audience; she has remained my most sympathetic supporter. My father, who carefully edited my manuscript, became my most reliable reader; his sharp eye helped me better to understand and to express my thoughts. This book goes to them with much love. Finally, this project gave me my most precious gift. Writing it led me to my wife, Diane Reis. Her love guided me through its completion and helped me to see beyond it to the beginning of our life together.

ABBREVIATIONS USED IN THE TEXT

AALD	American Alliance for Labor and Democracy
AASERE	Amalgamated Association of Street and Electric Railway Employees
ACWA	Amalgamated Clothing Workers of America
AFL	American Federation of Labor
ALP	American Labor Party
AMWA	Amalgamated Metal Workers of America
ATWA	Amalgamated Textile Workers of America
CAC	Cantonment Adjustment Commission
CCF	Central Competitive Field
CFI	Colorado Fuel and Iron Company
CFL	Chicago Federation of Labor
CIO	Congress of Industrial Organizations
CIR	Committee on Industrial Relations
CND	Council of National Defense
CPI	Committee on Public Information
CTUA	Commercial Telegraphers Union of America
DNE	Division of Negro Economics of the U.S. Department of Labor
FAES	Federated American Engineering Societies
FLP	Farmer-Labor Party
GE	General Electric Company
IAM	International Association of Machinists
IBEW	International Brotherhood of Electrical Workers
IUMMSW	International Union of Mine, Mill, and Smelter Workers
IWW	Industrial Workers of the World
NAM	National Association of Manufacturers
NCOISW	National Committee for Organizing Iron and Steel Workers

NICB	National Industrial Conference Board
NLDC	National Labor Defense Council
NMTA	National Metal Trades Association
NWLB	National War Labor Board
NWTUL	National Women's Trade Union League
OBU	One Big Union
PMC	President's Mediation Commission
SLAB	Shipbuilding Labor Adjustment Board
SLC	Stockyards Labor Council
SMTC	Schenectady Metal Trades Council
TCI	Tennessee Coal and Iron Company
UGW	United Garment Workers
UMW	United Mine Workers of America
USCIR	United States Commission on Industrial Relations
USES	U.S. Employment Service
USRA	U.S. Railroad Administration
UTW	United Textile Workers
WLCB	War Labor Conference Board
WLPB	War Labor Policies Board

INTRODUCTION.
RECONSIDERING
AMERICAN LABOR
IN THE ERA OF
THE GREAT WAR

What is industrial democracy?
—*Leon C. Marshall, 1918*

On the morning of July 25, 1918, as newspapers headlined a long-awaited American offensive on the battlefields of France, a U.S. Shipping Board official penned a letter to fifteen men who were regarded as authorities on labor. Leon C. Marshall, whose agency coordinated wartime shipbuilding, sat down to write these letters out of his concern about another battle reported in newspapers that July. Across industrial America, strikes were erupting that threatened the nation's war effort. Even as American soldiers fought through the Châtelet Forest, nearly forty thousand New England workers led a campaign of their own, marching out of the massive General Electric (GE) plant in Lynn, Massachusetts, out of the shoe factories in nearby Brockton, out of the shops of Smith and Wesson in Springfield, and out of Rhode Island textile and rubber mills. Although outraged politicians insisted that strikers "be treated as we treat others who give aid and encouragement to the enemy," the walkouts continued.[1]

Marshall was agitated by the threat that these work stoppages posed to his nation's effort in Europe, but he was also disturbed by a pattern that he began to detect in the demands of the strikers. The Lynn GE workers, for example, described themselves as seeking "democracy in industry." This was a perfectly patriotic demand, they insisted, and if a walkout was the only way to secure it, then such a drastic action was "the only course of action that true

Americans can pursue," whatever its consequences overseas. But this demand seemed enormously ambiguous. Indeed, outside Lynn, in hundreds of other settings, workers with diverse aims—those who sought higher wages or union recognition, even those who demanded that the government nationalize their factories—also phrased their demands as pleas for "industrial democracy." So often was that one demand repeated that a perceptive contemporary was soon to describe it as "the most ecumenically satisfying phrase now at large." Marshall was alarmed. To what did this perplexingly protean phrase refer if it could mean all these things? So, with a war raging "over there" and another erupting in the workshops of his nation, Marshall wrote to his correspondents with an urgent question. Just what is "industrial democracy"? he asked. No record of their replies survives.[2]

In a larger sense, however, the years between 1912 and 1921 resounded loudly with responses to Marshall's query, as I will show in this book. And, as I will also argue, on that troublesome question—what is industrial democracy?—much turned, including the fate of progressivism itself and the course of twentieth-century American labor relations.

During the era of the First World War, as the United States embarked on a crusade to make the world "safe for democracy"—in Mexico, in Europe, and finally in the former Russian empire—Americans fought at home to define the content of their own democracy. In this other war there was no more important theater of battle than the workplace. There was no trench warfare more militant or diplomacy more complex than that practiced by the corporate managers, government administrators, trade unionists, and rank-and-file working people who fought for power on the industrial battlefield. And there was no more important question to be decided than the one posed by Leon Marshall.

The English historian Eric Hobsbawm once noted that social movements tend to progress through brief "explosions" rather than gradual evolution. Certainly this was true for American labor in the era of the Great War.[3] The strikes that swept the United States during World War I, reverberating with greater force in 1919, were social explosions that momentarily lit the darkened landscape of industrial America. Those flashes made visible a set of developments that were remaking the nation, developments that had set the context for industrial democracy's "ecumenical" wartime appeal.

Three such developments were most significant. First, American management was undergoing a process of profound change. Indeed, the Great War marked a turning point in the history of labor management. Just before the war, a process that some historians call the "homogenization" of labor—the spread of mass production and the "drive system" of management—reached full bloom. And Frederick Winslow Taylor's authoritarian system of scientific management—"Taylorism"—secured its place as a ruling ideology (if not necessarily a dominant practice) in American industry.[4] But the war also saw the new factory system face its first crisis. Labor turnover that soared during wartime, bitter industrial strife that peaked after the armistice, and the conflict that accompanied managers' quest for efficiency ultimately forced employers to reconsider questions of power, authority, and organization in the workplace. From this turmoil emerged reforms ranging from corporate welfare programs to employee representation plans that were intended to make the employment relationship more orderly and stable. Out of the Great War came new philosophies of management that would endure for much of the century.

A second critical development was occurring within the labor movement, as the demographic composition of the working class was changing, opening the door to new models of union organization and radical ideologies that challenged the pure-and-simple craft unionism of the American Federation of Labor (AFL). The war accelerated these trends. Wartime saw the entry of women and African Americans into waged labor on a scale previously unmatched, the first glimmers of modern industrial unionism, the cresting of mass-based radical movements in the Industrial Workers of the World (IWW) and the Socialist Party, and a profusion of initiatives ranging from independent labor parties to workers' cooperatives and trade union banks. Perhaps at no time in American history did radical ideas penetrate the mainstream consciousness more deeply than in this era when calls to "conscript capital" gained serious hearings. To be sure, radical dreams died amid the postwar reaction, leaving behind no short-term alternative to the "business unionism" of the American Federation of Labor. But the developments of these years also changed the AFL itself. During this period most of its leaders abandoned their traditional nonpartisan stance to ally themselves with Woodrow Wilson's Democratic Party, forging ties to liberals that would weather the tumult of 1919 and shape labor politics for decades to come.

The third development was related to the new role that the federal government was beginning to assume in American life. Under the Wilson administration, progressivism reached its apogee, and what Stephen Skowronek has called the "new American state" came into its own. Nowhere was this development more observable than in the government's regulation of labor relations. The role that the state played in the workplace was significantly altered by the organization of a cabinet-level Labor Department; the passage of the Adamson Act, the Seamen's Act, and the Clayton Act; and the creation of wartime labor agencies. But just as it set precedents that would shape subsequent periods of reform, Progressive-era regulation also engendered conflict.

Spurred on by a rising faith in the powers of the state or prodded by fears of an emerging Leviathan, Bull Moosers and Brandeisians, social-control advocates and civil libertarians, social democrats and Southern Democrats, industrial planners and conservative jurists battled over contending visions of the state. In their conflicts—particularly as they were shaped by the war—belief in the federal government as an instrument of social reform would be put to its first great test (and suffer its first great disappointment) in this century.

As the narrative in the following chapters will show, each of these developments—the growing crisis of workplace management, the transformation of the labor movement, and the rise of an increasingly powerful national state—both allowed and encouraged Americans to recast the labor question around the demand for industrial democracy during the era of the Great War. Each set the context that made calls for industrial democracy so ubiquitous and so "ecumenically satisfying" that Leon Marshall felt the need to seek expert advice on the meaning of this phrase.

Surprisingly, however, the question that preoccupied Marshall in 1918 has largely escaped the curiosity of most historians. To date, few scholars have remarked on the powerful appeal of industrial democracy in the era of the Great War. None have made a close study of the subject. In large part, this failure can be attributed to the tendency of the historians of the Progressive era on the one hand and labor historians on the other hand to view their subjects in isolation from each other. To comprehend the significance of Marshall's question requires a synthesis of labor and political history that no historian has yet attempted for this period. It requires both "bringing the state back in" to labor history and uncovering what E. P. Thompson might have called the "working-class presence" in Progressive-era political reform.[5] Both labor and political history can benefit from such a synthesis.

To a great extent the history of Wilsonian progressivism has been dominated by three historiographical schools over the past generation. One, best represented by Arthur S. Link, has located in the Wilson years both the culmination of progressivism and the antecedents for subsequent reforms, including those of the New Deal. Another interpretation, developed in the works of Stephen Skowronek and Ellis Hawley, sees the Wilson era as primarily significant for contributing to the development of modern institutional structures—the rise of a "new American state," according to Skowronek, or an "associative state," according to Hawley. A third interpretation, associated with Martin J. Sklar, James Weinstein, and Gabriel Kolko, turned the notion of progressive "reform" on its head, finding in the Wilson era the triumph of a conservative "corporate liberalism."[6]

While these schools differ significantly in substance and interpretation, they share a common orientation. Most of their adherents have looked at Wilsonian progressivism from the perspective of developments in Washington, without deeply probing the interrelationship between government policy and civil society, especially that part of civil society bounded by the walls of the workplace. Even historians who have ably examined Wilsonian labor policies, such as Robert D. Cuff, David M. Kennedy, or Valerie Jean Conner, have not shed much light on the interplay between labor reforms and workers' struggles or shown how each of these shaped and constrained the other. The result has been to leave workers in the background of the narrative and to neglect an important element of the indeterminacy that infused the Progressive era.[7] Whether genuinely democratic or not, Wilsonian policies were not simply handed down from above. They were not inevitable, nor did they occur without producing a host of unintended consequences that demand examination. They were rather the product of conflict and accommodation at a variety of levels, and their unfolding entailed surprises for all concerned.

Several, more recent scholarly trends have made a reconsideration of Wilsonian progressivism on this score imperative. Political sociologists such as Theda Skocpol and Fred Block have urged scholars to consider the state as a relatively autonomous force shaped by and responsive to social conflict.[8] Historians such as Victoria Hattam, William Forbath, Christopher Tomlins, and Melvyn Dubofsky, meanwhile, have explored the complex relationship between labor and the state, drawing attention to the ways in which labor struggles shaped the law and the law shaped labor.[9] And historians of labor politics, such as Gwendolyn Mink and Julie Greene, have pulled back the curtain of official AFL voluntarism and nonpartisanship to reveal the complex relations among unions, the Democratic Party, and the state before the Great War.[10]

These scholarly developments have helped revise our understanding of Wilsonian progressivism. But to date no sociologist has looked at Wilsonian reforms in light of new theories of the state, no legal historian has been able to shed much light on the tumultuous years between 1916 and 1920 when the courts played a lesser role in defining labor policy than during any other period of reform in this century, and no historian of labor politics has examined the consummation of the Wilson administration's alliance with the AFL in wartime.

Just as any attempt to come to terms with the struggle over industrial democracy requires a revision of the history of Wilsonian progressivism, so too does it demand a rethinking of the labor history of this period. Since the 1960s, labor history has enjoyed a spectacular rebirth; the institutional tradition associated with John R. Commons has been profoundly revised by a new labor history that brought forth fresh insights into Progressive-era labor.[11] Whereas the old labor history dwelt on the AFL's triumph over the IWW or Socialism, the new labor history offered nuanced studies of working-class communities, rich portraits of shop floor militancy among union and non-union workers, men and women, blacks and whites. So rich has been the harvest of this literature that the problem of synthesis has increasingly haunted the field—a mark of its maturity.[12]

No historian of Progressive-era labor has left a more indelible imprint on this literature than David Montgomery. In two widely influential books, Montgomery advanced an interpretation that did more to shape the new labor historians' approach to this period than any other. Montgomery's work shifted the focus away from labor leaders, policymakers, and national unions and toward the rank and file, and it organized the labor history of the Progressive era around workers' search for control of production on the shop floor. Locating an impulse for "control" even among ostensibly conservative craftworkers, Montgomery freed historians from the relentless dichotomy between "pure-and-simple" craft unionism and "utopian" radicalism that enmeshed much of the old labor history. At the same time, he helped direct the attention of a generation of students toward the Progressive era as the fulcrum of American labor history, stimulating a plethora of case studies that have immeasurably enriched historians' views of these years.[13]

According to the interpretation advanced in Montgomery's first book on this period, *Workers' Control in America* (1979), the years around the First World War saw a rising wave of working-class militancy in which strikes to achieve workers' control of the shop floor became "especially prominent." During those struggles, "the phrase 'workers' control,' seldom heard before that time, became a popular catchword throughout the labor movement."[14] This movement was defeated after the war, however. And the defeat of the workers' control movement signaled a decisive—and tragic—turning point for American trade unionism. Montgomery elaborated on the significance of that turning point in a second book, *The Fall of the House of Labor* (1987). In this complex narrative, he argued that the years following the war witnessed a "decisive confrontation between the working class and the state." When the dust of that battle had settled, he suggested, "corporate mastery of American life seemed secure."[15]

In recent years, three streams of scholarship have begun to lay the basis for a reexamination of Montgomery's thesis. The first comes from such historians as Jonathan Zeitlin and Michael Kazin, who have argued that "rank-and-file" labor histories tend to romanticize shop floor militancy, assume that workers "must be endowed with a vast reservoir of latent power," or isolate the workplace as a "cockpit of social consciousness."[16] The second comes from scholars of management history such as Sanford Jacoby, who contend that employer behavior in this era was shaped by more than "a monomaniacal search . . . for control of the shop floor" and who are increasingly replacing a model of unrelenting conflict between workers and managers with one that recognizes nuanced patterns of conflict and accommodation.[17] The third comes from historians such as Gary Gerstle, who have shown how American political culture infused the language and consciousness of working people and their organizations.[18]

Although I acknowledge and build on David Montgomery's pathbreaking research, I borrow insights from this other scholarship to depart from Montgomery's interpretation at two points. First, I argue that Progressive-era labor conflicts were not significant because they witnessed the defeat of workers' struggles for control of the shop floor. Such a contest was illusory in most industries and among the vast majority of workers.[19] Rather, I contend that the labor conflicts of this period were primarily significant for giving voice to a widely expressed demand for industrial democracy, which was linked both to new union efforts to organize mass industries and to the emerging regulatory potential of the federal government. More than the demand for workers' control of the shop floor could, the call for industrial democracy resonated among a broad spectrum of actors. It appealed to the pure-and-simple trade unionists who advocated what David Brody has called "workplace contractualism," to the skilled metal trades radicals whom Montgomery has studied, and to unskilled laborers for whom gaining a predictable rule of law on the job made more sense than gaining "control" over the workplace. Moreover, because it was protectively rooted in what Gerstle calls "working-class Americanism," this demand transcended class to appeal to "American" values, a crucial asset in a political culture that persistently denied the reality of class. It should not be surprising, therefore, that workers gladly adopted a phrase— industrial democracy—first popularized by progressive reformers. Nor should it be astonishing to find that even the most militant unionists examined in this book called not for workers' control but, as one group of cigar makers tellingly put it during the Great War, for "self-government in the workshop . . . part of the democracy for which our armies are fighting in France."[20]

I depart from Montgomery's interpretation on a second count as well. I argue that the outcome of the labor conflicts of this period was far more ambiguous than his interpretation implies. Those struggles did not witness the destruction of a workers' control impulse so much as they saw the triumph of an ideal—industrial democracy—the meaning of which remained open to contest well beyond this period. Appreciating this permits us to see the labor history of these years as something more than a narrative of decline and fall. Indeed, doing so allows us instead to see more clearly in this period the origins of those patterns that have shaped American labor relations for much of the rest of this century.

Only a narrative rooted in both the workplace and the political arena allows us to recapture the question that seemed so crucial to Leon Marshall and yet so invisible to most subsequent scholars. This book offers such a narrative. By restoring the struggle to define industrial democracy to its proper place, this narrative in turn suggests three ways that we ought to rethink the history of these years.

First, it urges us to recognize anew just how fertile and fluid was the progressive moment before the Great War. During the years between 1912 and 1917, an extraordinary thing occurred. A diverse lot of Americans suddenly, simultaneously began calling for the democratization of industry. Apparently, the first to do so were progressives such as the colorful labor lawyer Frank P. Walsh, who burst on the national scene in 1913 as chairman of the U.S. Commission on Industrial Relations. "Political Democracy is an illusion," Walsh argued, "unless builded upon and guaranteed by a free and virile Industrial Democracy." [21] Words like these resonated deeply in Walsh's America, and not only among progressives. They also attracted forward-looking management consultants who sought a more rational workplace and more stable employment relations, AFL unionists who demanded collective bargaining, wartime government planners who sought to balance the deeply rooted American concept of voluntarism with the need for increasing state intervention in the workplace, and even radicals who wished to restructure the economic system itself. By the time America went to war, members of these groups had adopted industrial democracy as the name of their vision. Although this phrase spoke to their separate (often conflicting) hopes, it also possessed an electric appeal precisely because it promised to harness contending interests to what seemed to be shared goals: a more powerful state, a more democratic workplace. During this pregnant prewar moment, paths crossed, relationships were struck, and ideas were formulated that would influence American labor history for the remainder of the century.

Second, building a narrative around the struggle for industrial democracy allows us to appreciate just how deeply the Great War shaped modern America. It was the wartime mobilization itself that finally recast America's labor question as a question of how industry ought to be democratized. Wartime conditions eroded managerial control and ignited explosive labor militancy. This in turn triggered an abrupt, vast extension of federal government power expressed by both the repression of radicals and an unprecedented commitment to the democratization of the workplace. Although the latter development has been less fully probed than the former, ultimately the war's reform impulse may have been more significant than its repression. Carried on by a dozen new agencies, the government's war labor program sped the AFL's penetration of open-shop industry, transformed workers' expectations, and even briefly served the interests of militants (such as many of the strikers of July 1918) who wished to substitute a more radical vision of industrial democracy for AFL orthodoxy. By the time of the armistice, government intervention had shattered prewar patterns of labor relations, had made industrial democracy an objective to which all parties from union militants to corporate managers paid homage, and had laid the basis for a postwar struggle over what it meant to democratize industry that would permanently change employers and unions alike.

Finally, rooting this narrative in the struggle for industrial democracy reminds us that the labor battles that followed the Great War were not nearly as conclusive as they were bitter. Although conservative AFL leaders rooted out many of those who had advanced a militant vision of industrial democracy during the war, marginalizing labor radicalism for decades to come, they were no more successful in achieving their own vision. The war-induced fragmentation of progressivism, combined with a postwar open-shop offensive, allowed employers an opportunity to offer company unionism in place of the AFL's collective bargaining as a viable means to democratize industry. Workers and their allies were neither strong enough nor united enough to resist this development. But they had succeeded, as the employers' postwar embrace of company unionism confirmed, in making industrial democracy the goal of American industrial relations. It would be left to subsequent generations of Americans to decide whether company unionism and collective bargaining were compatible and to determine just what industrial democracy was to mean. In many respects, this problem has been central to American labor relations ever since.[22]

The narrative that follows conveys this story. The first three chapters begin by illuminating the developments that made the era of the Great War such a crucial historical juncture for the history of American labor. Chapter 1 sets the political context. I argue that three related developments—an alliance between the Wilson administration and the AFL, the probe conducted by the U.S. Commission on Industrial Relations (1913–15), and President Wilson's 1916 reelection campaign—helped forge an influential coalition of labor Democrats, AFL unionists, and left-wing progressives. Together they succeeded in injecting the issue of industrial democracy into American politics prior to World War I. Chapter 2 shows how the wartime labor crisis of 1917 sharpened demands for the democratization of the workplace and precipitated a struggle among Taylorist efficiency experts, AFL leaders, and union militants over the vision of democracy that ought to prevail in industry. In Chapter 3 I examine how the intervention by the federal government in wartime workplaces transformed industrial relations, weakened "authoritarian" management, and created opportunities for AFL leaders and labor militants alike to advance their own visions in the workplace.

In the next two chapters I consider how profoundly the wartime mobilization subverted prewar patterns of management and trade union action. Chapter 4 suggests the degree to which workers' expectations were altered by wartime conditions. It shows how workers co-opted wartime propaganda, manipulated favorable action from federal agencies, and initiated their own campaign for what one trade unionist called "the de-kaisering of industry," a struggle that helped bring about—within limits—a new vision of industrial citizenship. In Chapter 5 I examine how these developments unloosed strong currents of change within the labor movement itself. I argue that while wartime conditions reinforced the conservative tendencies of most union leaders, those same conditions also offered advantages to union militants in such industries as coal mining, munitions, and electrical manufacturing who sought to challenge the AFL's conservatism.

The final three chapters attempt to explain why the explosive changes triggered by the war achieved such apparently modest and ambiguous results. In Chapter 6 I probe the limitations of both federal regulation and union leadership, contending that federal intervention made possible industrial union initiatives in such industries as steel and textiles. But these initiatives were thwarted by the inherent weaknesses of federal agencies, the shortsightedness of craft union leaders, and the resistance of canny employers. Chapter 7 shows how postwar demobilization destroyed the fragile reform coalition; fragmented relations between AFL leaders, union militants, and left-wing progressives; and destroyed for the foreseeable future the possibility that industrial democracy could be defined in the political arena. In Chapter 8 I argue that, as unions retreated and government agencies retrenched after the war, employers and their allies in the nascent field of industrial relations privatized the debate over industrial democracy, defusing it with company unionism and welfare capitalism. Employers' success in equating company unionism and industrial democracy weakened trade unionism's claim to the ideal, forcing succeeding generations to battle over the legacy of labor's Great War.

In bequeathing that problem to posterity, the events described here also shaped those political, managerial, and trade union leaders who would carry on that struggle, which would finally reach a (temporary) resolution in the New Deal order. Labor's "great war" provided a moment of searing political and cultural transformation for the generation that would come to power under this order. Indeed, in many ways, the foundations of that New Deal order are to be found in the story to which we now turn.

BUILDING A POLITICS OF
INDUSTRIAL DEMOCRACY

1

Our liberation has just begun. We are far from free,

but the new spirit of democracy is the angel that

will free us.

—*Randolph Bourne, 1913*

"Political freedom can exist only where there is industrial freedom; political democracy only where there is industrial democracy." In many ways the roots of the labor struggle that shook America between 1912 and 1921 can be found in those words, the circumstances that led to their dissemination, and their subsequent political impact. They came not from the mouth of Bill Haywood, leader of the radical Industrial Workers of the World, or even from the picket signs carried by striking members of the American Federation of Labor. Rather, those words were contained in the 1915 report of the United States Commission on Industrial Relations (USCIR) written by a young attorney named Basil Manly under the supervision of USCIR chairman Frank P. Walsh. They made this document one of the most remarkable ever released by a federal agency. The "Walsh Report," as it was popularly dubbed, caused a sensation in the midst of a decade of labor upheaval by condemning the maldistribution of wealth, calling for measures to stem unemployment, and arguing that the "only hope for the solution" of labor conflict lay in "the rapid extension of the principles of democracy to industry."[1]

Not since Reconstruction had the report of any federal body seemed more radical. As the *New Republic* observed, the USCIR had gone well beyond its charge to investigate the "cause and cure" of labor unrest. In promoting industrial democracy, it offered a "tonic" for American democracy itself.

This prescription certainly touched a resonant chord among the pre–World War I Left. According to the *Masses* it signaled "the beginning of an indigenous American revolutionary movement." To the *Seattle Union Record* it meant "an indictment against organized capital." To a group of Christian socialists, it was on a par with the Declaration of Independence and the Emancipation Proclamation, the two "great documents" that marked previous "great epochs" in American history, and its publication augured the dawn of America's "third and greatest epoch."[2]

Because of its seemingly radical demand for the extension of democracy to industry, the Walsh Report also earned many loud critics. One business journal concluded that the USCIR could be judged a success only if the purpose of creating the commission "has been to foment unrest." The *New York Herald* agreed, characterizing Frank Walsh as nothing more than a "Mother Jones in trousers" for his conduct of the investigation. Even some of the progressive reformers who had originally sought a federal commission to investigate industrial violence in the aftermath of the bombing of the *Los Angeles Times* in 1911 disowned Walsh's report. And, more significant, so too did a majority of the USCIR commissioners who served under Walsh. Rather than signing their chairman's report, they affixed their names to two separate rump reports. One of those was written by commissioner John R. Commons, who feared that the Walsh Report's call for democratizing industry would end up "throwing the [labor] movement into politics." Commons's report therefore stopped short of calling for "industrial democracy," advocating instead the creation of impartial mediation boards.[3]

The profound controversy that attended the Walsh Report in 1915 indicated the arrival of an important moment in American political history. The USCIR investigation had made workers' rights a central focus of national reform efforts, placing the issues of authority and consent in the modern workplace on the national political agenda for the first time in the Progressive era. The debate triggered by the USCIR was all the more fiery because it coincided with three other important developments: the emergence of a partnership of a sort between the AFL and President Woodrow Wilson's Democratic Party; the Wilson administration's increasing interest in finding legislative solutions to labor strife; and the formation of an alliance—fostered in part by the USCIR itself—between labor progressives, nonrevolutionary radicals, and liberal Democrats, all of whom supported President Wilson's reelection in 1916 in the hope that it would speed the democratization of industry. Together, these developments set the political context for the profound labor struggles that would rock the United States during World War I and its aftermath. Together, they helped determine that those struggles would be waged over the idea popularized by the Walsh Report: industrial democracy. But how did this important historical moment come about?

THE AFL AND THE WILSONIAN DEMOCRACY

The significance of the Walsh Report's call for industrial democracy must be understood in the context of a pragmatic alliance between the AFL and Woodrow Wilson, struck during the 1912 presidential election. The four-sided campaign of that year, which pitted incumbent Republican William H. Taft against Democrat Woodrow Wilson, Progressive Theodore Roosevelt, and Socialist Eugene V. Debs, resulted in the election of Wilson, the first president who enjoyed the backing of the AFL. That was a precedent of no small importance for either Wilson or the labor movement.

Since its founding in 1886, the AFL had remained formally nonpartisan despite its repeated forays into politics. But, jostled by a hostile judiciary that wielded injunctions to cripple labor's right to strike, by the early twentieth century the AFL was increasingly anxious to make its political will felt. The federation's political strategy grew from the philosophy of its "chief," Samuel Gompers. This British-born cigar maker of Dutch Jewish parentage, who had formed his political views during the sectarian left-wing squabbles of the 1870s, imbued the AFL with the philosophy of nonpartisanship, turning this stand into a weapon against his Socialist rivals within the movement. Under attack by open-shop employers and antilabor judges, however, Gompers modified his nonpartisan stance in the early twentieth century.[4]

Beginning in 1906, the AFL embarked on a legislative campaign seeking relief from injunctions. Rebuffed by most Republican leaders, especially antilabor Speaker of the House Joe Cannon, the AFL drifted ever closer to the Democratic Party. The Democratic takeover of Congress in 1910 helped cement an alliance between AFL leaders and Democrats. The naming of Congressman William B. Wilson, a former official of the United Mine Workers (UMW), to the chair of the House Committee on Labor helped make the Congress, in Gompers's words, "a potent power responsive to social and economic conditions." William Wilson himself would later argue that under Democratic control, Congress had passed a string of pro-labor legislation that had "never been equalled by any party, at any time, or in any country in the world."[5]

This alliance between the AFL and the Democrats survived a close call in 1912. Before the Democratic National Convention, Gompers and other AFL leaders had worked diligently for the nomination of Speaker of the House Champ Clark of Missouri. Woodrow Wilson's nomination on the forty-sixth ballot was a blow to their plans. Neither training nor temperament prepared candidate Wilson for the task of pursuing an alliance with the AFL. An Anglo-philic Presbyterian, with southern lineage and a preacherly manner, Wilson was steeped in liberal individualism and instinctively shunned the collective consciousness of organized labor. Throughout his academic career, Wilson had retained an innate suspicion of unions, thinking them "economically dis-astrous" and socially divisive.[6]

But political life had moderated Wilson's views. Elected governor of New Jersey in 1910, Wilson built a commodious relationship with the New Jersey State Federation of Labor, undergirded by his support for a workers' com-pensation act. Although Wilson had not been his first choice, Gompers was determined to work with this nascent friend of labor, and he pointed to Wil-son's record as a reform governor in urging AFL members to follow suit. Even if belatedly, Gompers helped swing the majority of AFL union leaders behind candidate Wilson, making the federation's national office a virtual clearing-house for Democratic efforts to woo the labor vote in 1912.[7]

The rewards for the AFL's backing were sweet and immediate. Victory's fruits were most visible in the constitution of two new federal bodies vital to the labor movement: the Department of Labor and the USCIR. On his last day in office, lame-duck president William H. Taft had signed an act creating a cabinet-level Department of Labor. He left his successor to name its first secretary. President Wilson lost little time in nominating Representa-tive William B. Wilson to head the new department. In naming the former UMW secretary-treasurer and snubbing critics who charged that the appoint-ment came "virtually at the instigation" of Gompers, the president openly embraced labor as a constituency of his administration and his party.[8]

The Labor Department soon became emblematic of the developing rela-tionship between the AFL and the administration. Secretary Wilson, who was born in Scotland in 1862, had arrived in the United States at the age of eight to labor in the coal mines of north-central Pennsylvania. He was a longtime labor activist who had served as a masterworkman of the Knights of Labor in the years before he joined the UMW and ascended through its ranks. Wilson had gained election to Congress from Pennsylvania's 15th District in 1906. A staunch Democrat—"I donna like to dilute my democracy," he was wont to say in an affected Scottish burr in stump speeches—Wilson had led the in-vestigation conducted by the House Committee on Labor into the scientific management practices of the AFL's nemesis, Frederick W. Taylor. And under his leadership, the Labor Department symbolized the increasingly close con-nection between the AFL and the Democrats.[9]

President Wilson hoped that his administration would effect cooperation between labor and capital for the common good. At least formally, the secretary of labor subscribed to the president's goals. But the Labor Department under William Wilson's leadership was soon perceived by critics as a frank partisan of trade unionism. It is not difficult to understand why, for Secretary Wilson gathered an unusual assemblage of reformers and trade unionists into his department. Assistant Secretary Louis F. Post was a longtime friend of labor, a former Freedmen's Bureau official, and a supporter of single-tax theorist Henry George. Post hoped to have a hand in creating "a democracy that ignores all privileges of race and class." Joining him in Washington were a large number of AFL friends. John Densmore, former editor of the UMW's journal, enlisted as the department's solicitor, and Samuel Gompers's son headed the department's division of publications and supplies. Although the Congress refused until 1916 to create the full-time conciliation service that the secretary desired, Wilson scavenged congressional funds to pay the salaries of a growing number of part-time conciliators before the war. Generally they were trade unionists. Joseph R. Buchanan, an AFL pioneer; William R. Fairley and Patrick Gilday of the UMW, Elmer E. Greenawalt of the Cigar Makers; and John B. Colpoys, a labor editor: each worked for the Labor Department settling strikes. Such personnel ensured that the department's conciliation work would enjoy "a splendid future," as noted in one trade union journal.[10]

The close connection between the Department of Labor and the AFL concerned many contemporaries. As one observer put it, an "impression became current in many places that the Department was controlled by the labor unions, and that practically all of its personnel were or had been connected with organized labor." Nor did Secretary Wilson dispel such thinking when he addressed delegates to the 1913 AFL convention as "fellow trade unionists." Alarmed businesspeople demanded that the president "restrain this anarchist" cabinet member. "Why is Mr. Wilson allowed to take the stand he does with the American Federation of Labor?" groused one employer who thought William Wilson the "sole cause" of "the uneasiness now existing" in the business community. To the AFL's satisfaction, the president not only brushed aside such criticism but also resisted attempts by Democrats to draft Wilson for a U.S. Senate campaign. Instead, he sought to keep this symbol of his ties to labor close at hand.[11]

But the president's commitments to the Labor Department and the AFL could not be given without reservation, for he sat astride a contradictory coalition in which Gompers or William Wilson played only a small part. Conservative southern Democrats provided a strong counterweight to labor's influence. Congressmen from the former confederate states, for example, furnished thirty-eight of the forty-two Democratic votes mustered in 1915 against

Samuel Gompers stands between two allies, President Woodrow Wilson and Secretary of Labor William B. Wilson, at the July 4, 1916, dedication of the AFL's new Washington headquarters. (George Meany Memorial Archives, Silver Spring, Maryland)

an AFL-supported bill outlawing child labor. Senators James A. Reed of Missouri, Ben Tillman of South Carolina, and Hoke Smith of Georgia closely monitored the expansion of federal labor regulation, especially in the South. Indeed, Tillman had blocked the president's attempt to name Charles P. Neill to the Bureau of Labor Statistics in 1913 because Neill had once investigated southern textile manufacturers, making "many bitter enemies in the South." When Wilson was not being prodded by congressional heavyweights from his own party, he could count on hearing such views at his cabinet's conference table from the likes of Postmaster General Albert Sidney Burleson of Texas.[12]

The tenuousness of the administration's alliance with organized labor was starkly illustrated when the Congress considered action on antilabor injunctions, the issue about which AFL leaders were most anxious. Although Gompers labeled the resulting Clayton Act of 1914 "the greatest measure of humanitarian legislation in the world's history," a veritable "Magna Charta of American workers,"[13] it scarcely protected unions from antitrust action at all, as the president had implied it would. Judges had little trouble widening the loopholes that powerful congressmen—with the president's acquiescence—

had inserted into the act. This led some astute trade unionists, most notably Andrew Furuseth of the International Seamen's Union, to write the bill off as a dead letter even before it was signed.

In the face of the Clayton Act's failure, Gompers's critics were quick to point out that neither he nor William B. Wilson held much influence in Washington's halls of power. Indeed, by 1914, critics from each side of the political spectrum questioned the AFL's support for the administration. From the Left, Socialist Robert Hunter railed against "the political helplessness of Labor in America." William H. Johnston, the Socialist who presided over the International Association of Machinists, and John Fitzpatrick, head of the Chicago Federation of Labor (CFL), among others, echoed Hunter and called for an independent labor politics. From the Right, such union leaders as Republican "Big Bill" Hutcheson, of the United Brotherhood of Carpenters and Joiners, demanded a closer adherence to the AFL's traditional nonpartisan orthodoxy.[14] Such stinging attacks might have totally undermined the AFL's political strategy if not for the choices President Wilson made in constituting another body formed in 1913, the USCIR.

THE U.S. COMMISSION ON INDUSTRIAL RELATIONS

One of organized labor's greatest triumphs in the Progressive era was made possible by one of its greatest tragedies. In the early morning hours of October 1, 1910, two bombs exploded in the building that housed the antiunion *Los Angeles Times*, killing twenty-one people. "The crime of the century" was traced to two brothers: John J. McNamara, secretary-treasurer of the International Association of Bridge and Structural Iron Workers, and James McNamara. The bombing capped a long struggle by the McNamaras and their union to organize construction in open-shop Los Angeles in the face of the violent opposition of that city's Merchants and Manufacturers Association. Although the AFL initially proclaimed their innocence and hired Clarence Darrow to defend them, the brothers surprised the nation—and Gompers—on December 1, 1911, pleading guilty to the crime. Shocked by the case, muckraker Lincoln Steffens wondered, What could have caused "healthy, good-tempered boys like the McNamara boys" to believe "that the only recourse they have for improving the conditions of wage-earners is to use dynamite against property and life?"[15]

The *Times* bombing provided a potent catalyst for reform. Members of the Committee on Standards of Living and Labor of the National Conference of Charities and Corrections, many of whom were social workers affiliated with *Survey* magazine, mounted a petition drive calling for a federal commission to investigate the causes of industrial violence. "Today, as fifty years ago, a house divided against itself cannot stand," Jane Addams, Reverend Lyman Abbott, Rabbi Stephen Wise, and other petitioners wrote. America must "solve the problems of democracy in its industrial relationships," they insisted.[16] In response, Congress passed a bill in 1912 sponsored by Republican senator William Borah and Democratic representative (and former AFL member) William Hughes that provided for the creation of the USCIR. Facing a bruising reelection battle in which he needed to stem Progressive defections from his party, President Taft signed the bill. He then went on to set an important precedent by nominating three union officials to the nine-member commission: John Lennon, the AFL treasurer; James O'Connell, head of the AFL's Metal Trades Department; and Austin B. Garretson, of the Order of Railway Conductors. His choices may have been intended to make the AFL chief's support for the Democrats more difficult in 1912. Both Lennon and O'Connell, close allies of Gompers, had recently been driven from office in their own unions by socialist opponents. Naturally, they enjoyed Gompers's full support.[17]

Taft, however, was unable to secure the confirmation of these appointments by the Senate before the election. This development set the stage for an odd historical event that unfolded following Taft's defeat. Worried that president-elect Wilson's liberal adviser Louis D. Brandeis might engineer the appointment of a member of the radical IWW to the USCIR, Gompers lobbied quietly alongside a strange bedfellow, the National Association of Manufacturers (NAM), seeking the confirmation of Taft's original nominees from the lame-duck Congress. Gompers's ploy failed. Patronage-hungry Senate Democrats were reluctant to confirm Republican appointees, the AFL's desires notwithstanding. They shelved Taft's nominations. Ironically, this temporary setback for Gompers produced an unanticipated consequence that redounded to the AFL's favor. It paved the way for the elevation to the USCIR's chairmanship of the man who more than any other would make industrial democracy a political issue during the Progressive era: Frank P. Walsh.[18]

Two months after settling into the White House, President Wilson turned to Labor Secretary Wilson for advice on the makeup of the USCIR. The secretary recommended that Taft's labor appointees to the commission be retained, but he proposed nominees for the USCIR's other seats who were acceptable to Democrats. Named to the commission to represent employers were Henry Weinstock, a progressive California businessman; Thruston Ballard, a Kentucky Democrat who operated a flour mill; and Frederick A. Delano, a railroad executive (and uncle of Undersecretary of the Navy Franklin D. Roosevelt). To represent the public, Wilson tapped Florence Jaffray

("Daisy") Harriman, a prominent Democratic fund-raiser, and John R. Commons, the University of Wisconsin labor economist. To serve as chairman of the commission, Secretary Wilson offered a name sure to meet with the president's approval: Louis D. Brandeis, the architect of the administration's New Freedom. But, when the president offered the post to Brandeis, the "People's Lawyer" declined.[19]

Left without a nominee in late May 1913, it was President Wilson himself who first raised the name of Kansas City labor lawyer Frank P. Walsh. Wilson had known Walsh for less than one year at that point. He met him during the previous July at the urging of Daisy Harriman, who believed Walsh could help Wilson's campaign in Missouri. Before journeying to meet candidate Wilson, Walsh, a staunch reformer, had toyed with the idea of supporting the Bull Moosers. Upon meeting the New Jersey governor, however, Walsh concluded, as Mrs. Harriman later put it, that "Mr. Wilson's progressiveness was more progressive" than Roosevelt's.[20] Walsh threw himself vigorously into the campaign, running a bureau for social workers at Wilson's Chicago headquarters, where he impressed future Treasury secretary William G. McAdoo and others.

Still, the president found little support among his advisers for Walsh's nomination. Brandeis feared that a chairman who "lacks a national reputation" might undermine the USCIR, failing "to command the attention which the Chairman of the Commission should." Nor could the president look to the social workers affiliated with the *Survey* magazine for support; they desired one of their own to head the commission. Democratic senator James A. Reed of Missouri, meanwhile, constituted another obstacle. Reed, the protégé of Kansas City's famous Pendergast political machine, had been a bitter political rival of Walsh's for over a decade. Such considerations no doubt contributed to the president's delay in making a decision.[21] But when Wilson did offer the post on June 20, 1913, he opted for Walsh despite the misgivings of others. In part his decision appears to have been shaped by the personal regard for Walsh he had developed during the campaign, in part by a desire to build a stronger relationship with the AFL, the one significant group that supported the selection. Whatever the reason, the appointment would rank with the subsequent elevation of Brandeis to the Supreme Court as among Wilson's most lastingly influential.

Frank P. Walsh wired his acceptance to Wilson, and to his associates he unselfconsciously remarked, "I'll be an excellent chairman." Walsh's enthusiasm remained undimmed during the battle for Senate confirmation that followed. Chairman of the Senate Committee on Education and Labor, Hoke Smith of Georgia, with the encouragement of Senator Reed, let Walsh's nomination languish in committee for nearly three months, and he might well have killed it had not Walsh undertaken his own campaign to pry his name loose. In a move that foreshadowed the aggressive style with which he would conduct himself in Washington over the next seven years, Walsh enlisted the help of Democratic boss Joe Shannon of Kansas City and Senator William J. Stone of Missouri, Shannon's ally, in bringing his nomination to a successful vote. He was finally confirmed on September 19, 1913.[22]

In approving Frank P. Walsh, the Senate had elevated no ordinary, platitude-spouting political appointee. The *Masses* considered Walsh an American original. His tenure on the USCIR was enough to convince even "discouraged observers" that American politics were not hopeless if out of them "could emerge a figure like that of Frank P. Walsh," the radical journal concluded. That this journal warmed so to Frank Walsh helps illuminate the role Walsh and his commission would play in shaping labor politics in the Wilson era. And the reason why Walsh was embraced so easily by radicals had much to do with the history of this complex man.[23]

Walsh was a bootstrap success story. Born in 1863 to Irish immigrant parents in St. Louis's ramshackle "Kerry Patch," he had known strenuous labor. After he lost his father at a young age, Walsh worked as a messenger, a factory hand, and a railway cashier to put himself through Bryant and Stratton's night school, where he learned shorthand. He later recalled that only three among the thirty boys he had grown up with lived to a "normal, useful manhood"; but Walsh himself was luckier. At age twenty-one he secured a job as a legal stenographer and began reading law in his spare time. By 1888 he had joined the Missouri bar and moved to Kansas City. Two years later he married Katie O'Flaherty, the organist at St. Aloysius Church, with whom he was to have eight children. He soon parlayed his skills as a courtroom orator into a successful criminal practice. But Walsh earned his bread and butter as a corporate lawyer in a booming city. "I represented every corporation worth . . . representing in Kansas City," he later recalled. Nor was his practice hurt by his affiliation with Boss Shannon's "Rabbit" faction in the Kansas City Democratic Party, the rivals of the Pendergast machine's "Goats." Believing in those years that "it was immodest for a man to set up his own opinion against that of his party," Walsh profited amply from his political ties.[24]

But, like David Levinsky, the character in Abraham Cahan's famous 1917 novel, Walsh's rise had not brought him inner peace. On January 1, 1900, therefore, the thirty-six-year-old lawyer made a radical break that altered the rest of his life. As the new century dawned, Walsh "resigned from every corporation with which I was connected," thereafter becoming "a free hand in the legal profession." He continued to represent wealthy clients on occasion, "but only in particular cases" that he felt he could take up "with a more or less easy conscience." Thereafter he devoted himself to a range of causes: he fought to end corporate contributions to the campaigns of the Missouri Democratic Party; he took a post on Kansas City's Tenement Commission; he helped establish a municipal Board of Public Welfare; and he was elected president of the Kansas City Board of Civil Service. In general, he busied himself "piercing every weak point in the armor of the crowd that was out for booty," as one journalist put it. Walsh's new career brought him into conflict with future Senator James Reed, who played county prosecutor to Walsh's impassioned defense counsel and machine mayor to Walsh's renegade reformer before moving on to Washington. When Walsh's admirers urged him to follow Reed into higher office, he brushed them aside. "What we need more than lawmakers and law governors," he said, "is agitators."[25]

Walsh was indeed an agitator, driven by deep passions and attracted to radicalism in many forms. Regarding capitalism, he often expressed the hope that the "heart-destroying, soul-shriveling idea of production solely for . . . profits may give way to production for the good of all mankind." He held liberal views on race as well. "You know how close the troubles of the colored brother in industry are to my heart," he wrote to one trade union friend. "They always get the dirty end of the industrial stick handed to them by the employers, and, I am sorry to say, also from the unions." Nothing good could "finally come out of the Democratic Party," he feared, as long as it was "controlled . . . by the reactionary South." Walsh was also an early supporter of women's suffrage, and he counted radical feminists among his dearest friends.[26]

"I hate like hell to be so respectable," Walsh once told feminist friend Doris Stevens. Rather, he thought himself something of "a poet and a revolutionist." Perhaps that is why one historian observed of Walsh that no figure of his time "so clearly personified the possibility and the potential character of a labor party." But Walsh also personified the forces that would frustrate the emergence of such a party in America. For although he was an agitator, from his square jaw and boxer's build to the shrewd political sense he had honed since his days in Kerry Patch, he was scarcely a "revolutionist." He would never completely break his ties to the legal profession, the Democratic Party, or his Irish Catholic culture. Indeed, even as he railed against the dangers of an autocratic bench, he confessed privately that he loved "this crooked old profession of mine so dearly." Even as admirers praised Walsh for abandoning his corporate practice, accepting the myth that the gesture had imperiled his finances, Walsh's practice thrived, his income ranging as high as fifty thousand dollars in the year he took the reins of the USCIR. Even as Walsh was attracted to radical feminists like Stevens, he was repelled by "that awful mix-

Frank P. Walsh photographed at the start of his tenure as chairman of the U.S. Commission on Industrial Relations, 1913. (Library of Congress)

ture of beliefs, books, causes, and sex" among the avant garde, and he sent two of his own daughters to the convent. And though Walsh portrayed himself as a political independent "travelling in the direction of human justice," one who was "never going to be a member of any party," he remained bound by ties of culture and years of political footwork to the Democratic Party. It was a bond he could not easily break.[27]

On one occasion when Walsh reflected on his attempt to play simultaneously the roles of agitator and insider, he likened himself to "a cross between Jesse James and Lew Dockstader," a prominent vaudevillian of his day. The comparison was revealing. Part outlaw, part actor, Walsh constructed a public persona as a militant maverick, which was calculated to give him maximum leverage in the world of pragmatic politics. It was his skill in pulling off this role that made Walsh so attractive to both the reformers and the radicals of his time. Comfortable among Democrats and anarchists, among haughty AFL craft unionists and hardscrabble Wobblies, among Catholic prelates and Greenwich Village bohemians, Walsh was a unique figure, "as much called to this labor," as one of his feminist friends told him, "as ever a prophet was to his." "You are a phenomenon for which there is no precedent," another friend concluded, "that imaginary being that appears once in a great while in fairy tales."[28]

THE USCIR AND INDUSTRIAL DEMOCRACY

Certainly there was no precedent for what Frank Walsh did with the USCIR. Shortly after he convened the commission, as the *New Republic* observed, it became clear that Walsh would make "no pretense of judicial poise" in running it. Walsh did not intend to conduct a traditional investigation or to turn the USCIR into what he called "a smelling committee." This stand chagrined fellow commissioners, including John R. Commons, who would soon become Walsh's chief rival. Walsh instead saw his role as a chance to conduct his most sensational case, this time before a jury of millions. Between its formation in the autumn of 1913 and its final public sessions in the spring of 1915, Walsh guided the USCIR through 154 days of public hearings. The commission probed the flashpoints of labor conflict, from the silk strike in Paterson, New Jersey, in 1913 to the "Ludlow massacre" in Colorado's coalfields during the following year; it studied industrial violence from New York's needle trades to the shops of the Illinois Central Railroad; it launched investigations into the laboring conditions of migrant farm workers, oil field hands, and tenant farmers; and it documented repressive company towns and scientific management techniques. Some 740 witnesses, ranging from John D. Rockefeller to Vincent St. John, the secretary-treasurer of the IWW, came before the commission.[29]

What the commission found was shocking. Only 2 percent of the nation owned 60 percent of its wealth. Sixty-five percent of the population owned but 2 percent of the wealth. And while one-third of the nation's laborers took home less than ten dollars per week and most toilers in basic industries were jobless for more than two months each year, employers regularly used private detectives, spies, and blacklists to prevent workers from organizing. In some areas the exploitation was especially evident. The USCIR found that lumber workers in the Northwest labored at their dangerous jobs for ten hours a day at only twenty cents an hour. Seasonal unemployment dumped tens of thousands of laborers into the streets of the Pacific Coast cities, where only the fortunate averaged more than one meal a day. In California, migrant laborers stooped over crops in temperatures as high as 105 degrees on farms where growers refused to supply them water in the fields. And one Paterson, New Jersey, silk mill fined workers fifty cents for talking and fifty cents for laughing on the job. In an era of ubiquitous muckraking, the USCIR raised the technique to an unprecedented height, uncovering the deepest recesses of the nation's social structure and, in the process, breaking all molds for federal investigations.[30]

Three themes shaped the USCIR's work under Walsh: political independence, sensational publicity, and a deep concern with the problem of authoritarian management. Through the course of Walsh's leadership of the commission, he succeeded in using its investigations to raise a demand for the democratization of industrial life in the absence of a strong national political commitment to such an endeavor. Ironically, it was Walsh's success at this task that would also contribute to splitting the commission into rival factions by the end of its work.

Walsh quickly established the political independence of the USCIR. Only months after taking his seat, he showed that he was even willing to risk embarrassing the president who had appointed him if doing so would aid the cause of America's outcasts. In February 1914, even as Republicans were criticizing the Underwood Tariff for driving up unemployment, Walsh substantiated their claims. Without consulting anyone, he announced that the USCIR would investigate the "hundreds of thousands" of "poorly nourished and thinly clad" jobless swamping America's cities. The administration was furious. As the president disputed Walsh's statement on the levels of unemployment as "not an established fact," Wilson's secretary, Joseph Tumulty, fumed, and Daisy Harriman scrambled to refute her own chairman's charges.[31]

For anyone who still needed proof of his independence, Walsh provided plenty in his relations with sensitive southern Democrats in Congress. The skepticism of southern conservatives, who looked askance at Walsh from the beginning, was compounded in the first months of the commission's work when Walsh hinted that the South was "a prime place to make a study" of abusive working conditions. Suspicious of Walsh's intentions, Senator Hoke Smith led a group of southerners who attempted to cut the commission's budget by 75 percent in 1914, contending that the USCIR had so extended its inquiry that there was practically nothing in industrial America "it had not contemplated investigating." Smith termed the entire USCIR "a mistake." Senator Thomas S. Martin of Virginia agreed, arguing that "we should abolish it." Though their measure failed, southerners cast twelve of the eighteen votes against the commission in the Senate. Undeterred, Walsh promptly dispatched investigators to Smith's home state when a textile strike erupted in Atlanta in July 1914. And he instructed his staff simply to ignore the senator's subsequent angry phone calls to the White House and the USCIR office alike. Full hearings never grew out of the Atlanta strike, nor did the USCIR ever undertake an investigation of the working conditions of southern blacks as commission staffers had recommended it should. But what Walsh did do was enough to make lasting enemies among powerful southern politicians— and to gain for himself a lasting reputation for honesty and independence.[32]

Walsh was as adept at garnering publicity as he was in establishing a maverick political course. He soon laid to rest the fears of Brandeis and others that his lack of national visibility might consign the USCIR's work to the margins of public consciousness, for Walsh, as the *New Republic* dryly observed, "was not a shrinking violet at the thought of modern advertising methods." With a vaudevillian's instinct for the dramatic and with the help of such friends as George Creel, Walsh demonstrated an uncanny ability to attract press coverage, both favorable and otherwise. In the manner of evangelist Billy Sunday, he sent staffers to cities in advance of commission hearings to line up witnesses and publicize the commission's impending arrival. And when the commission came to town, it rarely disappointed. As Walter Lippmann commented, "An atmosphere of no quarter" pervaded the hearings when Walsh skewered mighty industrialists such as John D. Rockefeller Jr.[33]

The chairman's focus on publicity dismayed some USCIR members, especially Commons. A proponent of the "Wisconsin idea," Commons had hoped the USCIR would engage in careful, systematic inquiry, culminating in the drafting by experts of specific legislative proposals. USCIR research director Charles McCarthy shared that vision. Drawing on his experience as director of Wisconsin's Legislative Reference Library, McCarthy brought to Washington a remarkable staff of budding industrial relations professionals that included W. Jett Lauck, William Leiserson, Sumner Slichter, and Selig Perlman. But Walsh did not make as much use of these experts as McCarthy had hoped. Rather, he spent most of the commission's budget on public hearings, steering clear of "interminable 'bill-drafting,'" which, he believed, would "throw the legal profession into spasms of delight, and the proletariat into despair."[34] To organize hearings, Walsh relied less on the industrial relations professionals than on partisans and publicists such as Basil Manly of the Bureau of Labor Statistics, newspapermen George P. West and George Creel, and Women's Trade Union League activist Helen Marot.

The USCIR's public hearings instantly made Walsh notorious. They prompted workers to write the president to commend Walsh's "attack on the enemies of . . . democracy" and to praise Wilson's "nerve" in standing by his chairman "in the face of what Walsh is doing to the Masters of America." They also led his enemies to label Walsh a cheap demagogue and a "glib-tongued ward politician." But as his critics well realized, Walsh's flamboyant style only enhanced the commission's utility as a vehicle for molding public opinion.[35]

Toward what end should public opinion be shaped? There is no evidence that Walsh took the reins of the USCIR with a clear answer to this question. "Maybe we have been seeing our industrial problem through the haze of tradition," he told Creel as he prepared to take up his work, "and will find that it isn't so appalling after all." Over the course of his hearings, however, Walsh came to focus on one central problem: the lack of democracy in the workplace. As he did so, he began to build a case for "the absolute and inalienable right of workers" to exercise "a compelling voice" in determining their working conditions. By the end of his probe, Walsh was arguing that only "industrial democracy" offered a solution to the nation's labor problem.[36]

Walsh was by no means the first American to champion industrial democracy. Industrial democracy was an idea first popularized by American social gospelers such as Lyman Abbott and English Fabians such as Sidney and Beatrice Webb, who published a book on the subject in 1898. By the early twentieth century, however, the term had gradually crept into the discourse of reformers ranging from Henry Demarest Lloyd to Richard T. Ely. In the first decade of the century, Louis Brandeis emerged as the most prominent progressive proponent of the notion that "industrial democracy should ultimately attend political democracy." Through Brandeis, perceptive businesspeople such as the retailers Edward and Lincoln Filene were converted to the idea that workers had a right to representation in the workplace. The liberals associated with the *New Republic* magazine—Felix Frankfurter, Walter Weyl, and Walter Lippmann—were also among the most influential apostles of the ideal of industrial democracy before the war. Lippmann's *Drift and Mastery* (1914) and Herbert Croly's *Progressive Democracy* (1914) both discussed the necessity of democratizing industry, while by 1914, industrial democracy had become Weyl's "main theme," according to historian Charles B. Forcey. Such reformers came to believe, as Lippmann put it, that "without democracy in industry, there is no such thing as democracy in America." Yet, industrial democracy was a term rarely employed by trade unionists prior to the Wilson era. It was Frank Walsh who did the most to change that.[37]

If others before Walsh had invoked industrial democracy as a solution to the labor problem, none had done so with more mass appeal. As Walsh used it, industrial democracy became a slogan attractive to those beyond the parlors of progressives and farsighted businesspeople. Walsh, more so than any others who grasped the term, linked industrial democracy to the right to join unions and tied this right to the nation's democratic heritage, suggesting a vision of a new and just workplace. It was a vision calculated to appeal as much to AFL members, rank-and-file workers, and even radicals as it was to progressives. And in his legendary battle with John D. Rockefeller Jr.—a conflict that became the central drama of the USCIR's hearings—Walsh perfected his ability to inspire Americans with this vision.

Just as President Wilson was naming the USCIR, the UMW called a strike in Colorado, seeking recognition from the Rockefeller-owned Colorado Fuel and Iron Company (CFI). That bitter conflict resulted in a series of clashes between strikers and militia members that ended on April 20, 1914, when soldiers raked a strikers' tent city in Ludlow with machine-gun fire before torching it; men, women, and children alike died in the infamous massacre. The news shocked America. To refurbish his name, Rockefeller hired the Canadian labor expert W. L. Mackenzie King to devise an industrial relations plan for CFI. King subsequently designed a representation plan that would allow the company to hear workers' grievances without recognizing a union; the "Rockefeller Plan" soon became the model company union.[38]

In Walsh's eyes such sham representation was simply "a menace" to real industrial democracy, and it could not be allowed to stand unchallenged. He decided to investigate Rockefeller and CFI even though doing so again placed him at odds with President Wilson, who had appointed his own commission to mediate the Colorado conflict. Issuing subpoenas for both Rockefeller and Mackenzie King in October 1914, Walsh determined to make the Colorado case "a laboratory for an extensive study."[39]

On January 25, 1915, in a packed city hall in New York City—a location chosen to maximize the publicity of the event—Walsh began grilling John D. Rockefeller Jr., subjecting his taciturn witness to three days of rough handling. Marshaling evidence of CFI influence over churches, schools, and politicians, he questioned whether Colorado was really a democracy. He asked Rockefeller whether he believed workers' organizations "should be created and maintained democratically" and whether workers ought to have "the right to set up the organizations themselves." Rockefeller was evasive. When Mackenzie King took the stand, Walsh handled him so harshly that King later called the proceedings "disgraceful."[40]

But Walsh had accomplished what he wanted. The CFI hearings allowed him to make a case to the widest possible audience that unless industry were democratized, unless workers were allowed to choose their own representatives and bargain collectively with their employers, then autocratic management would corrupt political democracy itself.

Yet Walsh made his case at a cost. His pursuit of Rockefeller finally brought to the surface tensions that had been long roiling within the USCIR itself. Commons and several other commissioners felt that he had handled Rockefeller unfairly. They objected. When the dust settled, Walsh had ousted McCarthy, and an embittered Commons had returned to Wisconsin disgusted with the turn the USCIR's investigation had taken. When the commission adjourned in May 1915 to prepare a final report, there was no unanimity within its ranks. The commission's three trade unionists signed the report that Basil Manly drafted under Walsh's direction, the report calling for industrial democracy. But Commons, who believed that Walsh was leading unions, "by way of politics, into socialism or communism," drafted a rump report. His proposal for the creation of national mediation boards was also endorsed by Daisy Harriman, who found Walsh's report "incendiary and revolutionary."[41]

The differences between the Walsh and Commons reports were instructive, illustrating an important split in Progressive-era thinking on the labor question and the state. Where Commons sought government-sponsored mediation, Walsh sought the protection of workers' rights to organize. Where Commons sought an expansive state administrative capacity, Walsh sought only the "rapid extension of the principles of democracy to industry," hoping that trade unionists would then capitalize on the right to organize. And, significantly, where Commons hoped to keep the unions free of politics, Walsh envisioned a new politics constructed around workers' rights to industrial democracy. Indeed, as he would later show, Walsh hoped to translate the momentum of the USCIR's investigation into a political movement that could achieve the reforms he sought.

Most observers thought that its divided final reports signaled the USCIR's failure. Walsh was condemned by the editors of the *Survey* and the *New Republic* alike for preferring theatrics to sound social policy and for failing to craft a consensus within the commission. Hoke Smith, Walsh's old foe on Capitol Hill, contended that "much of the work of the Commission was useless." Only those on the Left, it seemed, approved of Walsh's work. Among them the verdict was unanimous. Carl Sandburg lauded Walsh's "tremendous ideas," Denver workers proclaimed him the "*only* man who has ever forced the Rockefellers to acknowledge the supremacy of the law," and even such customary foes as Samuel Gompers, Eugene Debs, and Bill Haywood found rare common ground in endorsing his report.[42]

Although the USCIR's work met a mixed reception outside of the Left, the commission still exerted some lasting influence nonetheless. Indeed, in some respects because of its failure to reach consensus, it served to profoundly shape some broader political developments. Its investigation had given the Wilson administration a more favorable image among unionists and workers than it had been able to win through the legislative achievements of its first three years. This fact was certainly an irony, given that Wilson was often troubled by Walsh's ways and that the president remained silent as critics assailed Walsh's final report. The commission had also propelled Walsh toward the center of the political stage just as progressivism's most dramatic moment was arriving. Indeed, it seemed to the *New Republic* that Walsh was fast becoming "the leader around whom American radicalism has tried to rally." [43] As a result of these developments and Walsh's almost unique ability to appeal to radicals, unionists and left-wing progressives alike, the USCIR had helped lay the basis for a courtship between the Wilson administration and broad segments of the Left prior to the 1916 election. Out of that courtship, it seemed to many at the time, emerged a reform politics in which the quest for industrial democracy was destined to assume a central place.

DEMOCRATS, INDUSTRIAL DEMOCRATS, AND THE 1916 ELECTION

Shortly after the USCIR concluded its work, Frank Walsh set out to link his call for industrial democracy to a political program. Passing up an opportunity to serve as counsel to the railway brotherhoods, Walsh turned instead toward the more exciting task of building a broad-based movement linking progressives and trade unionists in common cause. In November 1915, Walsh announced the formation of a private Committee on Industrial Relations (CIR). Walsh's hope was to bring together "leaders of every school of economic belief, from the so-called most conservative to the so-called wildest radical" to sound "one harmonious note for justice to labor." [44] The CIR did that. The group included Basil Manly, John Lennon, James O'Connell, and Austin Garretson, each of whom had served on the USCIR. But, in organizing the CIR, Walsh also reached out to a broader coalition of activists, trade unionists, and progressives, including Agnes Nestor and Helen Marot of the Women's Trade Union League, Immigration Commissioner Frederick C. Howe, liberal lawyer Amos Pinchot, Bishop Charles D. Williams of the Episcopal Diocese of Detroit, newspaperman Dante Barton, and President John P. White of the UMW.

In the CIR the advocates of industrial democracy found a common ground.

FRANK WALSH: "HAMMER ON THAT DOOR UNTIL YOU GET WHAT YOU ARE ENTITLED TO — A FAIR SHARE OF WHAT YOU PRODUCE!"

A political cartoonist for the Denver Post *felt that Frank P. Walsh's new Committee on Industrial Relations would be a potent force on the political scene in 1915. (Frank P. Walsh Papers, New York Public Library, Astor, Lenox and Tilden Foundation)*

The CIR linked conservative AFL stalwarts, such as Lennon and O'Connell, with left-wing sympathizers like Marot, who wrote frequently on labor topics for the *Masses*; Howe, who served as director of the radical People's Institute at Cooper Union; and Pinchot, who became active in the antiwar American Union against Militarism. This was a varied group of allies, to be sure. But most of its members understood that their influence would come in part from their diversity and agreed that "the Committee should not be labeled, that the public should be kept guessing" about their politics. Over the next year they hung together despite their differences, and Walsh expressed pleasure that "our circle is constantly widening." It is likely that Walsh's friend Dante

Barton was right in his assessment of the CIR's success. It stood a fair chance of building a coalition "for the sole and single reason," thought Barton, that the immensely popular Walsh was "at the head of it."[45]

The CIR cast itself as "an agency at Washington through which democratic thought on industrial problems can make itself felt," as one of its staffers put it. Under Basil Manly's day-to-day direction, the CIR opened offices in the Southern Building, where the USCIR had been housed, and capitalized on the illusion that it was simply an extension of the earlier federal body. Its inaugural statement noted that there was "every indication that the next few years will be the critical years in the history of American labor."[46] Walsh and his industrial democrats determined to figure large in the coming events.

Union leaders applauded the new organization, urging the "undivided support of organized labor." The radicals at the *Masses* hailed the CIR as "a permanent bureau of publicity for the American revolt." Stirring the fears of its foes and raising the expectations of its friends, the CIR soon took up a wide range of activities: planning motion pictures, founding fifty-six local groups around the nation, coordinating a national "Industrial Relations Day" on January 16, 1916, proposing an amendment to restrict the courts' right to judicial review, and campaigning for the "Americanization" of immigrants through union organization. San Francisco organizers expressed the hope that local committees of the CIR might become "a medium through which the Committee on Industrial Relations, from its headquarters in Washington, can quickly and effectively reach the 2,500,000 organized workers of the country." Such plans led conservative critics to allege that Walsh had simply formed a new "body of mischiefmakers" in order "to bring about a reincarnation of the [USCIR]."[47]

What first attracted national attention to the CIR, however, was its support for strikes. Among its early endeavors, the CIR publicized the plight of striking Pullman workers in Chicago and striking cloak makers and streetcar drivers in New York City. But it was its response to two walkouts—one that erupted in East Youngstown, Ohio, on December 27, 1915, and another that rocked the Pittsburgh area in April 1916—that made the CIR notorious. In each case, CIR-generated publicity on behalf of strikers outraged well-organized employers. The *Iron Trade Review* blamed "Walsh agitators" for Youngstown's labor trouble and demanded that "the administration at Washington . . . suppress this mischief-making coterie." One spokesperson for Pittsburgh employers even suggested that Walsh "should be assassinated."[48]

The work of the CIR only enhanced Walsh's reputation for radicalism. Since his service on the USCIR, Walsh had developed a friendship with the IWW's Vincent St. John and a growing respect for Bill Haywood. Although

Walsh had once faulted the IWW leader for falling "victim to the passion for short and effective sentences," by 1915 he was praising Haywood as a "rugged intellectual." Neither Haywood nor St. John joined the CIR; but other labor militants did. Among them were three men who later became Walsh's confidants: union dissident Alex Howatt, of the Kansas UMW; John Fitzpatrick of the CFL; and anarchist Anton Johannsen, the West Coast building trades organizer. Johannsen, who had been indicted in connection with the bombing of the *Los Angeles Times*, had refused to condemn that act in testimony before the USCIR. Walsh embraced him nonetheless. Although he hoped to work with Gompers, in choosing such allies Walsh showed that he was also prepared to enlist in Johannsen's fight against "the narrow and selfish interests of our labor leaders."[49]

Some trade unionists joined the *Seattle Union Record* in praising the CIR's ecumenism, congratulating it for gaining "the united support of all 'outsiders,' who acknowledge labor's leadership." But Samuel Gompers was not one of them. Because of Walsh's radical associations, the AFL leader closely monitored the CIR's activities and the relationship of the AFL to the organization. Even as he publicly hailed Walsh as "a great tribune," an "unwavering seeker of justice," Gompers privately sought to rein in his meddlesome group. When the CIR appealed to unions for funds, Gompers "invariably" advised them not to contribute. Meanwhile, Gompers used Lennon to voice his concerns within the CIR. In its executive meetings, the AFL treasurer argued that the CIR could ill afford to be "identified in opposition to the labor movement," and he urged CIR members to let the AFL's Executive Council "approve our work." Neither Walsh's assurances that the CIR would not "encroach upon the field occupied by organized labor" nor his decision to leave people "whose names might give the trade unionists a wrong impression" off the CIR's letterhead assuaged Lennon's or Gompers's fears. The continued obstructionism of the AFL's leaders periodically led Walsh to consider severing ties with union conservatives in order to put the CIR "on the basis of the less divided sort of radicalism." But ultimately Walsh judged the CIR's association with the AFL too valuable to sacrifice.[50]

Important in Walsh's calculations were the approaching 1916 elections and the growing threat that the United States might be drawn into the war in Europe. These two developments reconfigured the nation's political terrain in the final year of Wilson's first term. Both developments also created political opportunities that Walsh hoped to exploit with the help of trade union allies. When he did seize those opportunities, he was able to turn the CIR's reputation for radicalism to his own advantage in an attempt to bring the Left and Wilson together.

Political winds began shifting within the Wilson administration in 1915. Before that time the administration had stocked a bare legislative cupboard for labor. In the final two years of his first term, however, President Wilson signed four important bills—the La Follette Seamen's Act, the Keating-Owens Child Labor Act, the Kern-McGillicuddy Federal Workmen's Compensation Act, and the Adamson Act—into law. Together these constituted a veritable "Second New Freedom." Previously critical of such measures as a federal law prohibiting the interstate transportation of goods made by child labor, Wilson suddenly emerged as a strong friend of labor legislation.[51]

How far Wilson was prepared to go in this direction was best revealed by his support for the Adamson Act, for it was this action that earned him the harshest criticism. Seeking to "protect the pockets of our men," as one railroad brotherhood leader put it, the four great railway operators unions threatened to walk out on Labor Day 1916 unless they were granted an eight-hour workday. To avert this conflict, which would have endangered both his preparedness program and his reelection, President Wilson signed a bill rushed through the Democratic Congress by Senator W. C. Adamson. Following a signing ceremony on his private railroad car in Washington's Union Station, the president symbolically handed one pen to each of the heads of the four railway brotherhoods. Wilson received thunderous condemnation from Republicans for this seeming "capitulation" to union blackmail.[52]

Frank Walsh hailed the Adamson Act, with characteristic hyperbole, as the beginning of a "worldwide" movement that meant "the beginning of the end" for "industrial despotism." Wilson's move to the left led Walsh to believe that the cause of industrial democracy could be advanced through Wilson's Democratic Party in the next election. "I may exaggerate it," Walsh told a friend, "but I believe [it is] the most important thing that has happened in my time." As Wilson shifted his stance, Walsh and his allies sought ways to magnify their influence within the administration, throwing themselves into electoral politics in the summer of 1916.[53]

Their first step was to send CIR delegations to both the Republican and the Democratic conventions to urge adoption of the Walsh Report's "fundamental propositions" in each party's platform. Not surprisingly, the Republican convention coldly rebuffed the CIR. Indeed, Republicans chose to make Walsh a prime campaign target in the presidential campaign of Charles Evans Hughes. Terming the USCIR "one of the tragic incidents of the present administration" and claiming that its investigation had "accomplished nothing," Republicans criticized Wilson for having allowed Walsh to use the commission as a platform for "his socialistic theories and ideas." Again, as expected, Democrats reacted more warmly to the CIR, listening attentively as Walsh delivered testimony to their platform committee designed to "kick the profit system down stairs," as one newspaper put it. Walsh called on the Democrats both to recognize workers' right to "control their share in industry through the power of collective bargaining" and to condemn militarism, Taylorism, and the concentration of wealth. Democrats responded by endorsing the USCIR's report and distributing party literature that called it a "Great Charter of industrial as well as political liberty." [54]

Not all members of Wilson's party approved. As the *New York Call* observed, many leading Democrats regarded Walsh "as an overly enthusiastic person who must be gently kept from monkeying with the machinery." And a smaller faction held still more hostile views. Walsh's old rival, Senator Reed, for one, warned that Walsh was nothing but a "viper upon the bosom" of the party. In a screed to Joe Tumulty, Reed raged against the "broad and unmistakable" inference that if its leaders did "not bow to the policies of Mr. Walsh and his cohorts that the Democratic Party will be appropriately punished by the withdrawal of their support." Many right-wing Democrats harkened to Reed's words. [55]

But Woodrow Wilson did not join them. As the 1916 election neared, the president sought to shore up his support among progressives. Though the distant thunder of war in Europe proved to be the most crucial campaign issue in 1916, Wilson could ill afford to neglect the votes of reformers who desired an ambitious domestic legislative agenda. So Wilson cast the Democrats as "the party of reform" in 1916, and by so doing, he lured trade unionists, social workers, erstwhile Bull Moosers, and even Socialists into his column. [56] The AFL played an important role in this process, and Wilson courted its support by, among other things, dedicating the new AFL headquarters on July 4, 1916. Gompers repaid Wilson's solicitation of labor with editorials in the *American Federationist* that urged unionists to reelect the president. Many unionists responded. But Walsh and his friends in the CIR—because of the reputation for radicalism that had begun to adhere to them—were in a position to deliver to Wilson something Gompers could not: credibility on the left.

So, in August 1916, over the violent objections of such conservatives as James Reed, President Wilson summoned Frank Walsh to a White House meeting in the midst of the railway crisis. The man whom Pittsburgh industrialists wished "assassinated," the same man who had embarrassed Wilson on more than one occasion as chairman of the USCIR, was called in to advise the president on the railway brotherhoods' eight-hour demand. Rather than ignoring Walsh, the president embraced him. And he later expressed his "peculiar pleasure" to the CIR for its support of his reelection campaign. In return, CIR members threw themselves into the Wilson effort. It was, Walsh concluded, "the only game there is." Basil Manly agreed. "It seems to me now plainly the duty of every radical to do everything possible to re-elect Wilson," Manly reasoned, "and . . . to put as many *real democrats* in close to him for the next term as can be squeezed in."[57]

Manly hoped that the CIR's "radical democrats" working in "closest harmony" with the Democratic National Committee would create a faction within the Wilson camp that would outlast the election, and Walsh was well positioned to aid such an undertaking. According to the assessment of one Democratic operative, he "could do more good in labor circles than any other man in the United States." Walsh was prepared to exploit his position. "I want to help Wilson mightily," he confided. With Walsh's help, CIR members took up the Wilson banner without regard to ordinary partisanship, distributing press releases and organizing a speakers' bureau to crisscross New York, the Republican candidate's home state, attacking Hughes's labor record.[58]

The presence of CIR members tilted Wilson's campaign leftward. For example, it was George P. West—a man who had joined the CIR in hopes of "throwing Gompersism out" of the labor movement—who was tapped to run labor publicity for the Democratic Party during the campaign, not a Gompers man. Nor did the stump speeches that Frank Walsh delivered for Wilson on a swing through industrial cities dampen the potential support of radicals for the Democrat. Walsh characterized Charles Evans Hughes as a "cowardly politician" and urged listeners to vote for "the great liberator," Wilson. Only Wilson, Walsh suggested, could lead the way toward industrial democracy. Such arguments caught many of Walsh's recent Socialist Party allies by surprise. The *Cleveland Citizen* attacked the CIR leader for arguing that Wilson was "the best man" and for soliciting Socialist votes for him. But at least one Socialist daily understood the power of Walsh's appeal. In lauding Wilson's virtues, Walsh used arguments "entirely identical with those used by the average Socialist campaigner," the *Schenectady Citizen* reported. Indeed, Walsh made Wilson seem radical.[59]

It is difficult to gauge the role that the AFL played in delivering the close 1916 election to Woodrow Wilson. The labor vote, combined with Republican infighting, may have helped put California into Wilson's column. But, on the whole, workers did not constitute a coherent bloc, as Irish American opposition to Wilson stemming from his well-known Anglophilia vividly demonstrated. Therefore, any attempt to assess the CIR's influence on the election would be even more difficult to sustain.[60] What cannot be contested, however, is that the president saw the support of Walsh and the CIR as worth having. This fact made the results of the 1916 contest sweet news for the partisans of industrial democracy.

The CIR was quick to claim some credit for the outcome. "I am the happiest man in America over the Wilson victory," Walsh announced. His colleagues were every bit as breathless. Rabbi Stephen Wise believed that the Democratic Party had finally freed itself "from the racial and social Toryism of the South." Dante Barton thought the election was "the most notable political happening" in American history. "It seems to me that now pretty nearly anything is possible for radicalism and real democracy," he noted, "now that Wilson has won, after he and those supporting him had put the issue on such a radical plane."[61]

Members of the CIR may not have elected a president, but their attachment to Wilson completed a process that had unfolded over the previous four years. As he prepared to take the oath of office again in March 1917, President Wilson not only had recemented his alliance with the AFL but had also built ties to an influential community of progressives, labor militants, and radicals who advocated the democratization of industry. In the war crisis that would explode in the following month, that alliance would take on a greater significance than anyone could have foreseen.

WAR AND ORDER
IN THE WORKPLACE
2

Industrial democracy is on the way.

—*John Dewey, 1917*

Had America not entered a "war to make the world safe for democracy," a conflict that would deeply destabilize existing labor relations, as the reverberations from the USCIR investigation still echoed, then the work of Frank Walsh and his friends may have had little lasting significance. But America went to war at precisely the moment when industrial democracy was in vogue. It seemed to labor relations student Ernest M. Hopkins that everyone was speaking of the democratization of industry once the USCIR concluded its work. In an essay for a 1916 volume dedicated to the subject, Hopkins noted that he had "heard industrial democracy talked about within a few months among others by a trade unionist, a syndicalist . . . and an employer." Each of them, Hopkins marveled, used the term to signify what that person desired: to the trade unionist, it meant collective bargaining; to the syndicalist, "that industry belonged solely to the workers"; and to the employer, it implied merely a company union "permeated with a common zeal."[1]

Whatever Americans meant by it, they increasingly invoked industrial democracy as their answer to the labor problem on the eve of war. "Nearly all Americans to-day are willing to concede that business absolutism has its dangers," wrote Professor Frank Tracy Carlton. He predicted that the industrial world was "emerging from the era of industrial autocracy." Reformer

Harry F. Ward foresaw an end to "despotic ownership" and the emergence of "the elective control of industry." Louis D. Brandeis argued that the time had arrived for workers to gain "not merely a right to be heard, but a position through which labor may participate in management." Even Socialists and Wobblies found themselves speaking of government ownership and syndicalism as industrial democracy. William English Walling argued that only socialism could really "lead towards industrial democracy" in the "fuller and ordinary use of the word." Meanwhile, the IWW's newspaper ran a six-part series on the subject. As one Wobbly put it, only the IWW bore "the glorifying promise . . . of industrial democracy."[2]

A sure measure of the popularity of prewar industrial democracy talk was the criticism it earned from conservatives. In 1915, University of Chicago economist J. Laurence Laughlin, who had originally gained fame by debunking the Populist pamphleteer William "Coin" Harvey, turned his guns on what he perceived to be the most dangerous fad since "free silver." The demand for "industrial democracy," he warned, was spreading "like water in a lump of sugar." An idea hostile to the "system of property," it was to be resisted if America would preserve its heritage. Ernest Hopkins too wondered whether, under the weight of growing demands for democracy in the workplace, "authority has been weakened" until it commanded "even less respect than obedience."[3]

For those who fretted about a growing crisis of authority in the workplace, wartime was a nightmare. "This is a hell of a time to strike in America," one U.S. Army corporal complained to a hometown reporter on a French battlefield during World War I. Although he may not have liked their interpretation of his comment, doubtless many workers back home would have readily agreed with the corporal: wartime conditions had indeed made it "a hell of a time to strike." And strike workers did. Rather than anything resembling a *Burgfrieden* (the German "truce of the fortress"), the year 1917 brought unprecedented labor turmoil to the United States. Tight labor markets, an improving economy, and the consequent rise in union militancy combined to unleash a mammoth strike wave. An astounding 438 strikes took place during the first full month after the United States went to war. And during the first six months of the war, 6,285,519 workdays were lost to nearly 3,000 strikes. Overworked federal conciliators could scarcely keep up with the requests for strike mediation submitted to the Labor Department. As one ship engine builder saw it, strike fever was simply "in the air."[4]

The years around 1886, which saw the meteoric rise of the Knights of Labor, are often termed the "Great Upheaval." It would not be inaccurate to describe the turbulence of 1917 as a "Second Great Upheaval." As in that earlier period, the context for the upheaval of 1917 was set over a period of years; and when it burst forth it tested old forms of labor organization, spawned numerous radical initiatives, briefly threw open to question the future organization of the workplace, and triggered a furious employers' counterattack. During the Great Upheaval, many workers had been animated by the Knights' vision of a "Cooperative Commonwealth." Because of the developments that preceded America's entry into the First World War and because President Wilson waged this war as a democratic crusade, it would be around the ideal of "industrial democracy" that most workers would rally in the Second Great Upheaval. But old patterns of workplace relations first had to collapse before such a development became possible.

THE DISORGANIZATION OF THE WARTIME WORKPLACE

Four factors contributed to the explosiveness of the 1917 labor unrest, shaping the context within which industrial democracy would be debated. They were the extent to which labor and consumer markets were altered by mobilization, the zeal with which open-shop employers defended the status quo, the enthusiasm with which workers pursued efforts to better their own lots through collective action, and the degree to which the industrial workforce was reshaped in wartime. These factors ensured that the war did not submerge class antagonism as much as it accentuated what Secretary of Labor Wilson called the "traditional cleavages between employers and wage earners."[5]

The most immediate fuel for labor militancy was inflation. Between 1913 and 1919, the price of twenty-two basic commodities increased by 92 percent. Food prices alone rose 52 percent between 1916 and 1918. Housing costs also shot up—more so in those wartime boomtowns that contained shipyards or munitions plants. Thus, although real wages had risen between 1914 and 1916, wage gains by the end of 1917 began to lag behind inflation. A trip to the market or a glance at newspaper reports on the profiteering of munitions manufacturers punctured any illusion that Americans were sacrificing equally to win the war and undermined simplistic appeals to patriotism. Indeed, inflated price tags and rising stock dividends made it easy for strikers to fend off attacks on their Americanism by blaming "the poor patriotic profiteer who must work his help at least sixteen hours a day in order to clean up his millions."[6]

The Wilson government's decision to award key war contracts on a "cost-plus" basis further contributed to the problem of inflation by indemnifying contractors against any profit squeeze from rising labor costs and encouraging employers to "scamp" scarce labor from one another, bidding up wages in the process. Cost-plus contracts encouraged workers to demand higher wages and assuaged employers' fears about granting them. And while some in the administration joined presidential secretary Joseph Tumulty in criticizing policies that "multiplied time and again" the "prices to be paid by the consumer," no consensus emerged among Wilsonians for tackling the cost-plus problem. A conference that was to have been held in the summer of 1917 to hammer out methods of containing inflation was scrapped by the administration.[7]

Accentuating inflation's bite on workers' pocketbooks were wage rates that wildly fluctuated from region to region and industry to industry. By 1918, common labor could fetch twenty-two cents per hour in the South; forty cents in New England, where munitions and shipyard work bulked large; and fifty cents on the West Coast, where drastic labor shortages hampered all industries. Within these regions, shipyards or wartime boomtowns acted as magnets pulling workers toward high-waged war jobs. The resulting turbulence perpetuated a cycle of wage competition, and the ensuing chaos disrupted labor agreements and altered workers' expectations, encouraging organized and unorganized workers alike to strike for wage increases. Not surprisingly, wage disputes accounted for nearly 40 percent of all strikes during the first six months of the war.[8]

Taken together, these developments helped draw attention to the role that simple power politics played in structuring wartime markets in goods and labor. Skyrocketing housing costs, booming munitions industry profits, and the unpredictability of wages taught an increasing number of Americans that markets were driven by more than mere supply and demand. They were also shaped by the political power of builders, war contractors, and employers. Nothing drove home this point more clearly than the capriciousness with which conscription was often implemented. Recent scholarship suggests that the draft was often wielded as a tool by local employers whose interests frequently dominated local draft boards: they sought more control over labor markets through the draft, and they usually got it. The fact that as many as 80 percent of eligible registrants in some otherwise patriotic counties sought to avoid active service by requesting exemptions or joining a military organization not likely to see action suggests that workers understood this fact well enough. They took what measures they could to protect themselves from a lottery that was scarcely shaped by blind luck alone.[9]

Another source of wartime labor conflict during the first year of the war stemmed from employers' spirited attempts to undermine trade unionism. In at least seven states—including such war production centers as New York, Massachusetts, Pennsylvania, and Connecticut—business groups fought to weaken labor laws designed to protect women workers. Only the firm opposition of the Wilson administration saved such legislation from repeal. Undaunted, industrialists attacked on other fronts. On the national level, the American Iron and Steel Institute urged that coal miners be drafted into an industrial army; locally, such companies as Wagner Electric of St. Louis forced employees to sign loyalty oaths that pledged them to "do nothing in word or deed detrimental to the interests of the company." [10]

Nothing better illustrated how far employers were willing to go in attacking unionism than the "Bisbee deportation," the most infamous antiunion episode to come from the first year of the war. A strike of copper miners in that Arizona town provided a pretext for Sheriff Harry Wheeler, once a member of Teddy Roosevelt's Rough Riders, to form a vigilante posse supported by copper mine interests. On July 12, 1917, Wheeler and his posse rounded up over one thousand striking copper miners, loaded them onto cattle cars, and "deported" them into the New Mexico desert. This action outraged Secretary Wilson and Labor Department officials who were trying to cooperate with AFL leaders in achieving labor peace and full production. But the administration lacked the resources and the political consensus that might have allowed it to control vigilantism. [11]

The extent of antiunionism in the United States stunned foreign observers unacquainted with American ways. One British coal operator, on tour for the Ministry of Munitions, was surprised to find "hostility to a quite unbelievable extent against organized labor." "I do not think it is an exaggeration to say," he reported, that American employers were so intent on preserving the open shop that "the winning of the war is almost a secondary consideration for them." [12]

Employer attacks on trade unionism were matched by workers' own vigorous counterattacks. Strikes erupted at an unprecedented rate in the first months of the war. Two factors tended to account for their pattern. The first was the degree of connection of an industry to the war effort. The crucial, war-related metal trades, shipbuilding, coal mining, and copper mining industries together contributed 61.8 percent of all strikers during the first six months of the war (see table 1). The second factor was the percentage of union members in the workplace. Workplaces where more than 75 percent of workers were unionized accounted for almost one-half of all strikes early in the war. Meanwhile, partially organized workplaces where less than one-quarter of the workers were in unions accounted for less than 5 percent of strikes (see table 2). Together, these statistics reinforce an important point: wartime strikes were not so much spontaneous eruptions of workers seeking higher wages or giving voice to other grievances as they were planned actions by strategically placed, well-organized workers who sought to exploit favorable conditions.

TABLE 1. STRIKES BY INDUSTRY, APRIL 6–OCTOBER 6, 1917

INDUSTRY	NUMBER OF ESTABLISHMENTS STRUCK	PERCENTAGE OF ESTABLISHMENTS STRUCK	NUMBER OF WORKERS IDLED	PERCENTAGE OF ALL WORKERS IDLED
Metal trades	375	32.4	78,727	27.8
Shipbuilding	75	6.5	47,174	16.7
Coal mines	59	5.1	31,973	11.3
Copper mines	24	2.1	16,911	6.0
Textiles	122	10.6	20,708	7.3
Lumber	65	5.6	11,136	3.9
Clothing/shoes	59	5.1	10,396	3.7
Railroads	46	4.0	10,684	3.8
Foods	45	3.9	20,228	7.1
Building	22	1.9	1,780	0.6
All others	264	22.8	33,685	11.8
Total	1,156	100.0	283,402	100.0

Source: National Industrial Conference Board, *Strikes in American Industry in Wartime.*

Where workers were well organized, their actions could be quite effective indeed. If the Bisbee deportation of July 1917 symbolized the power of anti-union employers during the early months of the war, a union-organized "deportation" in Kansas City only one month later showed how forcefully organized workers could defend their interests during the war. On August 7, 1917, more than one thousand employees of Kansas City's metropolitan streetcar company struck for union recognition. A coalition of trade unionists and their political supporters rallied behind the strikers—including the mayor, who had supervised the destruction of a local IWW office a month earlier. Rather than see their city's transit system crippled by the walkout, politicians demanded that the transit company negotiate, refusing to deputize the company's security guards in the meantime. When the defiant employers attempted to import strikebreakers on August 10, strikers—with the support of the police—overturned streetcars bearing the "finks," escorted them to the train station where they were expelled from the city, and gladly accepted Police Chief Thomas Flahive's congratulations for their efforts.[13]

TABLE 2. STRIKES BY PROPORTION OF UNION MEMBERS IN WORKPLACE, APRIL 6–OCTOBER 6, 1917

PERCENTAGE OF UNION MEMBERS AMONG STRIKERS	NUMBER OF WORKPLACES STRUCK	PERCENTAGE OF ALL STRIKES	NUMBER OF WORKERS IDLED	PERCENTAGE OF WORKERS IDLED
None	161	13.9	18,999	6.7
1 to 25%	51	4.4	18,852	6.7
26 to 50%	96	8.3	42,620	15.0
51 to 75%	113	9.8	58,609	20.7
76 to 100%	561	48.5	117,664	41.5
Unknown	174	15.1	26,658	9.4
Total	1,156	100.0	283,402	100.0

Source: National Industrial Conference Board, *Strikes in American Industry in Wartime.*

Pitched battles such as these were the exception rather than the rule, of course. But they hinted at a less visible, more diffuse guerrilla war that spread in wartime workplaces throughout the country—a war whose battles went unreported in newspapers, whose clashes erupted and evaporated too quickly to attract union organizers and federal mediators, too quickly to merit inclusion in official strike statistics. The course of that war was shaped by a labor market tightened by mobilization, conscription, and the virtual suspension of immigration. Such conditions left wage earners free to protest working conditions or quit work in search of a better job—driving turnover rates up over 300 percent annually in some war-related workplaces and curbing the effectiveness of such time-tested employers' weapons as yellow-dog contracts, labor spies, discriminatory firings, and lockouts.[14]

These less visible battles were not merely economic in nature. They were about power in the workplace. Perhaps nothing better showed this than workers' collective efforts to battle the injustices of the piece rate system. Piece rates were a source of continuous frustration to large segments of the World War I–era workforce. Screw machine operators at General Electric, for example, complained bitterly that their wages fluctuated between nine and thirty dollars per week because of unpredictable piece rates. But just as important to them was the indignity of the time-motion study. Efforts by GE to time workers were a constant source of irritation. "You can never tell," one worker explained, when the boss "would be putting the stop watch on you." The result was almost invariably a downward revision in the rate designed to speed up the work. Resistance naturally grew in such an environment. As Margaret Crough later recalled of GE, "When you worked in there as long as I have and seen things reduced, you feel kind of provoked."[15]

Most often workers resisted piece rate exploitation by concealing from their bosses their true rate of output. As J. Edwin Doyle of GE later explained to federal investigators, "No matter how much we made we would stick in only so much [on our pay card] for fear of getting the job cut." Employers such as H. H. Edge of the Locomobile Company of Bridgeport, Connecticut, thus often complained to the government of their workers' "restriction of output" on "account of piece-rate earnings." But they found themselves increasingly unable to combat restriction of output successfully as the war went forward. Remington Arms found this to be the case. When the company locked out fifty bayonet straighteners for resisting a piece rate cut in October 1917, machinists generally threatened to reduce output and take "drastic action."[16]

The extent to which such action was often successful in restoring piece rate cuts was evidenced by two short, unorganized strikes involving between 250 and 300 women workers at the Lynn GE plant in 1917. When these Lynn GE women found that a rate setter had been placed in their midst to time out a new piece rate, they took swift action. They "got very excited," one of them remembered, "and well they started what I would call a rough house, and it was some rough house." After shutting down their department for over an hour, during which time the foreman "couldn't do a thing with the women," they succeeded in having the rate setter removed. Subsequent attempts by a foreman to bribe one of the shop women into setting a new rate herself provoked another short shutdown and met with no success.[17] Clearly, battles such as these were waged as much over the pace of work and the power to determine that pace as they were over wages.

The effect of such running guerrilla battles was to accelerate the erosion of management authority in many wartime workplaces. This reality persistently confounded managers, as an episode experienced by one official at Lynn's GE plant illustrated. Following the loss of a number of the "red-blooded men" in his plant's turbine division to enlistment in April 1917, this manager claimed that the company was held hostage by those who remained behind. "These men came to the foreman who in charge at that time and demanded an increase in pay or they would get through at once," he later reported. General Electric had little choice but to appease these "green men." Wage increases were immediately granted. As that official saw it, GE was "simply held up" by its workers.[18]

Adding to the turmoil in workplaces produced by inflation and the battle between workers and managers was the extent to which the face of the industrial workforce changed during the war. In some ways, mobilization confirmed existing patterns in industry. More than one-half of all war contracts, for example, were awarded to companies in just four heavily industrialized states: Massachusetts, New York, Illinois, and Ohio. Yet in other ways the war profoundly altered existing patterns, especially the racial, ethnic, and gender boundaries that had so structured the prewar labor market. Although the number of immigrants arriving in the United States fell from over 1.2 million in 1914 to only 110,618 in 1918, war industries siphoned off skilled and semi-skilled labor alike. Some 378,000 workers flocked to government shipyards alone during the war.[19] The resulting turbulence broke down commonly accepted patterns of employment, opening opportunities for recent immigrants to advance beyond the lowest rungs of industry and allowing more women and African Americans to enter the industrial workforce than ever before. These changes initiated friction among war workers along ethnic, skill, gender, and racial lines. Ultimately, such conflict could contribute as much to the deterioration of orderly workplace relations as battles between workers and managers.

Ethnic conflicts, for example, often produced explosive results. If the Bisbee deportation signified the tenacity of employer antiunionism, and the Kansas City deportation, the persistence of working-class solidarity, a third "deportation" that occurred in the lead-mining district of Missouri forty miles north of St. Louis in July 1917 indicated how violently native-born white workers could resist the wartime gains of previously subordinated groups. Two days after the Bisbee affair, native-born miners seized on the wartime hysteria to seek a racial monopoly on lead-mining work in their region. A mob of one thousand "freeborn American" miners chased an organizer of the International Union of Mine, Mill, and Smelter Workers out of Missouri; stoned the homes of foreign-born miners; and rounded up Italian, Russian, and Polish immigrants, pinning American flags to their lapels and loading as many as two thousand of them on trains out of the district. As such incidents make clear, in wartime America workers could fight one another just as bitterly as they fought their employers—and oftentimes far more effectively.[20]

Another continuing area of friction throughout the war ran along the fault line of skill. Skilled workers feared, as one union man put it, that the "trades, with the exception of a few, have practically disappeared" as a result of government training programs and the demand for war workers. Veteran carpenters complained of those who rushed to claim high wages building Liberty ships, men who entered shipyards "under the guise of a carpenter" with "a

Four wartime workers at the Westinghouse Electric Company, ca. 1918. (Hagley Museum and Library, Wilmington, Delaware)

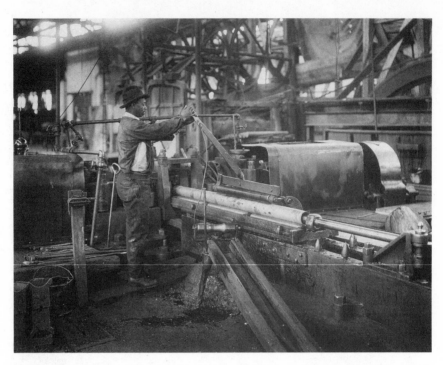

A black worker in an Ohio rolling mill, ca. 1918. (National Archives II, College Park, Maryland)

rusty saw and a hammer wrapped up in a newspaper, who come in from the woods without hardly any experience." Electrical workers also criticized green hands, who, they claimed, had yet to learn the habits of solidarity. "It seems a hard job to get wiremen to stick together," one electricians' organizer reported, since companies were hiring anyone "with nerve enough to call himself a wireman." [21]

Gender bias also complicated wartime work relations. One formerly male bastion, the metal trades, saw an explosive growth in women's employment. By the summer of 1918 some 100,000 women were employed in munitions plants and airplane factories—up from only 3,500 in 1910. In theory, AFL unions welcomed women on equal footing where they were perceived as necessary to the war effort. In practice, the story was much more ambiguous. For example, the International Association of Machinists (IAM) passed a resolution in April 1917 calling for the organization of women war workers. But IAM members continued to be among those most resistant to working alongside women. Railroad shopmen around the country resisted the organization of semiskilled female "specialists"; tire factory machinists in Akron blocked the hiring of women as "an entering wedge" that would debase their craft; and

Waynesboro, Pennsylvania, metalworkers pressured employers to fire women trainees.[22]

African Americans, of course, received the least enthusiastic reception from skilled whites. Most northern trade unionists agreed with one speaker at the AFL's 1916 convention who termed the "Great Migration" of blacks from the South a "menace" that had to be stopped. The East St. Louis race riot of July 1917, which left fifty dead, was in large part triggered by the reaction of that city's Central Trades and Labor Union to the influx of thousands of black workers. Race riots in Erie and Chester, Pennsylvania, sparked when blacks and whites competed over jobs on the docks and in shipyards, testified to the ubiquity of wartime racial tensions in the northern labor market. Further evidence came from GE, where white workers successfully kept blacks from employment. When the Schenectady GE plant hired a black machine specialist in June 1917, three thousand white machinists and helpers struck— apparently over the objections of their progressive local union leaders. They returned to work only after GE agreed to hire no northward-migrating blacks for the duration of the war.[23]

VISIONS OF ORDER

As wartime conditions disrupted familiar patterns of labor relations in the United States, employers no longer possessed as much power to compel obedience on the shop floor. Leading politicians began worrying about the consequences. Senator Porter J. McCumber of North Dakota was one of them. Arguing that workers were "slacking in a most shameful and disgraceful manner" and "drunken with power swelled with importance, guided by no standard but that of more, and more, and still more," he proposed creating a "civilian reserve" to discipline labor.[24] Many employers thrilled to the notion. But such proposals could scarcely receive a serious hearing in a nation that had construed its participation in this war as an effort to defend democracy. Rather, in keeping with the debate engendered by prewar reformers, most of those who offered solutions to wartime labor troubles presented them as models to achieve "industrial democracy."

As Ernest Hopkins had noted, at least three groups were advocating alternative visions of industrial democracy by the time the United States entered the war. One vision was advanced by a group of farsighted employers, influenced by renegades from the scientific management movement who had begun to recognize that workers' participation could influence the efficiency of production. Another vision, championed by the leadership of the AFL, posited the trade union collective bargaining agreement as the sine qua non of democratic industrial relations. A third vision, less fully articulated than the other two, emerged from the ranks of trade union militants and their allies. It linked industrial democracy to a radical restructuring of workplace and social relations.

Overlapping at some points, in clear opposition at others, these visions attracted adherents who were often bitterly at odds but who also occasionally shared ideas. As a brief overview indicates, proponents of each view shared the belief that the time had arrived to democratize the workplace.

A Corporate Model of Employee Representation

A growing interest in the merits of nonunion employee representation emerged among some American employers on the eve of World War I. That interest can be traced to two sources: a rebellion that took place within the ranks of the followers of the most influential management consultant of the prewar era, and the emergence of the company union movement.

The first of these was a most unlikely source indeed. Who could have predicted that the followers of the founder of scientific management, Frederick Winslow Taylor, would play an important role in promoting workplace representation by the time of World War I? Between the publication of his famous article "Shop Management" in 1903 and his 1911 book *The Principles of Scientific Management*, Taylor had led an effort to reorganize the American workplace. In doing so, he squared off against the principles of trade union representation in the most militant fashion. Utilizing stopwatches, time-motion studies, and differential piece rates, Taylor promised to increase productivity and raise wages to the point where labor-management conflict would dissolve; he felt that unions not only promoted inefficiency in the workplace but violence as well. By 1911 his followers, Frank Gilbreth, Henry Gantt, and Carl Barth, had founded the Society to Promote the Science of Management— later the Taylor Society—to educate others on Taylor's methods and philosophy. Although the extent to which Taylorist methods were actually adopted by businesses is debatable in this period, Taylor's influence is not. He was easily the most prominent management theorist of his time. Yet, by the time he died in 1915, a small revolution was under way among the ranks of his followers, and Taylorites had become "a burgeoning, uncontrollable family," according to one scholar.[25]

Two developments set the stage for a revolution among the efficiency engineers. The first occurred in 1910, when the Democratic Party captured the Congress and Representative William B. Wilson convened a special investigation of scientific management at federal arsenals. The hearings offered Wilson the opportunity to chastise Taylor for reducing workers to "automatons." Taylorism took its lumps in Washington, and by 1915, Congress had banned the use of "a stop-watch or other time-measuring device" for the purpose of time-motion studies in any federal workplace.[26] Then came a second setback. Taking up what John R. Commons termed "the most 'irrepressible conflict' before the Commission," the USCIR recruited Professor Robert Hoxie, a friend of the AFL, to conduct an investigation of scientific management. With the help of John P. Frey, editor of the iron molders' union journal, and Robert G. Valentine, a renegade member of the Taylor Society considered by Taylor to be "a consistent opponent of scientific management," Hoxie's investigation highlighted Taylorism's autocratic bent. Taylorists had routinely defended their methods as democratic, contending that they would eliminate "the old-fashioned dictator" and insure that work was "governed by rules and laws." Hoxie's report exploded this defense. Because Taylorists consistently opposed cooperating with trade unions, the report concluded, "democratic possibilities" of scientific management seemed "scant."[27]

But the blow that succeeded in splitting the Taylorists came from within their own ranks, when two friendly critics of scientific management, Robert Valentine, who had collaborated on the Hoxie report, and famed lawyer Louis D. Brandeis, broke with Taylorists on the question of workplace representation. Both men were recent converts to Taylorism. But their brief connections to Taylor did not dampen the influence of their critiques.

In many ways, Brandeis was the central figure in this story. Since the turn of the century, he had advocated the democratization of the workplace. His most notable contribution to industrial relations came in 1910 when, at the instigation of Boston merchant Lincoln Filene, he helped settle a conflict between New York City cloak makers and manufacturers. His mediation produced the "Protocol of Peace," an agreement that would influence industrial relations for a decade. The protocol constructed machinery for the settlement of grievances and effected a compromise on the divisive issue of the closed shop by creating what became known as the "preferential union shop"—an arrangement that saw employers hire union workers as long as they were available, while remaining free to hire whomever they wished when that supply was exhausted. The bugs were never worked out of the protocol. It collapsed on the eve of the war. But it served as the model for similar arrangements in New York's shirtwaist and Boston's cloak-making industries, and this "essay in industrial democracy," as Brandeis called the protocol, helped confirm his own belief in the efficacy of workplace representation.[28]

Shortly after crafting the protocol, Brandeis was converted to the ideas of Taylor. The occasion was the famous New Haven Railroad case of 1911. In the brief he filed against the railroad's request for a rate increase from the Interstate Commerce Commission, Brandeis drew on Taylor's theories to argue that an inefficiently managed workforce rather than low shipping rates was the cause of the railroad's profit squeeze. In this case Brandeis himself popularized the term "scientific management." He came away from the New Haven case desiring to combine Taylorism's insights on efficiency and the protocol's accommodation with trade unionism. Brandeis urged the Taylorists to realize that workers' opposition to their system could "be overcome only through securing the affirmative cooperation of the labor organizations." Such cooperation, Brandeis hoped, would lay the basis for a "full-grown industrial democracy."[29]

His prominent role as an adviser to the Wilson administration and his bitterly contested campaign for a seat on the Supreme Court made it difficult for Brandeis to carry his ideas further within the ranks of scientific managers. Robert Valentine stepped into the breach to continue the fight. A former teacher, civil servant, commissioner of the Bureau of Indian Affairs under President Taft, and Massachusetts minimum wage board official, Valentine possessed a web of connections among leading progressives. His Washington, D.C., residence—dubbed the "House of Truth" by Justice Oliver Wendell Holmes—was home base for a network that included lawyer Felix Frankfurter, enlightened New England shoe manufacturer Stanley King, and writer Walter Lippmann.[30] These men admired Brandeis. But it was Valentine who was best suited to transmit the kinds of ideas proposed by Brandeis through the ranks of scientific managers.

By the time he was hired by Robert Hoxie in 1914, Valentine had left politics, embarking on a career as a management consultant. Opening an office in Boston with Ordway Tead and Richard B. Gregg, this upper-crust New Englander joined the Taylor Society and hired himself out to conduct "industrial relations audits" for businesses, analyzing the "dissatisfaction costs" of their employees. Through his consulting business, Valentine came to the conclusion that workplace efficiency could not be improved without the consent of workers, preferably secured through unions. Among those interested in Valentine's work was Assistant Secretary of the Navy Franklin D. Roosevelt, who hired him to revamp management at the Charleston Navy Yard around "the principles of true democracy."[31]

Nine months after the death of its founder, Valentine brought his ideas before the Taylor Society. In a December 1915 speech he shocked his fellow efficiency engineers by attacking a central presumption of Taylorism: that more freedom for workers would result in increasing inefficiency in the workplace. A "consenting man" was a "more desirable worker," one likely to work to full potential, Valentine argued. The point for him was to combine "in constructively organized ways, the latest developments of efficiency in production with the latest developments of the science and art of democracy." To bring this combination about, he called for "shop-union councils" to serve as vehicles through which workers might offer their "consent to all that makes for efficiency."[32]

Valentine's case for "representative government in industry" sparked strong opposition and earned him few allies among Taylor Society members. And when he died suddenly in November 1916, his critique of Taylorism had barely taken root. But the movement he helped initiate began to flourish nonetheless. As testament to his lasting influence, a 1916 memorial service in his honor attracted trade union activists, New England employers, and political figures to hear a eulogy composed by Justice Brandeis that lauded him for teaching that industrial "discipline must be reconciled with industrial democracy."[33]

On the eve of the war, Valentine's ideas found an increasing number of advocates. His friend Felix Frankfurter was among those who took up the cause. In March 1917, Frankfurter urged Taylor Society members to spurn their fundamentalist reading of their founders' ideas as if those ideas represented a "dogmatic faith" that was "divinely inspired." It was time for efficiency engineers to make a "frank and candid recognition that organized labor" was "indispensable." By no means were most efficiency engineers prepared to accept Frankfurter's challenge regarding unions. But an increasing number of them began to think about ways of combining workplace representation and efficiency. In 1916, Professor Horace B. Drury of Ohio State set out to analyze "democracy as a factor in industrial efficiency," concluding that "rigid control" was "inadequate for mobilizing intelligence." Progress in efficiency proceeded "from the bottom up, and not from the top down," he insisted. Railway engineer Otto S. Beyer of the Rock Island and Pacific Railway Company reached a similar conclusion before the war. And even Morris L. Cooke, Taylor's prize pupil, began to rethink the assumptions on which his mentor's system had been built. In 1917 he argued that efficiency engineers ought to welcome workers' "growing demand for 'consent'" over the conditions of their labor "without any reservation."[34]

Advocacy of workplace representation came from a second direction before the war. Even as some engineers and consultants began rethinking the relationship between democracy and efficiency, employers such as Henry P. Kendall of Plimpton Press, Henry S. Dennison of the Boston Chamber of Commerce, and retailer Lincoln Filene (each of whom were also associates of Brandeis) began experimenting with nonunion workplace representation plans as a means of averting labor conflict and developing healthier relations between workers and managers. The trend toward "company unionism," however, received its greatest boost from the man who had taken the most heat from the USCIR, John D. Rockefeller Jr.

The representation plan devised by Mackenzie King for the Colorado Fuel and Iron Company in the wake of the Ludlow massacre made Rockefeller the most visible advocate for the democratization of the workplace through company unions. Rockefeller himself firmly believed that his system represented an important breakthrough. He defended it against attacks from two fronts. On one flank, the AFL lashed out at "Rockefeller unionism" and Frank Walsh attacked CFI's "so-called 'industrial plan'" for denying workers their "rightful opportunities of citizenship and of self expression." From the other flank Rockefeller was besieged by the complaints of his own reactionary managers who preferred not to deal with their employees collectively in any form. Still, Rockefeller held firm. "Paternalism is antagonistic to democracy," he told his skeptical subordinates, and "on the whole, democracy has far more in its favor." Not only did he continue King's plan at CFI, he soon extended similar plans to his Standard Oil refineries. By the time the United States entered World War I, Rockefeller was America's most prominent advocate of what Mackenzie King carefully termed "something in the nature of partnership" between management and workers.[35]

The rebellion of a rump faction of efficiency engineers and the experiments with company unionism under way as the United States entered World War I meant that a small but influential coterie of workplace representation advocates had begun to emerge. This development marked an important watershed in the history of American management. To be sure, a majority of employers worried that this preoccupation with industrial democracy might encourage those who felt that management ought to be "divested of its authority." But an increasing number were prepared to join Drury in applauding the move away from "German" management methods toward a more "democratic tendency." When industrial chaos spread in 1917, this latter group was prepared to offer answers.[36]

Trade Union Collective Bargaining

The leaders of the AFL were little impressed by the talk of employee representation among the followers of their late tormentor, Frederick Taylor. They were even less sanguine about "Rockefeller unionism," writing off its promises of employing workers without regard to their union affiliation as a ruse designed to achieve a closed, nonunion shop. "Democracy, even in America, has been a word rather than an idea with purpose and meaning," wrote

Samuel Gompers in 1916.[37] But he was confident that the AFL's vision could bring real democracy to the workplace. As the war began, the federation was emerging from a period of challenge and turmoil with its leadership more committed than ever to its traditional goals and better equipped than ever to achieve them.

The outbreak of war occurred at a propitious time for the AFL. Since the dramatic expansion of their ranks at the turn of the century, the federation's unions had seen their momentum wane. Thus, although the AFL claimed to speak for all the nation's workers, in 1910 it claimed only 10.9 percent of all nonagricultural wage earners as members, and it stood largely excluded from mass industry. Without union strongholds in the building trades, the federation would have been even more anemic. And, as Selig Perlman noted, with the exception of its organizations among miners and garment workers, the AFL was "mainly the organization of the upper and medium strata among native . . . wage earners."[38] This narrow craft basis had left the AFL open to attack by rival industrial union organizations, especially the IWW, founded in 1905, and the Amalgamated Clothing Workers of America (ACWA), founded by Sidney Hillman and others who broke away from the conservative United Garment Workers in 1914. Each organization was thriving on the eve of the war, posing strong challenges to the craft union vision that dominated the AFL.[39]

Further complicating the state of the unions were internal divisions within the federation. Gompers and his allies dominated the AFL's Executive Council. But "Gompersism" was not the only voice within labor's house. Critics attacked the AFL's direction from both sides of the political spectrum. The "Indianapolis Movement," led primarily by the Carpenters' leader Bill Hutcheson, drew together the unions with national offices in the AFL's first home city behind a critique of the AFL's growing alliance with the Democratic Party. Meanwhile, such unionists as Ben Schlesinger of the International Ladies' Garment Workers' Union, John Fitzpatrick and Ed Nockels of the Chicago Federation of Labor, and James H. Maurer of the Pennsylvania Federation of Labor criticized Gompers from the left for his continued resistance to industrial unionism and independent labor politics.[40]

Yet the fact that Gompers's vision continued to dominate the federation despite the rise of such alternative voices is beyond question. The AFL's 1915 San Francisco convention provided ample evidence of this reality. That meeting allowed Gompers to delineate once more labor's philosophy of "industrial statesmanship," even as artillery pounded European battlefields. Delegates to the San Francisco convention turned back a host of reforms proposed by the AFL's left wing, voting down proposals to elect AFL officers by referendum, to achieve the eight-hour workday through government legislation, and to put the AFL on record in favor of industrial unionism. As Gompers proudly noted, the "voluntary element dominate[d] the . . . policies of the movement."[41]

That element was loyal to the two central, overlapping principles of pure-and-simple trade unionism: voluntarism and economism. The AFL's voluntarism was based on the fear that government interference in workplace relations might enable the state to rob workers of their freedom of association; it held that improvements in workers' material conditions ought to be won by trade union bargaining rather than legislation. "The workers cannot be saved," Gompers often wrote; "they must save themselves." Political power, he contended, was a "secondary power." Real power was located in workplace organization. Voluntarism also described the federation's relations with its constituent unions: under Gompers's leadership the Executive Council largely refrained from interfering in the policies of the AFL's craft unions within their jurisdictions. The AFL's economism in turn flowed from its voluntarism. Rather than promising a social democratic paradise, the AFL sought what Gompers once famously described as "more, more, and more now."[42]

As America's entry into World War I neared, Gompers remained as committed as ever to protecting this vision from usurpers. Hence Gompers's suspicion of Frank Walsh and his allies. In seeking out radical associates and voicing support for such things as industrial unionism, Walsh necessitated careful handling. Thus Gompers's effusive words regarding the Walsh Report notwithstanding, the AFL never endorsed all the recommendations of the USCIR. Nor would it formally support the work of Walsh's CIR. Indeed, when the CIR approached the AFL for help, convention delegates adopted a resolution that accurately reflected Gompers's fears. It welcomed "the cooperation of all sympathetic individuals and organizations" with the labor movement, but it insisted that the AFL was "unwilling to be dictated to or dominated by an outside agency."[43]

The truth for the AFL on the eve of the war, however, was that Gompers's vision had been most successfully advanced when it was honored in the breach. Even as Gompers continued to preach his traditional voluntarism, the AFL was increasingly relying on the Wilson administration to advance its interests. The same AFL convention that endorsed the view that political power was "secondary," that real power had "gravitated slowly but surely from political to industrial agencies," also boasted of one hundred pieces of federal legislation enacted because of the AFL's lobbying. President Wilson's "Second New Freedom" and his reliance on the AFL in the 1916 election further cemented the ties between the federation and the federal government.[44]

The approach of war considerably heightened these contradictions in the

AFL's voluntarist approach. On one hand, the war consummated the federation's relationship with the Wilson administration and brought it into greatest conflict with its own professed voluntarist principles. On the other hand, that very alliance allowed Gompers an unprecedented opportunity to transform his collective bargaining vision into reality.

Gompers was initially horrified by the "unnatural, unjustified, and unholy" war that erupted in 1914. He thought it a ploy to "divert the peoples" from their "democratizing tendencies." By 1916, however, he had reversed course. Believing that it might be impossible to keep the United States out of the war, he began to consider how war might be made to serve the AFL's interests. Despite the objections of such leaders as John White of the UMW and Bill Hutcheson of the Carpenters, he persuaded the AFL's Executive Council to support Wilson's preparedness program. That support was soon rewarded. On October 11, 1916, President Wilson made Gompers a civilian adviser to the Council of National Defense (CND), an agency created to coordinate the preparedness program. This action set an important precedent, paving the way for AFL involvement in the coming wartime mobilization itself. In no previous national emergency, an AFL handbook later pointed out, had "the organized labor movement taken a directing part."[45]

Gompers took that directing role seriously. In early March 1917, as relations between the United States and Germany worsened, he called a meeting of the AFL's Executive Council and, after two days of debate, produced a statement committing the AFL to support war should the Congress declare it. Then Gompers summoned 148 union delegates to Washington on March 12 to discuss the statement. No record of that closed-door meeting was kept; only its results are known. According to the AFL's official version, delegates "unanimously" approved Gompers's document, "American Labor's Position in Peace or War." Several union leaders privately complained that Gompers rammed the proposal through, a view widely reprinted in angry rank-and-file circulars. But the AFL's official position was now clear.[46]

Once war was declared, Gompers was quick to assure the AFL's cooperation. "No strike ought to be inaugurated that cannot be justified to the men facing momentary death" on the battlefield, he declared in the *American Federationist*. But Gompers may have been too anxious to prove the AFL's loyalty. On April 7 he summoned a meeting of the CND's committee on labor, which he headed, and drafted a controversial statement. "Neither employers nor employees shall endeavor to take advantage of the country's necessities to change existing standards," it read. In this wording the AFL seemed to offer a virtual "no-strike pledge." Angry trade unionists swamped Gompers with complaints for seemingly surrendering their right to strike. "If you made any such pledge," Daniel Tobin of the Teamsters informed Gompers testily, "you had no right to do so." "Without the strike," a group of electrical workers informed the chief, their organization "would be seriously menaced." In response to the uproar, the CND subsequently issued a clarification, dispelling the "erroneous impression" contained in the original statement and maintaining that the freedom to strike remained as a weapon of last resort.[47]

As it turned out, the AFL was better able to wield that weapon during the first months of the war than ever before. This was due in part to the AFL's formal loyalty. On one hand, AFL leaders seconded Secretary of Labor Wilson's belief that because the "great union, the United States of America," had "declared a strike against the tyranny of the German government," it would be "a serious blunder for any man to scab" by himself going on strike. On the other hand, union leaders believed that by organizing workers they could stabilize war production and win lasting labor peace. So, as Gompers and Secretary Wilson argued that workers should strike only as a last resort, strikes abounded, especially in establishments where AFL members constituted a majority. And workers waged their most bitter struggles over issues of union power in the workplace, especially union recognition. The AFL's dominant vision of industrial democracy, then, was alive and well in the first months of the war. And union leaders had every reason to believe that it would advance still further in months ahead.[48]

Radical Workplace Democracy

Of course, Gompers's vision of industrial democracy, based on pure-and-simple trade unionism, was not hegemonic within the AFL as World War I erupted. A substantial Socialist minority continued to flourish within the federation, as did a wide spectrum of trade unionists who advocated such policies as industrial unionism, the amalgamation of trades, independent labor politics, and greater union democracy. It was among this faction of the movement that a more radical vision of industrial democracy took shape. Nowhere was that alternative vision more visible—or loyalty to "Gompersism" more tenuous—than in the metal trades. Metalworkers who labored in the transportation, munitions, and electrical industries on which the war effort depended were arguably those most affected by wartime conditions. They suffered the greatest threat from scientific management or "dilution," the replacing of skilled workers by semiskilled "specialists." This fact helps explain why they were more prone to labor militancy during 1917–18 than other workers and why among them radicalism found a congenial home.

The union to which the most influential portion of metal trades workers belonged during the war, the International Association of Machinists, among the most progressive in the AFL, was well suited to play host to labor militancy. In many ways the IAM had served as a bellwether for the "new unionism" in the years just before the war. In 1911, the union had dramatically shifted course after years of leadership by a conservative Gompers ally, James O'Connell. That year IAM members, disgusted by O'Connell's cooperation with big business leaders in the National Civic Federation, replaced their longtime president with a Socialist, William H. Johnston.

Under Johnston's leadership the IAM had embarked on a new era. The Canadian-born Johnston had worked his way to the top of his union from humble beginnings in a New England locomotive shop. The experience that had most shaped him began in 1909 when he was recruited to go to Washington as president of IAM District 44, which represented machinists at federal arsenals. In that post he forged a reputation as a tough trade unionist who commanded "the attention of audiences through his logic," an idealist whose politics were later described by one historian as "an amalgam of Progressivism, Populism, and grass roots American Socialism." Johnston embellished this image by becoming a staunch critic of Taylor's scientific management techniques, which at that time were being introduced into arsenal work. Johnston likened the "lash of the stopwatch" in Taylor's time-motion studies to a modern form of slavery. It was on the strength of such militant rhetoric that IAM members elevated him in 1911. He promised them change. The "craft organization can no longer cope with the new conditions of employment that have arisen," asserted the union's magazine following Johnston's election; "amalgamation of all the metal craft organizations is our only hope."[49]

For the most part, Johnston was true to his word. As he took its reins, the IAM faced dual threats of "dilution" and a militant open-shop movement waged by the National Metal Trades Association (NMTA). To meet the challenge, Johnston pioneered several measures. The IAM admitted semiskilled specialists to full membership. It joined other railroad shop craft unions— boilermakers, electrical workers, and carmen—to create system federations that could negotiate with railways as a bloc. And it fostered city metal trades councils, which brought together local federations of workers from a variety of metal trades unions.

The IAM was a union with a strong tradition of rank-and-file activism. So, on those occasions when Johnston appeared to contradict the cause of reform that he had campaigned on, he took heat from well-organized IAM militants. Such an occasion was provided by the failure of a bitter strike in the shops of the Illinois Central Railroad. That strike, which had begun in 1911, dragged on for the first three years of Johnston's presidency, draining the IAM treasury.

By 1914, Johnston had determined that for the sake of the union he had to end the disastrous walkout, even if strike leaders on the Illinois wanted to continue it. One of those leaders, the popular Carl E. Person, decided to oppose Johnston's move. Unfortunately for Johnston, he decided to expel the recalcitrant Person from the IAM. The backlash against his action was ferocious. Person himself contended that Johnston had "surrendered the democracy of the Machinists' organization to the autocratic decisions of himself." Legions of his followers from more than fifty IAM lodges agreed, contributing to Person's defense, passing resolutions on his behalf, and condemning the "unAmerican" and "distinctly autocratic" action of Johnston. "We believe that now is the time," wrote one IAMer from New Jersey, "for the rank and file to put their foot down and stamp out this simptom [sic] of autocracy in our movement." For years the Person incident provided fodder for Johnston's radical critics within the union.[50]

Obviously the IAM that entered World War I did so under strong leadership and with a vibrant, democratic rank-and-file culture. It should not be surprising, therefore, that IAM members laboring in war industries would emerge as among the most militant unionists in America early in the war. In two industries—munitions and electrical manufacturing—IAM militants were destined to have an especially deep impact, and a look at the centers of labor activism in these trades sheds further light on the militant nature of metal trades unionism during the war.

The first American strike associated with the outbreak of World War I occurred among machinists in the munitions plants of Bridgeport, Connecticut. On July 20, 1915, twelve hundred machinists from the four Bridgeport shops that serviced the giant Remington Arms Manufacturing Company struck for the eight-hour day. War orders from Europe had already begun to swell Bridgeport's population from its prewar figure of 120,000 upward toward the high of 190,000 that would be reached by the end of 1918. The "Essen of America," as Bridgeport was called, produced two-thirds of all small arms exported to European combatants. It also offered steady employment to metal trades workers who replicated this first strike many times to capitalize on the high demand for labor. By the end of the summer of 1915, according to one calculation, as many as fourteen thousand Bridgeport workers—including two thousand female corset makers—had joined the original strikers in staging walkouts for the eight-hour demand.[51] This strike wave was all the more dramatic because it emerged despite the initial opposition of Samuel Gompers, who feared that "Germans had found some labor representatives" among the Bridgeport strikers.[52]

In truth, the leaders of the Bridgeport movement were not German sympa-

thizers. But they were not Gompers sympathizers either. Indeed, foreshadow-
ing the complex impact that war would soon have on the larger American
labor movement, Bridgeport's prewar strikes had brought to the top a more
radical group of leaders in the Bridgeport IAM. War work and the campaign
for the eight-hour day attracted an increasing number of semiskilled operatives to the union. And with these new members came a new crop of leaders,
sympathetic to industrial unionism and standing to the left of the union's
Socialist president, William Johnston, on most issues. Three Bridgeport Machinists gained particular prominence: Edwin O'Connell, David Clydesdale,
and especially an eastern European Jewish immigrant named Samuel Lavit.
Lavit's election to the leadership of IAM Lodge 30 in 1916 came less than two
years after he joined the union. But by the time the United States entered
World War I, Lavit had emerged as one of the most visible union militants in
the country.

According to one military intelligence agent who spied on wartime union
meetings conducted by Lavit, the head of Lodge 30 was "an agitator of considerable cleverness." When he arrived in Bridgeport around 1914, Lavit was
already quite experienced. Federal investigators believed him to have been a
partisan of the IWW during the 1913 Paterson silk strike. But in Bridgeport
Lavit was an active supporter of the Socialist Labor Party. He found political
kinsmen in O'Connell, a Remington Arms machinist who had also arrived in
the city with the war boom, and Clydesdale, a Scottish toolmaker and veteran of Britain's Independent Labour Party, who was judged "the most radical
of all leaders in Bridgeport" by one military intelligence report. Together, the
three men reorganized the Bridgeport IAM on more militant footing.[53]

In early 1917, Lavit, O'Connell, and Clydesdale helped establish a new
district organization for Bridgeport's IAM lodges, IAM District 55. The new
organization joined the munitions-related lodges—Lavit's own Lodge 30,
Lodge 584 composed of recently organized Remington Arms workers, and
two ethnic lodges, composed of Polish and Scandinavian workers—under
Lavit's leadership. Lavit's election to the presidency of District 55 in May 1917
over a moderate opponent who believed "this is no time to talk strike" worried some national IAM officials. One of them even denied Lavit keys to the
union's Bridgeport office until Johnston intervened on his behalf. Over the
next two years Johnston was given ample cause to regret that intervention.
Once in office, Lavit became a critic of Johnston's leadership and turned District 55 into a center of militancy that often vexed the IAM's national leader.
Advocating industrial unionism, a forty-four-hour week, and even nationalization of some basic industries, Lavit was prepared to lead the IAM's Bridgeport
members in a new direction. He immediately stepped up his organizing in

the summer of 1917 by calling on employers to agree to a system that would end the "dilution" problem.[54]

The vision of Bridgeport's munitions industry militants was matched by the electrical industry unionists of Schenectady, New York, the home city to the giant General Electric company. GE machinists played an active role in the Schenectady Metal Trades Council (SMTC), one of the most successful and most consistently left-leaning metal trades organizations in the country. Led by three GE workers—President Raymond J. Leonard, a molder; Vice President Robert A. Jones, a machinist; and Secretary John C. Bellingham, an electrician—the SMTC provided the backbone of both the Schenectady union movement and the city's socialist politics. The machinists of the SMTC helped elect and reelect Socialist George R. Lunn mayor of Schenectady before the war. And even after April 1917, SMTC activists helped sponsor a full slate of Socialist candidates for local offices, perpetuating one of the most active working-class political organizations in the country.[55]

Matching their determination in local politics, SMTC leaders also worked to consolidate union ranks within open-shop GE. Long the site of union agitation (the IWW had staged a sit-down strike there in 1907), GE's Schenectady plant was the only one of the company's five major plants—including those at Lynn and Pittsfield, Massachusetts; Erie, Pennsylvania; and Fort Wayne, Indiana—where unions had an appreciable presence prior to 1917. The SMTC's skilled unionists gained concessions from GE that made their working conditions the best in the company. War orders further strengthened the hands of the Schenectady unionists, allowing them to dream of bringing organization to other GE plants.[56]

If Sam Lavit was the militant visionary among Bridgeport machinists, Schenectady's IAM members found their inspiration from outside the ranks of their union in electrician John Bellingham. A sharp-tongued Scottish immigrant who served as president of Schenectady's Electrical Workers' District Council, Bellingham was, according to one GE investigator, "the most radical and perhaps the most dangerous man in the Schenectady plant." As the SMTC's secretary, Bellingham advocated amalgamating the metal trades and creating a mass union of electrical manufacturing workers, views that influenced many Schenectady machinists. His radical vision was further evidenced by his stance on the war. In 1916 he helped persuade the Schenectady unionists to spurn a preparedness rally. And he supported the efforts of two GE activists, John I. Wickham and Jesse J. Finn, in organizing a chapter of the American Union against Militarism. When the United States subsequently entered the war, Bellingham caustically dismissed the arguments of those who maintained that "the class struggle idea should be suspended during the present crisis or war." This was "ridiculous advice," he announced. Workers "did not make the class struggle." Therefore, it would be "stupid in the extreme for us to try to stop this struggle of workers for their rights." Wars would continue unabated, he promised, "so long as workers tolerate a profit system of industry." [57]

To be sure, Samuel Gompers remained secure at the head of the AFL as the war began. But with a Socialist presiding over one of the unions that was most vital to the war effort and with radical militants dominating the movement in such war production centers as Bridgeport and Schenectady, Gompers's vision of industrial democracy as pure-and-simple collective bargaining was sure to be challenged as the war unfolded.

A DEEPENING CRISIS

But early in the war no one's vision of industrial democracy gained much ground. Only industrial chaos seemed to flourish. Labor turnover rates soared, managers continued to look for ways of diluting labor or undermining union strength, and strikes erupted without abatement. By the end of 1917, the United States had broken all records for work stoppages, threatening the entire war effort. Union discipline seemed to be waning. Leaders such as John Golden of the United Textile Workers and T. V. O'Connor of the International Longshoremen's Association found themselves battling wildcat strikers. As one Wilson administration official later noted in words that understated the depth of the problem, it seemed "that the national leaders of the American Federation of Labor did not in general exercise sufficient influence during those months to control their local unions." [58]

A member of the British Labor Commission who visited the United States in 1917 was aghast. If there had been one-eighth the degree of unrest in England that he had observed in the United States, he assured his hosts, England would have long before been "forced to conclude a disgraceful peace with Germany." [59] If the administration wanted to rescue its war effort, Washington officials began to realize, decisive action was necessary. When that action came over the winter of 1917–18, it saw the federal government assume more power over labor relations than anyone could have foreseen only months earlier. And as a war labor bureaucracy took shape, the struggle to determine what vision of industrial democracy would prevail in the wartime workplace assumed a new significance. That struggle soon became a battle to influence the state itself.

THE BATTLE TO SHAPE
WAR LABOR POLICY

3

*This is our day of grace and if we fail now . . . we shall
find out soon that our day is done. Can we not have
the vision to reorganize . . . our government into an
industrial democracy . . . in the common interest of
all the people?*
—Donald Richberg, 1917

      The Wilson administration's struggle between April
1917 and April 1918 to articulate a war labor policy was a defining event in the
history of American labor and politics. Before the war, the United States, perhaps more than any other major belligerent nation, possessed a weak central
government—a virtual "organizational vacuum" in the words of one scholar.[1]
This legacy of federalism was perhaps nowhere more significant than in the
realm of labor relations. The legislative and the executive branches had rarely
intervened in labor relations before, and when they had done so their role
was rarely mediatory. Restoring order to the wartime workplace, however, demanded strong federal action, and such action was forthcoming. During the
first year of the war, President Wilson presided over the birth of nearly a score
of new agencies and boards, staffed by hundreds of war labor bureaucrats
and dozens of trade unionists and businesspeople. These agencies betokened
a profound and sudden transformation of the role that government played in
industrial life. As one autoworker observed, "for once every citizen, no matter

how humble, was made to realize that the government was a real thing and that it wielded power, enormous power."[2]

These war agencies and their policies were not the result of a process of political or bureaucratic evolution. They were rather products of a complex struggle between factions that possessed different conceptions of industrial democracy and differing ideas regarding the role that the state should play in fostering it. As the power of employers to unilaterally determine workplace relations dissolved during the first year of American participation in the war and as the government stepped into the breach, a variety of groups argued over the direction that policy would take. Frank Walsh and his left-leaning allies in the CIR, AFL officials, Brandeisian progressives, and scientific managers each sought a role in policy making.

AFL officials seemed to emerge from that struggle with the upper hand. They ensured that the locus of labor policy making stayed within the Labor Department and that trade unionists would have a role in implementing that policy at virtually every level, especially through the most important war labor agency, the National War Labor Board (NWLB). But their victory was chimerical. In truth, Wilsonian war labor policy represented a compromise, many of the consequences of which were never anticipated by its framers. Indeed, while wartime federal labor policy ultimately sought two goals dear to the conservative leaders of the AFL—the destruction of the rival IWW and the federal protection of workers' rights to organize in "bona fide" unions— that policy gave more leverage to left-leaning industrial democrats than the federation's hierarchy liked. This fact in turn ensured that during the war, such federal agencies as the NWLB would play roles in workplaces around the country much different from what conservative unionists foresaw.

TURNING TOWARD THE STATE

American entry into World War I provided a watershed in the history of American labor and the Left. Both the relationship between Wilson and the AFL that had begun prior to 1916 and the flirtation between the president and some influential segments of the Left that had taken place during the election of that year were consummated in the early days of April 1917. "Only in a world where irony was dead," wrote Randolph Bourne, could so many liberals "enter war at the head of such illiberal cohorts in the avowed cause of world liberalism and world democracy."[3] But irony was not one of the Great War's many casualties. The AFL, Frank Walsh and his progressive friends, and even elements of the Socialist Party decided to support Wilson and war, believing that doing so would help them attain liberal ends. Their decision paved the way for both reform and repression. But as 1917 drew to a close and the struggle to define war labor policy reached its denouement, these groups were convinced that enough reform had been won to make the costs of repression tolerable.

War labor policy ultimately grew out of relationships forged in the battle for labor loyalty that unfolded in the first months of the war. When the Congress threw the nation into the conflict on April 6, Samuel Gompers threw down the gauntlet to trade unionists. "Each must stand up and be counted," warned the *American Federationist*, "for those who are not with us are against us." Despite vociferous rank-and-file objections to Samuel Gompers's prowar March 1917 declaration and the existence of strong pockets of pacifist resistance among some unions, public opposition to the war among trade union leaders virtually ceased. Such previously antiwar organizations as the New York Central Federated Union and the Chicago Federation of Labor fell in line behind the war, as did such prominent prewar skeptics as Andrew Furuseth of the Seamen's union and Sidney Hillman of the renegade ACWA. Within weeks it was clear that no sustained trade union–based opposition to the war was likely to emerge.[4]

That widespread trade union opposition to the war never coalesced must in the end be judged less surprising than that important segments of the Left also supported the war. Whereas unions would have had to persuade working people to risk their livelihoods to oppose the conflict, the risks for political activists were less immediate. Yet the great majority of progressives and a significant number of Socialists too supported the war. Among them was Frank P. Walsh.[5]

Before April 1917, Frank Walsh described himself as "what might be termed a pacifist," and the CIR attacked the preparedness movement as the tool of a "class of special interests" who sought an "undemocratic, militaristic, money-controlled" America. Encouraged by Walsh's well-known sympathies, Amos Pinchot contacted the CIR chairman during the hectic week leading up to the U.S. declaration of war. Pinchot despaired that America was being "driven into war by reactionary elements," and he urged Walsh to wire the president expressing his continued opposition to war. By then, however, Walsh had begun to weigh his pacifism against a broader political calculus. He demurred, and the CIR never took a stand against the war. In fact, several developments made it unlikely by April 1917 that Walsh would have done otherwise. First, Walsh had come to believe so strongly that the Wilson administration was committed to the democratization of industry that he considered a break with the president impossible. Indeed, as early as August 1915 he discussed with Basil Manly the impact of war on the CIR's work. At that time both agreed that their group ought to "do as we have always done," to use the drift of events "either to agitate or to put over some of our basic 'constructive proposals.'" Nothing had materially changed that analysis by 1917. Moreover, the benefits to the cause of industrial democracy that might come from a war against autocracy and the costs to that cause that would surely come from a break with either the AFL or the president weighed heavily in Walsh's thinking.[6]

"I am optimism incarnated," Walsh had claimed before the war. "I believe the world is getting better every day." He clearly had not relinquished that optimism in 1917. Shortly after the Congress voted for war, Walsh told friend Anton Johannsen that he did "not believe war will cut any figure unless to help the cause." Walsh's decision to ignore the pleas of pacifists who had asked him to rouse working people against the war stunned many former friends. Some broke with Walsh quietly, as did Amos Pinchot, who continued to aid pacifist efforts. Others broke with him more decisively. "You are lending them your name and influence," the prominent Socialist Scott Nearing wrote Walsh in disbelief. "The plutocrats are using your power to rivet the chains. How can you do it?"[7]

But Walsh was not alone in reading events differently from Nearing. He was joined in his stand by some like-minded colleagues from the Socialist Party. In the days after the party reaffirmed its antiwar stand at an emergency convention in St. Louis on April 7, 1917, a number of notable members bolted its ranks. Charles Edward Russell, William English Walling, Rose Pastor Stokes, Upton Sinclair, Robert Hunter, and John Spargo declared their support for the war. Together, these Socialists and their progressive allies provided crucial legitimation to Wilson's war.[8]

Both the Wilson administration and the AFL moved quickly to put Walsh and the Socialists in harness. Efforts by the antiwar People's Council of America for Democracy and Peace to capture New York City's Central Federated Union in July 1917 caused Gompers and prominent Wilsonians a great deal of concern. Their answer was an alliance of labor and the prowar Left that might counter any future such efforts. The mastermind of the alliance was Frank Walsh's former associate on the USCIR, George Creel, who acted as director of the administration's wartime propaganda arm, the Committee on Public Information (CPI). In the summer of 1917 Gompers and Creel formed the American Alliance for Labor and Democracy (AALD). Chaired by AFL secretary Frank Morrison, the AALD vigorously attacked labor "disloyalty" and promoted a democratic defense of the war. One AALD publication, authored by former USCIR commissioner John R. Commons, called the fight in Europe "an American workingman's war, conducted for American workingmen, by American workingmen." Antiwar unionists such as James Maurer derided the "paytriotism" of the AALD, pointing out that it received most of its funds from the government. But the organization attracted well-known prowar Socialists and Frank Walsh too. Walsh not only joined the group, he served on its board.[9]

The support of labor and significant portions of the Left for Wilson cleared the way for the defeat of the largest remaining antiwar organization, the People's Council. With the aid of a good number of trade unionists, that group planned a September 1917 convention in Minneapolis, where they had been invited by the city's Socialist mayor, Thomas Van Lear, an IAM union leader. The meeting was never held. Minnesota's governor, J. A. Burnquist, banned the convention from his state, and members of the AALD entrained to Minneapolis on the "Red, White, and Blue Special" to hold their own meeting on September 4–5, 1917. Only half of the 179 AALD delegates at this convention were actually trade unionists. And even some AFL stalwarts felt that the AALD's show was "an unnecessary display of super-patriotism." But the Minneapolis meeting effectively ended the People's Council threat. By the time the group finally held an abortive convention in Chicago later that year, it was no longer much of a threat to the war effort.[10]

More ominous, the AALD's formation paved the way for the repression of a labor organization that was not formally opposed to the war. AFL leaders, employers, and most members of the Wilson administration agreed that the IWW was a haven for dissenters, despite the fact that the organization had refrained from officially opposing the war. Pragmatic Wobbly leaders were instead intent on organizing workers. "Talk against conscription will get us nowhere," IWW leader Bill Haywood argued. "Power is what counts," he explained, and "power can only be developed on the job." The IWW had developed a good deal of such power in northwestern timber fields and south-western copper mines in 1916 and early 1917. Consequently, IWW leaders believed that they would harvest tens of thousands of new members because of wartime conditions. But the very success of IWW organizing so concerned industrial barons, government administrators, and craft unionists that action against the group was all but inevitable.[11]

What that action would be was not a foregone conclusion. Within the Wilson administration debate raged over how to handle the Wobblies. The Justice Department and the military favored repression. The Labor Department sought to curb the IWW by promoting responsible AFL unionism. As the government debated, however, wartime hysteria stoked the fires of paranoia. In Montana, vigilantes lynched organizer Frank Little, and around the country mobs ransacked IWW offices. As vigilantism sent the IWW reeling, Secretary

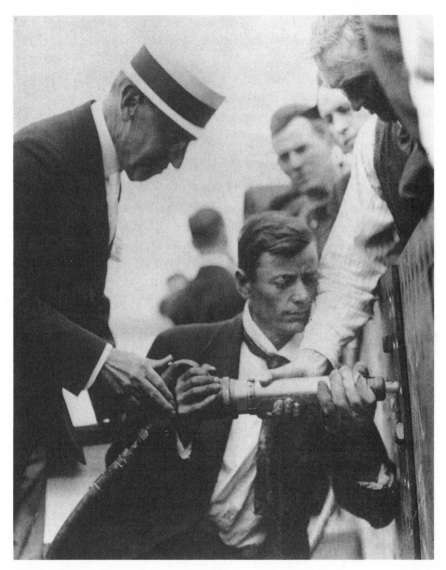

President Woodrow Wilson, with plenty of help, tries his hand at driving a rivet into the keel of a Liberty ship in Alexandria, Virginia, ca. 1917. (National Archives II, College Park, Maryland)

Wilson lost the debate in Washington. At the urging of Western governors and businesspeople, the Justice Department, thickly staffed by corporate lawyers, prepared a case against the Wobblies based on the recent Espionage Act. On September 5, 1917, agents raided IWW offices around the country, confiscating membership lists, printing presses, private correspondence, and more. On September 28, a Chicago grand jury indicted 166 of the IWW's top officials,

effectively killing the Wobblies and bringing the AFL one step closer to recognition as the sole bargaining agent of U.S. workers.[12]

The perceptive social critic Randolph Bourne was among those who first
foresaw the possibility of such repression and who consequently criticized
those progressives who supported war in 1917. His warnings to erstwhile
friends and allies that their actions might legitimize the forces of repression
were prophetic.[13] That the opposition of this minority could have prevented
the war or held back the repressive forces, however, was always doubtful.
Although aware of their limited influence, the prowar laborites thought that
they could preserve their freedom to pressure the government to enact reforms. Many realized how reliant the Wilson administration was on their
support. And they believed that this reliance would create genuinely democratic opportunities. Frank Walsh's associate Dante Barton was not alone in
thinking that "those who forced on this war have let loose something that
they cannot control."[14]

There was still good reason for such optimism in 1917. Even though the
IWW was crushed, progressives could console themselves with the thought
that AFL conservatives had gained no monopoly over labor activism. The
trade union activities of Frank Walsh and his industrial democrats, undertaken as the war began, bore witness to this fact.

In the fall of 1916, Walsh had decided that the time had come to form
a new organization. His experience organizing support for the prewar steel
strikes in Youngstown and Pittsburgh led Walsh to believe that the CIR had
been "holding out hopes to too many poor devils in different parts of the
country which might never be realized." Frustrated by the subterranean harassment of AFL leaders, Walsh decided to form a group expressly dedicated
to promoting the mass organization of unorganized workers. The new group
was called the National Labor Defense Council (NLDC); it was composed
of left-leaning lawyers and activists. Among its counsel were Edward Costi-
gan, the UMW's lawyer in Colorado; Clarence Darrow; C. E. S. Wood; and
Austin Lewis. Its publicity staff included Lincoln Steffens, Fremont Older,
Carl Sandburg, John Reed, and two veterans of the CIR, Dante Barton and
Helen Marot. The purpose of the organization was to offer legal and fund-
raising support to strikers or, as the NLDC's inaugural statement put it, to
defend "the *unorganized workers* in their insurrection." Indicative of the new
organization's bent, Walsh retained the notorious Anton Johannsen—a man
AFL officials would not allow on the CIR staff—as its field organizer.[15]

The outbreak of war in April 1917 immediately forced the NLDC to inter-
pose itself between the antiwar labor militants and their foes. Walsh and
Johannsen were angered by the tendency of employers "wherever labor makes

a protest" for better conditions "to say 'IWW! Anarchy! and Anti-patriotism!' "
Under Walsh's leadership, the organization attempted to aid labor militants
while officially supporting the war. Privately, Walsh expressed his disgust at
the "naked use of brute force" against the Wobblies and declared as "shocking to all my ideas of justice" the treatment accorded to Emma Goldman and
other war resisters. He offered quiet legal advice to both Goldman and Bill
Haywood. Publicly, meanwhile, Walsh fought some of the worst instances of
repression. When Postmaster General Albert Burleson began removing antiwar periodicals from the mails, for example, Walsh defended their publishers
before Burleson, warning of the "grave danger to free expression" inherent
in "the ultra-bureaucratic method adopted by you for suppressing newspapers."[16]

But resisting these examples of repression was not all that occupied the
NLDC. The group aimed to become, in the words of another Walsh associate, William Harvey, "a confederation of alert democrats, with the happi-
ness and well-being of the great masses at heart," a group that could "step in
and take charge of the wake," helping masses to organize. The NLDC's members valiantly attempted to live up to this hope in the summer of 1917. After
receiving a desperate plea from the Arizona Federation of Labor in August
1917, Walsh dispatched Harold Callender to investigate the "Bisbee deportation" on behalf of the NLDC. From Arizona, Callender circulated a widely
reprinted account detailing the abuses of local authorities in a mining town
that he called "the Belgium of America." NLDC investigators were also sent
to California to look into the case of labor radical Tom Mooney, who had
been jailed on dubious charges that he had set off a bomb at a preparedness
rally. Carl Sandburg was soon dispatched to publicize the plight of Omaha
trade unionists who suffered under a vicious open-shop campaign launched
under the cover of wartime patriotism. After several months of work, Walsh
remained confident that the forces of democracy would win out over those of
repression. Even "counting the frightful cost of life and the necessary breakdown of democratic safeguards, in spots," Walsh still believed that this "war
for democracy in its broadest aspect" would bring "a wonderful advance for
the human family along the lines of democracy."[17]

The activity of the NLDC drew the concern of Samuel Gompers. Careful
to protect the ability of the AFL itself to influence labor organizing, Gompers
was suspicious of the NLDC from the beginning. As one NLDC staffer saw
it, AFL "leaders instinctively fear[ed] the Council" and would have liked to
"have something against it." During the summer of 1917, Gompers went on
the offensive against the NLDC. He urged AFL unions to refrain from supporting the organization. He then reminded constituent unions in no uncer-

tain terms that an "organization for the defense of workers, if it is to receive the support of the organized labor movement, ought to first receive the approval of the movement itself." Unions "ought not to be asked to contribute to an organization to which the national labor movement has never given approval," Gompers told his members.[18]

NLDC members were confident that they could deflect Gompers's behind-the-scenes attacks. Walsh retained an enormous reservoir of goodwill among AFL trade unionists. Additionally, he could count on Ed Nockels, of the Chicago Federation of Labor, to act as a point man within the AFL, alerting the NLDC to Gompers's attacks and helping defuse them as best he could. Helen Marot, for one, was convinced that "we have the labor people where we want them just now," that they could not "take hold of anything which gives them a handle for their opposition." She believed that the NLDC could "count on the rank and file realizing that they have a force behind them" and that with this realization they would "carry forward their fight against the reactionary leaders and official policy." Nor was she alone in so believing. In the early autumn of 1917, the NLDC, confidently looking toward future campaigns, planned a journal and even secured a tentative pledge from Jack Reed to edit it.[19]

That journal never came to fruition. Indeed, by the end of 1917 the NLDC itself was dead. There were two reasons for these disappointments. The first could be traced to Gompers. By September 1917, it was clear that the NLDC's funds—largely coming from Walsh's own pocket to that point—were not being replenished as quickly as they were being spent. To survive, the organization needed financial support from the unions. But Gompers's opposition complicated the task of soliciting this support. "I wish he would be more public in his opposition," Johannsen complained, "for then we could organize the opposition to the Executive Council . . . and that would be sufficient to sustain our organization." But Gompers was too clever an opponent. So the NLDC decided to confront Gompers and the AFL's Executive Council directly in October 1917. Johannsen wrote Gompers with assurances that the NLDC did not propose to "in any way interfere with the policies or programs of the labor movement." He then secured the help of allies who brought before the AFL's Executive Council a resolution supporting the NLDC. Ever loyal to the chief, the Executive Council tabled it, to the great frustration of Walsh and his friends.[20]

The NLDC may have kept up its fight, however, had it not been for a second development. During the late summer and autumn of 1917, the federal government had begun slowly extending its control over labor relations in war industries. The result was that a patchwork of jury-rigged government boards and agencies were putting in place a structure that promised to do more to protect the rights of unorganized workers than the NLDC ever could. Because they had remained formally loyal to the war effort, the former activists of the CIR and the NLDC now pinned their hopes on this apparatus and on gaining a voice in shaping its policies.

ORIGINS OF FEDERAL WAR LABOR POLICY

During the summer of the 1917 AFL leaders successfully delivered labor loyalty and cheered the destruction of the IWW. But gains within the administration in Washington initially proved elusive. The Advisory Committee on Labor of the CND to which Gompers had been appointed head in 1916 did not yield much fruit for the AFL in the first months of the war. Indeed, the apparent no-strike pledge offered by that committee in early April had if anything sown only confusion and discord. Theoretically, the committee should have rebounded to become a significant policy-making body in wartime Washington. On it sat a broad-based group, including such figures as AFL secretary Frank Morrison, National Civic Federation secretary Ralph Easley, and Lee Frankel of the Metropolitan Life Insurance Company.[21] But the committee never quite gelled. One important reason was the continued opposition of business leaders, who cringed at the elevation of Gompers to this influential post. Even one of his colleagues on the CND went so far as to refer to Gompers as an "agitator, anarchist, bomb thrower, and all around bad man."[22]

Opposition within the CND meant that labor's most significant policy-making victories in the first six months of the war would come from a surprising quarter: the War Department. Ironically, the organization that forced the War Department to act was the Carpenters' union of Gompers's political rival Bill Hutcheson. In the first weeks of May 1917, a dispute occurred between building trades unions and contractors hired to construct military cantonments. Carpenters and other skilled workers in the building trades demanded that the closed shop become standard on such jobs. Contractors countered that the emergency nature of the work and the shortage of suitable labor prevented them from hiring only union workers. The disagreement threatened to halt the building of bases just as conscription began. Naturally, the federal government was pulled in. The progressive secretary of war, Newton D. Baker, sought to work out a compromise with Gompers that would become precedent setting for the remainder of the war. On June 19, 1917, Gompers and Baker signed a controversial accord. The agreement ensured that cantonment construction workers would be paid the prevailing union scale in return for a promise by Gompers that the unions would not seek the closed shop on the construction projects. As one of the administrators of the accord later observed, "Roughly speaking, it was a bargain for union scales in exchange for the open shop." The agreement was concluded over the vociferous objections of Hutcheson, who opposed any retreat on the closed shop. With both the government and Gompers arrayed against him, however, Hutcheson was in no position to contest this fait accompli.[23]

The consequences of the cantonment agreement were profound. Its surrender of the closed shop set the tone for future agreements. Still, Gompers felt this a bargain worth making. Confident in his belief that the administration would not support a closed shop and that surrendering it would not diminish union power in a tight labor market, Gompers made the trade. Ultimately, his judgment in the case of the cantonments proved sound; construction unions continued to gain members throughout the war (elsewhere the concession would prove more problematic). At the same time, the agreement set the precedent for the creation of a federal war labor agency to administer the agreement, the Cantonment Adjustment Commission (CAC). A half-dozen similar boards would soon spring up in other war industries. Finally, the cantonment accord that created the CAC precipitated the arrival in Washington of the first war labor bureaucrats. Significantly, the labor experts to whom Secretary Baker turned were part of the extended family of Brandeisian advocates of industrial democracy. It was Brandeis's nephew, Louis Brandeis Wehle, who negotiated the cantonment accord between Gompers and Baker. Robert Valentine's former tenant, Walter Lippmann, was named the government's first representative to the CAC. Wehle and Lippmann would soon be followed to Washington by many others who shared their views.[24]

By the end of 1917, the CAC model had been extended with modifications to other wartime workplaces. An August 10, 1917, agreement between Gompers and Secretary of the Navy Josephus Daniels extended the provisions of the Gompers-Baker accord to the building of naval cantonments. Later that month, threatened walkouts in the nation's shipyards produced another path-breaking agreement, this one signed by the heads of the relevant AFL unions as well as by Gompers. Like the CAC accord, the shipbuilding agreement created a mediation agency—the Shipbuilding Labor Adjustment Board (SLAB)—composed of corporate, labor, and public representatives. According to James O'Connell, who then headed the AFL's Metal Trades Department, that agreement was "practically a union contract signed between the government and the officers" of the AFL. O'Connell boasted that it required "the ship builders of America [to] come to Washington and put their feet under the table with the labor leaders."[25]

AFL leaders had good reason to approve of the trend in Washington. By early autumn, strikes by New York and New Orleans dockhands led to the creation of a National Adjustment Commission for the nation's wharves. Acting under the authority of the Lever Act, President Wilson had also created the Fuel Administration and named Harry A. Garfield as its head. UMW president John P. White then joined the agency as an official labor representative, giving the union a powerful role in determining its labor policies. By the end of the year, snarling railroad traffic forced the president to create the U.S. Railroad Administration (USRA), with Treasury secretary William Gibbs McAdoo as its director general. McAdoo authorized the USRA's famous General Order No. 8, prohibiting discrimination against union members. Then he named three separate boards, each with union representation, to settle disputes on the operating lines, in railroad shops, and among maintenance-of-way workers.[26]

Joining these agencies were others that grew up within the Labor Department's ambit. A vastly expanded U.S. Employment Service (USES), under the leadership of former trade unionist John Densmore, undertook the task of matching workers to jobs. The solicitation of the USES for union interests frustrated employers to no end. Nor were employers necessarily fond of such new agencies as the U.S. Housing Corporation, the Division of Women in Industry, and the Division of Negro Economics—the last of which would soon prove particularly galling in the South.

THE NEW STATE: WAR LABOR ADMINISTRATORS

In an influential 1918 book, Mary Parker Follett proclaimed the arrival of a "new state." With its coming, "forms, images, moulds," Parker wrote, "all must be broken up and the way prepared for our plastic life to find plastic expression." It certainly must have seemed this way to those who watched the rise of the war labor apparatus in a nation with scant precedent for such an instrument. In a matter of months, a far-flung labor administration had come into being, incorporating labor union representatives and business leaders into its structure, setting basic labor standards, and enlisting the aid of a growing corps of war labor administrators. This new regulatory state had been emerging haltingly over two decades; now its sudden ascendance was chief among the developments that led John Dewey to describe the Great War as a "plastic juncture" in American history.[27]

The most immediately striking features of the rise of this new state were the faces of those who came to administer it. Two groups that had never before received an appreciable role in determining government policy suddenly found themselves on the inside of the government apparatus. One was a new group: the labor relations experts who had recently emerged from the scientific management movement, the front offices of progressive enterprises, and the academy. The other was an unlikely group: self-schooled trade union men and women. Representatives of these groups would not always see eye-to-eye. But they would profoundly influence the course of wartime labor policy.

The rise of the war labor agencies called forth a new breed of government administrator. These agencies attracted to Washington a generation of idealistic public servants whose role has too often been glossed over by references to the "dollar-a-year" executives whose influence in wartime Washington was far more obvious. For the most part, the war labor administrators were progressives who thought of themselves as what one scholar calls "classless men of a voluntary state." Interested in ameliorating labor conflict and promoting their conception of the public interest, efficiency engineers, personnel management experts, labor economists, and industrial relations consultants alike boarded trains to Washington.[28]

Leading the way were many of Frederick W. Taylor's followers. The Brandeis-Valentine critique of Taylorism seemed to have profoundly affected the thinking of the scientific management advocates who came to Washington in 1917. Among them were Charles E. Piez, Morris L. Cooke, Henry L. Gantt, and Otto S. Beyer. Piez, chairman of the Link-Belt Company, received the most influential appointment of this bunch. He was named general manager of the Emergency Fleet Corporation. A German-born engineer, Piez had introduced scientific management at Link-Belt; he ranked among Taylor's most ardent followers. Cooke, Taylor's prize pupil, came to work for the CND and later the U.S. Army's Quartermaster Corps. In his work for the government, he emerged as a foremost advocate of industrial democracy, hoping that the war would promote "the enfranchisement of the human spirit." Gantt devised an efficiency system for the Ordnance Bureau of the Army. Beyer, a railroad construction engineer before the war, was commissioned as an army captain and charged with training technical ordnance personnel. And two Taylor Society members close to Robert Valentine, Henry Dennison and Henry P. Kendall, also came to Washington, Dennison as assistant director of the CND's Central Bureau of Planning and Statistics and Kendall in the storage section of the War Industries Board.[29]

Joining the efficiency engineers were academicians schooled in the fields of personnel relations and labor economics. Leon C. Marshall, an economics professor at Ohio Wesleyan, took a post as director of industrial relations for the Emergency Fleet Corporation. A. B. Wolfe, a professor of economics at the University of Texas, headed investigations for the Fleet Corporation's industrial relations division. Ernest M. Hopkins of Dartmouth College handled the War Department's mediation efforts in the aircraft industry and directed industrial relations for the Quartermaster Corps. William Leiserson, the Estonian immigrant who had worked for the USCIR before moving on to the University of Toledo, took charge of the Labor Conditions Service of the Department of Labor.

Also important in the war labor administration were friends, followers, and admirers of Justice Brandeis. In addition to Louis B. Wehle, who served as both assistant to Secretary Baker and counsel to the Fleet Corporation, three others played major roles. One was Stanley King, a Boston lawyer and partner in the W. H. McElwain Shoe Company, an enterprise that had absorbed Brandeis's philosophy of labor relations. King served as Baker's secretary. A second was a former Boston settlement house worker named Meyer Bloomfield. Along with Lincoln Filene, Bloomfield had enticed Brandeis into the negotiations that produced the Protocol of Peace in 1910. He joined the Fleet Corporation's industrial service section. The third man became the most prominent Brandeisian in the wartime government. He was Brandeis's "half brother, half son," Felix Frankfurter.[30]

Perhaps nothing better illustrated how suddenly the state had changed in wartime than the rise of this Jewish immigrant from Central Europe. Frankfurter came to Washington in May 1917 at Baker's invitation, thinking he might stay only a few days to help "straighten out the clothing industry." That weekend trip became a two-year sojourn. Frankfurter took a leave from his Harvard Law School post and immediately made himself indispensable, writing policy memos on industrial relations for Baker and other top administrators. Where Frankfurter felt policy should go was never in doubt. Early on, he began to lobby for a coordinated war labor administration to replace the patchwork of boards and agencies. "Just relations between management and labor do not enforce themselves," he told Gompers. "We must provide authoritative machinery, representative of the interests of the whole country, for working out sound conditions, and constant supervision of such conditions." Such machinery, he believed, "cannot be established too soon."[31]

Within three months the peripatetic Frankfurter had his chance to shape policy. His opportunity arrived with the news of vigilante violence in the Arizona copper district and in the spruce forests of the Northwest. Fearful that such violence would disrupt war production, President Wilson created a President's Mediation Commission (PMC) in September 1917 to investigate and recommend solutions. The move seemed to confirm Frankfurter's own contention that existing agencies were inadequate to the challenge at hand. What is more, the thirty-five-year-old lawyer, whom President Wilson personally singled out for some special assignments, was named the PMC's secretary, serving under its chair, William B. Wilson, and members John H. Walker of the UMW, Colonel J. L. Spangler of Pennsylvania, Verner Z. Reed of Colorado, and G. P. Marsh of Washington. Of these, none exercised as much influence on the commission's work as Frankfurter.[32]

Frankfurter transmitted the Brandeisian message well. Under his guidance, the PMC investigated vigilantism in Arizona and the complaints of Pacific Coast telephone workers, Chicago meatpackers, and other aggrieved toilers. His diagnosis of the labor problem was matter-of-fact. "Autocracy and anarchy," he argued, were "the basic evils" that promoted unrest. Of these two, Frankfurter judged autocracy—as practiced by most employers—as the more dangerous. When the commission presented its final report to the president on January 9, 1918, it expanded on this assessment. In language redolent of the industrial democracy debate that had preoccupied Brandeisians before the war, the report stated that the "failure to equalize the parties in the adjustments of inevitable industrial contests is the central cause of our difficulties." Labor strife could be stemmed only by promoting "some form of collective relationship between management and men." Capitalists who opposed this relationship, the report implied, were hypocrites who highlighted "a glaring inconsistency between our democratic purposes in this war abroad and the autocratic conduct of some of those guiding industry at home." Bringing these strays into the fold necessitated the "unified direction of the labor administration of the United States" as quickly as possible.[33]

What did Frankfurter mean in advocating "some form of collective relationship" between management and labor? Frankfurter believed that the time was ripe for expanding workplace representation. The prewar debate concerning the democratization of industry echoed more loudly than ever among the labor relations bureaucrats who followed Frankfurter to Washington in 1917. In Cooke's estimation, "group leadership" would improve productive efficiency. Gantt argued that the war machine could produce "immeasurably more by democratizing industry." The vision that "group organization is to be the new method in politics," as Follett put it, went virtually unchallenged among war labor administrators. But, though he was a partisan of trade unionism, Frankfurter, like these others, did not think it possible that employers could be forced to deal collectively with workers through unions. Thus the PMC helped foster a compromise solution through which the war labor administrators would have their most significant impact on wartime labor relations: the shop committee or works council.[34]

Shop committees were to be bodies elected by workers themselves, under impartial supervision. They were to operate in a milieu in which discrimination against union members was forbidden; and they were to provide vehicles

The "War Cabinet" of the secretary of labor, 1918. Secretary Wilson is seated behind the desk. Felix Frankfurter is just to the right of Wilson. Directly behind Frankfurter sit Mary Anderson and Mary Van Kleeck of the Women in Industry Service. Assistant Secretary Louis F. Post is the bearded man across from Wilson. George E. Haynes of the Division of Negro Economics is standing in front of the door. (Library of Congress)

through which open-shop employers could collectively bargain with workers without being forced to recognize a union. In many ways, they were a perfect solution to the problems that plagued American war labor bureaucrats. Shop committees provided a way to secure workers' consent to the terms of their labor without upsetting the delicate balance that had been struck between trade unionists intent on securing the right to organize and industrialists equally committed to retaining the open shop.

Even before the PMC recommended a shop committee organization as a way to help settle labor turmoil in Arizona, other war labor agencies were turning to this device. The most influential was the Emergency Fleet Corporation's SLAB. In his own effort to "harmonize Scientific Management with Trade Unionism," as he put it, Piez of the Fleet Corporation had experimented with shop committees at Link-Belt before the war. During the war, the Fleet Corporation became the first testing ground for shop committee organization as the SLAB introduced committees into shipyards. The idea quickly spread to other agencies, culminating with an agreement concluded on March 22, 1918, between the Railroad Administration and the unions in which shop committees were promoted along the railways. By the end of the war, Louis Wehle judged the shop committee "the most important contribution" of the war labor agencies. "The local shop committee has been planted so well and so broadly throughout industry by these various governmental adjustment agencies," Wehle wrote, "as hardly to seem eradicable." [35]

THE NEW STATE: LABOR IN THE HALLS OF POWER

A common joke made the rounds in Washington during 1917. With reference to the AFL chief's frequent visits with the president, it held that "Gompers had a key to the back door of the White House." This image spoke to one of the most startling developments of the war—the relationship it consummated between the AFL and the Wilson administration. Evidence of the new reality was everywhere during the first year of the war. President Wilson frequently consulted Gompers on policy matters. He sent prominent AFL officials to Europe on the administration's behalf. He deemed it a "great privilege and a real honor" to become the first president to address the assembled delegates of an AFL convention when he came to Buffalo on November 12, 1917, to make his first speech outside Washington since war was declared. In that speech he proclaimed that "while we are fighting for freedom, we must see, among other things, that labor is free." Amazingly, he also spoke out against "various processes of the dilution of labor" and other abuses that "ought not to go on." "I am with you," Wilson told the AFL, "if you are with me." [36]

Nor was the president's solicitude the sole sign of labor's maturation as a political force. A February 1918 article in *Survey* pointed out numerous "outward and visible signs of change" in organized labor's position: meatpacking executives patiently waiting to see a secretary of labor who was too busy conferring with trade unionists to see them; Gompers informing employers that he could not work them into his schedule for he had business with the Railroad Administration; a government agency calling for a new trial for labor prisoner and accused terrorist Tom Mooney. Trade unionists understood what such scenes betokened, and they relished their newly won influence. Referring to the SLAB's policy of sponsoring the trips of shipyard shop committees to Washington, one union official boasted, "Uncle Sam is paying the expenses of union committees to come to . . . meet the employers. Isn't it a pretty good union agreement?" [37]

Employers too were very conscious of the shift in power that had taken place. To John Dodge of the Dodge Motor Car Company and to many others, it seemed that the government had become the crass agent of trade unionism. When federal officials arrived to conciliate a strike at his company's Detroit facility in January 1918, Dodge sneeringly asked, "Do you represent the government and Sam Gompers?" When the conciliators assured him of their impartiality, Dodge retorted, "Every employer knows President Wilson is playing politics with Sam Gompers."[38]

Dodge's prejudice was widely shared by business leaders. The vice president of the Illinois NAM, for one, heaped scorn on "the partnership . . . between the two presidents, Messrs. Wilson and Gompers." It was a partnership that, he remarked, "should read the other way—Presidents Gompers and Wilson." And he guessed that union men must be saying to themselves, "Now, boys, *we* own the United States: just watch Congress and President Wilson! Sam Gompers is the *real* President of this country." More circumspectly, Judge Elbert Gary, chairman of U.S. Steel, simply concluded that "no one can tell what is going to happen with respect to the labor question, because the Government is very powerful."[39]

Were such examples as these representative of a significant shift in the balance of political power in wartime America? Or did they simply obscure a more painful truth: that, in return for a junior seat of power in Washington, the AFL acquiesced in labor policies that were self-defeating and destructive of its militancy? A number of critics at the time (and many scholars afterward) have opted for the latter reading.[40] Evidence supporting such a critical interpretation is not lacking, to be sure. From the beginning, for example, some federal officials hoped that merely "calling labor leaders into council" would "go far toward paving the way for the concessions labor leaders would be expected to make" and would "serve mightily" in bolstering the "sane, loyal, and reasonable leaders." But the rise of a war labor administration ultimately held consequences too complex to be easily dismissed by the critics of the AFL's policy. Nothing better illustrates this truth than the fact that some of labor's most progressive and militant factions were those that most benefited from the Wilson administration's war labor policies.[41]

One of those beneficiaries was the renegade Amalgamated Clothing Workers of America. Throughout his tenure in wartime Washington, Felix Frankfurter argued that the government ought to work with "responsible radicals" such as Sidney Hillman of the ACWA as well as with AFL leaders. It would be a mistake to rely solely upon the AFL hierarchy, Frankfurter told Newton Baker, since the federation had "shown itself thus far unable to organize and direct the policy of . . . non-English speaking workers." Frankfurter urged as well that the government reach an accommodation with "the radical wing of the AF of L who are opposing Mr. Gompers."[42]

It was thanks in part to the lobbying of Frankfurter and ACWA allies such as Florence Kelley of the National Consumers' League that the War Department moved to eliminate the sweatshop conditions under which military uniforms were made. On August 24, 1917, Secretary Baker created a Board of Control for Labor Standards to oversee government contracts in the needle trades. On the board sat Louis Kirstein of the Filene retailing interests, Florence Kelley, and Captain Walter Kreusi of the Quartermaster's Department. Under Kirstein's leadership, the board tried to eliminate contractors who did not grant the eight-hour day, prohibit child labor, pay women equally for equal work, or recognize the right of collective bargaining. The practical result of the policy was to contribute to the spread of the ACWA's brand of militant unionism. Kelley and Kirstein, both friends of Hillman, established a close relationship with the union, and the latter even used his influence to help the ACWA organize the elusive Rochester, New York, market during the war. When the Board of Control was later replaced by a more powerful Administrator of Labor Standards for Army Clothing, that organization too came under the direction of a friend of the ACWA, labor mediator William Z. Ripley. Indeed, so favorable were federal policies to the ACWA that its AFL rival, the United Garment Workers (UGW), demanded an investigation of pro-ACWA bias within the War Department.[43]

An even greater boost to labor progressives and militants came from federal intervention in the meatpacking industry. On July 23, 1917, John Fitzpatrick of the Chicago Federation of Labor joined with William Z. Foster of the Brotherhood of Railway Carmen to sponsor a new initiative to organize stockyard workers. Modeled on the successful federations that railroad crafts had built on the railways, the Stockyards Labor Council (SLC) was composed of representatives from twelve unions that acted as one body, with one ruling board and one set of business agents. With innovative neighborhood locals that organized the diverse stockyard workers along racial and ethnic lines, the SLC received a particularly enthusiastic response from eastern European workers. By November 1917, just as the war labor agencies were mobilizing, the movement gathered steam, and packing companies retaliated by firing activists. Ultimately, Fitzpatrick and Foster would rely on the government to crack employer opposition. With a strike threatening, the President's Mediation Commission intervened in late November.[44]

When the PMC came to Chicago in December to mediate an end to the conflict, commissioners succeeded in hammering out a Christmas Eve agreement calling for binding arbitration of the workers' grievances. Packers balked at this settlement, refusing to sit down with union officials. So Fitzpatrick and SLC members raced to Washington to demand that the government seize and operate the yards. Under pressure, William B. Wilson named federal judge Samuel Alschuler to arbitrate the case in return for a no-strike pledge from the union.

It was the government's intervention in the stockyards case that ultimately gave Frank Walsh and his allies an opportunity to influence the course of the labor movement that they had been unable to get on their own. Walsh, whose ties to the Chicago activists had grown increasingly tight over two years of work with Fitzpatrick and Nockels through the CIR and NLDC, offered to represent the SLC before Alschuler. His work on the case would help change the course of the war labor administration.

The stockyards case allowed Walsh suddenly to recapture much of the attention he had received during his tenure on the USCIR. He was at his melodramatic best in the case. He brought Alschuler on tours of the plants and the workers' housing. He called immigrant laborers to the stand to testify emotionally about their hardships. He raked packer J. Ogden Armour over the coals, presenting figures that suggested that the meat baron could have doubled his employees' wages and still made a profit. Then Walsh made an eloquent case for the right to "a living wage." "Why should industry be made safe for autocracy," he asked, "while soldiers are dying on a thousand battle fields to make the world in general safe for democracy?" The question answered itself. When Alschuler announced his award in March, it gave meatpackers throughout the Midwest wage increases and an eight-hour day. As a result of the decision, Fitzpatrick predicted, "the harvest will be reaped in the industries throughout the nation."[45]

The packinghouse movement was the first great victory of previously unorganized industrial workers during the war. It would have been impossible without federal help. The federal intervention that made this victory possible in turn helped catapult Walsh once again toward the front ranks of public consciousness. With "the honored name of Frank P. Walsh," the *Butcher Workman* reported, "will be linked the most stirring struggle for emancipation from wage slavery since the inception of our national body and since Labor first combined to reap a more equitable reward for its efforts." In celebration of the victory, five thousand workers in St. Joseph, Missouri, paraded through the streets of their city carrying banners hailing Walsh and Alschuler: "cheer after cheer filled the air whenever one of the banners referred to our champion, Frank P. Walsh."[46]

What Walsh and his allies had been unable to gain on their own—influence over the mass organization of industrial workers—the government helped them achieve through the meatpacking effort. Even more important, their rejuvenation came at precisely the moment when the jury-rigged framework of federal labor agencies was beginning to teeter under the pressure of mounting labor unrest. When the president finally authorized the consolidation of those agencies that Frankfurter had been calling for, Frank Walsh and his friends would emerge with more influence over government policy than anyone could have imagined. By then, as his former law partner would later joke, Walsh had come to resemble "Achilles or whoever that mythical character was that got twice as strong each time he touched earth."[47]

THE CRISIS AND TRANSFORMATION OF
WILSONIAN WAR LABOR POLICY

By the time the PMC submitted its final report in January 1918, it was widely acknowledged that the federal war labor program was in disarray. Ad hoc adjustment commissions and decentralized boards, without overall direction, proved incapable of controlling militancy. So, against a backdrop of mounting labor unrest, one wing of the administration battled another over solutions. Secretaries Baker, Wilson, and Josephus Daniels of Navy favored working with the unions. But the Justice Department, military intelligence, and many within the CPI tended to equate all labor activism with disloyalty. Indeed, at one point Secretary Wilson had to squelch a CPI film that blamed battlefield losses on striking coal miners. "The Germans did not defeat us," said one character in the offending film, *King Coal*. "We were defeated by the miners at home." When government propagandists weren't treading on the Labor Department's toes with such pieces as this, intelligence agents were on its trail, claiming that department personnel were "strongly biased" in favor of both unions and strikes.[48]

While the war labor program creaked and tottered, congressional sniping and judicial fiats further challenged administration policies. Just as the war agencies were granting labor the right to organize, for example, the Supreme Court delivered its decision in *Hitchman Coal and Coke Co. v. Mitchell, et al.*, which confirmed the legality of the yellow-dog contract, a favored weapon in the struggle against that right. Southern Democratic leaders, such as Senator John Sharp Williams of Mississippi, wondered whether in establishing its liberal policies "the Government has invited [workers] to strike." Republicans added their voices as well. A vocal Wilson critic, Senator Porter J. McCumber of North Dakota, railed against the "unlimited power" wielded by AFL union leaders through government agencies. Senator John Y. Sherman argued that since the AFL found it impossible "to control the locals or the individuals in the locals," it was time to consider "despotic measure[s] of industrial efficiency." In May 1918, the director of the Selective Service Administration, General Enoch Crowder, took a step in that direction by announcing his famous "work or fight" order. To one perceptive observer, it was as if the three branches of government were "pursuing three radically divergent and hopelessly conflicting policies." [49]

But a resolution of the conflict was in the offing. When it came, the administration moved in a liberal rather than a conservative direction. Although they would generally disapprove of its outcome, the Brandeisians sparked the transformation. In November 1917, a group of liberals within the administration began to formulate plans to revamp the entire war labor policy. The key figures were Louis Wehle, Stanley King, Felix Frankfurter, and Assistant Secretary of the Navy Franklin D. Roosevelt. On November 2, the group won their first victory when the CND created the Industrial Service Section under the guidance of economist L. C. Marshall, giving him leave to coordinate mediation activities through the CND. On November 11, Wehle fired off a memo to the president arguing for the creation of "a separate, centralized labor agency." Three weeks later, the CND took another step toward this vision by establishing the Interdepartmental Committee, chaired by Roosevelt, which was to study the labor relations machinery with an eye toward reorganizing it. [50]

Alarmed, Gompers and his allies in the Labor Department ultimately defeated the scheme. They believed that any reorganization directed by this group would weaken Secretary Wilson, possibly promoting interests antithetical to the pure-and-simple vision of the AFL leaders. As Assistant Secretary of Labor Louis Post saw it, the Roosevelt effort aimed at nothing less than to "abolish the Department of Labor during the rest of the war." Roosevelt put up a strong fight—supported behind the scenes by Brandeis and Frankfurter—but in the end Gompers and Labor prevailed. After smashing the Roosevelt plan in a meeting of the Interdepartmental Committee on January 3, 1918, Secretary Wilson went to the president with a proposal that he turn over responsibility for the nation's labor policy to the Labor Department. His timing was fortuitous. Having just taken drastic action to solve the nation's railroad and fuel crises, the president was reluctant to create the "labor czar" that the Brandeisians sought. He decided instead to entrust the formation of future war labor policy to his labor secretary. [51]

On January 4, 1918, the president issued an executive order creating the War Labor Administration, which was to be headed by William Wilson. With that action, he gave the secretary a mandate to reorganize the war labor agencies as he saw fit. Secretary Wilson knew what kind of machinery he wanted. During the first months of the war, a variety of groups, ranging from reformers associated with the *Survey* to business leaders associated with the National Industrial Conference Board (NICB), had begun calling for a special tripartite national board—including representatives of business, labor, and the public—that would be given wide authority to settle labor disputes. When the AFL later endorsed such an idea in November 1917, the way toward such a board was clear. On January 28, Wilson asked the NICB and the AFL each to nominate five individuals to sit on the War Labor Conference Board (WLCB) to take a hand in devising the agency.

The Brandeisians had been outflanked. Later that spring, Secretary Wilson softened the blow by creating the War Labor Policies Board (WLPB)—an agency to coordinate policies between agencies—placing Frankfurter at its head. But Frankfurter's agency would never gain the influence he sought. The trade unionists thus thought they had a victory over the Brandeisians. But that victory did not mean that the WLCB would simply become a vehicle for the AFL's vision of industrial democracy.

Ultimately, it was the makeup of the WLCB that would determine how well it upheld the AFL's views. The NICB named Leonor F. Loree of the D. & H. Railroad, C. Edwin Michael of the Virginia Bridge and Iron Company, Loyall A. Osborne of Westinghouse Electric, Illinois manufacturer William H. Van Dervoort, and B. L. Worden of the Lackawanna Bridge Company to the WLCB. Gompers named Frank J. Hayes of the UMW, J. A. Franklin of the Boilermakers, William Hutcheson of the Carpenters, Victor Olander of the Seamen, and Thomas A. Rickert of the United Garment Workers. But in a twist of fate with lasting consequences, Franklin removed himself, citing the demands of his union office. Under the circumstances, Gompers could no longer ignore the union leader with the most members in the war industries. So he named the IAM's William H. Johnston as the final labor member of the WLCB. The delegates from each group were then asked to nominate a representative of the public who would serve as cochairman of the board. The business leaders chose former president Taft. The labor men turned to the most visible public defender of trade unionism in America, Frank P. Walsh, who was fresh from his victory in Chicago.

Never had the federal government sponsored such an entity as the WLCB. Gathered around its conference table were some of the staunchest open-shop advocates and some of the most militant trade union leaders in the nation. Worden, a "hard-line" member of the National Erectors' Association, and Osborne, whose Westinghouse Electric had violently resisted a strike outside Pittsburgh in 1916, sat on one side of the table. Hutcheson, who had opposed any compromise on the closed shop in cantonment construction, and Johnston, an avowed Socialist, sat across from them. As divided by philosophy, temperament, and experience as the WLCB members were, it is unlikely that they could have worked together without the strong leadership of Taft and Walsh.[52]

There was no small irony in this pairing. If Walsh was arguably the best-known labor lawyer in the country, Taft, from his service on the federal bench through his term as chief executive, had earned a reputation as a union foe. Nor did the history of their relationship to each other bode well. Were it not for the Senate's shelving of Taft's appointees to the USCIR, Walsh would never have gained the national spotlight. Taft, meanwhile, had criticized Walsh's work on the USCIR, believing that it illustrated the extent to which the AFL was able to use its influence in ways "detrimental to the public weal and the good of society." Taft had declined to appear before the USCIR to discuss labor law. But Walsh had not been shy about turning investigators loose on the Taft family. The USCIR looked into a sprawling Texas ranch owned by the former president's brother. "Democracy is as dead as it is in Siberia," Walsh concluded, at that "agricultural sweatshop."[53]

Not surprisingly, Taft was wary of collaborating with Walsh. But with his own son, Charlie, in Europe with Pershing, Taft had come to believe that a "truce between labor and capital" was necessary to win the war. He resolved to try to fashion that truce. At the same time, Walsh knew that Taft's vote would be necessary if labor was to get favorable action from the WLCB. He therefore turned his considerable charm toward winning over Taft. The former president was surprised to find Walsh "mild and . . . full of flattery." "He is a curious fellow," Taft observed. "His emotions he has cultivated so that he becomes intoxicated with his own feelings." But, said the old judge, "I can not help liking the Irishman in him."[54]

Taft soon found himself in "curiously agreeable relations with the labor men." The work of the WLCB and its successor agency was possible largely "due to the personality" of Taft, Basil Manly later concluded. Whereas Walsh was often given to blunt informality, Taft was diplomatic. Whereas Walsh spoke with urgency, Taft possessed a calming judicial temperament. Whereas Walsh enjoyed the role of an impassioned advocate, Taft assumed that of the prudent jurist. Mindful of detail, attentive to precedent, and always conscious of procedural questions, Taft was also skilled at smoothing over divisions among the conferees with his sense of humor. He played the part of compromiser with utmost tact. Astonishingly, as their relationship deepened, Walsh seemed to influence Taft. As one staff member later recalled, Taft "frequently remarked to Frank Walsh, as they toiled on some decision during a hot Washington night, that he was being forced to abandon the time-honored dicta of Adam Smith."[55]

During this period Taft acted, as some sociological theorists might have it, "on behalf of" rather than "at the behest of" capital, sacrificing the short-term interests of employers for long-term stability. But the subtlety of this distinction would have escaped Taft's colleagues. The employers were simply outraged at Taft's betrayal. They vainly tried to rein in the errant former president throughout the remainder of the war.[56]

Meeting in March 1918, the WLCB drew up the outlines of a new war labor program. The cochairmen took the lead in the process. Taft drafted guidelines for a new labor board. Walsh drafted the principles that would guide its actions. On March 28, the WLCB met to discuss the chairmen's proposals. In short order the conferees agreed on Taft's outline of the board's function. But, as Taft put it, "the greater difficulty came with Walsh's principles." The businessmen on the board deeply distrusted Walsh and were alarmed by the pro-union content of his draft. Only after two days of wrangling, during which Taft sided with Walsh and "read the riot act to my people once or twice," did the conferees agree to the principles on March 29.[57]

The agreement was groundbreaking. Both sides signed on to a simple proposition: "There should be no strikes or lockouts during the war." To insure labor peace, the conferees agreed to eight principles. The first affirmed that the right of workers to organize and bargain collectively "shall not be denied, abridged, or interfered with by the employers in any manner whatsoever" so long as unions did not "use coercive measures" to recruit. The second called for the maintenance of existing conditions insofar as possible. Union shops were to remain union, open shops open, and protective labor laws untouched. That women receive equal pay for equal work was stipulated in the third principle. The fourth called for the eight-hour day in all cases where the law mandated it, leaving the issue open to settlement based on "governmental necessities and the welfare, health, and proper comfort of the workers" in other cases. The fifth proscribed practices that delayed or limited production. The sixth called on both unions and corporations to cooperate in distributing the limited supply of skilled workers throughout war-related industries. The seventh—a concession to the business leaders' worry that unions might overturn the status quo in nonunion regions—held that in fixing wages, hours, and conditions, "regard should always be had" for "conditions prevailing in the localities involved." The last principle recognized "the right of all workers" to "a living wage" that would "insure the subsistence of the worker and his family in health and comfort."[58]

In all, labor gained more than it gave up in the agreement. Though some

The War Labor Conference Board with Secretary Wilson, March 14, 1918. From left to right are B. L. Worden, W. H. Van Dervoort, Loyall A. Osborne, Leonor F. Loree, Frank J. Hayes, Thomas A. Rickert, William L. Hutcheson, William H. Taft, Secretary Wilson, C. Edwin Michael, Frank P. Walsh, and Victor Olander. William H. Johnston had not yet joined the board. (National Archives II, College Park, Maryland)

principles acknowledged business's concerns—especially the prevailing conditions principle—on the whole the program pleased the unions. Walsh's influence was particularly evident in the document. The right to bargain collectively was featured as the first principle. Businesspeople, therefore, accepted the program only reluctantly as their best chance of reducing unrest. "I am most hopeful that . . . it will become a stabilizing influence and a rock of refuge in spite of some of the things in which we would like to have the Board do differently," offered Walter S. Drew of the National Erectors' Association. Drew judged the WLCB program to be "safer" than anything that might come from Frankfurter's WLPB, expressing relief that it would "greatly minimize the danger from Frankfurter and his crowd." Regarding the board's stand in favor of collective bargaining, Drew was hopeful. As long as workers bargained through government-fostered shop committees and the right to the open shop was protected, "what object is there in paying dues to a union?" [59]

On March 29, 1918, the WLCB submitted its report to Secretary Wilson. A little more than a week later, on April 8, Woodrow Wilson issued a presidential proclamation ratifying the WLCB's principles and reconstituting its members in an agency charged with implementing those principles, the National War Labor Board. True to their personalities, the cochairmen looked at their handiwork differently. "Whether the thing will work is of course in the womb of the future," Taft cautiously concluded. Walsh called the program "a new deal for American labor."[60]

THE NATIONAL WAR LABOR BOARD

The NWLB turned out to be an agency different from that anticipated by either its employer or its labor members. Employers were especially pleased that the board was a voluntary agency. Not created by legislation, it had no legal authority. Rather, when a strike or lockout occurred or when a complaint was lodged, it would dispatch investigators, some representing the employers, others labor, to gather facts, hold hearings, and present the evidence to the NWLB for a decision. One employer and one union representative would then recommend a settlement, subject to ratification by the full board. Only in cases where each side in the dispute had agreed jointly to submit to NWLB arbitration would decisions be enforceable at common law. Otherwise, the NWLB would publish its findings in hopes that public opinion and patriotic feeling would compel acceptance.

Technically, the NWLB was a voluntary agency. Its voluntary structure simply codified what one scholar called the "curious arrangement" first arrived at in the CAC agreement, the compromise that permitted unions to exist but assured them no recognition. Nor did the NWLB legally wield "real power" of its own, as another scholar has noted. The way the board developed, however, makes it difficult to characterize the NWLB as simply a voluntary agency. Rather, the board ended up straddling the line between voluntarism and coercion in ways that surprised many of its creators. Two factors were crucial in making the NWLB a more powerful institution than its founders had envisioned: its field staff and its vigorous support by the administration.[61]

Quite simply, there had never been a staff on any previous government agency like that which represented the NWLB in the field. The NWLB set up its offices in Washington's Southern Building, the former home of both the USCIR and the CIR. The location must have been familiar to many of its staffers, for to a great extent they were simply recruited from Frank Walsh's circle of acquaintances. Walsh left an indelible stamp on the NWLB. In many ways the agency merely connected the networks he had built over the past several years. For the most important staff position, that of secretary to the NWLB, Walsh overcame the objections of several of the board's employers and hired economist W. Jett Lauck, who had worked for him on the USCIR.[62] Lauck and Walsh then began hiring the NWLB's labor field investigators.

Although the NWLB staff included investigators chosen by employers and a smattering of industrial relations professionals—such as Francis H. Bird, formerly of the USCIR, and Richard B. Gregg, Robert G. Valentine's former partner—the rest of the staff was thick with Walsh's friends. Basil Manly served as Walsh's alternate on the board. The NWLB's chief investigator was William P. Harvey, who had worked for both the CIR and the NLDC. The board's investigators included Kansas City single-tax advocates Carl Brannin and Vernon Rose; Robert S. Buck, a former Chicago alderman with close ties to the Chicago Federation of Labor; Harold Callender of Kansas City, an NLDC veteran; Raymond Swing, a liberal Chicago newspaperman whom Walsh had befriended in 1918; and Anton Johannsen. Female staffers included chief of women investigators Elizabeth Christman of the Chicago Women's Trade Union League. The chief of women examiners was Marie L. Obenauer, formerly of the USCIR. Also joining the staff were Bertha Nienburg; Olive Sullivan, who had aided Walsh during the meatpacking case; and Hazel Hunkins of the National Woman's Party, an acquaintance of Walsh's suffragist friends.

Walsh's influence in picking its staffers made the NWLB the most left-leaning government agency that Washington had ever seen. That fact did not escape labor enemies both within and outside the board. Over time, the NWLB's employer members became convinced that the labor staff was actually fomenting labor unrest rather then stemming it. The NWLB eventually mounted investigations into more than one NWLB staffer's actions, and by the autumn of 1918 Taft demanded an accounting of "exactly whom we have in the employ of the Board and why." He came to believe that "partisan agitators" had been appointed by Walsh and Lauck. Indeed, Taft thought such staffers had "abused the function of their office by attempting to organize the trade union side" and addressing "meetings with a view not of alleviating trouble, but of stirring it up."[63]

The attention of enemies outside the NWLB proved more ominous. Military intelligence agents conducted regular surveillance of many of the NWLB's officials, including Johannsen, Rose, Harvey, and even Walsh himself. Agents knew that Rose was with antiwar activist Rev. Herbert S. Bigelow on the night Bigelow was abducted by a tar-and-feather mob. They believed Rose was working with the People's Council. Agents also reported that Harvey might be a Wobbly and that Johannsen applauded U.S. military defeats that would "hasten our dream of a revolution." One intelligence brief even suggested that "most of the men on the NWLB are ex-dynamiters." Although such frenzied conclusions were apparently rejected by superiors, agents regularly spied on Walsh, opening his correspondence with the likes of civil liberties activist Roger Baldwin and debriefing reporters who covered him.[64]

For the duration of the war, however, such secret harassment had little discernible impact on the NWLB, largely because of the strong support that President Wilson himself gave the agency. That support was required early. In April 1918, the Commercial Telegraphers Union of America (CTUA) launched an organizing campaign at the Western Union Company that ultimately drew the NWLB into its first great controversy. The company's anti-union president, Newcomb Carlton, summarily fired eight hundred unionists in response to the drive. The CTUA retaliated by threatening a strike that would have paralyzed the nation's communications. The NWLB swiftly intervened, assigning the case to Taft and Walsh.[65]

The Western Union case represented a turning point for the untested agency. Throughout May 1918, complex negotiations between Taft, Walsh, and Carlton unfolded. The normally impetuous Walsh hoped to secure the immediate reinstatement of the fired employees, but he deferred to Taft's more moderate approach. Because Carlton had not requested NWLB intervention, the board could not require Western Union to heed its decision. Taft therefore hoped to persuade Carlton to accept a compromise. But when the "very obstinate" Carlton rejected Taft's cautious entreaties, the angry former president brushed aside the objections of the employer members of the board and sided with Walsh and the union members in a finding that demanded the reinstatement of the employees and a recognition of their right to organize.[66]

The NWLB's employers were outraged. They "had it out" with Taft in private, leaving him to conclude that they were "very tired of what they have gotten into" in signing on to the NWLB. Alarm soon spread beyond the board. Briefed on the cases before the NWLB by board member Osborne, the NICB decided that it had better open a Washington office to provide services to the NWLB's employer members, with staff to be paid out of a special fund. Behind the scenes, meanwhile, the NWLB's employer members connived with Carlton to resist the implementation of the NWLB's decision. Encouraged by dissension within the board, Carlton informed President Wilson that the Taft-Walsh recommendation would harm his company's ability to carry on its vitally important business and that he would therefore not comply with it.[67]

Carlton was on firm legal ground in taking this stand. Had President Wilson merely accepted it, the NWLB would have been thwarted and consigned to insignificance for the remainder of the war. Employers in future cases would have followed Carlton's lead, and the NWLB's employer members would have held it hostage. But Wilson did not accept Carlton's stand. He opted for a course of action recommended by Walsh weeks earlier: the emergency nationalization of the telegraph lines. He announced his action on July 16, 1918. To those who read newspaper accounts of the decision, the message seemed unmistakable. The president would brook no defiance of the NWLB. That was clear to Walter Drew. "The action of the President in putting the war-time powers of the Government back of the National War Labor Board," he later observed, "has fundamentally changed the nature of the Board."[68]

When it came, government control of the telegraph lines was something of a Pyrrhic victory for the unions. The administration of the lines fell to Postmaster Albert Sidney Burleson; he was no friend of labor, and his administration of the award would frustrate CTUA members in later months. But this outcome did little to assuage the fears of employers. They had cooperated in the creation of the NWLB, as Taft surmised, thinking that they could "maintain a *status quo* of . . . the closed non-union shop" through its principles. The Western Union case challenged that assumption. Employers would spend the rest of the war seeking to undo this precedent. In the meantime, they advised friends "not to get your case before the Board if you can help it." So long as Taft continued to vote with Walsh and labor, the NWLB was a new power to be reckoned with.[69]

In July 1918, Walsh rejoiced that the NWLB was "growing beyond my wildest expectations." He believed that it would "be not only a big thing for the country during the war, but that perhaps it will furnish a basis for a real industrial regime thereafter."[70] So it seemed a little over one year into America's participation in the war, as longtime advocates of industrial democracy gained ground in Washington generally and as Walsh and his friends enjoyed the height of their influence on Washington's most powerful war labor agency. But the NWLB helped shift the locus of the struggle to democratize industry once again to shipyards, mines, and mills around the country, and there the battle was destined to take some surprising turns.

TOWARD THE "DE-KAISERING" OF INDUSTRY

4

We are doing all that we are able . . . so that
Democracy in the true sense of the word will be
a reality.

—*Resolutions Committee, UMW Local 517, 1918*

Workers' struggles to improve their conditions had been the driving force behind Progressive-era labor reforms. And it was on those occasions when their efforts had resorted to or been met by appalling violence—the bombing of the *Los Angeles Times*, the Ludlow massacre, the Bisbee deportation—that workers had seen significant political gains materialize, from the creation of the USCIR to Frank Walsh's championship of industrial democracy and to the expansion of the war labor agencies. The emergence of federal agencies during World War I, designed to foster labor peace by granting basic rights to workers, transformed the context within which their struggles would be fought for the duration of the war. The war labor agencies did not determine what kind of industrial democracy would emerge during the war; in many ways they lagged behind events. But by wrapping this ideal in the mantle of federal policy, they influenced workplace struggles and set the parameters within which workers themselves would mobilize to define industrial democracy.

Judged by its impact on labor unrest, federal labor policy must be considered a failure. On the whole, strikes were not significantly dampened by it. Indeed, during April 1918, the first month of the NWLB's tenure, the Bureau of Labor Statistics measured a 25 percent increase in the strike rate. Workers, long restrained by larger forces, took advantage not only of tight labor markets but also of federal labor policies that protected their right to organize. They acted aggressively to capitalize on the federal machinery. Almost 90 percent of the cases submitted to the NWLB therefore originated in complaints by workers. Often those complaints were elicited by the board's own pro-labor rulings. As one contemporary explained, the NWLB's decisions "looked so good to workers that they were stirred to instigate" disputes so as to "secure the good offices of the Board."[1]

Unions profited immensely under the Wilsonian war labor agencies. In coal mines, steel mills, electrical manufacturing plants, and shipyards, in industries in which unions had a toehold before the war and those from which they had been excluded, the tide of organization rolled on. By January 1, 1919, AFL membership figures soared past the 3.2 million mark—one million more than in 1917. And those unions most closely regulated by the government seemed to profit most. During the NWLB's fifteen-month reign, for example, the IAM virtually doubled its membership. The all-but-moribund Amalgamated Association of Iron, Steel, and Tin Workers also mushroomed. Totaling only seven thousand members in 1915, the union recruited tens of thousands within months of the NWLB's creation. Unions ranging from the Electrical Workers to the Hod Carriers registered similarly spectacular figures.[2]

But to grasp fully the impact of the war labor agencies on workers and unions, one must move beyond the statistics to consider stories such as the one told by IAM organizer Robert Corley. While sitting in a hotel lobby in Kokomo, Indiana, one evening some months after the creation of the NWLB, Corley was approached by a stranger. "Can you help me out tonight?" he asked. "There is a bunch of men . . . and they have crowded the carpenters completely out of [their] hall . . . and they want to be organized." A bit skeptical, Corley followed his new companion to the meeting. That night, without any forethought or planning on his part, he organized two hundred employees of Ross Gear and Tool. Shortly thereafter, they brought their complaints against their company to the NWLB.[3]

This story, which was replayed in different ways throughout the war, indicates something important about the labor upheaval of World War I. Wartime conditions, including the presence of agencies such as the NWLB to which complaints could be directed, helped stir workers in ways not even union leaders were prepared for. Why did this happen? War labor agencies helped legitimize three things that resonated deeply among working people: their demand for a rule of law in the workplace, their call for a voice in determining the conditions of their work, and their desire to claim their rights as citizens through their labor. Though these could be conservative goals in themselves, in mobilizing to achieve them, workers did not always construe them as such.

Nor for that matter did employers who found themselves battling the erosion of their authority.

World War I did more than any previous event to rationalize the chaotic, idiosyncratic, and arbitrary American workplace. Prewar scientific managers, welfare workers, and personnel experts had done little to ameliorate the labor discontent that flowed from authoritarian managerial decision making, the uncertainty of wage rates, and a host of other problems. War labor agencies, however, helped change these conditions by attempting to promote what one government committee called a "rule of reason and justice" embodied in "standards . . . appropriate to American citizens devoting their energies to the successful prosecution of a righteous war." Mackenzie King advised his corporate clients during the war that an "entirely new situation has been created for American industries" by the government's effort "and the jurisdiction it has assumed." That situation saw workers fight for and gain a level of rationality and justice on the job that they had not previously known.[4]

A look at three important cases decided by one agency, the NWLB, helps to clarify the significance of this development. Two cases involved the problems of "dilution" and job classifications in the machine shops of Waynesboro, Pennsylvania, and Cambridge, Massachusetts. The other dealt with the use of yellow-dog contracts by General Electric at its Pittsfield, Massachusetts, plant. In each case, NWLB decisions helped promulgate a crude rule of law in the workplace.

The NWLB's most important decisions affecting the internal labor markets of companies were delivered in the Waynesboro and Cambridge cases. The Pennsylvania case emerged when machinists complained that employers were using lower-paid, semiskilled workers to depress wages, de-skill work, and in general erode working conditions. When some three thousand machinists left the shops of Waynesboro on May 23, 1918, the NWLB speedily intervened. This case ultimately served as the basis for a crucial decision. An investigation of working conditions in Waynesboro conducted by NWLB staffers pointed out the inadequacy of wages for the unskilled workers in that community, a factor that encouraged employers' efforts to de-skill jobs. Frank Walsh used this study to argue for a minimum wage rate—a "living wage"— in Waynesboro that might stabilize conditions there. Taft agreed to go along. With Taft's assent and over the objection of the NWLB's employer members, on July 11 the board set minimum wages for Waynesboro workers at forty cents per hour. (They had previously averaged only twenty-two cents.) Through the decision the board effectively authorized the government to impose a wage structure on the Waynesboro shops.[5]

On this same day the NWLB also set another critical precedent regarding job classifications and their relationship to the problem of dilution. In May 1918, machinists threatened to strike the Worthington Pump Company in Cambridge, Massachusetts, unless their jobs were classified according to their level of proficiency and their wages determined by a standard that would protect them from dilution. Employers insisted on retaining the right to determine a worker's classification, job category, and job content. Their allies on the NWLB defended that right. But again, on July 11, the unionists prevailed. The NWLB issued a finding in favor of the machinists' request. As part of the settlement, a federal administrator was dispatched to classify all the jobs at Worthington Pump's Cambridge plant.[6]

Decisions such as these significantly curtailed the ability of managers to regulate their own internal labor markets, while also lessening existing tensions between skilled workers and semiskilled workers. Too, such precedents tended to encourage other workers to seek a measure of order and fairness from the war labor administration, contributing to a tendency about which Mackenzie King warned employers during the war. Once workers found an effective "avenue of appeal to outside intervention," King expected, they would seek "incessant government intervention, involving submission to the fiats of National and State Boards." The Manufacturers' Association of Southern Connecticut absorbed that lesson, warning employers "to use utmost diligence and discretion" in their business before the "Taft-Walsh Board" so that "present conditions remain unchanged."[7]

The fears of Connecticut employers were hardly assuaged by the NWLB's decision in a case brought by the Pittsfield Metal Trades Council against General Electric. Although the United States Supreme Court had upheld the constitutionality of yellow-dog contracts in its *Hitchman* decision in 1917, the NWLB refused to sanction any such contracts signed after the war had begun. A series of strikes at GE in Pittsfield in 1918 in which the use of these contracts became the main issue led the board to ban yellow-dog contracts at GE on June 28, 1918. Two months later the board confirmed that precedent at the Smith and Wesson Company of Springfield, Massachusetts. In other cases, the board further strengthened the right to organize by forbidding discrimination against union members, ordering the reinstatement of fired unionists, and proscribing blacklisting. Peaceful participation in strikes was deemed no basis for an employee's dismissal, and the NWLB prohibited the threatened use of the military draft against union members.[8]

To be sure, these precedents were not implemented across the board. By the time the armistice was signed, the NWLB had resolved only 72 of the 847 cases it had received. This fact, however, was less significant than that the board rolled back managerial prerogatives in several highly publicized decisions, thus altering the expectations of managers and workers alike during the war. Following these decisions, an increasing number of workers sought the "living wage," job classifications, and the right to organize. And they did so with the expectation that the government would protect them. This perception led employers to claim, as Jett Lauck later explained, "that the unions were using the principles of the board as a basis for propaganda or union organization, claiming that the Government put its approval upon the recognition of unionism as a basis of industrial relations during the war."[9]

Nor was the NWLB the only agency that helped bring rationality and justice to the wartime workplace. Consider the rulings of the USRA's Railway Board of Adjustment No. 2, the union-management body created to settle grievances in railway shops. This board enforced the USRA's General Order No. 8 and a host of other rulings that protected workers against unjust discharge or transfer, forbade supervisors from interfering with the selection of shop committees, and ensured payment of overtime and back pay. Board No. 2 was swamped by complaints from individual workers, unions, and railroad shop committees. For the most part, it was a boon to workers. Indeed, a sample of 165 decisions rendered by Board No. 2 shows that 63 percent of decisions rendered favored labor, less than 24 percent favored management, while the remainder fell somewhere in between. By far the most common complaint received by the board involved workers' appeals against unjust firing by employers in violation of General Order No. 8. In such cases, railway shop employees found that they could consistently rely on Board No. 2 to order reinstatement.[10]

The federal government may have shaped workers' fight for a workplace rule of law, but in doing so it did not necessarily create order in the workplace. Rather, the possibility that the government might intervene to settle workers' complaints often resulted in engendering more complaints. The instructions one USRA official gave to union leaders on the Pennsylvania Railroad are telling on this point. While the federal agent reminded the unionists that "it is the duty of every man to obey" the supervisor, he also qualified what he meant by obedience. "Now, I do not mean by 'obeying' that you are supposed to jump into a red hot firebox, or something of that sort," he explained. "But you understand what I mean. If the order is such that it is going to work a hardship on you, there is a way . . . to take it up. Go with it to your foreman . . . and, if necessary, Washington will come and hear the grievance and sit on the job."[11]

Getting Washington to "sit on the job" became a prime activity for workers in shipyards, mines, and mills during the war. Many learned that the best way to do that was to strike or threaten to do so. This was the paradox of the war labor administration: in offering workers a means of stabilizing their working lives, it contributed to the destabilization of workplace relations and the growth of labor militancy. Again, Mackenzie King foresaw the problems that might flow from government intervention tendered in this fashion. Militancy would breed militancy, he predicted, and once triggered it would prove difficult to contain. "The effect upon all," he warned in picturesque language, "is bound to be that which comes from 'having once tasted blood.'"[12]

LEGITIMIZING THE DEMAND FOR REPRESENTATION

Nothing stirred workers more during the World War I era than their demand to a voice in determining the conditions under which they labored. By fostering workplace representation through shop committees, the war labor agencies helped promote that demand. First implemented by the SLAB in 1917, shop committees or works councils were subsequently adopted by other war labor agencies. The Fuel Administration created pit committees to help spur production in coal mines. The PMC introduced committees into Arizona's embattled copper mines. And, most important, the NWLB implemented them in the war industries over which it had jurisdiction. Before it expired in the summer of 1919, the NWLB issued 226 decisions that called for collective bargaining. In 125 of those cases, the board provided for the creation of shop committees to achieve that goal. Because the NWLB decisions affected such historically nonunion industries as steel and electrical manufacturing, its decisions had resounding impact. As staffer Richard Gregg noted, the NWLB gave collective bargaining "a great impetus in all American industry."[13]

War labor administrators had first turned to shop committee representation as a means of dampening labor militancy. As one staff member of the PMC explained, it was hoped that the "establishment of a system of domestic shop committees to represent these men might help in getting hold of them." In some cases shop committees did function in this way, funneling labor militancy into manageable channels. One example of this comes from the stockyard committees instituted after Judge Alschuler's decision, one of whose members told of shop representatives who "would go down there [on the shop floor] and keep them working, settle whatever dispute there was." But such instances were not the rule. More often, the committees provided what one scholar has aptly described as an arena within which workers' struggles "clashed with the government's quest for a mechanism to mediate industrial disputes and increase productivity."[14]

Rather than simply diverting labor militancy into acceptable channels, wartime shop committees promoted several unanticipated results. Often they operated as Trojan horses, easily captured by labor unionists and converted by them into instruments through which they could bargain collectively with open-shop employers. On other occasions they acted to facilitate the organization of unskilled workers into unions in settings where skilled trade unionists had previously neglected them. Most important, they raised powerful expectations among workers that they had a *right* to representation. Once raised, such expectations were not easily met. Again, a look at examples taken from the records of the war labor agencies helps to clarify the significance of this phenomenon.

Every record of NWLB shop committee elections indicates that unionists took control of these committees. "Those elected were practically all union members," one NWLB examiner explained of the election he conducted, "and it was reported to me that two or three who were not union members when elected, joined immediately thereafter." Moreover, once they controlled shop committees, union militants frequently used them as front organizations through which to present union demands to their open-shop employers. When he led a committee into the office of W. J. Lloyd, supervisor of the meters and instruments department at Lynn GE, John F. Peterson, a union leader at the plant, demanded a meeting and informed his stunned supervisor that he was aware of the government's stand on collective bargaining. "You know what this means, Mr. Lloyd; we're here under the guidance of the War Board; we're here under their policy, as I understand, that employers should treat with committees." Lloyd's angry response—"Get two officers and drag this man out," he called to his secretary—only inflamed the GE workers, led them to strike, and brought the NWLB into the case.[15]

When unionists controlled them, shop committees rarely served to dampen labor militancy. Coal mines provide a case in point. Early in the war many mine owners of the Alabama Coal Operators Association believed that the election of pit committees would increase production and decrease unrest. The spread of Fuel Administration pit committees, however, quickly disillusioned them. They found that UMW activists dominated committees. One operator complained that the leader of his pit committee "at all times assumed the air of a dictatorial master" who was "void of the principles of conciliation and patriotism." Another told of an Italian committee member who "at times goes around like a raving maniac, stating that he is running the mine." A Fuel Administration investigator found that a "radical element" had taken over the mine committee at Coal Brook Collieries in Carbondale,

Pennsylvania, staging a strike over wages despite the criticism of the UMW's former president and then Fuel Administration official John P. White.[16]

Shipyard and railway committees were also susceptible to co-optation by militants. One SLAB investigator in the South informed his superior that he feared the committees under his supervision "might become dangerously radical." Shipyard supervisors and railway administrators were exasperated by committees that demanded wage increases, shorter hours, and the reinstatement of workers fired for union affiliation. When the Florida East Coast Railroad laid off one unionist in March 1918, for example, it was the chairman of his shop committee that rallied to his support. The committee took a strike vote and the company backed down. On other occasions, like one at the Terry Shipbuilding Company in Savannah, Georgia, yard committees called for the firing of hated foremen. Foreman Harry Downing of the Terry yard was himself bewildered by a turn of events that seemingly left workers with the expectation that they could have him canned. "All I have done," he muttered, "is to require these men to earn the money that the Government is paying them."[17]

In the mass production factories under NWLB jurisdiction, shop committees also seemed to facilitate broader organization in settings where workers had been previously divided by skill level. Typically, the NWLB called for the election of a plantwide shop committee rather than separate committees consisting of workers of varying trades and skills. The system set up at GE's Lynn plant, for example, set electoral districts of two hundred employees each; two representatives were to be elected from each district. Committee representatives thus selected would in turn elect four of their number to a Joint General Council. The practical effect was to bring together in one organization workers of all skill levels, making the Joint General Council representative of the entire plant.[18]

This trend played a significant role in broadening unionization. Records show that in the industries regulated by the NWLB, militancy tended to originate among skilled workers. Hence fully 45.3 percent of the 1,125 cases that made it to the NWLB's docket originated among members of just five crafts: machinists, molders, carpenters, electrical workers, and street railway drivers. Only 4.3 percent of the cases, meanwhile, originated among members of the federal labor unions, laborers' unions, or city central bodies that most often represented unskilled or semiskilled workers.[19] Skilled workers, then, tended to act as "spark plug" unionists, initiating organizing. But the structure of shop committees encouraged them to act in concert with less skilled workers if they wished to control the shop committee elections that might come from federal intervention. For without wide electoral support—Lynn GE saw 82.2

percent of eligible voters turn out for shop elections—skilled unionists would have little chance to influence committees. So emerged a frequently repeated dynamic in NWLB cases: a small group of skilled unionists initiated a strike, the NWLB intervened and called for collective bargaining, and union members then swept into office, turning the shop committee into a de facto union council.[20]

In some cases where skilled workers still preferred to remain aloof from their less-skilled colleagues, war labor agencies discouraged them. In shops where women worked, for example, the NWLB mandated that women serve on committees. In one case where local craft unionists attempted to keep unskilled workers off of a shop committee, NWLB examiners even stepped in to stop them. Most war labor administration staffers agreed with one SLAB investigator that their purpose was to build "really democratic shop committees."[21]

In promoting the right to representation, shop committees also stirred something more intangible. They contributed directly to the surging demand for democracy that marked so much political discourse during the era of the war. As the counsel for one group of union workers explained, workers cherished "the right to choose their own committees in their own way; in other words to exercise their own discretion." An electrical worker explained that while he and his colleagues "were thankful to the Board for bringing our wages up," the board's most important contribution was the shop committee—"giving us poor devils a chance to go to the old man and tell him about conditions without the risk of being jumped for it." Those who had never worked with him, he said, could not possibly "appreciate what this new deal meant to the rank and file." Munitions workers apparently understood what he meant. "The interest of the employees was so great as to strike me as almost pathetic," reported one federal investigator about the shop committee elections he conducted in Bridgeport.[22]

No industrial workers had labored in an environment more impervious to their expression of a collective voice than steel workers. They were especially captivated by the prospect of workplace representation. "It would be impossible to overstate the change for the better that has occurred in the morale of these folks," observed one NWLB official on hand for shop committee elections at Bethlehem Steel. He found steelworkers "joyful" as they set about electing committee representatives. Later, AFL secretary Frank Morrison confirmed as much. He reported that he was furnished "with one of the badges which was worn by the elected shop committees when they held their convention to elect a Local Board of Conciliation in Bethlehem." It was, the steelworkers told him, "'the first Badge of Democracy ever worn in that city.'" Morrison had it framed.[23]

The very factors that made shop committees attractive to workers during the war led managers to begin to fear their spread. Most employers soon seconded the conclusion of Detroit auto parts makers who guessed that "the demand for shop committees . . . is mere camouflage. The effort is being made to force the closed shop down the throats of Detroit manufacturers." Nor did managers' complaints subside after committee elections. One employer groused that his delegates "spent most of their time going from department to department and keeping things upset generally." Such stories inspired the resistance of some employers to the free election of committees. The Fuel Administration received reports from the UMW that many operators of Kentucky and Tennessee mines were taking it upon themselves to appoint pit committees rather than have them elected. Where they could not actually appoint the committees, mine operators were "interfering in the internal affairs of meetings by having their superintendents participate." [24]

But employers' blunt resistance to workplace representation was difficult to sustain during the war to make the world safe for democracy, as GE officials realized. When workers at Lynn demanded that GE meet with their committees, company officials felt very much on the spot. "Having in mind the whole situation, both in Washington and Lynn," general counsel Owen D. Young told GE's president, it would be prudent not to allow the company's actions to be "construed as a refusal to meet representatives of the employees." Pressed by such considerations, farsighted employers focused on minimizing the threat posed by shop committees rather than on opposing them outright. Two strategies proved popular. One saw employers rush to create their own shop committees before the government stepped in to do so. Hence by September 1918, the Manufacturers' Association of Southern Connecticut was recommending that its members "proceed to have their employees elect proper employees' committees at once." The other strategy saw employers fight for certain concessions from government administrators. One of their most frequent demands was that committee elections be held on company grounds rather than in the community, where union activists could presumably more easily influence their outcomes. According to the NICB, employers ought to see "that such elections be held on the premises of the employer," with voting by secret ballot and "the votes counted in the presence of representatives of both the management and the employees." [25]

Attempts by employers to defuse the independence of shop committees often drew fierce opposition from workers whose appetite for representation had been whetted by their own government's pronouncements. They did not give in easily to intimidation. Thus when GE officials at Lynn tried to implement a committee plan designed by Mackenzie King, in lieu of an

NWLB shop committee, they met a nearly unanimous rejection. An election to select delegates to the King-designed committee drew only 230 out of 14,000 eligible voters. In Lynn and elsewhere the constitution and function of shop committees emerged as a central issue of contest between managers and workers. Rather than encouraging quiescence among workers, then, representation issues stirred them.[26]

REDRAWING THE BOUNDARIES OF INDUSTRIAL CITIZENSHIP

When one of the Lynn GE workers who was most active in resisting management's attempts to rein in representation was asked by government officials whether he had to hide his union sympathies on the job, his answer surprised them. "In a way, I didn't have any," he replied, "only—I might say I had an American feeling, that is all. . . . I didn't have much thought in the matter . . . of union stuff." Further questions revealed that indeed this employee saw his unionism as simply an extension of the war effort that he loyally supported. That response was emblematic of an important tendency in the wartime workplace. As workers mobilized to demand representation, they did so in a climate charged by the propaganda of democracy and citizenship. During the period of the war, unionists and militants were remarkably successful at employing such rhetoric in defense of their goals. Patriotic appeals that urged toilers to shoulder the burdens of a war against autocracy afforded them as well a rationalization for action, as they sought to make real the talk of democracy. In the minds of more than this Lynn worker, the concepts of good citizenship and workplace organization were fused.[27]

The propaganda of the government's own agencies lent itself to co-optation by workers. In the era when sauerkraut was rechristened as "liberty cabbage," Bridgeport, Connecticut, machinists began referring to Remington Arms as "the American Junkers!" The steelworkers of Birmingham, Alabama, called the Tennessee Coal and Iron Company (TCI) the "Kaiser of Industrial America." Others flung the more colorful epithet "American Hohenzollerns" at their employers. Pennsylvania coal miners attacked mine operators for their "hunnism." Most common of all, however, were the terms "Prussian" and "autocratic." Thus, the German *Kultur* excoriated by George Creel's CPI offered a perfect analogy for industrial management, and bossism became "kaiserism" in the language of union activists. Utica, New York, textile workers thus contended that "the United States was the land of the free until it became Kaiserized," whereas a Mississippi railroad shopman complained that while working for the Illinois Central "I was nothing more than a subject of the Kaiser, and as far as a right I had none." By using such language, trade unionists portrayed their movement as seeking the "de-kaisering of industry," as one union newspaper put it, rather than merely higher wages and shorter hours.[28]

Workers were aided in claiming this broad language of citizenship by an important development. During the war, the American workplace as never before became a public space. War work was the people's work, and the boundaries between private industry and the demands of the commonweal were blurred. Reminders of the conflation of the workplace and public space were everywhere. Government agents—whether labor investigators, the "four-minute men" who gave patriotic speeches at the behest of the CPI, or Liberty bond promoters—crowded into shipyards, mines, and mills. And the flag was flown more often over, in, and around factories than anywhere else. This virtual worship of the flag on the job, promoted by employers who were eager to foster "100% Americanism," saw flag raisings and rallies become a staple in most war-related industries. One such event staged for Bethlehem Steel workers in Steelton, Pennsylvania, on July 3, 1918, saw company officials engaging workers in a series of chants so loud "that the men in Bethlehem [could] hear them," according to the company paper. GE erected a flagpole on each of the twenty buildings in its Lynn complex. Some departments at Bethlehem Steel's main facility required workers to salute a huge flag every time they entered or left their workroom. As one Lawrence textile worker reported, everywhere one turned in her mill "there was a poster or a picture. 'Buy a Bond' and 'Be Patriotic.'"[29]

Consecrated by the flag, government posters, speakers, and rallies, the workbench, the loom, the mine, and the blast furnace were no longer purely private property: they were on the front lines of the war. As the workplace was increasingly transformed into public space, it became easier for activists to attack employers' autocracy and defend union organizing as being an act of good citizenship as much as one of self- or class-interest. Their ability to make such an equation undoubtedly strengthened the resolve of many workers. The case of Mrs. C. W. Brooks, an operative in the magazine department of a Colt factory in Connecticut, is illustrative. When asked by her boss if she had been to a union meeting, she replied to him with a degree of confidence that he must have found surprising. "Yes," she said, "and as a free American citizen I have a right to go if I want to."[30]

It was a short step from identifying union organization as a citizen's right to defining it as a citizen's responsibility. Throughout the war, unionists cast their movement as the agent of industrial democracy, making unionization a patriotic act. Thus the authors of union leaflets often found it unnecessary to mention the union in their appeals. In New Jersey, workers were urged to "AMERI-

This flag-bestrewn workroom in a munitions plant indicates the extent to which the workplace became a public space, no longer purely private property but an arena of the wartime struggle itself. (National Archives II, College Park, Maryland)

CANIZE, DEMOCRATIZE, and usher the New Freedom into every machine shop in the Newark district." "Wake up! Machine Shop Workers, Wake Up!" read a similar appeal to Akron tire factory workers. "No longer fear the employers who have been so un-American in denying us the right to Organize. Uncle Sam proclaimed to the World that the freedom and democracy we are fighting for shall be practiced in the Industries of America. And wherever Kaiserism has been practiced it must go." Those who refused to join the union, in the language of the Akron leaflet, were not "scabs." Rather, they were "INDUSTRIAL SLACKERS!" The story was much the same in Bridgeport, where the IAM's organizing slogan was simply, "Wake Up! Be Real Citizens!" Bethlehem Steel unionists reinforced this message that opposing the union was tantamount to un-Americanism. When a nonunion candidate ran for a shop committee post in their plant, they trashed his campaign leaflet by drawing a kaiser's mustache and helmet on his picture. He finished near the bottom of the polls.[31]

If unionizing was evidence of good citizenship, so too, under some circumstances, was striking. So the Resolutions Committee of one UMW local defended wartime walkouts with this potent argument: "We are doing all that we are able to do so that Democracy in the true sense of the word will be a reality and that Monarchy, Aristocracy, and Autocracy shall be forever banished from the Earth." Lynn GE strikers defended their actions by simply contending that they had "ambitions common to all Americans, and proclaimed as just by our honored President."[32]

Workers also showed themselves adept at using the material symbols of patriotism to advance trade union agendas. The case of African American shipyard worker Amos Henderson reveals something of the power that workers could derive from making the flag the symbol of their aspirations. In the midst of work one day in May 1918, Henderson, a general utility man on a New Jersey shipway, put down his work and circulated through the yard to collect money from his fellows to purchase a large flag for display. Henderson did not request—he demanded—a ten-cent contribution from one foreman. For his pains, he was fired. But the foreman could not make his action stick. One patriotic clerk refused to make out Henderson's discharge slip. Meanwhile, a committee of workers left the yard, entrained to Philadelphia, and appealed directly to the U.S. Shipping Board for their mate's reinstatement. These committee members were, in turn, fired. But, fearing increasing unrest from a yard full of shipbuilders who grumbled about this affront to their patriotism, the government ultimately reprimanded the superintendent and ordered reinstatements all around.[33]

Unionists also quickly grasped both the power of the military uniform and the persuasive value of President Wilson's speeches. So frequently did striking New York City clothing workers solicit the participation of their uniformed comrades on picket lines that Secretary of War Baker's staff was compelled to develop a policy on the issue. Baker's assistant Stanley King beseeched William Z. Ripley, the administrator of labor standards for army clothing, to forbid the practice. President Wilson, meanwhile, was shocked to discover that one Newark, New Jersey, IAM organizer used excerpts from the president's speeches in newspaper advertisements designed to convince workers to organize. Enraged, Wilson wondered, "Who is by quotation from me [trying] to dragoon men into his organization"?[34]

Employers, of course, battled to identify their own cause with Americanism. One coal operator complained of the disloyalty of striking miners. "You can't impress upon them patriotism," he claimed. "All they seem to think of [is] money." "They positively have not patriotic feeling," complained another mine operator, who offered that his "miners only work when they want to." During a laundry strike, Arkansas employers defended their right to hire strikebreakers. "We don't call them scabs," explained the lawyer for the laundry owner. "We call them patriots." But most employers would have agreed with their contemporary Gordon Watkins that in "light of the present world movement for political democracy, autocratic government in industry assumes an extremely unbecoming aspect." The onus was clearly on employers. As one Illinois manufacturer explained, "Such catch-phrases as . . . 'democratization of industry' " demonstrated an "effectiveness as slogans of demagogy, whose appeal to the average unthinking, liberty-loving American must indeed be conceded, and can hardly be overestimated."[35]

Without doubt, U.S. entry into the First World War triggered reactionary impulses. As the Espionage Act was invoked to silence the Wobblies, as Postmaster Burleson removed Socialist Party publications from the mails, as the superpatriots of the American Protective League conducted "slacker raids," and as racists ranted against hyphenated Americans, a chilling conformity spread over the land. Yet the very drive for ideological unity also unexpectedly fed workers' demands for full industrial citizenship. As journalist John Graham Brooks noted, workers seemed to have "learned the troublesome liturgy about 'self-determination' " and they showed every intent of demanding "something of it for themselves."[36]

Perhaps nothing better illustrated the power of Brooks's "liturgy of self-determination" than the efforts of the nation's most marginalized workers to lay claim to their own industrial rights. One of the most significant contradictions of the Great War was that while it triggered rising xenophobia, race riots, and widespread male resentment of women war workers, it also offered the most favorable conditions that the nation had yet seen for the creation of a pluralistic, democratic culture in the workplace. To be sure, such a culture never quite took shape during the war; indeed, workers would spend the rest of the century wrestling with the divisions of ethnicity, gender, and race that were so obvious during these years. But the same immigrants, women, and African Americans who may have suffered from the war's reactionary impulses also found opportunities in wartime workplaces not only to demand equality for themselves but also to secure a greater measure of it than they had theretofore.

Immigrants who supported the U.S. war effort were one group that derived a powerful sense of entitlement from their stance. As Fred Teluchik, a Russian who worked in a Lawrence textile mill, explained after the war, his "greatest resentment [was] being called 'foreigner.' " He and his coworkers demanded that their contributions be recognized. Two sisters who labored with Teluchik, Rose and Grace Santora, reported proudly that "in war work Italians were first. They marched ahead in the parade because they bought so many liberty bonds." In deference to such sentiments, some Lawrence mills began to fly Italian and American flags together. But, most important to the Santora sisters, for the first time the "bosses . . . called all Italians 'American people.' " When employers were less sensitive to immigrants' desires to meld

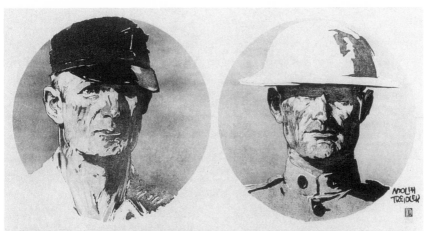

The COMBINATION
THAT WILL WIN the WAR

Every piece of work done in this plant has a direct bearing on the outcome of the war.

Our finished product goes to France.

The men who face for us weariness, hardships, death, depend upon us.

Our work here, fits their work over there, like a cog in a giant machine.

Without our product they are helpless. With it they are invincible.

They fight with what we make. We are their resource and reliance, the American workman and the American soldier, the combination that will win the war.

Issued By
Ordnance Department
U.S. Army

⊗18593

During the war, as this poster makes clear, workers were as essential to the war against autocracy as were soldiers. It was a short step for many from acknowledging the importance of "our work here" to denouncing "employers who have been so un-American in denying us the right to Organize." (National Archives II, College Park, Maryland)

It is doubtful that those who commissioned this U.S. Army Ordnance poster anticipated the extent to which workers would not only "roll up their sleeves" for the flag during the war but also use the flag to advance their own agendas in the workplace. (National Archives II, College Park, Maryland)

their ethnic and American identities, immigrant toilers displayed their anger. Such was the case with a Salt Lake City coal operator who told of an "entire Greek colony" that demanded the "dismissal of American mine foremen" who they felt treated them with disrespect.[37]

The war labor agencies served in many ways to legitimize immigrants' aspirations for a full portion of America's promised liberties. American citizenship was not a prerequisite for one to file a complaint before the NWLB or other war labor agencies. Nor were any of the rights they were designed to protect to be guaranteed for only the native-born. Furthermore, the principles enforced by the war labor agencies disproportionately benefited immigrants, who tended to labor in industrial settings. The minimum wage decisions of the NWLB, the SLAB, and other agencies, for example, boosted the earnings of the immigrant laborers who were concentrated in unskilled occupations. Moreover, immigrants regularly appeared before the hearings of such agencies as the NWLB. When they did, their testimony revealed how they had come to equate the war in Europe with their personal struggles for self-determination. As John Cemka, an immigrant laborer at Schenectady GE, explained at one hearing, he only desired to "live as Americans ought to live." Because he supported the war effort and bought a Liberty bond every week, he told the board, he believed he merited a raise.[38]

Shop committees also provided an important validation of immigrant claims to full industrial citizenship. Typically, immigrants voted in shop elections without regard to their American citizenship and served on committees as long as they held their first papers. Indeed, to solicit their participation, the NWLB enlisted the aid of translators and used multilingual forms and announcements for shop committee ballots. In part because of such efforts at Bethlehem Steel, where one-third of the plant's thirty thousand employees were foreign-born, immigrants voted in large numbers and served as committee delegates.

Women too constructed their own case for full industrial citizenship in wartime. Federal labor policies regarding women war workers tried to balance competing interests. In a tight labor market, employers wanted women. Women, for reasons shaped by patriotism, their material needs, or desires for adventure or fulfillment, sought jobs previously dominated by men. But skilled male workers feared that the women's entry would both degrade their crafts and ultimately drive them from their jobs. To ensure that these competing interests would least disrupt the status quo, the NWLB and other agencies stipulated that women ought to enjoy the same rights and be paid the same wage as men for the same work, theoretically removing the incentive for employers to replace men with women. Out of such policies, women labor activists and their allies in the war labor agencies were able to fashion a powerful argument for workplace equality. Although their gains were limited, they were also significant.

That workingwomen responded enthusiastically to the right to workplace representation granted by such agencies as the NWLB cannot be denied. Although women had yet to win the suffrage amendment nationally, the NWLB shop committee elections offered them the chance to vote for and serve on shop committees. They seized this opportunity. In elections held at the Corn Products Refining Company's plant in Argo, Illinois, women's turnout far exceeded men's. At Pittsfield's GE plant, an investigator noted that women voted in even larger numbers when they had a chance to cast their ballots for another woman for the shop committee. When they did not have that opportunity, women sometimes demanded that the NWLB name women representatives to their shop committees, as did women at the Willys-Overland auto plant and at Hartford's Colt factory.[39]

To a large extent the women staffers on war labor agencies strove to make the ideal of industrial citizenship more than mere rhetoric for women workers. Many of those staffers were part of a network of what one contemporary author called "industrial feminists"—activists whose feminism had a distinctly working-class orientation. Such women predominated among the NWLB's female staffers. When the board dispatched staff to the munitions plants of Bridgeport, for example, among them were Mildred Rankin of the National Women's Trade Union League (NWTUL), Elizabeth Curry of the Boot and Shoe Workers Union, and Hazel Hunkins of the National Women's Party. Only weeks before her departure for Bridgeport, Hunkins had been arrested for her role in a White House protest honoring suffrage martyr Inez Mulholland.[40]

Such women offered strong support to working sisters who claimed their rights. "Equal pay, of course!" Curry told one meeting of munitions workers. "No self-respecting woman is willing to be used by an avaricious employer as a means of lowering the wage of her brother workers, much less of forcing them out of their jobs. She will not permit herself to be used to break unions or debase living conditions in her community." But women should not stop at seeking equal pay, she counseled. "The one protection against the exploitation of women . . . is . . . collective bargaining in which women have proportional representation."[41]

The Railroad Administration's Women's Service Section was also stocked with women's advocates who worked under the leadership of Pauline Goldmark. One such agent, Florence E. Clark, was emblematic of the kind of women attracted to government agencies during the war. Appointed in September 1918 when she was twenty-eight years old, she was single and a graduate of the University of Chicago and the Chicago School of Civics and Philanthropy, where she had studied under Robert F. Hoxie and Sophonisba Breckinridge. Clark was an activist staffer who told railroad women that union organization has "come to stay and both men and women ought to be in the same organization if they are working together." Start "getting control of the polices of the Union and trying to get justice for every one," she advised the women who contacted her. Naturally, employers tried to keep their women away from Clark. "I hear that some of the women are going to the hotel to see the government women. Are you one of them?" Clara DeGuilo, the Pennsylvania Railroad worker to whom this question was put, decided to "do as I pleased" and saw Clark anyway. Her example was emulated by many, all of whom found encouragement and understanding in Clark. Cora Knisely, a materials handler in a Pennsylvania trainyard, complained of sexual harassment. "They treated me like a *beast*," she wrote. But, inspired by Clark's example, she "would not give up." Katherine Hagen, an oiler in a Jersey City yard, stayed in regular contact with Clark. She reported how she and her coworkers joined the railway clerks union "to show the men that we could be as business like as they."[42]

Despite the best efforts of such people as Florence Clark, women were never able to institutionalize great gains in the war labor agencies. A conference on October 4–5, 1918, at the Southern Building in Washington, organized by Mary Van Kleeck and Mary Anderson of the Labor Department's Women in Industry Service, attracted sixteen women union leaders and such speakers as Secretary Wilson and Felix Frankfurter. But it yielded little. While Wilson expressed support for the "equal rights of women in industry," he also cautioned that the "maintenance of standards" meant keeping women from dangerous work. When he was pressed by conferees to pledge strong enforcement of the equal pay principle by the WLPB, Frankfurter made no promises. Nor did women fare better within the NWLB. When women's groups demanded that two women be named to the board, the president ignored their suggestion, despite a letter from Frank Walsh, who observed that "the women in the presentation of their grievances are not fairly and vigorously represented by the men." And when Marie Obenauer, chief of the NWLB's Division of Women Administrative Examiners, asked Jett Lauck to expand her division and clarify NWLB policy by stipulating specifically that women serve on shop committees anywhere they did work previously done by men, her requests set off a power struggle. Lauck won that struggle. On October 29, 1918, the NWLB approved Obenauer's shop committee policy, but only after Lauck was given power over her division.[43]

Such failures must, however, be judged against a broader context. Despite political setbacks, women made gains in workplaces around the country. With the aid of federal guidelines and helpful government staffers, many working-women emerged as forceful activists, demanding industrial equality. One of them, Laura Cannon, of GE's Fort Wayne plant, reportedly signed one thousand women into the union during 1918. At the Worthington Pump plant in Cambridge, another unheralded activist, Mabel Parmer, led coworkers in demanding that an NWLB award originally granted to skilled men in their shop be extended to cover women as well.[44]

With the support of federal agents such as Florence Clark, women also sought rights within their unions. "I am out of patience with our Lodge. The men would be only too glad if we girls have to go," complained Anna Crosson, a member of the Railway Clerks. Rather than back down, however, she was determined to express her own vision of self-determination. "If you don't stand up for the girls," she told the president of her lodge, "you yourself may be in danger of losing your own job." To one leader of the NWTUL, such courage signaled a watershed. "This is the women's age!" declared Margaret Drier Robbins. "At last, after centuries of disabilities and discriminations, women are coming into the . . . festival of life on equal terms with men."[45]

African American workers too staked claims to full industrial citizenship in the midst of a war that unloosed violent racial reaction. They found less support from federal agencies than did women. Labor agencies focused their attention away from the South, where most blacks still worked. (The NWLB handled 121 disputes in New York alone; but it took up only 85 cases in nine southern states and the District of Columbia combined.) Neither did the NWLB or other major labor boards employ black investigators, even as those agencies gave seats of power to unions—such as the IAM—that barred blacks. Additionally, federal agencies often simply winked at discriminatory practices, as did the SLAB when it created two wage scales for laborers in southern shipyards to accommodate a custom whereby blacks were paid less. But despite these limitations, the war labor administration unintentionally laid the groundwork for blacks' claims to equality in three significant ways. Wartime labor agencies brought several white racial liberals to positions of influence in Washington. Their stands for the freedom to organize, equal pay, and a workplace rule of law helped legitimize blacks' demands for justice. And the elevation of industrial democracy as the defining goal of wartime reforms allowed blacks to express their demands in a patriotic vocabulary that was difficult to deny.

To be sure, African Americans did not gain positions in wartime Washington labor agencies commensurate with their importance to the war effort.

A move by Frank Walsh to hire black lawyer W. C. Hueston as a permanent member of the NWLB who would handle cases involving blacks did not gain the support of Lauck or other NWLB members and thus never materialized. The lone exception to black exclusion was Dr. George E. Haynes, a founder of the National Urban League. In 1918, Haynes was named director of the new Division of Negro Economics (DNE) within the Labor Department. The DNE gathered data on black workers, promoted their employment in war jobs, and set up local committees to address their problems. These committees won few concrete gains, but the DNE did promote the administration's labor reforms among blacks. A staff of 134 black DNE investigators eventually took to the field in six southern states, even attempting to integrate some worksites in Mississippi. Still, the DNE was a lonely outpost for black America in Washington.[46]

Although African Americans were denied places of influence in wartime Washington, several white racial liberals did take posts in the war labor administration. Walsh was one of them. Since his work on the USCIR, he had hoped to spread trade unionism in southern industry, opening unions to blacks. He brought several like-minded individuals onto the NWLB's staff: liberal journalist Raymond Swing, who once described himself as "an abolitionist to the core"; Robert Buck, who had connections to the interracial meatpackers union movement in Chicago; and Mildred Rankin, who as an NWTUL organizer had helped black women tobacco stemmers organize in Norfolk, Virginia, in 1917. Even those agents who may not have shared the sympathies of Walsh and his friends found that implementing federal labor policy occasionally led them to challenge aspects of the nation's racial caste system. Thomas E. Carroll of the SLAB, for example, informed his supervisor that he intended to "make no distinction [as to] color, creed, or affiliations in my attitude" toward shipyard workers "and no amount of threatening or bulldozing will swerve me one inch." Motivated by such simple idealism, one of Carroll's colleagues in the South was led to breach the etiquette of segregation: he invited a group of "colored laborers" to "congregate on the front porch" of his hotel for a meeting on their grievances. "We would much prefer that this not be done in the future," wrote enraged hoteliers to his superior in Washington. That such signs of respect encouraged black workers in their demands for justice is probable. That white southern politicians thought so is certain. Governor Sidney Catts of Florida likened labor agents to "white carpet bag officers" who "inflamed . . . the minds of the negroes."[47]

Where the staffs of federal labor agencies fell short, the broad principles on which the agencies based their work still aided black workers. Even in agencies with poor racial records, the government's interest in preserving labor peace could sometimes serve black workers' interests. When black shipbuilders saw whites walk out rather than work in the same yards with them, for example, the government attempted to get white union leaders to accept the entry of black workers. "You gentlemen who hold the situation of labor in your hands in the South are charged with a very grave responsibility," shipbuilding administrator Charles Piez told leaders. "Personal differences and personal prejudices must yield absolutely to the needs of the nation."[48]

Once on the job, blacks found it possible to invoke the principles of the war labor program to their advantage. The USRA, for example, upheld the principle of seniority even at the expense of prior agreements between unions and railroads that guaranteed whites jobs ahead of blacks. In one case involving the Nashville, Chattanooga, and St. Louis Railroad, Railway Board of Adjustment No. 2 ruled against sixty-four white machinist's helpers who protested that they were laid off while twenty blacks kept their jobs following the armistice. Although the railroad had signed an agreement that stipulated that "white machinist helpers will help machinists," the board ruled that "any reduction of the force shall be according to seniority." This action preserved the black helpers' jobs.[49]

Undeniably, such decisions helped raise expectations for justice among African Americans. Wrote one appreciative boilermaker's helper to USRA administrator McAdoo: "I am getting more to day then I ever made in all my past life. I thanks you so mightily for seein to it." What made such decisions more remarkable was that they ran counter to some bitter resistance. This same black helper also reported that "since you had granted us as colored mens of the South the 45 cents per hour and back time," it was "a hard matter to get along with the [white] man I am helping. . . . he says that 45 cents per hour is entirely too d—— much for a negro to have."[50]

Sadly, however, the same federal agencies whose decisions served to encourage black workers regularly failed to live up to their own principles of fairness. This fact was starkly revealed in one case that came before the NWLB. In 1918 the NWLB was drawn into a dispute involving New Orleans streetcar drivers and mechanics. In this case the board issued a decision, based on its "living wage" principle, that called for the New Orleans Railway and Light Company to establish a forty-two-cent minimum wage for all its workers. But not all streetcar workers celebrated. This decision trebled the wages of black laborers, closing the distance between their wages and those of skilled whites. Both white unionists and New Orleans politicians, who argued that they would have to raise streetcar fares to pay for the wage increases, objected strenuously to the decision's breadth. "The way the thing stands," a lawyer for the unionized white streetcar workers told the board, "the people at large in

New Orleans can not quite understand how is it that the negroes are making more money than the whites." Cochair Taft sympathized with the racist logic in this complaint. "I am in favor of equality of opportunity," he told Walsh, but "the cost of living of a negro in a southern city, even when he lives in reasonable comfort, is less than that of a white man, as we would wish it to be." He urged that the NWLB rewrite its ruling. Faced with Taft's defection, Walsh reluctantly acceded, and the NWLB reduced its minimum wage award in this case to thirty-eight cents.[51]

The New Orleans case aptly illustrated the ambiguous impact of wartime mobilization and federal labor regulation on African Americans. On one hand, the NWLB's decision reinforced racial discrimination and legitimized a Jim Crow practice. On the other hand, the board's revised thirty-eight-cent award still significantly raised wages for poorly paid blacks. Perhaps that is why black workers continued to look to the federal government for help. To be sure, blacks were often forced to cite the inconsistencies between the government's pronouncements and the treatment they received. But they still hoped for justice from Washington agencies. So it was that railroad firemen complained to the USRA that whites were granted runs ahead of them regardless of seniority. "It is a shame Mr. McAdoo the way they doing us for white men," said one. "I stand for [the job], and I want it," wrote another. "Please advise why I cannot have it." A black brakeman from Palestine, Texas, asked simply for "the protection that is guaranteed by the U.S. government." Two boilermaker's helpers reminded McAdoo that he had said that "no discrimination will be practiced." Our "boys in France," they told him, were "not fighting for any individual but for the entire world." And when black freight handlers in Petersburg, Virginia, thought their union guilty of "unjust dealings against us," their spokesperson, John Dailey, demanded a USRA investigation. "To begin with," Dailey wrote, "we have put up fight after fight . . . to reach some justice." They had "a right to organize," Dailey claimed, "and we demand the . . . AF of L to now take proper steps to defend us in defending its principles." Voicing feelings that must have been broadly shared, Dailey concluded, "We are tired of such men who seem to think we are ignorant."[52]

As Dailey's frustration suggests, industrial democracy remained largely an unkept promise to African American workers during the era of the Great War. As did immigrants and women, blacks grasped that promise as it was articulated by war labor agencies, and they used it to frame their own demands for full industrial citizenship. Throughout the war, black workers continued to appeal to flawed agencies such as the NWLB for relief from employers who "don't want to pay us poor negro . . . and want to fool us to work or fight," as one New Orleans worker put it. Even in the face of repeated disappointments, many persisted in framing their requests with the same degree of hope evident in a letter from I. Ross, the black president of Federal Labor Union 15355 of Beaumont, Texas. Asking that the U.S. Shipping Board help him improve conditions in Gulf Coast shipyards, Ross wondered whether Washington could "send me some government words so that I can be guided." More black workers had joined Ross in the ranks of organized labor by war's end than at any time in U.S. history, many of them inspired by those "government words." But, as John Dailey well knew, those workers entered a labor movement that was then no more interested in achieving a nonracial industrial democracy than the nation was in achieving a nonracial political democracy.[53]

THE POWER OF INDUSTRIAL DEMOCRACY

In attempting to promote labor peace by rationalizing the wartime workplace, offering workers the right to representation, and incorporating a diverse working class into a contest against autocracy on the behalf of democracy, the Wilsonian war labor agencies triggered developments that few anticipated. These developments would leave a lasting imprint on the American workplace, altering substantially the expectations of a broad swath of American workers. John Dewey was one of those who anticipated where events were heading. "The wage-earner," he wrote in 1918, "is more likely to be interested in using his newly discovered power to increase his own share of control in an industry, than he is in transferring control over to government officials."[54]

Dewey was right. When the workers at Ross Gear and Tool sought out Robert Corley in 1918, they were probably driven by complex factors, including a desire to win a more rational and just workplace, to have their voices heard, and to have their citizenship acknowledged on the job. In many ways, their actions were both legitimized and made possible by the war labor agencies that Frank Walsh and other reformers had constructed. But if the war labor agencies had helped trigger their mobilization, those agencies did not determine its course. Nor were workers willing to cede that power to Washington.

In the federal labor agencies that emerged in 1917 and 1918, AFL leaders who defined industrial democracy as pure-and-simple trade union collective bargaining were forced to compromise with liberals for whom industrial democracy meant workplace representation that could salve labor strife and spur productive efficiency. As it turned out, their compromise—as embodied in agencies like the NWLB and such policies as shop committee representation—lent itself more easily than they could have realized to the uses of those who defined industrial democracy in more radical terms.

The minutes of a mass meeting of the employees of the Eugene Diet-zen Company of Chicago in 1918 reveal something important about wartime labor militancy. These minutes show Dietzen workers demanding an end to the "Prussian" methods of their superintendent and angrily rejecting a wage increase proffered by management because it did not address their concerns about abusive treatment. After laying out their problems with the boss, the workers moved beyond a pure-and-simple discussion of grievances to debate "the meaning of industrial democracy."[55]

Like the Dietzen workers, many toilers who fought management abuses during World War I ultimately found themselves considering what it would mean to have democracy in their workplaces. Those discussions often led to interpretations of industrial democracy different from the one held by AFL officialdom. Ed Galloway, an Illinois trade unionist, concluded that indus-trial democracy implied "more than a living wage." It also meant "a good share of [the employers'] profits." To John Fitzpatrick of the CFL, true indus-trial democracy demanded government control of industry. He granted that owners had a "reasonable right" to run their enterprises, but workers needed the "final say" on working conditions—a say that could be guaranteed only when the government ensured it. To some New England Telephone workers, "government ownership" was not "inconsistent with representative govern-ment in industry." And to one group of cigar makers, industrial democracy meant their control of the workplace. As they saw it, "Self-government in the workshop" was "one part of the democracy for which our armies are fighting in France."[56]

Of course, radicals rarely constituted a majority in the workplace, even in industries like the metal trades where they were sometimes concentrated. Moreover, in those places where toilers followed radicals, they did not nec-essarily share the expansive vision of industrial democracy offered by those leaders. The power of the demand for industrial democracy—what allowed it to transcend particular immigrant groups, industries, skill levels, and political persuasions—was that it remained for most workers an inchoate and diffuse vision, one that did not directly challenge the ideal of voluntarism that was so deeply rooted in American political culture, one that did not demand a resolution to the ambivalence with which many working people viewed the state. Still, the fact that radical demands were so easily voiced in this popu-lar idiom dispelled any certainty over the outcomes that would flow from wartime labor struggles. What did it mean to "de-kaiser" industry? To that question there was yet no answer in the summer of 1918, and from that un-certainty, labor militants took heart.

THE DYNAMICS OF WARTIME LABOR MILITANCY

5

From the moment that the National War Labor Board commenced its hearings, the American labor movement passed into the stage of semi-governmental protection. . . . Organization then became a matter of local willingness and no longer of international trade union strategy.

—*Laurence Todd, 1919*

Shortly after the armistice, leftist writer Laurence Todd assessed the impact of the war labor agencies on organized labor. In an article for a publication brought out by the Rand School, a socialist institute in New York City that would soon be targeted by Red-baiters, Todd presented a fascinating thesis. During the war, as the government-sanctioned AFL began "gathering in hundreds of thousands of new members with scarcely an effort," Todd argued, the security and power of union leaders was not necessarily bolstered, nor was labor militancy dampened. Instead, "authority and responsibility within the American labor movement, to a very great degree, passed over from the executive offices of the international unions and the executive offices of the American Federation of Labor to the meetings and local councils of the rank and file." With the government prepared to investigate their complaints, with a tight labor market adding leverage to their strike threats, local leaders found that the aid of national unions "had ceased to be essential." The result, Todd thought, was to shift "initiative and the power of action" from "the national leaders' hands" toward the "masses of workers who have gained a new self-confidence and self-respect since April 1917."[1]

Laurence Todd understood an important feature of wartime labor organizing. AFL leaders had helped shape the war labor administration that emerged during World War I. For the most part they considered its creation to be an enormous victory. But they found some of its fruits to be bittersweet. As they attempted to establish their vision of industrial democracy through the aid of the war labor agencies, union leaders sometimes found that their own organizations were transformed into arenas of conflict over just what kind of democracy ought to be established in industry.

AN INDUSTRIAL "NO-MAN'S LAND"

During the war, trade unionists found that government regulation was fraught with opportunity and complexity. AFL leaders reasonably hoped that their cooperation with the administration's war labor agencies would help them consolidate their own organizations. Long excluded from mass industries, unions had been unable to overcome the organized might of employers or the prejudicial application of the law on their own. But war labor agencies weakened those obstacles, providing an unequaled opportunity for unionists to expand their organizations. AFL leaders rushed to make the most of this situation. To most of them, the war would be worth fighting if it yielded a labor-capital détente codified in collective bargaining agreements, what Samuel Gompers called "the mile-stones of industrial progress."[2]

But advancing toward that goal was not easy, nor did the war labor agencies — by creating opportunities for rank-and-file initiative — necessarily make it easier. Rather, government intervention tended to highlight the ambivalence with which most union leaders viewed labor militancy. In some ways labor militancy strengthened their hands, encouraging more government reforms, weakening the resistance of employers to collective bargaining, and allowing union leaders to portray their organizations as a bulwark against something worse. "Whatever other difficulties we might have," John Golden of the United Textile Workers assured the employer members of the NWLB, "we will line up together against Bolshevism and all that it means." But militancy was also a tiger on whose back AFL leaders rode. To retain their credibility, they had to manage discontent and show that they would honor the principles of the war labor agencies. Yet these very agencies complicated that task by lifting the hopes of rank-and-file workers and providing them the means for quick action. That combination could be explosive.[3]

An incident that disrupted one executive session of the NWLB serves to illustrate how complex the dynamics of labor militancy became during the war. After unions struck General Electric's Pittsfield plant in May 1918, the NWLB promised to address their demand that they be freed from the yellow-dog contracts they had been forced to sign. The board asked Loyall Osborne of Westinghouse and Tom Savage of the IAM to decide the case. But Osborne and Savage, occupying opposite ideological poles, found it impossible to agree. One month later impatient Pittsfielders decided to force the issue. They sent delegates to Washington on June 28 to threaten a strike if their demands went unmet. Standing in the hallway outside the NWLB offices, the Pittsfielders refused to leave until they were heard.

Thus confronted, the board allowed the delegates into their meeting and told them that Taft and Walsh would write a decision nullifying the yellow-dogs. Once in the meeting, however, the Pittsfielders refused to be placated. They demanded "a decisive answer" on wage demands as well. Taft pleaded for patience. "We are Americans as you are," he told the guests, "and it is a little trying . . . to have a gun put at your head when you are trying to do justice." Victor Olander of the International Seamen's Union, who usually found himself fighting the NWLB's employer members for swift action on cases, sprang to Taft's defense. Assuring the protesters that they were "getting a rather decided action now," Olander finally persuaded the Pittsfielders to leave—but not before they "just bothered the life out of us," as Walsh put it. In the end, the Pittsfielders got what they sought: they won wage increases as well as an end to their yellow-dog contracts.[4]

The confrontation was revealing. Militancy helped national union leaders such as the IAM's Savage wring concessions from employers and the government, including protection of the right to organize. Government intervention helped focus labor militancy into demands for "decisive answers." Once triggered, however, militancy threatened to disrupt both the government agencies that sought to regulate it and the union hierarchies that sought to exploit it. Time and again unionists who served on war labor agencies were pressed by angry activists who demanded immediate resolution to their problems, refused to wait for established procedures to run their course, and seemed, as one IAM official delicately put it, "in such a mood that they are rather eager for strikes."[5]

No leader found the effort to balance the stimulation of militancy with its constraint more vexing than the IAM's William Johnston, who himself served on the NWLB. When asked by employer colleagues on the board why he could not control his union's renegade strikers, he could only throw up his hands and exclaim, "We wish we could sometimes." Johnston, whose union sought more decisions before the NWLB than any other, grew increasingly concerned about rank-and-file militancy by the war's end. He feared that the frequent walkouts of his members had eroded leadership and discipline within the union. "When you have a lot of people on the street" engaged in strikes, he confided to his brethren on the NWLB, "they drift away from the influence of the so-called conservative, constructive element and go to the very extremes to follow the advice of the extreme."[6]

As Johnston's travails suggest, the operations of the Wilson administration's war labor agencies did as much to create a "no-man's land" within unions — space within which union leaders' powers were contested — as they did to confirm the authority of national union leaders. No group conquered that terrain during the war. But numerous forays into that territory by local union activists demonstrated the extent to which "authority and initiative" within the labor movement remained contested.

The complexity of union organizing under the war labor agencies was especially evident in three industries. In one of those, coal mining, federal intervention was crucial in spreading organization to nonunion fields in the South. But regulation also fed conflict within the UMW. Similarly, in the electrical manufacturing industry a group of farsighted militants were able to capitalize on federal intervention to launch something resembling an industrial union at General Electric, virtually independent of their national leaders. In the munitions industry, meanwhile, militants were successful in surmounting the limits of government regulation to exploit its strengths in their efforts to build a militant union that ultimately challenged national labor leaders. A closer look at these cases indicates the degree to which wartime conditions promoted rather than contained labor militancy.

COAL MINERS, THE GOVERNMENT, AND THE UMW

Historically, labor relations in coal have been very responsive to government policies. This was certainly true during the Great War. As the United States entered World War I, the UMW was emerging from a decade in which it was virtually confined to the Central Competitive Field (CCF) in the states of Ohio, Indiana, Illinois, and western Pennsylvania. The main obstacles to the union's expansion were the nonunion southern Appalachian coalfields. Since a bitter strike in Alabama in 1908, during which Governor Braxton B. Comer invoked charges of "social equality" against the biracial UMW and used the militia to break its walkout, the union had struggled for simple survival in the South. But the war turned the tide. In the CCF, miners quickly capitalized on the rising demand for coal to win improvements in their working conditions, staging frequent strikes. "This morning our men went on one of the stampedes," complained one typical Illinois operator. "No demands were made. They simply had a meeting on top of the shaft . . . and talked until the whistle blew, then went home." As unrest spread, CCF operators feared that they could not "stop the striking business."[7]

Southern miners were not far behind their northern counterparts. On June 3, 1917, the UMW inaugurated an organizing drive in Alabama's Warrior Coalfield with a large rally in Brookside. Within three weeks, 12,000 Alabamians had joined the union, and by August perhaps as many as 23,000 of the 25,000 miners in the region had become UMW members. In only three months the union gained in Alabama what had eluded it for decades: near total organization of the coal miners. When operators refused UMW demands for an eight-hour day, the election of checkweighers, and wage increases, the union confidently set a strike date for August 18, 1917. Fearing that a walkout would endanger vital coal supplies, William B. Wilson intervened, and UMW leaders postponed the strike. Wilson dispatched former UMW official William Fairley to Alabama to conciliate. Scarcely a neutral party, Fairley sought advice from the union's former president, John Mitchell, throughout his work. Officials of the UMW could hardly have been more pleased with this turn of events.[8]

The Alabama effort illustrated how ambivalent union leaders were about wartime strikes. Even though UMW leaders, like the rest of the AFL, had committed themselves to averting strikes, they did not rush to head off the Alabama walkout. Instead, they made the most of the threat. Since April 1917, the union had lobbied unsuccessfully for a joint union-operator plan for maximum coal production. This initiative had been vetoed by the CND's Committee on Coal Production, which was composed only of operators, most of whom were antiunion. Although UMW protests prodded Secretary Wilson to add a union representative to the CND's subcommittee, the union's voice was largely ignored in Washington prior to the Alabama disturbance. The threatened strike helped change that situation. On August 17, Secretary Wilson persuaded UMW leaders to call off strike plans in return for his pledge to mediate the dispute personally. Thousands of Alabama miners refused to heed the last-minute truce called by their leaders. They struck anyway on the appointed day, August 18. But the promise of an agreement soon coaxed most of them back into the mines.[9]

Federal intervention did ultimately bring an agreement. On August 23, 1917, as Secretary of Labor Wilson negotiated with Alabama UMW leaders, President Wilson, acting under the authority of the Lever Act, created the Fuel Administration and named Harry A. Garfield as its head. UMW president John P. White was named the Fuel Administration's official labor representative, thereby securing the union a powerful role in determining the labor policies of the new agency. Their position in Washington thus strengthened, UMW officials were more willing to come to an agreement in Alabama, and mine operators were more likely to give them one. On August 28, William Wilson, officials of the Alabama Mine Owners Association, and a UMW team led by John L. Lewis negotiated that agreement. In it the union made several concessions, surrendering its demands for the eight-hour day and the closed shop. In return, mine operators agreed to install checkweighers chosen by the miners and to refrain from discriminating against union members. But, contending that they could not grant wage increases because of the government's fixed price for coal, the operators refused to deal with wages until Washington officials considered the relation of miners' wages to coal prices. The UMW agreed to this compromise.[10]

Most rank-and-file miners in Alabama viewed the agreement as a disaster. Anxious for immediate wage increases, they staged sporadic wildcat strikes throughout early September 1917. So incensed were the miners that they soon mounted an effort to overthrow J. R. Kennamer, leader of Alabama's UMW District 20. In a stormy district convention held to ratify the agreement, they nearly succeeded in that effort. Nor was their rage quieted by subsequent events in Washington. On October 6, 1917, mine worker officials and operators in the CCF negotiated the Washington Agreement, which shaped coal mine labor relations for the remainder of the war. Not only did this agreement put off raises for the foreseeable future, it also elaborated a widely unpopular penalty clause that mandated fines of one dollar per worker per day on any union or coal mine operator that closed a mine through a strike or lockout.[11]

Nothing better symbolized for miners the limitations of federal regulation during the war than the penalty clause in combination with their lagging wages. Indeed, the penalty clause set off a virtual civil war within the UMW. The union's 1918 convention saw former UMW president White, his successor, Frank J. Hayes, and UMW district officials scrambling to defend their leadership against the attacks of irate delegates led by Alex Howatt, who encouraged miners to "serve notice on the coal operators . . . that you are not deceived and hoodwinked by the cry of patriotism." Howatt's supporters were many. The penalty clause robbed miners of their rights, one delegate pointed out, and they ought to "resent it in order to defend our Americanism and our patriotism." A Kansas miner complained that since companies "have got the penalty claus [sic] in their hands they will impose all kinds of bad conditions on the miners to try and rais [sic] trouble." The fight spilled over into UMW district conventions as well, as miners attacked not only the agreement but the fact that they had not been allowed to approve it. "At this time we are fighting for the great principles of democracy," stated one Indiana union member. "It behooves us to . . . preserve that same democracy within the ranks of our own organization." Despite such protests, the clause remained.[12]

In the minds of many critics the penalty clause and UMW leaders' efforts to enforce it starkly illustrated the extent to which federal regulation sapped labor militancy during the war. Evidence for this view was certainly abundant. UMW leaders were for the most part, as one Colorado operator found them, "ready and anxious to live up to their obligations." Faithful to their agreements, they were even prepared on occasion to side with operators or the government against miners in order to keep them at work. "In no spirit of vainglory or egotism, I take occasion . . . to say that we have done well to control our constituency," district leader W. D. Duncan of Kentucky boasted. Even a rank-and-file hero such as John Brophy, president of Pennsylvania's District 2, tried to "manage discontent" under the penalty clause. Brophy's diary entries during the war reveal a great deal. "Advised Springfield miners to return to work," read one entry. "Addressed meeting at Portage. . . . Advised men to return to work," read another. "It was agreed . . . to advise the men to return to work," read a third. So went the refrain. Elected in 1916 as a militant, Brophy found himself criticizing the growth in "unauthorized strikes that has occurred in the district lately" and warning that his union might degenerate into a "disorderly rabble."[13]

But this view must be tempered by an understanding of the ways in which UMW leaders also made use of coalfield militancy to gain increased leverage in Washington or with operators. Often union leaders predicted "the end of our ability to control the situation" as they pressed the Fuel Administration for more vigorous enforcement of union rights. At the same time, workers found so many ways around the penalty clause that operators thought that unions were not the problem: "the difficult element is the ordinary miner." Miners flaunted the penalty clause directly—by walking out over issues such as filthy washrooms—or through ruses. One operator complained that miners used the funerals of fellow union members as a cover for strikes, another that send-offs for comrades headed into the army served the same purpose. When strikes were inadvisable, miners often "worked-to-rule." At one Pennsylvania tipple, they refused to push loaded cars more than the eighty yards beyond the mine head, the distance called for in their hastily drawn contract. They pushed the cars eighty yards and two feet and left them, much to the operator's dismay.[14]

The truth was that government regulation provided some new opportunities for labor militancy even as it foreclosed others. Perhaps nothing demonstrated that better than the UMW's progress in Alabama, where miners had been so disappointed with the settlement that had arisen from their 1917 conflict. Alabama miners would have had great difficulty sustaining their organization in that state without federal support, for federal intervention aided them in overcoming the most significant obstacle to their organization in the South: opposition to the construction of a biracial union. Charges that it sought "social equality" had led to the UMW's destruction in Alabama in 1908. The UMW's wartime partnership with the administration, however, temporarily blunted attacks on its biracial character during 1917 and 1918. Federal involvement served the dual purpose of restraining state-level repression and allowing the UMW to deflect the charges of operators such as Erskine Ransey, of Pratt Consolidated Coal, who contended that the union was stampeding "ignorant negroes" into its ranks.[15]

The union played government intervention off against the race issue quite cautiously. To avoid potentially fatal racial attacks, District 20 leader Kennamer (who, of course, was white) was careful to reassure Alabamians. He told one gathering: "If I thought the negroes wanted social equality I would not be here today. All the negro wants is an opportunity to work under decent conditions." The union had made such protestations in the past with little success. This time, however, union leaders were able to add to their argument the contention that they only sought to defeat what Americans were fighting in Europe. The "non-union mines of Alabama are as much an industrial autocracy as Russia was a political autocracy or Germany a military autocracy," claimed the UMW. As long as such an equation was possible, as one chagrined Alabama coal operator realized, the union could persuasively suggest that its efforts enjoyed "the approval of the . . . Congress."[16]

The UMW's growth in Alabama belies the notion that federal regulation operated solely to transform the union into a pliant instrument that served the interests of operators or the administration. Even the suggestion that UMW leaders had established an ingratiating compact with the government would have seemed ludicrous to Alabama mine operators. Instead of sitting back while the UMW held its members' militancy in check, operators petitioned the Fuel Administration to "call off the Union organizers who have been loafing around." Organizers, meanwhile, continued to trade freely on their association with the government to promote the union, even as workers manipulated patriotism to justify their own militant actions.[17]

The overall effect of the war labor administration on the UMW, then, was quite complex. Federal policies effectively underwrote the growth of the UMW into the nation's largest union, securing it a foothold in the southern Appalachian fields and increasing its leaders' influence in Washington. In return union officials attempted to contain the militancy of their members. At the same time, however, federal policies continued to provide a rationale for miners' protests without significantly dampening their militancy, and federal intervention helped them solidify their organization against significant opposition. Thus when John L. Lewis, who had negotiated the Alabama accord, rose to lead the UMW after the war, he inherited a union that was more reliant on federal policies than ever before but whose membership had scarcely been tamed by federal regulation. Both realities would do much to shape his early tenure as UMW president.

BUILDING THE ELECTRICAL MANUFACTURING
INDUSTRY LABOR FEDERATION

The impact of federal regulation in the electrical manufacturing industry was far less ambiguous than it had been in the coalfields. Among the workers of General Electric, for example, the emergence of the war labor administration had a profoundly positive effect on unionism and labor militancy. Although several spontaneous strikes aided by tight labor markets had flared in 1917, no broadscale movement of electrical workers had gelled at GE's Lynn, Pittsfield, Erie, and Fort Wayne plants. Only Schenectady workers were well organized, and GE continued to use aggressive tactics, including blacklisting, espionage, and yellow-dog contracts, to keep it that way. "At that time," reported one Lynn worker, "it was dangerous to ask your neighbor if he belonged to the union." But the creation of the NWLB changed this atmosphere, unintentionally giving metal trades councils in the GE cities a mechanism through which to organize a broad union movement. John Bellingham and the Schenectadians, who had long wanted to unionize the entire electrical manufacturing industry, immediately sought to manipulate NWLB intervention to accomplish their aims.[18]

Their campaign began only days after the NWLB was established. On April 23, 1918, the Schenectady Metal Trades Council presented demands to GE that included a forty-four-hour workweek and a 25 percent raise. When GE did not respond—which likely surprised none of the union people— the SMTC acted. In concert with unionists from the Pittsfield Metal Trades Council, the GE workers arranged for a coordinated walkout of crane operators at both facilities on May 1, 1918. It was a brilliant ploy, effectively halting production at the two crucial war factories, even though the union had a bare presence in Pittsfield. Strikers were determined to stay out until the NWLB agreed to hear their case. Surprised GE managers had little time to respond before the NWLB announced, on May 6, that it would investigate.[19]

What then transpired can only be characterized as remarkable. Once activists secured NWLB involvement and returned to work, they began to exploit the board as an organizing tool to stage a company-wide union offensive against GE in a mere six weeks' time.

The NWLB held hearings in Schenectady in late May on the crane operators' strike. The SMTC followed up those hearings with a warning: if the board did not hear the grievances of all the plant's employees, the vital Schenectady plant would be shut down on June 10. Only the cajoling of exasperated NWLB secretary Lauck kept the Schenectady workers on the job until the board had a chance to schedule more hearings in Schenectady in late June. Those hearings, opened on June 22 by NWLB cochairs Taft and Walsh, were a political coup for the GE activists. They used the well-publicized event both to make a case against GE and to build their organization, detailing the company's autocratic management and rallying unorganized workers into unions. During four days of testimony, Bellingham and the SMTC leaders brought forth workers from all parts of the plant to tell their stories of favoritism, piece rate cutting, overwork, and underpay. Sheet metal truckers, blacksmith's helpers, foundry laborers, armature winders, and many other semiskilled or unskilled workers testified. Men and women, native and immigrant, laid their grievances before the board. The SMTC also demanded that the board hear the cases of GE's scrubwomen, clerks, and secretaries. None of these workers were previously organized, yet they attacked GE for profiteering and called for higher wages and a voice in determining the conditions of their work.[20]

Following the entry of the NWLB, the Schenectady activists succeeded in organizing most of their plant's unskilled and semiskilled workers. By the conclusion of the hearings, the SMTC leaders had accomplished more than they had in the previous year of organizing. Workers flooded into the SMTC's union locals even before the NWLB's favorable decision, rendered in July, forced GE to raise wages and ban discrimination against the union. Among the most enthusiastic new members were the office workers who formed the Bookkeepers, Typists, Stenographers, and Assistants Union shortly after the NWLB hearings. Within two months their local contained fifteen hundred members.[21]

The SMTC's success in using the NWLB to build its organization immediately inspired activists in other cities. Pittsfield workers, who had cooperated in the initial work stoppage, followed Schenectady's lead and threatened to strike in mid-June unless the NWLB also granted their demands, which included an end to their hated yellow-dog contracts. The Pittsfield Metal Trades Council also asked that shop committees be established so that collective bargaining might commence at the plant. The Pittsfielders too were successful.

On June 28, after Pittsfield delegates stormed into the NWLB's Washington offices, the board agreed to their demands and called for shop committees to be elected at a neutral site. In one swift stroke, the NWLB opened the door to the unionization of Pittsfield GE.[22]

The most dramatic organizing, however, took place at Lynn. Shortly after the NWLB was formed, members of the Lynn Central Labor Union won permission from their city council to leaflet workers at GE plant gates. Organizers from the IAM and the International Brotherhood of Electrical Workers (IBEW) distributed leaflets that implied that the president himself was urging GE workers to "get busy and join the Machinists' or Electrical Workers' Union." To block growing interest in the unions, plant manager Walter Fish discharged fourteen activists on July 13, 1918. In the past such actions discouraged union campaigns. No longer. This time the firings gave Lynn unionists the issue they needed to pull workers from their plant and force the federal government to intervene.[23]

GE workers were unquestionably galvanized by the prospect of federal intervention. On the evening of the firings a mass meeting of GE employees decided that "as the company was violating the rules laid down by the W. L. B. by discharging men for union sympathies . . . there was nothing left to do . . . but to strike." On July 15, only days after the NWLB announced its decision at Pittsfield, fourteen thousand Lynn GE workers did strike. The almost unanimous walkout exceeded the most sanguine hopes of its organizers. In a telegram to President Wilson, strike leaders attempted to "assure you and all our fellow citizens of our loyalty and of our realization of the serious situation brought about by the present strike." But they also expressed their determination to "carry out your proclamation of April 8th" creating the NWLB. The SMTC sprang to the aid of the Lynn strikers. A telegram from Bellingham informed them that Schenectady had voted overwhelmingly to support them "to the point of a strike, if necessary." Though unorganized at the time of the walkout, Lynn workers flocked into the IAM and the IBEW, signing pledge cards at huge meetings conducted in English, Polish, and Italian. Over the next three weeks these hastily marshaled strikers displayed remarkable solidarity and froze vital war production as pressure mounted on them from state officials and a hostile press.[24]

Their solidarity paid off. During the tense standoff, GE attempted to get the strikers to agree to a settlement brokered by the Massachusetts Board of Conciliation and Arbitration, which would have allowed GE officials to set up their own shop committee plan. But strikers held out for the same award the NWLB had applied in Schenectady and Pittsfield. When plant manager Fish informed them at a public hearing on July 25 that he would not accept such a settlement, they hooted him down. The key point for strike leaders was that an NWLB decision would stipulate "that the employees be allowed to elect committees of themselves, by themselves, in their own way." "If we are to have democracy in industry," read a statement by strike leaders, "workers must be permitted to elect their own committees without interference on the part of the management of the company." Like the Pittsfielders, they sent a delegation to Washington, met with their counterparts from Schenectady and Pittsfield, and lobbied for NWLB action. They achieved their goal. The NWLB decided to intervene over the objections of Massachusetts officials and against the wishes of the NWLB's employer members. When GE strikers finally returned to work on August 2, they did so in return for an NWLB investigation.[25]

Once that investigation began, Lynn organizers, like their colleagues in Schenectady, exploited it to recruit union members. With government agents on hand, organizers finished the work of unionizing the Lynn plant. By Labor Day, the complex was 90 percent organized, one investigator concluded. "Lynn is now an organized city," strike leader John F. Peterson proclaimed, "and the outlook for workers is bright." Peterson's optimism was apparently contagious, for by the end of September workers in Erie and Fort Wayne also began to stir. As one Fort Wayne activist explained, they "expect the same kind of an award from the War Labor Board that was given at Lynn." Erie workers were also ready to claim what was rightly theirs. "The time is ripe and the griddle is hot in Erie," one organizer reported.[26]

Within six months, GE metal trades activists had manipulated federal intervention to initiate a movement across five cities. As the movement coalesced, the leadership of the Schenectadians was evident. Their vision was to build an organization capable of bargaining with their giant company the way railway system federations bargained with railroads. They sought to federate the metal trades union locals of the GE cities, especially those of the IAM and IBEW, into a single unit. These federations then would act much like the Stockyards Labor Council had done in Chicago, organizing workers who fell outside craft jurisdictions — unskilled, semiskilled, white-collar workers — and putting their own federation organizers into the field. With encouragement from Schenectady, the Pittsfield Metal Trades Council took a step in this direction by commissioning such an organizer in September 1918. By the end of October, plans for a coordinated effort across GE's five main plants were taking shape. "Our aim is to get the big fellow solid," noted Erie organizer R. A. Parsons.[27]

This movement was fed by a new, more militant shop floor psychology at GE, a glimpse of which was visible in events that took place at Lynn following the intervention of the NWLB. As they ended their July 1918 walkout in return for NWLB hearings, Lynn GE workers took very seriously the board's commitment to shop committee representation. They decided to elect their own committees before the NWLB stepped in to conduct the process. On the night of August 6, at the local Odd Fellows Hall, IBEW organizer Charles Keaveny organized elections in which GE workers—whether they were union members or not—voted for representatives who would take up future grievances with management. Unionists swept virtually all committee offices that night. Seeking to derail Keaveny's plans, plant manager Fish fired several of the committee members the following morning, during the midst of the NWLB's hearings in Lynn. This action might have been possible months earlier when it was "dangerous to ask your neighbor if he belonged to the union." This time it precipitated a battle in the plant.[28]

When news of the firings reached the floor of the meter shop where he worked, Peterson grew furious. Together with a colleague, William H. White, Peterson organized a spontaneous sit-down strike among the more than three hundred workers—mostly women—who toiled in their department. As NWLB cochair Taft later described the scene, "These two employees [went] running up and down the aisles . . . advising the hundreds of women employees who were working to stop work, sit in their chairs and do no work, but not to leave the factory." A supervisor summoned to the shop attempted to intimidate the employees back to work but without success, while Peterson telephoned the IBEW headquarters to inform Keaveny of what was occurring. Meanwhile, in another machine shop, a similar protest erupted. Workers from both shops eventually walked out, followed by thousands of others, closing the plant down again for two days. The NWLB was forced to adjudicate the dispute.[29]

This second Lynn strike indicated how much the war had served suddenly to shift power relations on the shop floors of GE. Company managers were appalled by the insubordination. In a brief to the NWLB, they derided Peterson's action as a "breach of discipline so flagrant that it became solely a question whether the business of the company was to be conducted by its proper officials." Nothing less than "the discipline and efficiency of the Plant" were at stake. When the NWLB later asked Peterson if he had considered shop discipline before he urged his colleagues to sit down, his response revealed a great deal about how the war had altered the balance of power on the Lynn shop floor. "Shop discipline? Yes," he said. "I think if we didn't [sit down] there would have been more serious trouble." Events of the following two months suggested that Peterson did not exaggerate his coworkers' willingness to make "serious trouble." When the NWLB held its own shop committee elections at Lynn, the federal official who conducted them found workers still vigilant in the assertion of their rights. "I had a little strike on my hands in the midst of the elections," William Stoddard reported. "An entire building, comprising some 200 employees, refused to work until a certain discharged girl had been reinstated."[30]

It was precisely this militant psychology that SMTC activists hoped to tap to build a movement across the company. After weeks of laying the groundwork, they finally brought their plans to fruition on November 25, 1918. Exactly two weeks after the armistice was signed, GE militants had built enough organization in all five plants to stage a convention in Erie. Delegates from each of GE's facilities journeyed to Pennsylvania, overcame an attempt by Erie GE officials to break up their meeting, and formalized a new organization, the Electrical Manufacturing Industry Labor Federation. The electrical federation brought together unionists with a variety of philosophies, including moderates and even conservative AFL stalwarts, such as William Purdum of Erie's IAM local. Yet the more radical delegates from Schenectady dominated the convention. As the most experienced trade unionists among the electrical federation's delegates and as representatives of GE's largest plant, SMTC activists gained election to the top offices in the new organization: Robert A. Jones, president of the SMTC, took the same post in the federation, and John I. Wickham, who organized Schenectady GE's office workers, was elected secretary-treasurer. And the man who did the most to shape the organization was John Bellingham of the SMTC.[31]

The SMTC leaders imparted a militant, socialist-leaning industrial union vision to the electrical federation. They approved a list of demands that included a call for a forty-four-hour workweek in the industry, a federal commission to examine unemployment after the war and to provide financial assistance to the jobless, 50 percent labor representation at the postwar peace conference, and freedom for imprisoned labor organizer Tom Mooney. Pledging to back up these demands with united action, the delegates made plans to extend their organization. Erie was targeted for an intensive organizing drive, as was a GE plant in Canada. The federation also considered plans to join with Westinghouse Electric workers in Philadelphia. General Electric officials took none of these moves lightly. A secret study commissioned by counsel Owen D. Young concluded that the situation was "fraught with great danger." The federation, according to this report, possessed "dangerous potentialities."[32]

If it worried GE managers, the founding of the new federation excited electrical industry radicals. Noting that the organization welcomed men and women, skilled and unskilled, Schenectady Socialists celebrated the birth of "one big union . . . in line with the great principle of industrial unionism." The electrical federation was not a dual union that sought to break from the AFL. Its founding convention was addressed by two national union officials, and its Pittsfield leader, David Kevlin, had consulted with AFL officials before his metal trades council put their own organizer into the field in September. But its militancy, its founders' socialist commitments, and its effort to organize without respect to craft or skill made it a potent alternative to cautious AFL strategies.[33]

These very characteristics also meant that the electrical federation would develop a delicate relationship with national union leaders, including the IAM's Socialist president William Johnston. By the fall of 1918, Johnston and the other labor members of the NWLB were beginning to worry that the board might be crippled by employer opposition arising from recent union gains. A flood of appeals and protests from anxious employers began to clog the NWLB's docket by October 1918. All this exasperated Frank Walsh. If such appeals continued, he warned, "it will mean simply a second trial of every case." Preserving their credibility in Washington and protecting the NWLB from the attacks of panicked employers required union leaders (even such left-leaning ones as Johnston) to show that they were willing to restrain their workers when their demands appeared unreasonable or excessive.[34]

When the cases of Peterson and White, the organizers of the Lynn sit-down strike, came before the NWLB in October, Johnston showed how far he was willing to go to carry out what he felt were his obligations. To GE officials, the two sit-down strike leaders were emblematic of the breakdown of proper deference. "Someone must have authority in a plant like ours," Lynn plant manager Fish told the NWLB. "Discipline is necessary." Naturally, Fish sought to prevent the reinstatement of these two. His argument resonated well with cochair Taft. "I think that the Company is entitled to maintain discipline on its grounds," Taft told Walsh. Peterson and White "flaunted the necessary supervisory control—the police control if you will—of the superintendents." Believing that it was time to "draw a line on a proper subordination to reasonable discipline within shop limits," Taft argued that GE certainly had a right to fire them. Neither Taft's nor GE's stance was surprising to the electrical federation. But Johnston's was. When Taft berated White and Peterson, Johnston offered no defense for these men. In fact, Johnston coauthored the NWLB finding that closed the door to their reinstatement.[35]

As the treatment that two of its activists were accorded by William Johnston suggests, Electrical Manufacturing Industry Labor Federation organizers could not necessarily count on the uncompromising support of national leaders. This made them all the more anxious to insist that they were not dual unionists. The federation was "decidedly not Bolsheviki," one of its press releases carefully stated. It was "but a labor organization, backed up by crafts having official representation" in the AFL. Still, the organization carved out

William H. Johnston, president of the International Association of Machinists, ca. 1921. (George Meany Memorial Archives, Silver Spring, Maryland)

an independent path, particularly in the realm of politics, that did little to ease the fears of more conservative union leaders.[36]

The federation elaborated its own political agenda in two GE cities. During the fall of 1918, Bellingham and Jesse Finn ran unsuccessfully for the New York State Assembly from Schenectady on the Socialist ticket with strong support from the electrical federation there. In Pittsfield, meanwhile, a remarkable effort unfolded as David Kevlin, a GE mechanic, staged two extraordinary campaigns. In October 1918, Kevlin failed in a hastily organized write-in campaign for a seat in the Massachusetts state legislature. He then mounted a campaign for the mayoralty of Pittsfield in November on an Independent

Labor Party ticket with the electrical federation as his base. Portraying himself as the "People's Mayor" in that rock-ribbed Republican community, Kevlin drew volunteers from among the "mostly young workers from the mills, who sacrificed two weeks pay to hustle for him," according to one reporter. His platform was, that reporter noted, "a straight appeal to class consciousness." The campaign shocked the city's political establishment. "Why if that man gets into City Hall," one resident of the wealthy fourth ward reportedly speculated, "he'll make himself head of the police force, and then we'll have a strike in the General Electric works every fifteen minutes." Whether that vision helped or hurt Kevlin's campaign is uncertain. What is clear is that he lost by a hair's breadth, sweeping a majority of wards but falling 360 votes short of election. The *New Republic* credited "the newly organized shop committees" for boosting Kevlin, "releasing latent ideals and desires for self expression."[37]

As the Kevlin campaign indicated, the impact of the NWLB's intervention in the electrical industry was quite surprising. In six months, using NWLB protection and capitalizing on shop committee organization, militants built a remarkable socialist-tinged union federation, nourished a militant shop floor culture, and launched a surprisingly successful, radical political campaign. As the electrical federation grew, its organizers found that their interests did not always coincide with those of union leaders who had joined Wilson's war labor administration in Washington. But it was still Washington's intervention that helped make their organizing "a matter of local willingness," as Laurence Todd would have put it.

The electrical federation's leaders were acutely sensitive to this fact. Thus, in the aftermath of the armistice, they did not celebrate the NWLB's loss of power. Rather, they feared that the armistice would bring only more "temporizing and stalling" from GE in the implementation of NWLB awards. And when, by the end of November 1918, they were forced to admit that it had become a "waste of time to take a case before the Board," it was with an enormous sense of foreboding. Without the NWLB, most of them well realized, there would have been no Electrical Manufacturing Industry Labor Federation.[38]

THE TRANSFORMATION OF IAM DISTRICT 55

In the vital munitions plants of Bridgeport, Connecticut, trade unionists learned that even flawed war labor policies could create new opportunities for militancy and mass organizing that would have been impossible without government intervention. Beginning with a strike at Lake Torpedo in August 1917, IAM District 55, under the radical leadership of Sam Lavit, made great strides in organizing machinists and toolmakers in Bridgeport munitions plants. Friday night "smokers" attracted hundreds to boxing matches and entertainment interspersed with speakers who harangued "food pirates" and urged workers to join the IAM. But over the winter of 1917–18, Lavit's movement remained largely confined to skilled men. For the most part, he failed to parlay the militancy of Bridgeport's women corset workers or that demonstrated by the eight-hour strikers of 1915 into a broadly based movement. Federal intervention, however, would help reshape District 55's strategy, first by dealing a blow to the skilled munitions workers and then by presenting Lavit with the means to attract semiskilled workers into his union's ranks.[39]

A series of events set District 55 on a collision course with the federal war labor program, which made all this possible. On February 7, 1918, machinists at Remington Arms demanded a minimum wage of eighty cents per hour for toolmakers and seventy cents for machinists. For months before this, District 55 had engaged in a fight to obtain minimum wages and job classifications that would protect skilled workers from "dilution." Past wage increases, members complained, amounted to little because after they were given, "new men are hired and those who get raised get displaced." Machinists in other plants echoed the demands, and rolling strikes to win them began when machinists struck Liberty Ordnance on February 20. On Good Friday, March 29, 1918, Remington's machinists also struck, bringing the conflict to a head. Employers responded by inducing the local draft board to revoke draft deferments for the strikers. Strike leaders went to Washington to appeal, and Lavit called machinists out of twenty-two subcontract shops on May 3 — over the objections of IAM president Johnston — finally to force government action.[40]

The NWLB's entry into the case was circuitous. On May 11, Lavit called off the strike in return for an investigation by Major William C. Rogers of the War Department. Rogers, who had recently settled a dispute in an aircraft factory strike by instituting job classifications like those demanded by the Bridgeporters, was a sympathetic mediator. He delivered a decision on June 8 that authorized raises and minimum rates for six classes of machinists. Members of the IAM overwhelmingly accepted the settlement. But employers balked at an award that would have ceded the power to define those classes of machinists to the government. Lavit asked the War Department to enforce its award, and his members staged several short strikes to keep the pressure on. But the War Department could not budge Bridgeport manufacturers, and so Secretary Baker turned to the NWLB in July. At that moment, the NWLB was considering minimum wage and job classification demands in the Waynesboro and Cambridge cases. Bridgeport, however, would prove to be a more complex affair.[41]

On June 27, a delegation led by Sam Lavit laid District 55's grievances before the NWLB, and the board took the case. One year of frustration in dealing with recalcitrant employers and slow-moving government agencies had bred cynicism among them, and the Bridgeporters were by that time "out of control of their International leaders here in Washington," as one official reported. Reflecting the urgency of the situation, the NWLB appointed a subsection consisting of Taft, Walsh, Johnston, and Loyall Osborne and promised fast action on the case. Bridgeport machinists thought that meant that their employers were "at last brought to bay." They were soon to learn otherwise.[42]

NWLB members could not agree on the case. Hearings held in Bridgeport during July saw both sides present lengthy arguments. District 55's witnesses told of blacklisting and coercion, including the manipulation of draft deferments. Employers, led by Walter G. Merritt of the American Anti-Boycott Association, presented a three-volume study of the machinists' incomes, asserting that they were prosperous indeed. Each side heard what they wanted in the testimony. Neither Johnston nor Osborne was prepared to compromise. Johnston for his part sought to aid his own members' efforts to win job classifications that would protect them from de-skilling, and he was solicitous of Lavit's needs during the board's deliberations. Meanwhile, Osborne, as a Westinghouse official, was determined to prevent any widening of the board's precedents regarding job classifications. The departure of the board's moderating spirit, cochair Taft, for a vacation in Canada thus virtually ensured a stalemate. Taft's alternate, Kansas City lawyer Frederick Judson, sided with Osborne. No prodding from Walsh could budge him. This left the NWLB perfectly divided.[43]

Events outside Bridgeport, however, soon pushed the NWLB to break its deadlock. As the board wrestled with the Bridgeport matter, unionists upped the ante throughout the munitions industry. In mid-July, Hartford, Connecticut, Colt workers asked the NWLB to investigate their conditions. Simultaneously, a dispute at Smith and Wesson in Springfield, Massachusetts, over yellow-dog contracts boiled over. Defying the War Department, Smith and Wesson began firing union members who broke those contracts. In retaliation, machinists struck the plant in early August. When the department tried to craft a settlement, Smith and Wesson ignored it. On August 13, the War Department asked the NWLB to mediate. Hoping to stave off impending chaos in the nation's munitions plants, the board voted on August 15 to turn the Bridgeport case over to umpire Otto Eidlitz, a New York City builder.[44]

By the time Eidlitz took the case, events had nearly spiraled out of control in Bridgeport itself. Since the NWLB hearings, Lavit had recruited over one thousand new members into the IAM. But the hopeful mood of the unionists turned to frustration as they vainly waited for Washington to act. Lavit had attempted to harness this river of frustration to prod the NWLB. But on August 14 it flooded over its banks. Ignoring Lavit's counsel, machinists resolved to strike the following day at noon. Only a telegram from Frank Walsh kept them at work: they stayed on the job "to show Mr. Walsh that we had confidence in him," said one. Walsh repaid their trust by visiting Bridgeport on August 23 to assure them that they would get what they sought. "I have criticized the laws of my country," Walsh told a rapt audience. "But all the time I knew that the education of the people would reach a point as I hope that it has now, when all men understand their rights and [have] the machinery to make this government as near to an ideal government as it could possibly be." Industrial democracy would soon reign in Bridgeport, he promised. (This speech led one Bridgeport employer to label Walsh "the head of the American Bolsheviki.") Yet Walsh spoke too soon.[45]

Eidlitz's decision on August 27 was a grave blow to Lavit and District 55. Walsh and Johnston were equally shocked by it. It provided for an eight-hour day, the election of shop committees, a local board of mediation and conciliation to be composed of workers and employers and chaired by an NWLB examiner, a minimum wage of forty-two cents for men and thirty-two cents for women, and a sliding scale of raises that increased the wages of the most poorly paid workers by the greatest amount. But the highly paid toolmakers—District 55's militant core constituency—received little from the award. Most important, Eidlitz did not mention the key issue in the case—job classifications. Walsh felt betrayed. Johnston was livid. But their anger could not match that of the Bridgeporters. When word of the decision reached them on August 28, union men mobbed Lavit demanding an explanation. At a mass meeting, five thousand District 55 members discussed their options. According to one description, "the mood of the meeting was such that nothing could get consideration but a strike vote." Machinists hissed Johnston's name, dismissed Lavit's organizing committee, and formed a strike committee to which Lavit had difficulty getting himself named. Resolving that they would "go back to the trenches to fight for Uncle Sam" before they would work under such an award, they voted to strike at noon on August 30.[46]

The Bridgeport strike imperiled the NWLB. It was the first by workers against an award of the board. Nearly six thousand men walked out despite the charges of local clergy who attacked them as "traitors." Complicating matters considerably, their action coincided with an employer's defiance of the NWLB. Only a week earlier on August 22, the NWLB decided the Smith and Wesson case, banning yellow-dog contracts there. Smith and Wesson refused to recognize the award, with company officials arguing they would rather see their "business lawfully taken over and conducted by the government" than submit to such terms. The board's crisis was further complicated by William

Johnston's actions in the aftermath of the Eidlitz decision. In the days after the walkout, he not only refused to condemn strikers but also publicly sympathized with them. On Labor Day 1918, Johnston journeyed to Bridgeport and mounted a podium with the radical Ella Reeve Bloor. While he still proclaimed President Wilson "the grandest man who ever lived," Johnston also shared his frustration with his members. "You have been robbed and exploited all your life. You will be robbed and exploited for the rest of your life if you don't . . . act together." [47]

Both Johnston and Lavit, however, had an interest in preserving the NWLB. Even as he excoriated Eidlitz, Johnston privately searched for a way to mollify his members. His union had gained too much from the NWLB to risk seeing it undermined. If employers were allowed to point to Bridgeport and say that the IAM "cannot be controlled by its own officers" and that its members regarded "an agreement as a mere scrap of paper," as the journal *Iron Age* contended, then the war labor program might crumble only to be succeeded by something worse. As much as he too objected to the Eidlitz award, Sam Lavit saw no more to be gained in his members' confrontation with Washington than did Johnston. Therefore, immediately after the Labor Day rally, Lavit joined Johnston in talks with the mayor of Bridgeport and NWLB staffer E. B. Woods to look for a way out of the strike. The four men soon concluded that the shop committees called for by Eidlitz could provide the key to a settlement. Johnston and Lavit agreed to end the strike on the condition that Eidlitz clarified his award by stating that the shop committees would have the authority to negotiate the job classifications that toolmakers wanted. Over employer objections, Eidlitz promptly agreed to this clarification. [48]

Lavit still had no success in putting this compromise over with his members. When he and Johnston requested that IAMers return to work to bargain through shop committees, they were attacked. According to one observer, a "mob psychology . . . that nothing could penetrate" took over the mass meeting that discussed the compromise. Angry machinists threw Lavit off the strike committee and, in the days that followed, denounced him and Johnston with equal ferocity. But the rank and filers' actions were motivated by narrow interests. District 55's base membership was among skilled machinists and toolmakers. While Lavit saw the possibility of using shop committees to broaden his organization in the munitions plants, many of these workers were simply impatient for immediate wage gains and protection against de-skilling. Scarcely revolutionaries, they turned to the only man they felt would help them. "President Wilson . . . understands the Bridgeport situation better than William H. Johnston, president of the IAM," said the strikers' statement. On September 5, they cabled the White House, asking "the strong arm of the government to intervene, and take over" the munitions industry so that arms manufacturing would no longer be conducted "for the private enrichment of a few men."[49]

By this point, Johnston's desire to quell the strike was clear, and he decided to act. On September 9, 1918, Johnston sent IAM official Fred Hewitt to Bridgeport to request that machinists resume work. When Hewitt informed the District 55 men that the union might revoke their charter, he was met with cries of "Take it!" The strike committee then made plans for a convention of dissident IAM lodges to depose Johnston. The situation, one NWLB official concluded, was "grave beyond expression." While the War Department dispatched a general to Bridgeport to pressure the manufacturers to give ground and military agents stepped up spying on strike leaders, Johnston himself spoke on September 10. Assuring machinists that the Eidlitz award was "just as distasteful to the International Officers as it is to our individual members in Bridgeport," he nonetheless demanded that they return to work to preserve the "honor of our Association." Strikers repudiated him, however, resolving to stand "like men without a yellow streak for our principles." Although he was now convinced that shop committees could prove to be an enormous boon to his union in Bridgeport, Sam Lavit was no more successful than Johnston in getting his members to return to work.[50]

Only the government was capable of ending the strike, confirming Johnston's control of the IAM, and rehabilitating Sam Lavit as District 55's leader. No one was more acutely aware of this than the man the strikers most trusted, Frank Walsh. Anxious to preserve the NWLB's integrity, Walsh now sprang into action by bringing the president to bear on the case. When Taft returned from his long vacation on September 9, Walsh was ready to move. He drafted a settlement with Taft that was forwarded to President Wilson on September 10. It called for the machinists to resume work so that "the authority of the War Labor Board shall be firmly established." "Your strike," the letter informed the Bridgeporters, "is a breach of faith calculated to reflect on the sincerity of National organized labor in proclaiming its acceptance of the principles and machinery of the National War Labor Board." The letter further warned that if the strikers did not resume work, their draft exemptions would be revoked. But with careful evenhandedness the letter also stated that the War Department would assume control over Smith and Wesson because of that company's refusal to honor the NWLB's Springfield award. President Wilson signed the letter on September 13.[51]

Wilson's statement—among his "finest and bravest," his secretary Joseph Tumulty thought—crushed District 55's rebellious strike. But it did not at all crush District 55. Rather, this move put the weight of the presidency behind the NWLB, preserving it as much as the president's July action against Western Union had done, and it persuaded District 55 members to give up their fight and follow the course of action that Lavit had already recommended. They did. On September 17, the Bridgeporters returned to work "not as driven slaves, but as hopeful Americans," as Lavit put it. And Lavit had reason to be hopeful, despite the disappointments of the Eidlitz decision. NWLB examiner Isaac Russell, on hand when the strikers went back to work, understood this point. Russell argued that the chance to elect shop committees would transform the "sullen beaten workmen into a buoyant force, aware at last of a method of spontaneous cooperation that is all they could desire." As Russell predicted, the Bridgeport IAM would soon emerge from Wilson's intervention stronger than ever.[52]

NWLB shop committee elections revitalized the Bridgeport labor movement. In September 1918, the board dispatched labor sympathizers Vernon Rose, Mildred Rankin, Hazel Hunkins, Agnes Johnson, and Elizabeth Curry to hold elections in Bridgeport schoolhouses for these committees. Company officials, foremen, and security guards were barred from the polls, voting was secret, and workers were free from managerial intimidation. When the voting ended on September 23, 116 shop committees had been elected by nearly ten thousand workers. Evidence indicates that they were overwhelmingly loyal to District 55. When these committee delegates in turn selected three representatives to the Bridgeport-wide Local Board of Mediation and Conciliation to negotiate the classification issue and settle unresolved grievances, they chose Lavit, his associate David Clydesdale, and Patrick Scollin, also a prominent union leader. Rather than seeing his power diminished by his confrontation with the NWLB, Lavit saw it enhanced. Now he presided over a council that could claim to represent all munitions workers in the city. Perhaps that is why the NWLB's Russell found no evidence of disgruntlement among District 55 members on the day after the shop committee elections ended. "The men feel fine towards the government," he reported.[53]

In the brief span of time between their election and the armistice, Bridgeport shop committees provided an effective voice for previously unorganized workers. Staffers such as Alpheus Winter, the NWLB examiner in charge of the Bridgeport case, helped ensure this. Winter issued a set of rulings that secured the autonomy of the committees, prohibited discrimination against union members, and called for all grievances to come before him. Employers were enraged by the pro-union bias they perceived among Winter and his colleagues. Only days after investigators arrived in Bridgeport, complaints were delivered to cochair Taft that Hazel Hunkins was organizing Bridgeport workers into the suffragist movement. Others alleged that Mildred Rankin and Vernon Rose had gone up to Hartford to instigate labor trouble at the Colt factory there. Though an NWLB investigation exonerated them, employers had ample reason to fear NWLB staffers. When he spoke to Colt workers, Rose, by his own account, "dwelt at considerable length upon the meaning of democracy; its translation into the terms of industry, and that while fighting for it abroad we should work unceasingly for it at home." It may have been due to the presence of such NWLB staffers that one observer found Bridgeport workers so enthusiastic about the shop committee. "They appeared to see in it," thought Hugh McCabe, "something of hope and betterment beyond anything they have heretofore had." [54]

Supervision of the Bridgeport shop committees by NWLB staffers like these did not hurt Lavit's efforts to broaden District 55's membership, particularly among women. In August 1918, Lavit had enlisted the aid of AFL organizer Mary Scully to initiate an organizing drive among women munitions workers. As the *Bridgeport Labor Leader* explained, "Men have at last wakened up to the fact that it is necessary to organize the women." As if to illustrate his union's commitment to equality, Lavit also offered support to the Connecticut branch of the National Woman's Party. It was not until the election of shop committees, however, that District 55 actually attracted significant numbers of women. When NWLB investigators arrived in Bridgeport, one of them reported, most women munitions workers were "afraid of the term unionism." The shop elections seemed to change that. In educating women workers before those elections, Elizabeth Curry ardently advocated "proportional representation" for women. Mildred Rankin found that such arguments, accompanied by "sympathetic understanding and patient explanations," resonated well among Bridgeporters. "These women are, as all working women of their experience, entirely without experience in elections of any sort," she found. But they were "eager to learn what the war labor Board wanted and ready to respond." [55]

Participating in shop committee elections seemed to energize women munitions workers. Rankin found that there were generally two groups of women. One was keen to join the IAM. The other, a larger group, was wary of the union but "anxious to take advantage of committee representation and [take] care of grievances." Among both groups shop committee elections had a profound effect. Rankin reported that when munitions women were "given any help they rise to a complete realization of their responsibility and are able and ready to do their share in making collective bargaining a success." Within a month of the shop committee elections, several women emerged from the ranks to lead munitions workers. Elsie Ver Vane, a forty-five-year-old mother who became an IAM member at the Union Metallic Cartridge plant, was the most prominent. Thanking the NWLB for giving her a chance to fight for "Industrial Democracy," Ver Vane was determined to show the "manufacturers how sincere and firm I am for the laboring class." She helped organize a new IAM lodge for women. The "Park City Women Workers Lodge" was chartered two weeks after the shop committee elections. Initially it contained 150 members, and it gained scores more before the armistice.[56]

The broadening of District 55's ranks following NWLB intervention reshaped the union. The organization of the women "comes at an opportune time," editorialized Lavit's paper, the *Bridgeport Labor Leader*, for "working women . . . are breadwinners for themselves and their families." But the transformation of the union also entailed some growing pains. Some vocal critics were not at all happy with the union's new direction. Several walkouts by men protesting the employment of women followed the shop committee elections. Nor did remaining conservatives support the two-pronged strategy that District 55's leaders embarked upon to secure a broader base for their union.[57]

The first prong of that strategy focused on the Local Board of Mediation and Conciliation. Lavit was determined that District 55 control that board. He took a leave of absence as IAM business agent to reenter the munitions workforce and qualify as a shop committee member so that he might be elected to it. When he, Clydesdale, and Scollin were sworn in, it meant that three of the staunchest militants in the city now had the authority to speak on behalf of all munitions workers. They attempted to use the local board to demand that shop committees assume increased authority over the work process in the munitions industry. At the first meeting of the local board, on November 7, Scollin informed the management that thenceforth workers would expect an equal voice in decision making. The local board should not be bound by past precedents, Scollin thought. "I don't think we ought to go back to the past on any matters that comes [*sic*] before us," he announced. Scollin's words were backed up by aggressive demands from shop committees themselves. They called for the reinstatement of fired workers, back pay according to the terms of the Eidlitz award, a forty-four-hour workweek in order to forestall layoffs after the war, clear grievance procedures, and job classifications.[58]

The second prong of District 55's strategy was political. On the same day that District 55 members were ordered back to work by President Wilson, Lavit and his supporters founded the American Labor Party (ALP) in Bridgeport. Asserting that the AFL had "fallen down" politically, Lavit urged Bridgeport workers to chart their own course. The Bridgeporters explicitly patterned their effort after the British Labour Party. Although only weeks old, the party fielded a slate of candidates for local office in November, including David Clydesdale and Elsie Ver Vane. Phil Deselets received the party's endorsement for a seat in the Congress. The election of Deselets, argued Lavit, would help "lay the corner stone for Industrial Democracy." Though Deselets and other candidates failed, the ALP made a respectable showing for a new political party.[59]

Its efforts through the local board and the ALP showed that District 55 had not only survived federal intervention but also in many ways thrived under it. What was more, federal intervention seemed to have substantially strengthened the militant Lavit's hand within the IAM. Lavit and Johnston collaborated during the September crisis that followed the Eidlitz award. They had reason to at that time. But tension marked the relationship between these men. Lavit stood to the left of Johnston politically, and he was dissatisfied with what he perceived as the IAM president's timid leadership. Early in 1918, District 55 announced its opposition to Johnston's reelection as president, endorsing instead a ticket headed by James A. Taylor of the Seattle Metal Trades Council in national union elections. At that time, the *Bridgeport Labor Leader* called on machinists to dump from office those who merely "style themselves as progressive." In the wake of the September crisis, Johnston's prestige was further diminished in Bridgeport and among IAM militants elsewhere around the country. Lavit, on the other hand, had managed to avoid most of the costs associated with the NWLB intervention at the same time as he capitalized on its benefits to increase his own power and influence.[60]

In the munitions industry, then, as in coal and electrical manufacturing, federal intervention had stimulated local organizing with unanticipated results. So it is not surprising that District 55 officials mourned the NWLB's growing impotency following the armistice. Just as Bridgeport was one of the first cities to feel the impact of war, so too was it among the first to feel the pinch of peace. Canceled war contracts, layoffs, and plant closings quickly endangered all that District 55 had built. The local board set up by the Eidlitz award was an early casualty. Employers refused to accept its authority after the armistice. And almost immediately an NWLB examiner detected "a certain amount of stalling" in the willingness of some employers to meet with their shop committees. Other employers were more forthright. Alleging that NWLB shop committees were nothing more than "recruiting agencies of the machinists," several employers fired committee delegates or created their own committees, providing no court of appeal for those bodies other than the plant manager's office. Lavit pleaded with the NWLB to step in and protect his workers' rights. "It's a question of whether or not these manufacturers are more powerful than the government," he argued. But, within weeks of the armistice, Lavit learned to his regret that the NWLB no longer had the power to intervene in his favor.[61]

As this survey of events in coal mining, electrical manufacturing, and munitions makes clear, government regulation had a complex impact on unions and workers during World War I. In many ways it strengthened unions as institutions, allowing them to broaden their memberships and build organizations in areas from which they had been excluded. That in turn served to bind national leaders, from John L. Lewis to William Johnston, more closely to the war labor agencies, their limitations notwithstanding. At the same time, Laurence Todd's thesis was not far off the mark. Federal regulation also created conditions under which local militants could seize the initiative and lead movements that ran counter not only to what Washington officials sought to achieve but also to what AFL leaders envisioned as the proper goal of industrial democracy. Of course, there was a glaring irony here, for labor's most successful radical-led efforts—including the Stockyards Labor Council, the Electrical Manufacturing Industry Labor Federation, and IAM District 55—were profoundly dependent on the same federal labor program that also destroyed the IWW and accommodated the demands of a conservative AFL hierarchy.

Finally, events in coalfields, electrical manufacturing plants, and munitions factories made something else clear. Wartime conditions had contributed to the breakdown of old patterns of labor relations, sparked new forms of militancy, and created fresh opportunities for radicals, but they had scarcely established a consensus within labor's ranks regarding how industry ought to be democratized. On that question, men like William Johnston often found themselves at odds with the likes of John Bellingham or Sam Lavit, even as they shared interests in building their movement. The absence of a consensus among trade unionists as the war ended would help shape the postwar order, ensuring that while the labor movement would never completely return to its prewar state, neither would it attain the acceptance hoped for by its leaders or the social restructuring dreamed of by its militants.

THE TENTATIVE RISE
OF MASS UNIONISM

6——————————————————

*The prospect of submitting grievances to a
Government board . . . has proved a vastly greater
stimulus to labor organizations than the prospect of
venturing a strike and a contest with the tremendous
physical, financial, and local political power of a great
industrial corporation.*

—George P. West, 1918

*The original plan of a dashing offensive went to smash
. . . and with it, likewise, the opportunity to organize
the steel industry.*

—William Z. Foster, 1920

        In August 1918, as the impact of the federal inter-
vention on union organizing around the country was becoming clear, Paul
Wallace attempted to analyze events for the Socialist daily the *New York Call*.
The *Call* had initially feared that America's entry into the war would produce state repression and destroy progressive labor organizations. Wallace had
since arrived at a different view. Looking at the Eidlitz decision that had been
announced recently in Bridgeport—a decision roundly condemned by most
labor sympathizers—Wallace found good reasons for radicals to be hopeful.
By dealing a blow to some of the most exclusive impulses of skilled machinists

and toolmakers, by refusing to consider their request for job classifications, and by calling for shop committees that would be elected by Bridgeport's entire munitions workforce, Wallace thought the Eidlitz decision had actually opened the door to a progressive mass union movement among munitions workers. The decision would accelerate "the death throes which have overtaken craft unions" and provide an "enormous stimulus to industrial unionism." Bridgeport's shop committees, he argued, would provide "the nucleus of a shop soviet through which workers may exert the full weight of their collective power."[1]

Certainly, no "soviets" emerged in Bridgeport. Yet, as Sam Lavit and the reinvigorated District 55 would show in following weeks, Wallace was not entirely wrong in his assessment of events. Wallace's specific observation regarding Bridgeport pointed to a broader phenomenon at the heart of the World War I labor upheaval. Federal labor policies provided an "enormous stimulus to industrial unionism" within the AFL. Some architects of those policies, such as Frank Walsh, who had aided the cause of industrial unionism through the CIR, the NLDC, and the stockyards movement, certainly hoped that they would do so. Clearly, though, the role that government policy played in this regard was, for the most part, unintended. Most administration officials, some AFL leaders, and certainly all the employers who helped design them, were surprised by the role that federal policies played in encouraging both unionism in open-shop industries and industrial unionism within the union movement. By the end of the war, open-shop bastions in steel, clothing, textiles, electrical manufacturing, and meatpacking played host to vigorous organizing drives that took on the cast of industrial union ventures, to the delight of radicals such as Wallace.

Yet those who dreamed of unionizing open-shop mass industries and transforming the labor movement in the process found organizing under the war labor agencies to be profoundly frustrating. Three organizing drives that took shape during the early months of the NWLB's tenure showed that federal intervention did not occur broadly, deeply, or consistently enough to enable industrial unionists to defeat open-shop employers at their strongest points or to accelerate magically the "death throes" of craft unionism. An attempt by Birmingham steelworkers to organize across the racial divide showed that while war labor agencies may have served to spark organizing efforts, they were not always strong enough to protect those efforts. In northern steel centers the halting rise of the National Committee for Organizing Iron and Steel Workers revealed that federal intervention ultimately aided craft unionists and company unionism as much as it did the cause of industrial unionism. And a campaign by New England textile workers illustrated the degree to which craft union leaders were willing to manipulate the threat of mass unionism to secure purely craft-oriented goals, stirring industrial union aspirations among workers only to quash them when it served craft union interests. Together, these cases suggest that while federal policies allowed workers to carry the battle for industrial democracy into industry's most impregnable strongholds, creating a remarkable moment in American labor history, those policies were themselves insufficient in helping workers impose their own vision of democracy on mass industry.

THE ABORTIVE EFFORT TO UNIONIZE BIRMINGHAM STEELWORKERS

Nowhere did the impulse toward mass unionism produce more sound and fury and yield more meager results than in the iron and steel mills of Birmingham, Alabama. Birmingham's mills, the epitome of the "New South," were strongly open shop, thoroughly segregated, and characterized by conditions of extreme exploitation. By the advent of war, Birmingham and neighboring Bessemer constituted a booming industrial corridor where steel production had risen from 320,000 tons in 1907 to 1,225,000 in 1916. U.S. Steel—operating two plants through its Tennessee Coal and Iron company (TCI) subsidiary and one through its American Steel and Wire Company—Sloss-Sheffield, Republic Steel, and the American Cast Iron Pipe Company were the backbone of the industrial South, a critical link in the wartime economy.[2]

Before the war, attempts to organize Alabama iron and steel had been frustrated by a host of forces. One of the most important impediments was the racial caste system that divided black and white workers, making solidarity nearly impossible. During the war, roughly 64 percent of the semiskilled workers and 89 percent of unskilled workers in the Birmingham region's mills were African American. Other than molders—48 percent of whom were black—skilled workers in the mills, including machinists, boilermakers, and patternmakers, were white. Birmingham's lily-white metal trades unions fought to preserve this distinction. This racial chasm helped sap the power of the 70 percent of skilled whites in the plants who were union members. Only 15 percent of these had won union recognition from their managers, in part because employers could draw on the reservoir of nonunion blacks to undermine walkouts by whites.[3]

But wartime and the growth of the federal war labor agencies provided an opportunity for steelworkers to surmount the barriers to organization. In 1914, one USCIR investigator dispatched to Birmingham by Frank Walsh had delivered a positive assessment of unionism's possibilities there. A. M. Daly believed that Birmingham steelworkers, including the thousands of blacks streaming into the mills, "can be organized provided the conditions are such that it will be possible."[4] At that time, the USCIR had no power to affect such conditions. Four years, later, however, the NWLB and other agencies seemed to have that power. Recent successes in Alabama's coal mines certainly suggested as much. So Birmingham's union workers took heart.

Birmingham's organized white crafts workers soon resolved to test how far power had shifted in the wartime steel industry. On February 20, 1918, the metal trades unionists of the iron and steel mills acted. Over three thousand white machinists, iron molders, boilermakers, patternmakers, blacksmiths, and electrical workers struck as part of a citywide attempt to win eight hours in the metal trades. As the first strike for the eight-hour day in the wartime steel industry, the Birmingham walkout was monitored closely by AFL leaders in Washington; they rushed to offer support. The mills, however, continued to produce essential iron and steel. To meet the walkout, TCI and the other companies had recruited both white and black scabs to take the strikers' places. Moreover, it appeared that U.S. Steel was digging in for a long fight: TCI shifted production to plants outside Birmingham and offered wage raises to lure workers back to the mills, and both George G. Crawford of TCI and Judge Elbert Gary of U.S. Steel turned aside conciliation efforts. Led by the intransigent TCI, Birmingham's mill operators were determined to wait out the strike, sure that their workers would not forego high wartime wages for long.[5]

As the fight stalemated, Birmingham's white steelworkers pinned their hopes for success on the government. Acting through their national leaders, they invoked federal aid. On March 30, as President Wilson prepared to appoint the NWLB, Samuel Gompers asked Secretary William B. Wilson to make the Birmingham strike a test case for the new agency, reminding Wilson that the new board had already declared in favor of the eight-hour day. In Birmingham, strikers made the same point. "We have been called slackers, pro-German, unpatriotic and everything else," they complained. Still, they were "merely asking for something that the government . . . had set its seal of approval upon." Confident that their demands were in line with the administration's goals, the metal trades unionists awaited Washington's action.[6]

Two considerations, meanwhile, reconfigured the union movement in the Birmingham mills. First, federal intervention could not be effectively secured unless the Birmingham walkout restricted iron and steel output enough for Washington to take notice. But, as the strike stretched through March, steel manufacturers were showing signs of rebuilding their production levels. Second, any gains made by white skilled laborers were imperiled as long as the threat of employing unorganized black workers could be held over their heads. Taking these factors into consideration, leaders of the Birmingham Metal Trades Council prepared to embark on a broader and more ambitious strategy in April. Local AFL unions, with a history of racially exclusive practices, had never been keen on organizing blacks. Yet to win the eight-hour strike, many concluded, necessitated organizing all production workers, especially blacks. As Bessemer patternmaker J. A. Lipscomb explained, this "battle concerns us all." The craft unions of the metal trades did not seek to lower their own barriers to the entry of unskilled or black workers, however. To accomplish the task, they instead secured the help of the International Union of Mine, Mill, and Smelter Workers (IUMMSW).[7]

The entry of the IUMMSW and the attempt to organize black steelworkers changed the character of the Birmingham walkout. The IUMMSW sent Edward Crough, a veteran white organizer who had spent 1917 with striking copper miners in Arizona, and both the IUMMSW and the AFL pooled funds to hire Ulysses Hale, a black organizer from Oxmoor, Alabama, to initiate the broader movement. AFL secretary Frank Morrison even journeyed to Alabama to confer with Birmingham trade unionists regarding strategy. By early May, Hale had begun making discernible progress. He organized two locals of black blast furnace workers, one containing one hundred members, the other sixty-three. Not surprisingly, his work soon attracted the attention of racist terrorists. Hale's residence was bombed. The bitter reaction against the IUMMSW and the union's determination to hold on made clear that both sides understood the importance of this first significant attempt by the AFL to organize black and white steelworkers in a coordinated effort.[8]

The Birmingham drive took place at a crucial moment for the AFL. One week before the metal trades strike erupted, federation leaders began considering the possibility of an alliance with African American civil rights leaders, which might help the unions organize blacks. On February 12, 1918, R. R. Moton, Emmet J. Scott, Eugene Kinkle Jones, and other civil rights leaders met with the AFL's Executive Council to urge that the unions end racial discrimination. A cautious Samuel Gompers explained that the AFL could not "rush too far ahead" of "the great mass of workers" on the issue of racial equality. Yet the AFL did hold out an olive branch. The Executive Council instructed Gompers "to appoint a committee to meet a like committee representing the colored workers to prepare a plan of organization." Even as a rapprochement between the AFL and black leaders seemed in the offing, another opportunity was arising. By April 1918, the AFL was considering a proposal from Ed Nockels of the Chicago Federation of Labor that a conference be held in order to initiate a mass organizing drive in steel. Morrison believed that the Birmingham effort, in the context of the AFL's negotiations with the civil rights leaders, might become the first step toward Nockels's vision.[9]

A great deal, then, seemed to turn on the Birmingham strike, and the IUMMSW component soon became the focal point of the eight-hour drive in the Alabama mills. Both AFL strategists and Birmingham union leaders realized that federal support was crucial to winning the campaign. President Wilson's proclamation of April 8, 1918, creating the NWLB provided the instrument they needed. Two days after the president acted, Frank Morrison urged B. W. King, head of the Birmingham Metal Trades Council, to contact the NWLB. King immediately forwarded a request for federal intervention. "After repeated efforts we have at last succeeded in making some progress toward organizing the negro and common laborers," King wrote. "Corporate gunmen," however, were determined "to prevent the organization of this class of labor." King predicted "bitter industrial war" in Birmingham "unless the government speedily interferes."[10]

The NWLB quickly considered King's request. National union leaders, including Gompers, Morrison, and James O'Connell, of the AFL's Metal Trades Department, brought their influence to bear. They found willing allies among the labor members of the NWLB, especially Johnston of the IAM, which had members on strike in Birmingham, and Frank Walsh. Since his days on the USCIR, Walsh had hoped to use the federal government to promote unions in southern industries. The Birmingham dispute offered an opportunity to accomplish that. With his enthusiastic support, the NWLB held a preliminary hearing on May 9, 1918, to gather the facts on the Birmingham case. During that hearing, Gompers asked the NWLB to assume jurisdiction of the case and apply its eight-hour principle in Birmingham. TCI's lawyer, Fortney Johnston, son of a former U.S. senator and a leading figure in Alabama's Democratic Party, argued that the board ought to keep its hands off Birmingham for two reasons. First, hours of labor in Birmingham were a matter of "local custom" that the NWLB (in line with its own seventh principle) ought not to disturb. Second, the strike had created no production crisis in Birmingham mills necessitating government involvement. Divided by these arguments, members of the NWLB determined to send examiner Raymond Swing to the scene to ascertain facts in order that they might decide whether to intervene.[11]

The mere prospect of federal interference was greeted with anger by union opponents in Alabama. Since the UMW's 1917 organizing campaign, the Labor Department had found that "numerous citizens' committees, vigilantes or Ku Klux Klan agencies" had come into being to combat unions with Redbaiting and race-baiting tactics. Antiunion Alabamians had begun contending that German propaganda was "getting a hold on the negroes . . . using the miners' Union as a channel." The threatened entry of the NWLB further inflamed such opponents, and the reorganized Ku Klux Klan weighed in. Three days before the NWLB was to hear arguments in Washington on the Birmingham case, the Klan staged a march down the "Magic City's" streets. One hundred fifty robed horsemen distributed leaflets directed at steel strikers, calling them "idlers and disloyalists." "Be respectful of the flag," read the leaflets. "Aid by every means at your command the suppression of disloyalty by either speech or action. There is no neutral stand! Take heed and go to work! The eye of scrutiny is upon you." [12]

Amid this repressive atmosphere, Swing's arrival in Birmingham offered needed hope to the IUMMSW campaign. The union was able to use the promise of federal protection to overcome the fears of workers who otherwise may have been reluctant to expose themselves to retaliation by joining the union. This strategy was apparently successful. On May 26, the Birmingham Central Labor Council threw its support behind the IUMMSW drive, and Hale reported to union leaders in Washington that he was on the verge of organizing another local union of blacks. Swing confirmed the success of Hale's efforts, reporting huge audiences at meetings in black neighborhoods. [13]

IUMMSW successes in Birmingham, meanwhile, seemed to ignite interest in the union among the iron ore miners of Russellville in northern Alabama who supplied the Birmingham mills. The IUMMSW began organizing ore miners at Sloss-Sheffield and the Suwanee Iron Company in March 1918. On the day after the NWLB was formed, the miners submitted demands to these companies for an eight-hour day, union recognition, elimination of the company store, and an end to discrimination. Five hundred ore miners later backed up these demands with a strike that quickly prompted NWLB intervention. At a hearing in St. Louis on May 25, Taft and Walsh heard testimony that confirmed that ore miners' wages had stagnated since the war began, even as the price of iron ore doubled. An NWLB ruling delivered in August favored the miners, calling for a wage increase and improvements in company housing. "Peonage in Alabama and elsewhere has been given a blow by the National War Labor Board," exalted the *Cleveland Citizen*. [14]

Government action did seem to reshape the contours of labor organizing in Alabama, but only on the surface. Alabama unionists believed that the NWLB intervention in Russellville and Swing's presence in Birmingham had vindicated their loyalty to the Wilson administration. "The war has to a considerable extent straightened all of us out," the editors of the *Birmingham Labor Advocate* proclaimed on June 1, 1918. Managers of the steel companies seemed to agree on the significance of federal intervention. They fiercely lobbied employer members on the NWLB to have Swing recalled. But, unlike the unions, the steel companies drew confidence from that fact that leading Alabama Democrats such as Fortney Johnston stood with them and from the knowledge that the Wilson administration was itself divided on the strike. They knew, for example, that the U.S. attorney for the Birmingham district, W. Murray Reese, like much of the Wilson Justice Department, was scarcely a union supporter. Indeed, Reese actively worked to defeat the IUMMSW drive, going so far as to organize a vigilante campaign against it.[15]

Adding to the unionists' trouble was opposition they encountered from the leaders of Birmingham's black community. Most black leaders viewed the AFL as "white man's unionism," a force that would confirm the exclusion of blacks from skilled jobs. "Emphasizing the virtues of racial solidarity, thrift, and economic development," as Joe W. Trotter Jr. found West Virginia's black middle class doing during the same period, Birmingham's black leaders fought to retain the loyalty of black labor and to maintain their own positions as power brokers for their community. Thus, the *Workmen's Chronicle*, a newspaper published by Reverend P. Colfax Rameaux with funds from TCI, advised blacks to shun the AFL "as one would a rattlesnake." Rameaux urged his readers further to eschew the AFL's industrial democracy for "the industrial Christian Democracy" that is "the Kingdom of God." "The methods of our warfare for industrial Christian Democracy are not carnal—they are intellectual and spiritual," wrote Rameaux. If blacks would stay at work and help win the war, he argued, "we will have Industrial Christian Democracy throughout this land of Dixie." Meanwhile, Oscar W. Adams, editor of the black-owned *Birmingham Reporter*, and Reverend M. H. Mixon, the leader of Birmingham's A.M.E. church, both believed that the "majority of the laboring classes—men and women—are satisfied."[16]

The reports of Ulysses Hale and Raymond Swing, however, indicate that a growing number of black workers were ready to reject the advice of their community leaders and to join the strike by early June 1918. Whether the trend would continue, virtually all participants understood, depended on whether the federal government would really protect their rights. Unfortunately for the strike leaders, the government's inability to do that became clear by mid-June. By then vigilantes began descending on union meetings in black neighborhoods, parking cars with headlights shining on meetinghouse doors to take down the names of those who entered. Meetings were broken up in Tuxedo, Ensley, and Mason City. At Bessemer, unions succeeded in passing a municipal ordinance forbidding interference with labor meetings, but they could find no one to enforce it; and a black woman who owned a meeting hall in Avondale received a bomb threat because she allowed the IUMMSW to meet there. On June 7, the violence peaked when vigilantes kidnapped organizers Crough and Hale. Although they released Crough after a beating, they singled out Hale for terrorism. He was told that he "was preaching the industrial equality of the Negro and that this would cause labor unrest, which was unpatriotic." He was savagely beaten, bathed in tar and feathers, and turned loose with the warning that "the next time it will be a necktie affair." The attack suspended the IUMMSW effort in Birmingham. When word reached Russellville, ore miners staged a one-day strike to demand a federal investigation. The *Birmingham Labor Advocate*, meanwhile, blasted the men who committed "this outrage," and the AFL lodged a protest in Washington.[17]

In the breach, though, the NWLB failed to come through for the Birmingham steelworkers. As B. W. King had hoped, Raymond Swing, shocked by the racist violence, did plead with the NWLB to intervene formally in the case, despite the sniping of steel company lawyers, who attacked him for being more concerned "with the tarring of a negro organizer" than with winning the war. Frank Walsh, also outraged, demanded immediate action, as did each of the labor members of the NWLB. Yet formal intervention required a majority vote, and cochair Taft showed no interest in Birmingham. Two factors may have shaped Taft's view. First, although he often supported labor on the NWLB, he was no advocate for expansive federal intervention and remained unconvinced that the NWLB should take a case that seemed to challenge the "local customs" principle. Also, Taft's stand may have been influenced by his racial views. His NWLB correspondence reveals the former president to be less than sympathetic to the plight of black workers. His observations regarding the rewriting of the New Orleans streetcar decision and his occasional derogatory references to those such as "a man named Taylor, with partly negro blood, whose temper and roughness and profanity justified his discharge," certainly suggest as much. In any case, Taft never voiced support for intervening in Birmingham. He departed for his vacation before the final vote was taken, ensuring the outcome of the affair.[18]

With Taft's alternate Frederick Judson sitting in, the NWLB met on July 9 to discuss Birmingham. Employer members argued that intervention there was unnecessary and hence would violate NWLB principles. Victor Olander retorted that the "general situation of discontent, suspicion, hatred and distrust" that prevailed in Birmingham necessitated federal involvement. "I think there is a strike going on," Walsh added, "and I think that . . . it has been repressed by physical violence which is still being conducted, and therefore I think we ought to take jurisdiction of it." But, try as he might, Walsh could not convince Judson to side with him. A vote deadlocked the board six to six.

Lacking a majority for intervention, Lauck was forced to inform the Birmingham workers that they were on their own.[19]

The effect of the decision was devastating to unionists. On July 20, Frank Morrison dropped Ulysses Hale from the AFL payroll and judged that any further support for the Birmingham drive would be "a waste of money." By September, the Klan was marching down the streets of Montgomery to warn "slackers" to "work or fight," and there were no longer any Raymond Swings on hand to report their terrorism. Shortly thereafter, NWLB examiner Edwin Newdick reported that in Birmingham "the menace of race riots always present [had been] increased by employers' tactics." Back in Washington, union leaders were bitter. As Olander saw it, the decision sent a counterproductive message to workers: "If you want action from this Board, you must . . . show that you have the power and the strength and the will to stop war production." This lesson would only undermine the authority of labor leaders who were trying to keep down unrest, he warned.[20]

Thus did one of the most promising union efforts of the World War I era die aborning. Birmingham steelworkers, encouraged by wartime federal labor policies, had mounted an ambitious effort to organize the mills of their city only to see federal agencies fail them at the moment of truth.

THE SLUGGISH START OF THE NATIONAL COMMITTEE FOR ORGANIZING IRON AND STEEL WORKERS

A more ambiguous story was told in northern steel mills. Surely the most important mass union effort of the early twentieth century began among northern steelworkers during 1918. Few could have predicted it even a year earlier. When members of a federal labor union of furnace hands at Pittsburgh's Jones and Laughlin plant staged the first wartime steel strike in September 1917, idling as many as seven thousand Slovak, Serb, and Polish immigrants for more than three weeks, their walkout was easily broken. This failure again illustrated the factors that ensured that steelworkers would be among the last to demonstrate militancy during the war: their employers possessed vast power, and they themselves suffered from interunion squabbles. Unions of skilled workers, such as the Amalgamated Association of Iron, Steel, and Tin Workers (AAISTW), ignored unskilled furnace hands and others, leaving the job of unionizing them to the few AFL agents in the field who tried to organize catchall federal labor unions. Their ethnic heterogeneity, moreover, made it difficult to weld steelworkers into a single movement.[21]

By the summer of 1918, however, these inhibiting factors were counterbalanced by other developments, especially in those steel mills most closely tied to the war effort. Tightening labor markets, federal protection of the right to organize, and the war's own tendency to draw a multicultural workforce together around a common language of democratic citizenship laid the groundwork for the emergence of successful organizing efforts in steel mills. Among the first places where this became clear was in the plants of the Bethlehem Steel Company. No contractor was more important to the war effort than Bethlehem Steel. With mills spread across seven Pennsylvania cities, the company produced armor plate, naval guns, and shells for the Liberty fleet. Its massive South Bethlehem works was one of the most essential war production plants in the nation. And it was right there that wartime steel unionism first took root.

As the war began, unionism in South Bethlehem faced large obstacles. Wide gulfs between skilled and unskilled workers were accentuated by ethnic divisions. Bethlehem's skilled workers were disproportionately Pennsylvania Dutch and stood aloof from the largely eastern European immigrant workforce occupying unskilled positions. One-third of South Bethlehem's thirty thousand workers were foreign-born, among them large numbers of Hungarians, Slovaks, and Czechs. The arrival of African American workers as a result of the Great Migration, first to work in the company's Lehigh Coal and Coke subsidiary in Northampton, Pennsylvania, and later in South Bethlehem, added a new element of racial tension. And the employment of hundreds of women in South Bethlehem's light machine shops, where they assembled artillery cartridges, further stratified the workforce by gender.[22]

Adding to these problems was Bethlehem Steel's political power. Arch Johnson, the company's vice president, was mayor of Bethlehem during the war, and the city's police chief was a former member of the State Constabulary—the infamous "Cossacks" who helped break union efforts. The company's support of churches, community organizations, and the foreign-language press, meanwhile, kept these institutions largely within its orbit. During the first year of the war, company officials exerted an even tighter grip on workers' lives in the name of patriotism. Posters equating labor organizers with "hun" agents went up in Bethlehem workshops. And, according to one worker, it was "either you do as I tell you or you go in the trench." Since the company controlled local draft administrators, this was no idle threat.[23]

This repressive atmosphere began to crack during the spring of 1918. As in other industries, the federal war labor program helped open the door for change. Even as the NWLB's members were hammering out their principles, a movement began among skilled machinists and electricians at the South Bethlehem plant. It was led by David Williams, a machinist and veteran of a failed 1910 strike in Bethlehem. Williams's movement gained ground in the huge Machine Shops No. 2 and No. 4 at the Bethlehem works, which together employed as many as three thousand metal trades workers who machined naval guns. Bethlehem's machinists and electrical workers provided the core of union support in the plant. On March 23, 1918, electrical workers sent their first committee to demand a meeting with plant managers. They were rebuffed and labeled as "Reds" when they tried to hold a mass meeting with Bethlehem's workers to discuss the situation. But they were not dissuaded.[24]

Ironically, the Bethlehem company itself helped the metal trades toilers crystallize their movement. In April 1918, company officials, citing a backlog of war orders, announced that a ten-hour day would replace the eight-hour day then in effect in the machine shops. Workers immediately seized on the NWLB's eight-hour proviso to mount a campaign to reverse this plan. When Bethlehem officials ignored their demands and tried to implement the new policy on April 16, three thousand machinists struck. Unlike the Jones and Laughlin strikers of the previous year, however, the Bethlehem workers could claim that the government sanctioned their demands. This gave them a new edge. After two days the company gave in. And when they returned to work, the machinists took with them a new spirit of self-confidence. Days later, when managers again refused to meet a committee of workers, machinists decided to strike on May 1, 1918, laying claim to the NWLB's promise that workers had the right to bargain collectively with employers.[25]

A strike of machinists at the critical Bethlehem plant attracted immediate attention in Washington. When word arrived that electrical workers were planing a walkout that would further disrupt the plant's operation, pressure mounted for the NWLB to intervene over the objections of the company's notoriously antiunion president, Eugene Grace. On May 11, 1918, the NWLB decided to assume jurisdiction of the dispute, guaranteeing strikers that they would not be subject to discrimination if they went back to work in return for an NWLB investigation.

NWLB entry soon profoundly reshaped labor relations at Bethlehem. As they returned to work, the Bethlehem strikers made three demands that struck at the heart of the company's authority. They sought an end to discrimination against union members, recognition of shop committees, and the dismantling of the company's complicated bonus system, a scientific management plan intended to spur production. Machinists claimed that the bonus plan fostered an inhuman work pace and left workers in constant doubt about their earnings. Bethlehem Steel defended its position on each issue. Furthermore, Eugene Grace made clear his belief that the NWLB had no authority over his relations with his employees since he had not invited the board's mediation of any dispute. Ignoring Grace's objections, Lauck dispatched Frank Walsh's associate, William Harvey, to Bethlehem to investigate. Grace refused to meet Harvey, but Harvey, a veteran of both the USCIR and NLDC, refused to back down. He delivered a slashing condemnation of the company's actions to his superiors in Washington, calling Bethlehem "rankly seditious." He urged an immediate settlement along the lines sought by the unionists.[26]

Yet the NWLB found the Bethlehem case a sticky one to resolve. Armed with Harvey's report, Walsh lobbied on behalf of the workers. Employer members, predictably, opposed him. As in the Bridgeport case, employers were reluctant to allow the board to intrude on the organization of the work process itself—in this case by dissolving the bonus system. H. H. Rice of General Motors was given the responsibility of protecting management's interests by the board's employers. He was paired with Tom Savage of the IAM (Johnston's alternate) in hopes that they could negotiate a decision. They could not agree. When Jett Lauck tried to break the deadlock with a proposal that also called for an end to the bonus system, he was rebuffed by Taft. As it would later be on the Bridgeport case, the board was split down the middle.[27]

It was the militancy of the Bethlehem machinists that finally broke the deadlock. As the NWLB argued the case, Bethlehem workers continued to organize throughout June and July. Police Chief Davis did his best to stop them by prohibiting public meetings. With moral support from Harvey, Williams's machinists gained enough strength to threaten a larger strike near the end of July. The U.S. Army's Ordnance Department grew so concerned that it dispatched nearly thirty officers to investigate, and the machinists' threats finally did the trick. Fearing that another strike would cripple production at the key facility, the NWLB met on July 31 to work out a compromise.[28]

The initiative came from labor's side of the table. Savage and Walsh persuaded employer members to agree to an award that would "eliminate or revise" the bonus system. That language gave the award enough "elasticity" to persuade Taft's alternate, Frederick Judson, to support it. In addition, the labor members agreed to leave the setting of overtime rates for piece workers, a point of rancorous contention, to be determined later by an examiner appointed by the board. To induce their employer colleagues to accept the award, the labor men also agreed to delay the payment of any wage increases that might come from a revision of the bonus system. In return the unions received protection against discrimination, the establishment of shop committees under NWLB supervision, and the creation of a local mediation board to supervise collective bargaining at the plant and negotiate many of the award's open provisions, including the length of the workday. In an unusual show of unity, the NWLB unanimously adopted the award on July 31, 1918.[29]

The award did not immediately grant the demands of the Bethlehem ma-

Arnold, E. W.	X	Lynch, William	X
Bachman, Ray	X	Martin, George	X
Blidberg, Adolph	X	McConlogue, Thomas	X
Bowe, Edwin	X	McLean, Everett F.	
Brown, Thomas G.	X	Mikitz, S.	X
Carr, George W	X	Mills, Agnes	X
Connelly, L. P.	X	Plank, William	X
Cox, Robert	X	Sabal, P. P.	X
Crossman, H. E.	X	Semprini, Edgar	X
Dower, James D.	X	Silfies, Warren	X
Erdman, Ray B.	X	Souders, Louis	X
Huber, Harry H.	X	Stein, W. W.	X
Hulshizer, Charles	X	Suter, Rose	X
Judd, Joseph	X	Woodring, T. A.	X

Directions to Voters

Place cross (X) opposite the names of the 27 persons whom you wish to serve as members of the committee.

(Two of the 27 must be women.)

The right to vote is limited to those who were in the employ of the company Aug. 31, 1918.

Those not wishing to vote for persons whose names are on the ballot may write other names in blank spaces provided.

(Additional space for names on back page.)

NWLB shop committee ballot, Machine Shop No. 4 DU, Bethlehem Steel Company, October 17, 1918. Note that the NWLB required voters to pick at least two women. Voters in this shop were also required to eliminate at least one nominee from their list. Eighty-eight percent of voters joined this one in skipping over the same man, Everett F. McLean. Such lopsided tallies were the norm in NWLB shop committee elections. This is one important measure of the degree to which union activists were able to control the elections by recommending delegate slates. (NWLB Records, National Archives, Washington, D.C.)

chinists, but the labor members still saw it as a significant victory. This may have had a great deal to do with its timing, for the award set a precedent for the right to bargain collectively at precisely the moment when steelworkers were rousing themselves. The strikes at Bethlehem Steel in April and May 1918 marked a turning point for trade unionism in steel. Even before the NWLB rendered a decision in the Bethlehem case, its examiners were scrambling from one steel mill to another to settle walkouts and to address the complaints of organizing workers. Moreover, the NWLB's award followed by a few weeks the AFL's approval of the Chicago Federation of Labor's proposal for a joint organizing campaign in steel; and it preceded by one day the meeting at Chicago's New Morrison Hotel that founded the National Committee for Organizing Iron and Steel Workers (NCOISW) under the direction of John Fitzpatrick and William Z. Foster.

At the time, the Bethlehem award certainly seemed to be a harbinger of a swelling tide of organization. NWLB records reveal the dimensions of the remarkable union movement that emerged in steel during June and July 1918. Within weeks, Pennsylvania plants were swept by agitation. Workers at Lebanon Valley Iron Company, Midvale Steel's Nicetown plant, the American Steel Works in Franklin, Eastern Steel in Pottsville, Bethlehem's North Lebanon plant, and Steelton all either struck or threatened to do so, precipitating NWLB intervention. Illinois and Ohio saw several strikes or threatened walkouts. The spreading union spirit even restored the withered AAISTW; the long-dormant union sprang to life, threatening a strike at the Reading Iron Company and leading two others in Ohio.[30]

Steelworker organizing was well under way by the time the NCOISW took shape. Though no records of its founding meeting survive, it is fair to speculate that the union leaders involved in the effort were encouraged by federal intervention in steel. The NCOISW was the brainchild of Foster and Fitzpatrick, each of whom had been instrumental in organizing Chicago stockyard workers under the Alschuler decision. Foster envisioned a federation of AFL unions that could accomplish the same goal in steel, the "masterclock of the whole war program." Walsh's ascension to the NWLB provided Foster an important ally in that effort. At the AFL convention in mid-June, Foster moved a resolution calling for the mass organization of steelworkers by a committee that would skirt the hoary jurisdictional squabbles that pitted union against union in the industry. Foster was surprised by the lack of opposition to his plan. "Everybody seemed to realize that now is the appointed time to do this big job," he concluded. Fitzpatrick was named temporary chair of the NCOISW, and Foster, its secretary. Foster promptly informed his Washington ally of what was in store. "Prospects look good for a big steel campaign," he told Frank Walsh following the convention.[31]

Unfortunately for Foster, however, the influence of Frank Walsh and the NWLB may have inadvertently sidetracked the NCOISW. For while the actions of Walsh and staffers such as William Harvey made the mass organization of steelworkers a real possibility, they may have also stiffened the resolve of craft union leaders who were unwilling to cede too much power to the joint NCOISW effort. Such leaders as Michael Tighe of the AAISTW were reluctant to commit resources to an umbrella organization, particularly when their own organizers began making steady progress under the NWLB. From the outset, the AAISTW's organ, the *Amalgamated Journal*, had followed the NWLB, reprinting and circulating its charter and principles and crediting federal policy for helping make an evident change in the attitude of steelworkers. "The toiler has been lost in a very thick fog," one union official noted, "but at last that fog is rising." In this heady atmosphere, Foster found it difficult to get Tighe and other union heads to cooperate.[32]

Ironically, then, the favorable atmosphere for organizing may have ensured that the NCOISW got off to a slow start. In Foster's estimation, the conference that founded the NCOISW, held on the day after the Bethlehem decision, "failed dismally." The steel unions assessed themselves a paltry one hundred dollars each to finance the effort, furnishing only "a corporal's guard of organizers." The AAISTW contributed less than twelve thousand dollars to the NCOISW over the next sixteen months; this was less than 4 percent of what the union reaped in initiation fees during that same period. Why should Tighe and the other craft union leaders have acted otherwise? Following the Chicago meeting, they continued to see their memberships grow and the principle of collective bargaining advance under the NWLB. On August 21, the board rendered a decision calling for shop committees at Pollack Steel in Cincinnati. Three weeks later a favorable award was delivered at A. M. Byers in Girard, Ohio, where the AAISTW had filed a complaint. The promise of victories in other mills was also on the horizon. Foster was embittered by the turn of events. As he later put it, the "original plan of a dashing offensive went to smash . . . and with it, likewise, the opportunity to organize the steel industry."[33]

Of course, by the time the armistice was signed, events proved that craft unionists had been unwise in withholding support for Foster's effort. Since mid-September 1918, employers who initially cooperated with federal agencies were increasingly dragging their heels and hoping that an armistice would rescue them. The first sign of resistance was visible at South Bethlehem, where the steel union movement had experienced its first big victory less than two months earlier. Bethlehem Steel simply refused to carry out the provisions of the NWLB award. The company stalled the shop committee elections, refused to meet workers' representatives, and fired sixteen IBEW members by September. Initially, the NWLB provided little relief. The philosophy of Lucien Chaney, the first examiner assigned to the Bethlehem case, made him atypical among NWLB staffers. He shared Bethlehem president Eugene Grace's suspicion of unions and refused to meet formally with their representatives. Ultimately, the NWLB had to send in Raymond Swing, fresh from his mission in Alabama, to repair the situation. But Swing could not get the company to implement the award either. A standoff developed, and two days before the government commandeered Smith and Wesson, machinists and electricians threatened a strike unless the government seized their plant.[34]

Because the Bethlehem crisis coincided with crises at Smith and Wesson and at Bridgeport, Eugene Grace had some leverage. Grace bet that the NWLB would do almost anything to avoid another major confrontation in September 1918. And he was right. As in other serious confrontations with

NWLB authority, the board's cochairs initially closed ranks to demand compliance with their decision. Walsh and Judson drafted a telegram to Grace on September 11, demanding that he implement their award. But Grace was ready to outmaneuver them. He came to Washington on September 13, the same day the government seized Smith and Wesson. No doubt realizing that the administration would be loathe to inflict the same punishment on him—thereby giving ammunition to those critics who charged that President Wilson was moving the nation toward some form of socialism—Grace offered to implement the NWLB decision on one condition. Bethlehem Steel would accept collective bargaining through shop committees, he said, only if the government picked up the tab. The company would bargain over the bonus system if it were reimbursed for any losses it might incur as a result. To justify this stand, Grace claimed that Bethlehem Steel had barely turned a profit in 1917—an amazingly brazen assertion.[35]

Grace's gambit paid off. NWLB labor members were anxious to get compliance without another controversial plant seizure. Behind closed doors, the board debated the offer. Sensing their strength, employer members raised another issue. They were concerned about the creation of a local mediation board to oversee the Bethlehem shop committees. They wanted assurances that shop committees would not undermine management authority. The union members were stunned that their colleagues would consider injecting a new issue into the controversy. "If you don't put that Award into effect immediately," one of them warned, "you are going to create a psychology there and every place where the Awards of this Board won't amount to anything." But the employer members held the high cards. It was either accept Grace's offer or hope that President Wilson might do to Bethlehem Steel what he had done to Smith and Wesson. That latter course, however, seemed unlikely, and union leaders well realized that unless some action were taken, workers would "pooh pooh this Board and its power," as one of them put it. So in the end the NWLB caved in to Grace's blackmail. Desperate to get raises for their members and compliance with their award, the NWLB's union members agreed to a compromise that was distasteful in the extreme. Accordingly, Taft and Walsh drafted a letter to the War Department on September 17 asking that the government subsidize raises at Bethlehem, a request that was accepted.[36]

Grace's successful game of brinkmanship only stiffened resistance against the wartime union movement in steel. Encouraged by the victory of their colleague, steel manufacturers prepared to undermine the movement by addressing two points that were crucial to the war labor program: the questions of the eight-hour day and collective bargaining. One week after Grace's appearance before the NWLB, Felix Frankfurter of the War Labor Policies Board met with Judge Elbert Gary of U.S. Steel to discuss the eight-hour question. The meeting, Frankfurter thought, yielded nothing. Days later, however, on September 25, Gary made a surprise announcement. The basic eight-hour workday would go into effect at U.S. Steel on October 1, 1918. Steelworkers won a major concession even before they had begun to organize in large numbers. Other steel companies soon followed suit. It was a brilliant "counterstroke," according to Foster. "Although this concession really spelled a great moral victory for the unions its practical effect was bad," he later wrote, for it robbed organizers of a powerful issue and it proved difficult for the unions to claim credit for this victory.[37]

On another front, steelmakers moved with alacrity to take the issue of industrial democracy away from the unions by exploiting the ambiguities of federal policy regarding collective bargaining. Although Judge Gary himself was not enthusiastic about employee representation, other steelmakers saw its uses and began to experiment with company unionism as a way of derailing something worse. Ironically, NWLB shop committees helped inspire these employers, and they soon sprang into action to implement their own version of the shop committees that the NWLB had been promoting. The first steelmaker to do so was William B. Dickson of Midvale Steel, who acted within days of Grace's victory over the NWLB. Dickson gambled that employee representation plans, administered free of government interference, could help stifle union spirit among employees and that federal resolve would not be strong enough to resist a company-sponsored form of collective bargaining. Acting on that belief, on September 22 Midvale Steel announced the formation of an employee representation plan hastily drafted by Dickson to avoid the tacit unionization of Midvale through meddlesome NWLB shop committees. Dickson's strategy worked. Elections at Midvale were supervised by foremen who also ran as delegates, and the resulting shop committees offered workers no avenue of appeal for their grievances other than to management. Workers expressed skepticism about the Midvale committees. Mill helper Paul McCleester of Midvale's Cambria plant, for one, felt that there was "something loose about the plan." But when Midvale machinists asked the NWLB to condemn Dickson's plan, the board's investigation bogged down, reaching no conclusion by the time of the armistice. A number of employers took heart from Dickson's experiment and considered following suit.[38]

At Bethlehem, meanwhile, the NWLB's award was implemented too late in the war for it to have any great effect in promoting the unionization of the plant. Shop committee elections were finally held in October 1918 in Bethlehem under the supervision of eight NWLB staffers. Enthusiasm ran high among employees during balloting, with turnout ranging as high as 92 per-

Midvale Steel workers assemble for a patriotic rally outside their plant. Speakers on the podium stand below the flags of all the allied nations, ca. 1918. (National Archives II, College Park, Maryland)

cent in some departments. Union delegates won in every department where they ran. Machine Shop Nos. 2 and 4, where the organizing had begun the previous spring, illustrated the strength of the union. In the sixteen departments of those shops, all 117 delegates elected to the shop committee were union members. Unskilled workers, immigrants, and women also participated enthusiastically in the elections. Staffers were particularly impressed by the enthusiasm with which immigrants voted. "I can say 'make a cross here' in seven different languages," one staffer remarked after the voting ended. According to another, the mood in the plant had been "changed entirely" by the voting. No one would ever really know, however, for the war ended before the NWLB shop committees began work.[39]

As the armistice was signed on November 11, steel unionism had as yet made little progress. After that date, the NWLB would be unable to protect its shop committees at Bethlehem from managerial domination or to guarantee the rights of any other steelworkers to organize. Meanwhile, the kind of employer-dominated shop committee pioneered by Midvale Steel was being taken up by other employers. Soon after the armistice, one of the cruel ironies that marked steelworker organizing during the war was becoming clear. The same NWLB decision for shop committee elections at Bethlehem that had given the supporters of the NCOISW such hope in July 1918 had also planted the seed of company unionism in the industry.

In October 1918, the NCOISW finally began an effort to break into the open-shop Pennsylvania steel mills. It had lost precious time, however, and the gods that had been "fighting on the side of labor" during the war, as William Foster put it, did not do so for long. Steelworkers would still make a courageous effort to organize their mills after the war, an effort culminating in the Great Strike that began on September 22, 1919. But, as the most astute observers understood, the limits of industrial democracy in steel had been determined long before that strike began.[40]

A LOST OPPORTUNITY IN TEXTILES

If the difficulties of coordinating the many craft unions that joined the NCOISW can be partly blamed for the failure of steel unionism to get a fast start during the war, no such problem afflicted textile workers. Still, their efforts at mass organization yielded meager results. The AFL granted jurisdiction to one textile union, the United Textile Workers (UTW), a union that contained both craft union locals of skilled workers, such as mulespinners or loomfixers, and industrial union locals of weavers and other semiskilled and unskilled workers. The UTW was led by two conservatives, John Golden, a former mulespinner who had emigrated from England and risen to the union's presidency as a Gompers loyalist and member of the antisocialist Militia of Christ, and Sara Conboy, its secretary-treasurer.[41]

Despite its sole jurisdiction in textiles, the UTW had made little organizing headway before the war. As late as 1914, the union spoke for only slightly more than 2 percent of all textile workers. Organizing in textiles continued to stumble on several factors: the movement of yarn mills to the nonunion South, an ethnically polyglot workforce in the Northeast, and long-standing divisions between skilled and unskilled workers. Nor had the UTW proved effective in bridging those gaps. While nearly one-half of the workers in the industry were women, they made up only 10 percent of delegates to UTW conventions during this period. The union was as slow to reach out to immigrants as to women. In the textile-rich state of Rhode Island, only two of seventeen UTW local officers had French Canadian or Franco-Belgian surnames as the war began, even though workers of these nationalities predominated in the state's mills. Moreover, UTW industrial locals were few and far between. In Rhode Island only three of seventeen locals were organized on an industrial basis.[42]

But wartime brought the opportunity for growth to the long-dormant UTW. Added to the factors that favored other unions during the war—labor shortages, cost-plus contracts, the propaganda of industrial democracy—the UTW possessed one more. On the NWLB sat an ally with a special interest in seeing the UTW grow: Thomas Rickert of its sister union, the United Garment Workers. There were indications in 1918 that the UTW would exploit these fortuitous circumstances to its advantage, as the union ballooned in membership and made some large gains in the South. The most important wartime victory came in August when nearly three thousand members joined an industrial union local of the UTW at the Swift spinning mills in Columbus, Georgia. Swift had responded by locking out those workers and recruiting scabs. Mill workers had battled back, forming a posse, mobbing the sheriff's deputies, and breaking their guns into pieces. To quell the disturbance, two companies of U.S. Army troops were dispatched, and the NWLB entered the dispute. NWLB intervention quickly salvaged the strike for the union. The UTW emerged with a settlement that granted most of its demands and consolidated a thriving local of five thousand members.[43]

What happened in Columbus, however, was not repeated on a larger scale. During the war the UTW never launched the kind of industrial organization in northern textile mills that many of its supporters hoped it would, even when opportunities arose for the union to do so. What illustrated this failure best was the union's inability to capitalize on a July 1918 strike of New England loomfixers that drew the support of thousands of semiskilled and unorganized weavers, a strike that also precipitated NWLB intervention.

This episode began in May 1918 when John Golden wrote to New England mill owners on behalf of the UTW's loomfixers—the elite mechanics who maintained mill machinery—demanding a 15 percent pay increase and threatening a strike if the demand was not met. Encouraged by the war labor administration's defense of the right to organize and determined to use their privileged positions in the mills to win what they could, these mechanics grew restless when the owners refused to concede over the following two months. The fact that mills in Lowell, Massachusetts, and Manchester, New Hampshire, proffered 10 percent increases to stave off the strike only whetted the appetites of these workers. They decided to strike to force the issue. On July 1, 1918, then, an unparalleled strike of loomfixers from Rhode Island to New Hampshire shocked the industry.[44]

The strike was effective. Focusing on mills in Rhode Island, Lowell, and Manchester, it threatened to idle thousands of textile workers. Nearly six hundred loomfixers walked out of twenty-five Rhode Island mills alone. Mills could not function indefinitely deprived of skilled maintenance workers. Making matters worse for the textile manufacturers were signs that the strike might spread beyond the ranks of the loomfixers. In Lowell, eighteen hundred weavers followed the loomfixers out, demanding that their grievances also be heard. Weavers also joined the strike at the giant Amoskeag complex in Manchester, prompting the largest walkout in thirty-two years at that plant. Enthusiasm for the union was particularly strong among semiskilled Polish and French-Canadian operatives at Amoskeag. Within a day more than thirty-five hundred of them struck. Immigrant operatives so swelled the strike meetings at Manchester's St. Cecilia's Hall in the following days that overflow crowds stood in the streets. By July 6, the UTW had received five thousand applications for membership in the union, which represented nearly a third of the Amoskeag force.[45]

Reports of the spreading strike alarmed Washington. NWLB secretary W. Jett Lauck, struggling to deal with a strike wave that seemed to spread from one New England industry to another, beseeched Gompers to end this "indefensible" walkout, explaining that the NWLB was swamped with work. In truth, it was unlikely that either Gompers or Golden could have stopped the strike had they wanted. With their labor in heavy demand, the loomfixers were not anxious to return to work until all their demands were met. They ignored Lauck's plea. And because the NWLB was so busy dealing with other cases, officials from the War Department decided to step in. Secretary Baker enlisted financier Henry B. Endicott, of the Massachusetts Committee on Public Safety, as a mediator. Endicott, who had settled major shipyard and coal-hauling strikes in Massachusetts in 1917, enjoyed the trust of both the manufacturers and the UTW. After only four days, he awarded the Lowell workers the 15 percent wage increase they desired and stipulated that future disputes be mediated by the NWLB. He settled the walkout in New Hampshire two days later according to the same terms. Thus, after only a week on the picket lines, Lowell and Manchester loomfixers returned to work with their demands met. Apparently, the union then suspended its organizing efforts among the weavers in those cities. It was a fateful precedent.[46]

The Endicott award did not settle the strike in Rhode Island. Mill owners in Providence and the Blackstone Valley proved intransigent in their resistance to the union. Rebuffing the overtures of Endicott, they preferred to "fight their own battles." NWLB mediation was also anathema. "What the War Labor Board should do, and do that very promptly," advised their trade journal, "is to pick out the ringleaders in the strike and send them to Camp Devens where the rigid training and the prospect of early shipment to France would give them a new viewpoint." Contending that they had raised wages significantly in recent months, mill owners dug in to resist the loomfixers' demands. Because the Rhode Island manufacturers refused mediation, a majority on the NWLB would not consider intervening in the controversy unless it could be demonstrated that production lagged as a result of the walkout. This factor shaped the rest of the course of the strike.[47]

The strike in Rhode Island soon became an endurance contest, and it was not long before UTW leaders understood that winning their demands would require enlisting weavers in the fight. Unless operatives joined the walkout in sufficient numbers to impair production, forcing NWLB intervention, mill owners might wait out the loomfixers. Yet, as recent experiences had shown, immigrant operatives were more than ready to join the fight if the union provided encouragement. As they had in Lowell and Manchester, once the loomfixers walked out, Rhode Island weavers also responded enthusiastically to the strike. The union estimated that four thousand operatives stayed away from the mills in the first days of the loomfixers' fight.[48]

The UTW soon found Rhode Island operatives quite eager to organize. Union fever spread along the densely packed mill towns of Rhode Island's Blackstone River, as textile workers seized what one UTW official described as "the only means at their command to obtain a wage sufficient to enable them to live as self-respecting citizens and examples of . . . Americanism." Solidarity had rarely characterized relations between textile operatives and loomfixers. Nor had the war magically created solidarity where there was none, as one Lawrence operative made clear. "If you do not buy [Liberty bonds]," she reported, "the loomfixer puts the belt off your loom, and you cannot work." Still, the July strike made it advisable for the UTW loomfixers to make common cause with the unorganized. So when weavers and beamtenders in Pawtucket requested organizers, the union quickly complied. And when it became clear that the strike would drag on, the union made a concerted effort to attract mill operatives. Within two weeks, organizing efforts were under way in the villages of Ashton and Berkeley, where immigrant weavers warmly received union organizers. Their response far exceeded the expectations of UTW vice president Thomas McMahon, who had come to feel that there was "more inclination to have unionism among the so-called foreign workers" than among the native-born mill workers.[49]

The UTW made a special effort to organize immigrant operatives during late July 1918. The union sent two organizers, a Pole named Antoni Janiec and a French Canadian named Horace A. Riviere, through the mill towns.

Janiec and Riviere received a hearty welcome. On July 17, three hundred Polish and French Canadian workers held a meeting in Jacques Cartier Hall in Manville to listen to them. That meeting was followed by several gatherings of French Canadians. By July 24, Portuguese workers also began joining the movement, and newspapers reported that "many Syrian, Armenian, and Greek workers became organized" as well. Mass meetings soon spread northward up the Blackstone Valley from Providence to Woonsocket and across the Narragansett Bay to Warren. Such meetings were occasionally followed by spontaneous walkouts, swelling the size of the overall strike. Manufacturers responded with repression. Evictions from company housing occurred in some towns. Police broke up solidarity marches, and officers demanded to see the draft cards of union picketers outside the mills. Some War Department officials, meanwhile, publicly disparaged the strikers' patriotism. The walkout spread nonetheless. By early August, the UTW estimated that over eight thousand workers, including several thousand immigrant operatives, were striking twenty-eight Rhode Island mills.[50]

From the beginning, though, it seemed that UTW president Golden was more interested in gaining NWLB intervention than in organizing immigrant weavers. Golden skillfully exploited the walkout of the operatives, threatening soon to put every textile worker in the state on the streets. He even went to Rhode Island on July 7 to direct the strike personally. Meanwhile, he pleaded with his allies on the NWLB to intervene. In mid-July, at Golden's suggestion, strikers voted to submit their case to the NWLB. Frank Walsh tried to get his brethren on the board interested. But the NWLB did not ultimately take action until mid-August, when the strike had attracted the support of still more weavers, significantly impeding production in the mills. On August 19, after more than seven weeks on strike, Rhode Island workers finally returned to their mills as the NWLB took up their case. Mill owners meanwhile pledged that they would not discriminate against union members. Once Golden secured the involvement of the NWLB, however, his interest in organizing operatives clearly waned. Newspapers carried no further reports of union meetings in the region. Nor did new dues-paying industrial union locals join the UTW. This reversal of course proved portentous.[51]

Suspending its efforts to organize weavers and placing its hopes in the NWLB in August 1918 was a tactical blunder for the union. Rhode Island manufacturers, it turned out, were well prepared to test the resolve of the NWLB during the autumn of 1918, when employers everywhere, fearful of government encroachment, began to fight back. First, mill owners, with the aid of the NWLB's employer members, succeeded in delaying their hearing before the board. Soon thereafter, they began systematically to fire more than sixty union activists who had helped organize the July strike. Although the union protested to Washington, mill owners continued to act with impunity. When the NWLB finally did hold hearings on the case in Providence on October 11, 1918, mill owners, thanks to their allies on the board, were able to secure yet another delay and a change in NWLB procedure that made it more difficult for textile workers to bring complaints before the government.[52]

In the context of a managerial counteroffensive against federal intervention across several industries, and without a strong organization among Rhode Island's semiskilled mill operatives, the UTW lacked leverage in Washington. Its claims languished before the NWLB. After two months of inaction, textile workers' faith in the government began to erode. By the time the armistice was signed, many workers were reaching the conclusion that only another strike would bring "quick action" on their demands, but the impulse toward mass organization had dissipated as quickly as it had arisen.[53]

If any faith in the NWLB remained among Rhode Island workers, it evaporated in the weeks following the armistice. As in other industries, the coming of peace sparked a full-scale managerial counteroffensive. Confident that the NWLB would soon be defunct, Rhode Island employers blatantly defied its authority. When one group of operatives approached a mill superintendent with a petition of grievances, as NWLB guidelines required that they do, they were told to "wipe your ——— with that paper." In the two months following the armistice, employers stepped up discriminatory firings. Nor did the NWLB effectively resist the onslaught. No decision calling for shop committee elections—the vehicle that aided unionization in other settings—was ever issued in the Rhode Island case. By January 1919 the UTW's wartime gains had been effectively scotched in Rhode Island. As the labor conflicts of that year began, the union was far weaker in New England mills than friends of industrial unionism had imagined it would be.[54]

INSTITUTIONAL SOURCES OF STIMULUS AND RESTRAINT

America's participation in World War I gave rise to impressive mass union movements in basic industries, but ultimately wartime did not see industrial unionists entrench their gains. Hundreds of thousands of unorganized mass production workers were drawn into the ranks of the AFL during this period, and the federation's unions stepped closer toward industrial organization than they ever had before; but as the war ended, some mass organizing campaigns were still struggling to get off the ground, whereas others had already collapsed. To be sure, the mass union impulse would spill into the postwar period, continuing to gain ground until disastrous postwar strikes in such industries as steel and meatpacking ultimately stifled it. But in many ways its trajectory had been determined by what had and had not happened during the war.

Several factors inhibited the consolidation of mass unions. The most obvious may have been the opposition of employers, but equally significant may have been the role that craft union leaders played. Union leaders such as Michael Tighe and John Golden proved that while wartime conditions helped stimulate industrial unionism, they did not necessarily undermine craft unions or the vision that guided them. In the end, craft unionists showed themselves to be more concerned with their own narrow institutional interests than with organizing the unorganized. Instead of provoking a crisis that may have led them to look beyond craft unionism, wartime brought opportunities that encouraged craft unionists to hold on to what they had.

Just as important was the role that the federal government played. Even at its strongest—as in an agency such as the NWLB—wartime federal intervention was neither consistent nor powerful enough to force open-shop employers to tolerate the growth of mass unions within their factories. In Birmingham, Bethlehem, or the Blackstone Valley, government protection was a prerequisite for the mobilization of workers. Yet government intervention proved to be insufficient. How could it have been otherwise? The fervent hopes of Frank Walsh aside, the war labor apparatus had been created to ensure labor peace, not the organization of mass industry. No political will to the contrary had been brought to bear in Washington. Thus emergency war labor agencies, created by executive order rather than bipartisan legislation and composed of warring employers and trade unionists, ultimately proved to be tantalizingly unreliable instruments through which industrial unionists might advance their plans.

Writing shortly after the armistice in *Reconstruction*, the journal edited by Socialist Allan Benson, Charles Wood argued that had "the war continued, labor must have gone on to more and more collective control of industry," and America in a short time would have "evolved into a pure industrial democracy." Whether Wood was right is arguable. But what cannot be denied is that by the time the armistice arrived, mass unionism had already begun to reach its limits. Wartime did see the battle for industrial democracy extended into mass production workplaces, as Frank Walsh and others had hoped. But it did not see workers or unions successfully democratize mass industry. And that failure helped determine the course of events following the war.[55]

RECONSTRUCTION
AND REACTION

7

For months, that word spelled a new world to me.

For months it suggested . . . a new deal all around,

a square deal all around. But now I see my mistake.

Reconstruction used to be the slogan of progress.

Now it is the watchword of reaction.

—Sam Lavit, 1919

Early on November 8, 1918, a whistle atop the GE complex in Schenectady roared with the news of peace in Europe. In minutes, reported the local newspaper, "hatless men in overalls with the grime of the shop still on their hands touching elbows with girls in bloomers and aprons" fell in line behind plant manager G. E. Emmons and a dozen men carrying a huge American flag. The factory shut down as workers and managers flowed out to celebrate on Schenectady's streets. Only later did they learn that the news of peace was premature; the war would continue for three more days. In a way, the "false armistice" that provoked raucous demonstrations throughout the country was a fitting epitaph for the rocky wartime détente in American industry. There, war also continued. The employers and trade unionists who had once rallied around Wilsonian labor policies found that those policies had scarcely ended their conflicts. So if workers and managers could join hands to celebrate a shared victory in November 1918, their celebrations were destined to be cut short. Rather than basking in labor peace, American industry braced itself for a bitter storm, with trade unionists reminding workers who had "been fighting for democracy" that there would be "no peace until you have obtained . . . industrial democracy."[1]

Few trade unionists anticipated just how far off peace was on those terms. Everywhere one looked in November 1918, evidence of labor's triumphs abounded. Membership in the AFL rivaled in numbers the army that the United States had sent to Europe. Where unions were established before the war, they had increased their power. And, where they previously had a weak foothold, they had made important inroads. Too, labor enjoyed a closer relationship with the Wilson administration than even the most fervent trade union Democrats might have predicted two years earlier. As the war ended, many administration officials joined Secretary of the Navy Josephus Daniels in crediting the "wise attitude" of the AFL's leaders for the U.S. victory. Nor was this sentiment confined to the administration. Because the AFL backed the war, its patriotism was beyond reproach, and the federation enjoyed vastly greater acceptance at war's end than at its start. So long a marginal force, labor now seemed to one commentator to have achieved "a moral and political strengthening" that would leave it "more entrenched in American life than it has ever been before."[2]

What better symbolized labor's arrival than the role trade unionists and their allies had played in designing war labor policies in Washington? Their handiwork had already paid enormous dividends, boosting union membership and—thanks to wartime repression of the IWW—confirming the AFL's control of the labor movement. "The labor policy of President Wilson's administration during the War," Frank T. Carlton predicted, would "mark a new epoch in the history of organized labor in America." That this epoch would firmly ensconce unions in Washington as well as in the workplace seemed certain enough to void the ancient warnings of the labor movement's voluntarists. "If this is what government control means," remarked one railway unionist at the end of the war, "let us have more and plenty of it." In partnership with a solicitous Democratic administration, labor evidently had crossed the Rubicon.[3]

American labor's gains were in keeping with trends in other combatant nations. In each nation reports confirmed that union organization surged during the war. Viewing the course of events throughout the West, British economist John A. Hobson predicted that the postwar era would see the laboring classes complete their efforts to "conquer the state" and usher in true democracy. As time would tell, however, American gains would be more ephemeral than those made by the workers of other Western nations.[4]

Indeed, in the postwar United States, Hobson's prediction regarding a workers' takeover of the state spoke to a reality that existed only in the fevered brains of Red-baiting, open-shop employers or the poignant dreams of hopelessly isolated revolutionaries. Far from attempting its takeover, American unionists learned anew how profoundly dependent they remained on the state. And they were reminded again of the degree to which their goals remained hostage to larger political forces.

Within months of the armistice, a multisided political struggle unfolded that would determine American labor-management relations for more than a decade and influence those relations for many years beyond that. This struggle dealt a series of stunning blows to those who had hoped to advance a vision of industrial democracy rooted in trade union collective bargaining, and it all but smashed the hopes of those who sought something more radical. In quick succession these blows fell. The war labor agencies that had promoted democracy in industry collapsed; the opponents of state regulation mobilized successfully in the electoral arena; planning for postwar "reconstruction" unraveled; the administration failed in its efforts to broker a postwar labor settlement; and Frank Walsh's influential circle of left-wing progressives split from their allies in the Democratic Party and themselves fell into disarray. These blows so radically restructured the political landscape by the end of 1919 that it was barely recognizable to those laborites who had believed only three years earlier that "pretty nearly anything" was possible for "radicalism and real democracy."

THE WITHERING AWAY OF THE STATE

The impact of peacetime on federal regulation of the workplace was first evident within the most powerful war labor agency, the NWLB. By November 11, the board had a backlog of close to four hundred cases that it was struggling to address. The overload was due in part to the stalling tactics of the board's employer members, who by the autumn of 1918 had come to believe that its decisions were breaking down the open shop. These employers responded by attempting to delay decisions whenever possible. Frank Walsh had grown increasingly frustrated with their obstructionism. "The employing members upon this Board, so far as their official duties are concerned, have absolutely failed," Walsh told his friend Victor Olander. "Without exception, they have sat like hawks upon the Board to pounce down upon any person making an effort to ameliorate the conditions of workers any place." Frustration had also developed among workers. By October 1918, one Chicago machinist concluded that he didn't know of "a better method for killing off a strike" than to give it to the NWLB. Even Walsh's ally John Fitzpatrick agreed. "The Board is not composed of supporters of labor," he concluded, "but of labor baiters and . . . crushers."[5]

The armistice allowed employers to weaken the NWLB further. Established by wartime executive order, it rested on an uncertain foundation. Although the board could technically continue until the war was ended by the ratification of a peace treaty, employers called for its quick termination. The board's supporters feared its demise. Thus, in a desperate attempt to salvage the NWLB for the postwar era, Frank Walsh and his friend Basil Manly drafted an ambitious plan to preserve its contribution to industrial life. They presented this plan on November 20, during a series of NWLB executive sessions in which employers and labor leaders argued over the future of the board. The Walsh-Manly plan was couched as a proposal that would allow the NWLB to dispense of its backlog quickly. But the employers who heard it must have seen its striking similarities to the USCIR report Walsh and Manly had authored three years earlier.

The Walsh-Manly plan called for the NWLB to lump together all the cases that remained on its docket and to issue a sweeping finding calling for shop committee elections in each company from which it had received a complaint. Shop committees elected under this finding would be empowered to bargain with management in line with the NWLB's principles. The NWLB, in turn, would act as a court of appeals, ruling on any impasses. The proposal could scarcely have been more dramatic. If adopted, it would have extended NWLB shop committees into hundreds of new workplaces, creating a national, federally supervised, collective bargaining apparatus that reached into virtually every corner of industry.

The import of the resolution was not lost on either Taft or the NWLB's employers. They were determined to kill it. Taft was loathe to see an emergency agency intrude into workplaces in peacetime, and employers had seen enough of NWLB shop committees. Still, Walsh used every device in trying to cajole Taft into joining him once more. He argued first that NWLB-created shop committees might save employers from a fate they detested more: having to recognize unions. But no one—least of all Walsh—really believed that federally administered shop committees would forestall unionism as much as they would foster it. In an attempt to strengthen his case, Walsh warned that the "wave of ultraradicalism sweeping through the world" could soon hit America if significant reforms such as those he proposed were not forthcoming. But the fear of "ultraradicalism" was more effectively employed by labor's enemies than by its advocates in the wake of the armistice and the Bolshevik revolution. Taft did not budge. A vote on the plan split the board evenly, permanently tabling the idea. Thus a bitterly divided NWLB would slog through case after case in its waning days, affording employers ample opportunity to disable the board.[6]

The death of the Walsh-Manly plan signified the end of the NWLB as a force in the workplace. Thereafter, the tenuous cooperation that had defined its work in wartime was torn asunder. As Valerie Jean Conner points out, by December 1918 "the NWLB members [had] dropped all pretense of harmony," opposing the designs of labor at every turn. Faced with this situation, Walsh decided to resign. On the day after his plan was defeated, he drafted his letter to the president. "This Board, in my opinion, has come to the point where it cannot be anything but a disappointing mirage to the working people of the country," he told Olander. Basil Manly was named to his place.[7]

Without Walsh, the NWLB was not the same agency. It began to retreat from the industrial field just as ominous conflicts loomed. On December 5, the board voted to cease taking up cases that were not jointly submitted, effectively keeping all new cases off its dockets. Still, the backlog of cases remained, as employers sought and received extensions and appeals hearings aplenty. Three disputes that erupted in the following months—with Bethlehem Steel, Western Union, and New York harbor workers—illustrated how helpless the NWLB had become before its enemies and how much its policies had fallen under attack.[8]

It should have surprised no one that the first blow delivered to the enfeebled NWLB came from Eugene Grace. Less than a week after the armistice, the truculent Bethlehem Steel executive informed the NWLB that thenceforth he considered its recent award dead. "As a result of the attitude of the company," one NWLB staffer concluded ominously, "there is no predicting what is going to happen in Bethlehem next." Grace cleared up the uncertainty in short order by "deliberately violating the award in a clear cut way," as examiner Richard B. Gregg reported. Grace refused to bargain with shop committees, declined to name representatives to serve on the local board of mediation, laid off committee representatives, and ignored NWLB staff protests. Gregg sensed such hostility that he feared the company might even break into his office. Nor was he calmed by Grace's announced intention to replace NWLB committees with a company union and his decision to seek out Frank Walsh's nemesis, W. L. Mackenzie King, as an adviser. It was to be, the *Pennsylvania Labor Herald* feared, a "dose of reconstruction à la National Manufacturers Association."[9]

Faced with this offensive, Bethlehem's electricians threatened to strike, drawing the NWLB's attention. Grace's effrontery offended cochair Taft's sense of judicial propriety. Though he was reluctant to lead a strong board in peacetime, Taft considered initiating contempt proceedings against Bethlehem. But the idea found no support among employers. On December 12, 1918, Grace informed the NWLB that he intended to ignore its committees. When the NWLB met to discuss Bethlehem, the board's employer members blocked any action. Taft acquiesced. The labor members were stunned. William Johnston thought Grace's behavior outrageous. The company was "flaunting its fist in the face of the board," said a colleague. This raised the question of "whether the Bethlehem Steel Company is more powerful than the government." When the board invited Grace to Washington to explain his actions, the Bethlehem executive revealed his own thoughts on that question. Refusing to appear himself, Grace sent corporate counsel, Guy W. Currier, with news that in peacetime his company would not abide a system where NWLB staffers "administer our relations with our employees."[10]

There was little that the NWLB could do. Even its labor members hesitated to take aggressive action against Grace for fear that the War Department would then withhold the payments to the company meant to cover retroactive wage increases. Without those payments Bethlehem would suspend raises, and union members might be left with nothing to show for their trouble over the previous ten months. As the NWLB's frustrated labor members fretted over the situation, Bethlehem Steel preempted them. It suspended payment of back wages and fired "practically all active committeemen" elected in the fall. Federal mediation in the steel industry was over.[11]

Steelmakers rushed in to make sure it was dead. As internal division crippled the NWLB, companies took the offensive. Lebanon Valley Iron Company began firing workers. Eastern Steel informed the board that its decisions were now considered moot; Midvale Steel eluded an investigation into its employee representation plan. Meanwhile, NWLB employers abetted their friends. Failure to deliver awards at National Enameling and Stamping, the Benjamin Iron and Steel Company, Carpenter Steel Company, and Lehigh Structural Steel, resulting from deadlocked votes and postponements, underlined the ineffectuality of the postwar NWLB. The dream of industrial democracy that had inspired steelworkers may not have completely vanished with the incapacitation of the board, but steelworkers could no longer rely on help from Washington to realize it.[12]

Encouraged by events in steel, other employers began snubbing the NWLB. When Smith and Wesson returned to private hands in early 1919, managers announced that they would employ no union members. Though Taft found such a stand "archaic," he concluded, "I don't know what you can do with them." Where NWLB action had produced small cracks in the open-shop wall erected around the auto industry, automakers moved quickly to repair them. Dodge fired workers who attempted to form a shop committee, and Willys-Overland blocked the implementation of a back pay award authorized by the prostrate NWLB. Having successfully avoided NWLB-supported organizing drives in their plants, automakers rejoiced at having "stood that damn War Labor Board on its head," as one unnamed executive put it.[13]

Western Union, which provided the pretext for President Wilson's first defense of the NWLB, helped illustrate the board's postwar impotency. Trouble had been brewing for months in telegraph offices, as Postmaster Burleson had yet to implement the NWLB's July award. Burleson, who was perpetually at odds with William B. Wilson and the entire war labor administration, made no serious attempt to comply with the ruling. By early November the CTUA was asking the NWLB to intervene once again. This time, however, the board saw its lack of authority rather than its power confirmed. Burleson simply declined to work with the NWLB. He argued that since the war had ended, telegraph operations were his sole responsibility. To prove the point, he announced a new pay scale for telegraphers to take effect January 1, 1919. It was less generous than the scale proposed by Western Union's Newton Carlton during the previous spring.

The efforts of some NWLB members to get Burleson to reconsider were to no avail. Despite Taft's "positively acid-tongued" criticism, Burleson simply ignored the NWLB, much to the delight of the board's employer members. Nor did President Wilson, who was preoccupied with his work in Versailles, intervene to tip the scales. The CTUA had no choice but to launch a suicidal strike in July 1919 seeking the justice that the government could no longer promise. The union's defeat in that walkout made clear that Burleson had triumphed over the CTUA as well as the NWLB.[14]

Any doubts concerning the NWLB's place in postwar Washington were settled in a battle waged by New York harbor workers. In November 1918 the Marine Workers Affiliation—a federation of New York harbor workers, 60 percent of whom were employed by private boat owners and 40 percent of whom worked for the Railroad Administration—asked for an eight-hour day and a "living wage." When the NWLB tried to act on the case in December, it hit a snag. William G. McAdoo, who had struck favorable agreements with unions throughout the war, had resigned from the Railroad Administration to reenter private business. After his departure, the Railroad Administration refused to accept NWLB jurisdiction in New York harbor, stiffening the resolve of the private owners to do likewise. Inaction from Washington prompted the walkout of sixteen thousand workers, the largest harbor strike to that point in New York history.

Only a cable from President Wilson in Paris got the USRA to cooperate with the NWLB, and then reluctantly. Even after the USRA agreed to NWLB jurisdiction, the NWLB's employers successfully deadlocked their agency, necessitating a ruling from umpire V. Everit Macy. Macy's award fell short of the marine workers' demands. Disappointed, they struck once again, this time winning on their own what they could not get the government to give them. The meaning of the episode was clear. The NWLB no longer carried any pro-labor clout within the administration. Reporting on the harbor strikes, the *Nation* wondered whether the NWLB was a dead letter and recommended that "immediate steps" be taken to salvage the agency.[15]

But the withering away of the wartime state was not to be reversed, and its consequences were soon felt in companies such as General Electric where state intervention had been most significant during the war. The rise of the NWLB had been instrumental in fostering the growth of the Electrical Manufacturing Industry Labor Federation, and the decline of the board helped precipitate its downfall. On December 7, 1918, GE began an offensive. Managers at Erie announced that they were creating a company union. Erie workers were given twenty-four hours to nominate candidates for the new body. Electrical federation leaders demanded a meeting to discuss the issue. Management refused. The Erie unionists had little choice but to strike, setting the stage for the destruction of the federation.

On December 10, Erie GE workers walked out. Realizing full well that if the protest failed their organization would be broken, the electrical federation's leaders in Schenectady demanded a meeting with GE executives. When they too were rebuffed, only one course of action remained. With Erie on strike and GE refusing negotiations, electrical federation leaders were forced to call out workers from all five GE plants. On December 15, federation delegates met in Schenectady and authorized that strike. It began on December 19, 1918.[16]

The electrical federation, however, was poorly prepared to confront GE for at least two reasons. First, it could not count on a great deal of support from national union leaders. Indeed, the IAM's William Johnston, who had grown irritated with what he considered the quick-tempered militants of the electrical and munitions industries, was particularly ambivalent about the federation's strike. When the NWLB met on December 18, he mentioned the impending strike at GE only as an aside, and he did not press the board to hear the Erie case. Although Johnston would later attack GE for provoking the strike, he was plainly slow to take up the cudgels for the electrical federation. Second, Lynn workers did not support the walkout. William Nealey, the conservative president of the Lynn Central Labor Union, opposed the goals sketched out at the federation's Erie convention. He accused federation organizers of being outside agitators who cared little for Lynn GE workers, and he urged Lynn workers to remain on the job. John Bellingham went to Lynn to counter Nealey and received a sympathetic hearing from Lynn workers. Yet Nealey's argument that a strike would void the NWLB shop committees that Lynn workers had recently elected seemed to turn the tide. In the end, no strike vote was taken in Lynn.[17]

So when fourteen thousand GE workers walked out of their Schenectady shops on the morning of December 19, led by two groups of men carrying American flags, the press noted that they were more "sober-faced" than they had been during their recent armistice celebrations. Although most GE workers in Fort Wayne and Pittsfield joined their walkout that day, bringing the total number of strikers to some thirty thousand, their chances of defeating GE were slim. The strikers nonetheless demonstrated surprising solidarity in this first big postwar labor skirmish. "The workers are beginning to realize that we must fight for Democracy over here, as well as we did for Democracy 'over there,'" declared the organization's press committee, and "the boys coming back say they are with us to win." Immigrants, women, and skilled and unskilled workers alike responded to such appeals. The walkout also brought together white- and blue-collar workers in common cause. "For the first time in the history of the local labor movements," argued one Schenectady leader, "clerks and office workers have taken their place side by side and shoulder to shoulder with their fellow workers in the factories."[18]

Yet brave words could not win out. Waged against a powerful employer in a demobilizing economy, this remarkable strike was doomed, and the NWLB would not rescue it. By the end of December the electrical federation was losing momentum as bitter cold thinned pickets and frustrated organizers railed against the "howling hypocrites" who had so recently yelled "so loudly for democracy and liberty that you couldn't hear yourself think." "You stood by them," one leaflet read. "Are they standing by you now?" The question, of course, answered itself. Without allies and with little hope of winning on their own, electrical federation leaders decided to end their walkout on January 6, 1919, simply for the promise of a hearing before the NWLB. That hearing gave federation leaders a forum to argue for the formalization of collective bargaining arrangements and the abolition of company unions. But it produced nothing else. The board predictably deadlocked on the case, effectively leaving GE free to impose its own settlement. GE promptly blacklisted federation strike leaders such as Laura Cannon, of Fort Wayne, who had personally organized hundreds of women. Erie officials, meanwhile, completed their company union. And in Pittsfield a foreman educated returning workers on the nature of the postwar order. "To Hell with the War Labor Board," he bellowed. "They are a snake in the grass." [19]

As the posture of the postwar state was reconfigured, erstwhile allies turned on each other within the halls of the Southern Building where the NWLB was located. During the war, Frank Walsh had staffed the NWLB with his brand of left-leaning progressives. Employers were not the only ones who had viewed these people with concern. Shortly after Walsh resigned, many of the field investigators he had hired were let go at the behest of the NWLB's labor members. As one staffer reported to Walsh, they were told simply, "You were Walsh's friends. He picked you without consulting us." The real reason may well have been, as that examiner feared, that the AFL suspected Walsh's friends of "lending aid and comfort to the Labor Party idea." In any case, their departure meant that in its waning days the NWLB was no longer a very progressive institution.[20]

The board's postwar political coloring became quite clear when the UTW —so plodding in its wartime organization of textile workers—was pushed by insistent workers into a national strike for the eight-hour day on February 3, 1919. Once that walkout began, the union lost control of it. Having a small base among the industry's multitudes of immigrant operatives, it was unable to guide them successfully. Workers in Lawrence, Paterson, Passaic, and other textile centers soon fell in line behind militant leaders who sought help from the Amalgamated Clothing Workers rather than the UTW. Eventually the ACWA helped them launch an independent union, the Amalgamated Textile Workers of America (ATWA), intent on bringing organization to the mills where the UTW had failed. The ATWA found enthusiastic support among the silk mills of Paterson, the periodic home of labor radicalism, where rank-and-file silk workers gravitated behind a militant umbrella organization known as the Eight-Hour Workday Conference. But even before the ATWA coalesced, the UTW grew alarmed by the specter of dual unionism.[21]

Faced with this threat, UTW leaders turned to the NWLB not to protect their workers from mill owners but from ACWA organizers. A week after the strike began, John Golden called on his ally Thomas Rickert of the NWLB, urging him to employ the board to stave off the insurgent challenge. Rickert needed little prodding to take on the hated ACWA. He asked his NWLB brethren to investigate the strike speedily, lest a "gang" of silk worker radicals wreck bona fide trade unionism in the industry. The argument aroused the interest of Taft, who frequently fretted about the radical threat in early 1919. Though he was reluctant to have the board take up postwar strikes, he urged it to look at the Paterson case, and as usual, his vote swung the issue.[22]

The postwar NWLB proved to be a pliable tool in the hands of the ACWA's opponents. Once it investigated the case, silk manufacturers and the UTW leaders sat down together to negotiate an end to the strike in Paterson under the cover of the NWLB. Neither party wished to see ACWA-style unionism flourish in Paterson; accordingly, they worked out an accord that would take the ground out from under the militants. It called for a temporary shortening of hours while the NWLB investigated the eight-hour demand. This proposal found support from Matthew Woll of the International Photo-Engravers' Union, who served as an alternate on the NWLB. He argued that the board ought to uphold the "legitimate" union movement.[23]

The UTW and the silk manufacturers seconded this view. In a hearing before the NWLB on February 11, James Starr, a Paterson UTW leader, urged the board to "kill off" the radicals by backing the joint UTW-manufacturers accord. Unless "we get some Board behind us," he warned, radicalism might take root in Paterson mills. The leaders of the UTW, he assured, "have got control," but dire consequences would follow "if we should lose control." A representative of the silk manufacturers agreed. Only an NWLB ruling would "control the IWW and other radical elements." Employers must have savored the irony of listening to Golden describe the "menace of Bolshevism" as "graver than 75 percent of the people in this country think." In the end, Golden got his way. The NWLB gave the UTW most of what it wanted in a ruling that granted a temporary reduction of the work week to forty-two and one-half hours.[24]

The action accomplished what silk manufacturers and AFL unionists sought. The bulk of silk strikers returned to work upon receipt of the decision, despite the pleas of the Eight-Hour Workday Conference. But if the silk operatives went back because they trusted the NWLB, they soon had reason to regret their decision. Once the board's initial ruling expired, neither Taft nor the NWLB employers were willing to endorse anything less than a return to a forty-eight-hour week. This "stunned" a great many silk workers and fueled the growth of the ATWA. By May 1920, the new union had translated disaffection in Paterson and the other textile centers into fifty thousand members in its ranks. Long before then, however, it was clear that the Paterson case had been nothing more than a sordid epitaph to the career of the NWLB. Once a boon to organizing workers, in its last days the NWLB was effective only as the instrument of reaction.[25]

By early 1919, the significance of the federal war labor agencies inhered less in what they did or failed to do than in their value as a political target. Republicans had zeroed in on that target in the 1918 congressional elections, the first skirmish in the campaign to restore the "status quo ante in governmental administration" sought by employers. Early in the campaign Democrats tried to rouse labor. "If the Republicans control the next Congress," one warned, they would undo "labor's most powerful ally—the National War Labor Board." During the campaign, William B. Wilson blasted "the partisan activity of the reactionary Republican element," and Frank Walsh praised Wilson for promoting "the principles of democracy as applied to industry." The NWLB, assured another Democratic National Committee election pamphlet, enjoyed "the fullest backing of the entire Administration."[26] But it was precisely this that drew conservative fire. Massachusetts manufacturers circulated a pamphlet flaying the NWLB as "an American Federation of Labor proposition, carefully guided by a Federation attorney." If let alone the board would "unionize all manufacturing plants in the United States doing war work." The best way to beat it was to elect a Republican Congress with which "the president's hands can be tied" and the "War Labor Board relegated to the rear."[27]

How important such arguments were in the 1918 elections is unclear, but how devastating those elections were for the war labor agencies and the unions is not. President Wilson's party took a drubbing on November 5, 1918. It may not have been a massive repudiation of Wilson. After all, Democrats did well in the South, in the Northeast—where the NWLB and other labor agencies had their greatest impact—and in the far West. But Midwestern wheat belt farmers disaffected with wartime price controls sent Democrats "down like dead timber," as one scholar put it. In the end, all that mattered was that both houses of the Congress were in the hands of Republican Party leaders for whom Wilson's labor policies were anathema.[28]

The election of the Sixty-sixth Congress sent shock waves through the American body politic, setting the stage for a critical congressional realignment. A delighted William H. Barr of the National Founders Association predicted a swift end to interference by "petty government officials and shop committees" in industrial life. Most trade unionists and their allies were appalled. To Basil Manly it was "the least enlightened, most reactionary Congress that this generation has known." Feeding the dreams of the businesspeople and the dreads of the laborites was an important reality: the Republicans were able to look across the aisle to find allies against Wilson's labor policies among many conservative southern Democrats. One astute observer of Alabama politics predicted after the election that "opposition to Wilson's progressive ideas will more and more find expression among our Rockbed Southern democratic members." His forecast was not long in being fulfilled.[29]

Republicans and employers who opposed Wilson's labor policies found it easy to establish common ground with southern conservatives. A speech by open-shop champion John H. Kirby to the National Lumber Manufacturers' Association following the armistice helps illustrate why. Speaking to a largely southern audience in New Orleans, in words clearly intended to recall the ghosts of reconstructions past, Kirby attacked a power-hungry Washington bureaucracy intent on crushing states' rights. "What do we find today, you Southern men?" he asked. Although the president was "nominally" a Democrat, the states were being "hourly trimmed of their reserve power." And the Department of Labor and the NWLB were "undertaking to build up, in Washington, strongly centralized powers, intervening between you and your employees." Indeed, there was "an effort made by the Department of Labor" to organize workers, "and mostly the colored people." In case anyone missed his reference, Kirby drove it home: "The Department of Labor in Washington when it sends these emissaries . . . for the purpose of organizing your labor and taking charge of the industrial force of this people, is sending carpetbaggers just as certainly today as they sent them" in 1867. There could be "no peace in any community in this country," he warned, "where this kind of thing is . . . tolerated."[30]

Many southern Democrats, chary of the administration's labor sympathizers since Frank Walsh first threatened to hold USCIR hearings in Atlanta, had long feared just such a scenario. Wartime events had only confirmed their distrust. They called on the administration to remove government labor agents from the field swiftly. If it did not, there would be hell to pay, warned Florida governor Sidney Catts. The "party has enough to answer for without also answering for the carpet bag negro Federal Officers going over this State engendering strife between the white and black race," he thundered. As another southerner explained to the Justice Department, the administration's "encroachment upon States' rights" was "engendering a spirit of protest" in the South.[31]

The armistice and the Republican landslide encouraged southern Democrats to come out into the open against the administration's labor program. They quickly did so. "South Aroused over Wilson's Labor Policies," blared an April 1919 headline in the New York Tribune. "Whole Political Structure Is Menaced by 'Carpetbag' Methods of Administration, Declare Senators." That article cited an unnamed senator who warned the Department of Labor to cease its efforts in the South. If Secretary of Labor Wilson "keeps on," threatened the anonymous assailant, "the South will cast its electoral votes for the Republican party next time, regarding that party as being less offensive both on the negro and on state rights." Representative Thomas Blanton of Texas, meanwhile, warned President Wilson that while Texas was "ordinarily 95% Democratic," if "there is any more truckling [to labor], it will take unusual efforts for us to carry it" in 1920. Such threats could scarcely be ignored, especially when southerners began collaborating with Republicans to end funding for the war labor agencies. "It is up to you, good Republican colleagues of mine," Blanton told the House, to take on Secretary Wilson's "department of union labor." [32]

With southern Democrats and Republicans allied, postwar congressional appropriations hearings became a forum for attacks on the Department of Labor, the NWLB, and other agencies. None proved more skillful at exploiting the process than racist Democrats. In an emotional tirade on the House floor, Congressman Blanton claimed that Washington "has sent these directors of Negro economics, or their agents, down to Denison, Texas . . . to organize the colored cooks of that town into a domestic union, telling them that they are foolish to stay there in Denison and draw $15 and $20 and $30 a month when by unionizing they can demand $75 and $100 a month, like the colored employees in Washington." Blanton accused federal investigators of "stirring up strife and animosity" among blacks against "the best friends they have on God's green earth." Representative Carlos Bee of Texas joined the chorus. The problem with federal labor regulation, he contended, was that there was a "disturbance caused by bringing in these men from New York and elsewhere, to teach different doctrines." [33]

Lending punch to such attacks was the postwar Red Scare, a development that forced labor's political allies to distinguish between state regulation and state socialism, collective bargaining and collectivism. In light of the October Revolution of 1917, these were distinctions without a difference in the minds of all too many politicians. Labor's very recent successes now boomeranged. During the war, radicals such as Paul Wallace may have praised the NWLB for having created "shop soviets," and workers may have petitioned Washington for "self-government in the workshop as one part of the democracy for which our armies are fighting in France." In 1919, the echoes of such language only fueled unreasoning paranoia. As one speaker told the 1919 convention of the NAM, employers were determined not to "let labor think that industrial democracy means anything like Bolshevism as it is run in Russia." Correcting this misimpression meant above all that employers intended to extinguish any role for the state in defining democracy on the job. [34]

Bolstered by these political winds, congressional attacks accelerated the demobilization of the war labor agencies and the transformation of the state. Employers cheered a series of victories that removed the "clumsy and partial hand of government from the shrinking and sensitive throat of industry," as one of their number claimed. In March 1919, the Shipbuilding Labor Adjustment Board ceased operations. By May, the U.S. Employment Service had seen the House Appropriations Committee drastically cut its funds and inform its head that "some of the Southern States" had "strenuously objected" to its projects. Nor did the weakened NWLB escape the budget cutters' axes; the board was denied the deficiency appropriation it sought to wind up its work. Even as progressive agencies were dismantled, less favorable agencies took their places: on the federal level came the Esch-Cummins Act's Railroad Labor Board, which exercised quasi-judicial powers over railway labor disputes, and on the state level Kansas experimented with a Court of Industrial Relations that the AFL feared would amount to nothing more than compulsory arbitration. Well before the 1920 election, it was clear that the remaining levers of state power were falling into the hands of labor's foes.[35]

A CHIMERICAL RECONSTRUCTION

The collapse of the war labor agencies in 1919 was one of the chief ironies of that annus mirabilis, for it occurred just as wartime state expansion had given flight to the fancies of progressive reformers. Mobilization had seemingly raised the possibility of the thorough reorganization of the American political economy. As the war ended, progressives hoped that this work would be completed under the rubric of what they termed "reconstruction." In the first months of 1919 this word, which had been uttered by few in recent years save the admirers or adversaries of D. W. Griffith, was again on the lips of millions. Out of the war, Alabama State Federation of Labor president William L. Harrison hoped, would come "progressive ideas on reconstruction." Come they did in a flood of books with such titles as *Reconstructing America*, *Democracy in Reconstruction*, and *Social Reconstruction*, as well as a new journal called *Reconstruction: A Herald of the New Time*. They came also from the AFL's Special Committee on Reconstruction, the pre-November 1918 Congress, and even from Gerard Swope of GE. Socialist commentator Harry W. Laidler thought that all this ferment offered "believers in industrial democracy" reason to take heart. Why then was optimism so quickly dissipated? Why was there no reconstruction in postwar America?[36]

The answer is certainly not to be found in a lack of ideas or advocates within the administration. Plans to shape a reconstruction policy were afoot well before the armistice. The administration's liberals led the way. In December 1917, Walter Lippmann called for the creation of a "Reconstruction Bureau" in Washington. His friends at the *New Republic* beat the drum for such an agency. And his affiliation with the Department of War gave Lippmann an opportunity to sound out the thinking of like-minded war bureaucrats on the question. Grosvenor Clarkson of the CND, meanwhile, set up a Reconstruction Research Division in May 1918. By the time the war ended, the liberals were ready to act. On November 11, 1918, Felix Frankfurter composed a memorandum for Secretary of Labor Wilson urging that the administration immediately create an agency to plan America's "reconstruction." Wilson found the memo intriguing.[37]

Nor could the failure of postwar reconstruction be attributed to a lack of allies outside the administration. From many quarters came calls to "reconstruct" the nation in 1919. Workers were among those who raised the cry for government action after the war. "Let us hold fast to such valuable things as the War Labor Board," advised one Ohio steelworker. Frank Walsh and his friends shared similar hopes. After Walsh resigned from the NWLB in November 1918, he worked with the labor members of the board to formulate a proposal for a new National Labor Board that they hoped the president would endorse. Such groups as the National Catholic War Council also lent their support to such thinking. The Catholic bishops argued for a reorganized NWLB that would be "endowed with all the power for effective action that it can possess under the Federal Constitution." Even Taft supported a postwar board to foster collective bargaining—provided that it was created by legislation. The "day of the industrial autocrats is passing and should pass," he wrote in one newspaper editorial.[38]

In the end, however, the reactionary political tide, in concert with divisions among progressive forces, scotched reconstruction planning before it got very far. The 1919 convention of the NAM set the tone for further political discussions regarding the perpetuation of wartime government agencies in peacetime: "We see no occasion for the further continuance of a body similar to the National War Labor Board," its delegates declared. Within the administration, meanwhile, the obstacles faced by those who wanted to build reconstruction agencies were no less formidable. The one man who seemed most committed to crafting a reconstruction policy within the administration, Felix Frankfurter, felt them acutely.[39]

Frankfurter, whose star rose quickly in the war labor administration, saw its luster fade after the armistice. AFL leaders, wary of his ties to Sidney Hillman and the ACWA, had harassed Frankfurter periodically during the war. After the armistice they sought to make sure that the would-be "labor czar" did not get control over postwar planning by circulating reports tarnishing his record with the WLPB. Besides AFL leaders, Frankfurter faced a more pernicious opposition. William Taft was among those who criticized the Harvard professor and his "little ring of power seeking Jews" and feared that they would "show us their cloven hoof" in the aftermath of the war. President Wilson, who had shown faith in Frankfurter in 1918, could have endorsed his ideas for a reconstruction agency. But as early as December 1918, Wilson intimated that he saw no role for such an agency.[40]

Clearly the political winds did not favor Wilson acting otherwise on reconstruction, particularly as it related to postwar labor agencies. As George P. West had guessed in the summer of 1918, Wilson's strong advocacy of such agencies as the NWLB was "a temporary and fortuitous circumstance of politics." To be sure, some Wilsonians considered continuing this advocacy after the war. In June 1919, the president's secretary, Joe Tumulty, urged Wilson to think about calling a postwar conference to concoct something "similar to the Whitley programme" of workplace representation and corporatist decision making that had taken shape in wartime England. Tumulty speculated that, if it received Wilson's "hearty support," such a program could "result in a realignment of parties" and "thus make the Democratic party the great liberal party of the country." But, like most politicians, Wilson was more concerned about reelections than realignments.[41]

The president nonetheless did decide to tantalize his labor supporters with a message from Europe. When the Sixty-sixth Congress convened in May 1919, Wilson sent a letter to its members. "The question which stands at the front of all others in every country amidst the present great awakening," it read, "is the question of labour." Then, in words that seemed calculated to appeal to advocates of industrial democracy, Wilson announced that the "object of all reform in this essential matter must be the genuine democratization of industry." Progressives rejoiced: the president had seemingly adopted Frank Walsh's rhetoric. Businesspeople panicked: Wilson was proposing not a "democratization of industry," declared one, "but a tyranny of Labor." Such fears were unfounded, of course. Clearly, Wilson did not expect the Republicans to pass sweeping labor legislation that would write the reforms of the NWLB into law. But it is likely that he hoped to preserve the alliance between Democrats and labor that he had done so much to forge. Indeed, one observer of that alliance concluded that the message was never intended to "have any other practical effect than the strengthening of Mr. Gompers's position, and the weakening of the demand for a national Labor party."[42]

Those who could not fathom such subtle politicking should have seen other signs that the president's support for the postwar democratization of industry would remain largely rhetorical. In addition to his growing preoccupation with peace negotiations and his problems with conservative Democrats, Wilson had to contend with the perception that his administration had unduly benefited unions, and he had to face opposition from powerful quarters in the banking industry.

By mid-1919, most Wilson advisers argued that the time had come to distance themselves from labor. They felt that since the appointment of the USCIR in 1913, Wilson had seemed to work too closely with the AFL. By war's end, the president was paying the price for this. Samuel H. Church, of the Carnegie Institute, was among Wilson's critics on this score. "For seven years," he intoned, Samuel Gompers "has sat at Washington and dictated the legislation which controls management, industry and labor alike." Such attacks saw Wilsonians backpedal. "If there is any class in this country to which we have been overgenerous," Tumulty advised the president, "it has been labor." Wilson evidently agreed, for he seemingly lost no opportunity to prove his independence from the unions in 1919. One chance came his way during an August wildcat strike of railroad shop workers. Facing a national rail shutdown, Tumulty advised Wilson to come down hard, placing the unions "in the eyes of the public and of their fellow-workers in their true position of a privileged group," separating union members "from labor as a whole." If Wilson did this, then the government could show that it was "not to be held in ransom to satisfy the claims of a class." In following Tumulty's advice, the president chose to treat labor as simply one more special interest, scarcely distinguishable from big business in its narrow self-interestedness. In a nation where union membership had still not spread far beyond the ranks of elite craftsmen, this was not a bad political strategy. But if it shored up the president's support among anxious middle-class voters, it also spelled doom for the massive steel and coal walkouts of 1919.[43]

Even if Wilson had been prepared to buck political perceptions to stand with labor, economic considerations intruded. Such men as Benjamin Strong, president of the New York Federal Reserve Bank, whose influence was muted by the war emergency, held increasing sway over the postwar economy. In the year following the armistice, inflation had soared to 15 percent, and Strong was determined to quash it. Ironically, this set the two parts of the New Freedom—its labor and banking reforms—on a collision course. The outcome was a foregone conclusion. Laborites had hoped that there would be a federal public works program and easy credit to cushion the transition to a peacetime economy. But Strong and the Fed desired fiscal austerity and tight money. In September 1919, the Fed won that argument, raising interest rates at ten regional banks. Interest rates were raised again and again until the economy was thrown into a tailspin, and manufacturing activity had declined by a staggering 42 percent by 1921. In the context of the bankers' actions, Wilson was in a poor position to support the demands of railroaders, steelworkers, and miners in the autumn of 1919 or to propose postwar agencies that might be seen as firming up wages.[44]

Unable to rally around a postwar reconstruction program that dealt frankly with the labor problem, the administration's progressives saw their clout decline. The Labor Department, once the symbol of the administration's ties with trade unionists, suddenly became a demoralized agency following the war. As such figures as Albert S. Burleson and newly appointed Attorney General A. Mitchell Palmer gained a greater voice in the shaping of domestic policy, Secretary Wilson saw his own influence ebb, and he was left alone to lament "the policies adopted by some of my executive associates."[45]

THE OTHER VERSAILLES

The costs of political reaction and the failure of the administration to formulate a reconstruction program became clear in two ill-fated industrial conferences summoned by the president to define a postwar answer to the labor question. That these conferences would so disappoint laborites and progressives was ironic, given that they had suggested the conference approach in the first place. In June 1919, Basil Manly called for Wilson to bypass the conservative Congress and present a reconstruction program directly to industrial and labor leaders at a national conference. A month later, W. Jett Lauck added his voice to those prevailing on the president to hold a "national industrial congress" to consider the "democratization of industry." The railroad shop workers' walkout and looming strikes in coal and steel finally pushed Wilson to act. When he did call a conference, however, it did not produce what Manly and Lauck sought.[46]

Wilson summoned a national industrial conference to open in Washington on October 6, 1919. The conference was to be composed of fifty-nine members divided into representatives of labor, employers, and the public. When the president named the representatives of the latter group, it became clear to many labor partisans that the conference was doomed. Rather than turning to Frank Walsh, William H. Taft, or V. Everit Macy, each of whom had helped lead wartime labor boards as public representatives, Wilson tapped such men as John D. Rockefeller Jr. and Elbert Gary. The composition of the public group virtually assured that the conference would not grant what AFL leaders sought—an unequivocal recognition of labor's right to organize.

Clearly aware of the difficulty of the task that awaits him, a dour-faced Secretary of Labor Wilson (center) arrives with staff to open the ill-fated President's Industrial Conference, October 6, 1919. (Library of Congress)

Moreover, it made it unlikely that any labor peace along the lines pioneered by the NWLB would emerge from the conference. So offended by Wilson's appointees was the UMW representative to the conference, John L. Lewis, that he resigned in protest prior to the first meeting.[47]

Lewis's judgment was sound. As the conference convened, the massive steel strike that had begun on September 22 formed its backdrop. With so much on the line, it is hardly surprising that the conferees split on the question of collective bargaining. Labor supported a resolution initially proposed by public representatives Charles Edward Russell and Henry Endicott, which endorsed the right to organize and to bargain collectively. A clear majority sided with labor on this. But conference rules stipulated that a majority vote mustered within any of the three groups could veto a proposal. A majority of business representatives did veto the Russell-Endicott proposal. When Endicott redrafted the resolution so as to appease this faction, the new wording recognized workers' right to organize in unions "and other organizations." No war labor agencies had adopted such language. Its goal was to allow employer-dominated shop committees or company unions to take the place of real unions. Rather than waste time in futile debate about the issue, Gompers led the labor delegates out of the conference on October 22.[48]

As the conference disbanded, the White House scurried to pick up the pieces. On the recommendation of the public members of the conference, President Wilson proposed a second conference for December 1919. This time William B. Wilson—who felt that Gompers's walkout had been too hasty—convened the affair, assisted by the man who recently had headed the Food Administration, Herbert C. Hoover. The second conference was composed not of representative members of labor and industry but of members of the business and government elite—including the former governors of New York, Massachusetts, and Virginia; the likes of Julius Rosenwald of Sears and Roebuck and Owen D. Young of General Electric; and individuals experienced in industrial relations, such as Stanley King of the W. H. McElwain Company.[49]

As the second conference convened, progressive laborites attempted to influence its deliberations. Basil Manly sent a memorandum to the conferees calling for a "national industrial judiciary." He would have the president appoint twenty-four "distinguished citizens" to an Industrial Judiciary for six-year terms. When labor troubles arose in transportation or communications or when they threatened manufacturing and mining interests employing over ten thousand workers, each party to the dispute would select a representative to sit on a temporary labor board along with three members of the Industrial Judiciary. The panel would then arbitrate the case. Improving on one flaw in the NWLB system, Manly's plan would require that the panel render a decision before it left the hearing room. The operation of the entire system would be overseen by a chairperson and two associates elected from among the twenty-four members of the Industrial Judiciary and one representative each from the AFL and the Chamber of Commerce.[50]

But hopes that the second conference would adopt this plan were ill placed. AFL leaders were not optimistic that an acceptable proposal could emerge from a conference that excluded them and included business members who felt that labor unions must be operated "so that capital can live with them," as Owen Young of GE phrased it. Nor were they surprised by what emerged from the conference. Although it resembled Manly's plan in some ways, the conference's recommendation, which Hoover played a leading role in crafting, was more modest and less protective of unions. It called for a National Industrial Board composed of individuals who served six-year terms, as Manly had suggested. But Hoover's board was to be a smaller body of nine members that would hear appeals from a lower set of temporary "regional adjustment boards." These were to be constituted by four members chosen by the workers and four by the managers who were party to a dispute. The proposal endorsed "the policy of collective bargaining," but it also sanctioned company-sponsored shop committees, maintaining that they might furnish "a new basis of industrial peace."[51]

The work of the second conference proved to be no more effective in settling the labor question in America than the Versailles negotiations were in preserving the peace in Europe. Although newspaper editors generally approved of the conference plan—one survey found that only three from a sample of seventy-five newspapers expressed opposition to it—neither business nor labor leaders lent it support. When it arrived on Capitol Hill, the report was greeted with a deafening silence—an eerie coda to the Wilson administration's promises to democratize industry.[52]

"THINGS FALL APART, THE CENTRE CANNOT HOLD"

Testifying before a Senate committee in 1920, W. Jett Lauck spoke of what "in the absence of a better term" he called "the movement for industrial democracy." There had indeed been such a movement emerging from the USCIR, gravitating to Wilson in 1916, helping shape labor policy during the war. It had included AFL trade unionists, Brandeisian liberals, some members of the non-revolutionary Left, and progressives. Most prominent among them had been Frank P. Walsh. Following the war, however, Walsh increasingly found himself out of step with the Wilson administration. By the time Lauck spoke to the Senate in 1920, Walsh had reevaluated his relationships with AFL leaders and the Democratic Party and determined on a new course. As he did, those who had once composed the "movement for industrial democracy" began to drift apart, adding another tragic dimension to the postwar reaction.[53]

The first evidence of Walsh's postwar evolution came shortly after he left the NWLB. On December 30, 1918, he resigned from the AALD, the patriotic-front organization set up by the AFL and the CPI to ensure labor loyalty. Significantly, the issue Walsh cited for his resignation was the AALD's "vicious onslaught" against the Soviet Union. Although he was by no means a Communist, Walsh believed the Russians were "a great body of people, fighting valiantly to control their own destiny whether right or wrong," and he objected to Wilson's dispatch of troops to Vladivostok. Walsh had first joined the AALD thinking that it might help advance the cause of industrial democracy. But he now believed that the AALD could only frustrate progressivism. "It seems that the Government took it over," he confided to Manly.[54]

Free of the AALD, Walsh was prepared to take on what he felt were some of the reactionary impulses that predominated within the postwar AFL. He lent his name to the National Association for the Advancement of Colored People's call for an antilynching conference, he supported the general strike in Seattle in 1919, and he called on the labor movement to "act for itself in politics as well as in industry." His popularity among rank-and-file unionists guaranteed him a hearing. William Johnston, for one, conceded that Walsh was more popular among IAM members than he was himself.[55]

His biggest victory against hidebound union policies came when women streetcar conductors asked him to defend them in a hearing before his old agency, the NWLB, in 1919. The women's complaint dated to a December 1918 decision by the NWLB authorizing the Cleveland Street Railway Company to fire 150 women conductors it had hired in previous months in order to give their jobs to men returning from the war. The decision had been sought by the all-male Amalgamated Association of Street and Electric Railway Employees (AASERE) and supported by the NWLB's labor members. A storm of feminist outrage greeted the NWLB decision. Walsh himself was indignant. "The organized workers seem to me to be playing right into the hands of the profiteering employers," he told a friend, exacerbating "old, heart-sickening . . . divisions on account of nationality, race, religion, and all the other points of difference between us humans, which have kept the workers unorganized." He decided to handle an appeal before the NWLB for the women. This angered some of Walsh's labor friends, but he brushed aside their criticism. If he passed up this case, Walsh explained to Anton Johannsen, "what sort of man would I be"?[56]

On March 13, 1919, Walsh represented the Cleveland women before his former colleagues. He was well prepared. Presenting as his star witness streetcar conductor Laura Prince, whose husband was with the army in Europe, Walsh insisted that women had "an elemental right" to keep the jobs they had taken during the war. The NWLB union members, who had okayed the dismissal of the women three months earlier, squirmed. Reversing their previous action, they ruled that the women must be rehired immediately. "If you had not taken it up," Manly told his friend, "I am quite sure that the labor members of the Board . . . would have stood pat and refused to permit the women to be reinstated." Yet Walsh's efforts to reeducate his labor friends went for naught. Although the NWLB issued the decision Walsh desired, it was too weak to enforce it. The Cleveland Street Railway Company, to the great relief of the male members of the AASERE, refused to comply.[57]

As Walsh reevaluated his relationship to the AFL hierarchy, he also reexamined his political commitments. Before 1919 was over he showed as much willingness to differ with his party as with his trade union friends. Out of that came a reevaluation of Woodrow Wilson himself. Woodrow Wilson had made Frank Walsh a national figure. Walsh in turn had helped define Wilson's presidency. But the two men were destined to break before the year was out.

For Walsh the cause was as much Ireland as labor. He was among those who had celebrated the "martyrs" of the Easter Rebellion of 1916 as "the very best and cleverest Irishmen of their day," and he hoped that Wilson's wartime commitment to self-determination would free his ancestral homeland from the British yoke. His resignation from the NWLB allowed him to throw himself into this cause. In February 1919 Walsh was named, along with Edward F. Dunne, former governor of Illinois, and Michael J. Ryan, of the Clan-na-Gael in Philadelphia, to the Irish shadow delegation at the Versailles conference. Walsh arrived in Europe on April 12, 1919, still a Wilsonian.[58]

After a promising start, the shadow delegates' mission met disaster. Upon arriving in Paris, Walsh met with Colonel Edward House and President Wilson. On April 17, Wilson gave Walsh assurances that he would raise the Irish question with the English. Buoyed by Wilson's pledge, Walsh and his colleagues, with the permission of the British, set off to visit Ireland. They were welcomed as conquering heroes. But in retrospect it seems that they may have stumbled into a trap. The *Times* of London soon carried reports that the Americans had roamed the island making "roaring speeches about a Republic." The inflammatory effect of these stories gave the English all the ammunition they needed to pressure Wilson, who in turn feared that the Irish question might torpedo the peace talks. When Wilson was forced to make a choice, he cut Walsh and his friends loose. "We had practically cleared the way for the coming of the Irish representatives to Paris," Wilson cabled Joe Tumulty, until the American delegates "so inflamed British opinion that the situation has got quite out of hand." When Walsh arrived back in Versailles, Wilson informed him that he had "overturned the apple cart" and that further efforts on behalf of Ireland would be futile. The two never spoke again.[59]

Returning to America to find labor under assault from all quarters, the NCOISW broken in a massive strike in which branches of the administration either stood idly by or conspired in its defeat, and the UMW forced by a federal injunction to suspend a strike to win its long-awaited wage increases, Walsh soon determined to take on Wilson. In January 1920, he landed his first blow in an article for the new journal *Reconstruction*. Walsh confessed that he had "always believed that the Democratic Party was the natural abiding place of economic justice." He also recalled Wilson's 1912 election, when he had thought that "a new day dawned." But this was true no longer. "We must face the fact, terrible as it is," he wrote, "that the present administration has absolutely turned its back upon the producing masses of this country."

This "swift and terrible change of front of the present administration is both shocking and pathetic." In a later article, he contended that the Wilson administration was "a labor-destroying and farm-baiting organization," and the Democratic Party was the "assailant of honest democracy."[60]

Walsh's disillusion was emblematic. By 1920, trade unionists, progressives, and prowar socialists who had banked on the promise of Wilsonian reform, as well as the belief that a war for democracy in Europe might democratize America, fell away from their former champion in droves. No doubt making their break with Wilson more bitter was their realization that they may have been partly to blame for their own travails, having underestimated how much the wartime mobilization would invigorate reactionary forces. In 1917, most of them felt that they had no choice but to stick with Wilson. In 1920, that was no longer true.

Many of those who had been involved in the "movement for industrial democracy" were drawn into third-party politics in 1920. Most of those were attracted to the effort launched by the Chicago Federation of Labor to found a National Labor Party. Encouraged by the upsurge of third-party organizing on the local level in 1918 and 1919, Frank Walsh had helped finance that effort undertaken by his friend John Fitzpatrick. Former staffer Robert Buck departed the NWLB for Chicago early that year to lend his support to the new movement, editing its newspaper, the *New Majority*. By mid-1919 Walsh had begun to convince himself that through the new party, Fitzpatrick might "swing the Irish Movement in this country to the radical movement."[61]

The Chicago initiative eventually evolved into the Farmer-Labor Party (FLP). This new party was born when a movement of progressives called the Committee of Forty-Eight, among whom Walsh's former ally Amos Pinchot played a principal role, proposed collaborating with Chicago's Labor Party activists on the national level. Walsh lent his approval to this plan. The effort was consummated in a Chicago convention in July 1920 that brought together many of those who had been allied in the struggle for industrial democracy since the days of the USCIR. Walsh, Pinchot, Fitzpatrick, Basil Manly, and Robert S. Buck were some of those who helped found the FLP. They took heart from the recent drift of the Democrats. In the summer of 1920, a delusional President Wilson entertained just enough hope of being drafted for a third term to discourage the one Democrat these progressives would have supported, William G. McAdoo, from declaring his candidacy. When the party offered its nomination to Ohio's conservative Governor James M. Cox, leaving the field open to a progressive alternative, Walsh's hopes rose. He rated the FLP as having "an excellent chance" of capturing the White House in 1920.[62]

His prediction was more wishful than wise not only because of the traditional handicaps that third parties face in America but also because the FLP was plagued by internal divisions from the beginning. "Forty-Eighters" and Labor Party delegates differed substantially in their conception of the proper stance for a third party. The most important bone of contention between them, as it turned out, was industrial democracy. Before the war, Walsh had been able to pull together trades unionists and progressives of a variety of hues around their common desire to democratize industry. No more. The Labor Party group endorsed a platform calling for industrial democracy. But the "Forty-Eighters" balked at this. As one observer reported, "The issue turned upon the advanced demand of the workers for 'the democratic operation of industry.'" Pinchot had hoped to draft Senator Robert M. La Follette as the FLP's candidate, and he feared that "hotheads" who sought "a class party" would derail this possibility. In a telling sign of the reactionary times, he concluded that a declaration on behalf of industrial democracy might make the platform too radical for "Battling Bob." The Labor Party faction rammed the industrial democracy plank through anyway. As Pinchot predicted, La Follette spurned the party, and the nomination went to little-known Salt Lake City attorney Parley Parker Christensen.[63]

The tiff over industrial democracy did not bode well for the FLP. Faction-ridden and poorly organized, it offered no threat, even as a spoiler. Those AFL union leaders who were loyal to the Democratic Party remained so, and in November Christensen polled a mere 200,000 votes. That tally underscored the dissolution of the "industrial democracy movement" that had once rallied to Wilson. Nor were there signs that it would soon reassemble. In December 1920, Pinchot withdrew from the Committee of Forty-Eight, believing that the "radical material" in the FLP's plank on industrial democracy had contributed to its defeat.[64]

By the end of 1920, despair reigned among those who had recently felt that the democratization of industry was imminent. "My attitude toward the state was changed as a result of these experiences," Frederic Howe, formerly of the CIR, later recalled. "I became distrustful of the state." Similarly, progressive Walter Weyl was no longer confident that "our democratic government" could effect "a real Industrial Democratization." But no one was more disillusioned than Frank Walsh, the man who had helped make industrial democracy a national byword. Following the election, Walsh's robust health deteriorated. In June 1921 he checked into a Baltimore sanatorium to recuperate from chronic stomach pains, complaining that "I seem to tire much more easily than I did."[65]

MAKING INDUSTRIAL
DEMOCRACY SAFE
FOR AMERICA
8

We believe that the greatest possible strength
lies in the right kind of democracy.
—*Henry L. Gantt, 1917*

   The political reaction that followed the war did not completely reverse the effort to democratize industry that had taken shape over the previous several years. But it did mean that the central question for postwar America—which the author Neil M. Clark defined simply as, "How far can industrial democracy go?"—would be settled outside the political arena.[1] On shop floors, in union headquarters, in the offices of government labor agencies that began disconnecting their telephones and packing files after the armistice, in boardrooms, and in managers' offices, most observers agreed that the age of industrial autocracy had passed. What kind of world would replace it was not, however, immediately clear.

  To be sure, the partisans of industrial democracy had many reasons for optimism, even amid postwar reaction and the defeated strikes of 1919. As the war ended, electrical worker John Peterson, who had been among the union leaders in Lynn, believed that GE workers were "enjoying a freedom that exceeds the expectation of the most sanguine advocates." Although the Electrical Manufacturing Industry Labor Federation was broken after the war, GE had not been able to turn back the clock on the company's labor relations. The impact that wartime organizing had on one Lynn worker serves to illustrate. After returning from the successful Lynn strike of July 1918 "a little more spunky" than she had been previously, one of Peterson's coworkers was asked to labor at what she considered an unfair piece rate. This woman simply "told the foreman she absolutely refused to do it." Even without the electrical federation, that woman, her foreman, and shop relations at GE could never be quite the same again. Frank Walsh was among those who were convinced that a war in which such confrontations abounded had permanently changed things. During the war, workers "were told in effect by their government that they were entitled to receive and had the right to demand . . . fundamental things," Walsh wrote. Once their right to a voice on the job was accepted by management—even if it was accepted only in principle—Walsh did not believe that it could ever again be withdrawn.[2]

Although they had not achieved their vision of industrial democracy during the war, AFL leaders also thought that the war had been a watershed. Matthew Woll of the International Photo-Engravers' Union located the most important change in the war's impact on the thinking of working people. "Men and women came to think of democracy as they had never thought of it before," concluded Woll in an analysis of labor's postwar outlook. "Democracy became the great, flaming religion of mankind." This development was not always comforting to Woll and other AFL conservatives. They well knew that democracy's "flaming religion" could be marshaled on behalf of those who were "sick and tired of Czar Gompers and his bunch of Grand Dukes" and who wanted "DEMOCRACY in the labor movement as well as in Politics and Industry," as one autoworker militant put it.[3]

No one had to convince businesspeople that the war had changed their relationship with their workers. Many agreed with one analyst that the precedent for collective bargaining through shop committees, if not unions, had been planted so widely in industry "as hardly to seem eradicable." Business leaders had to come to terms with a new set of unsettling expectations among their workers. Some employers subscribed to a theory articulated in Samuel Crowther's 1920 book *Common Sense and Labour*. Crowther believed that the war had "destroyed values" in the workplace. Wartime labor markets and wages "opened up to the unthinking mass of the population" a vision of life "without work," teaching workers that high wages could be "invoked" as a "kind of manna from above." Steelmaster James Bowron of Birmingham was one of those who agreed with this analysis. "Taking it as a whole," he soberly concluded, "we find that labor is much less efficient than before the war." So much had the war upset traditions of authority and deference in the workplace that E. S. Cowdrick, the vice president of the Colorado Fuel and Iron Company, questioned whether old-style managers any longer had a place. "What are we going to do with the boss?" he asked in one influential article.[4]

Virtually every commentator writing after the war seemed to agree that industrial democracy was the wave of the future. Religious authors from Catholic John A. Ryan to Baptist Samuel Zane Batten reflected on it. Politicos as diverse as Franklin K. Lane, Ray Stannard Baker, Henry L. Stimson, and Herbert Hoover held forth on it. In Oklahoma City a "Party of Industrial Democracy" even formed to promote it.[5] Indeed, the slogan was suddenly so ubiquitous that its earliest champions feared that its significance might be diluted. By 1920 W. Jett Lauck complained that "phrases such as 'industrial democracy' " were now "used loosely and without any general agreement as to their exact meaning." The worries of conservative commentators were hardly stanched by this seeming lack of agreement. Dr. Charles A. Richmond, president of Union College in Schenectady, had watched firsthand the rise of the electrical federation at General Electric, and he believed that the call for industrial democracy could mean only one thing. "It is not representation they want, but control," he insisted. "And if they should succeed in putting through their program it would mean a tyranny and a reign of terror which would make the French revolution look like a pink tea."[6]

Of course, Richmond's nightmare did not come to pass. Instead, those who sought to achieve a vision that resembled Richmond's feared workers' control saw the mantle of industrial democracy wrested almost completely from them and planted firmly in the hands of others—including those who advocated company unionism.

In the past, historians have looked at America's postwar labor battles through the lens of institutional history, recounting epic defeats in the great steel strike, the Seattle general strike, and the Boston police strike of 1919 to explain unionism's decline in the 1920s. These are crucial stories, yet they are best understood within the context of the larger struggle over the limits of democracy in the workplace. Workers certainly saw such battles in this light. "The workers gave up billions of treasure and thousands of lives to make this ideal of Democracy a real live thing," explained a writer for the *Auto Worker* in 1919. Labor's postwar demands were nothing more than efforts to secure "some of the 'Democracy' they have made so many sacrifices for." Managers too understood that postwar labor battles were struggles over the content of Americanism and democracy as much as over the question of union recognition. This was one reason why they abandoned what Walter Drew called "the controversial . . . term 'open shop' " to combat trade unionism behind the more patriotic "American Plan." This also helps explain why Samuel Crowther found "industrial democracy" the "most ecumenically satisfying phrase" at large after the war, used so often by militants and manufacturers alike that one could find "staid" businesspeople and "the craziest and most violent radical yelling and waving a red flag at the same utterance."[7]

The federal government—first through the USCIR and later through the war labor agencies—had helped promote industrial democracy as the solution to the labor problem. But the collapse of government regulation after the war destroyed any possibility that industrial democracy might be defined in the political arena. Its meaning would instead be determined in hundreds of individual workplaces, union halls, and personnel offices where conservative manufacturers, labor radicals, and those in between each sought to define industrial democracy in their own image. The outcome of that struggle was neither what crusaders like Frank Walsh hoped for nor what such conservatives as Dr. Richmond feared. In the absence of countervailing state power, employers successfully advanced their vision of democracy in industry, heeding the advice of businesspeople who warned that with "labor crying for democracy, capital must go part way or face revolution." Leading industrialists adjusted their management to the changes wrought by the war in order to recapture the legitimacy they had temporarily lost. In that effort, they were unfettered by federal government interference, they were aided by new industrial relations professionals who had honed their craft during the war, and they confronted a divided union movement that was itself marginalizing those who advocated a radical vision of industrial democracy. The results of employers' efforts to make democracy safe for American industry were therefore overdetermined.[8]

RESOLVING LABOR'S DIVIDED HOUSE

The mobilization of 1917–18 had a contradictory impact on the union movement. In some ways, wartime conditions strengthened the movement's conservative tendencies. The war empowered union leaders who sought business unionist goals, saddled progressives with political considerations that curbed their rhetoric, undercut syndicalist and socialist radicals, and reinforced the dependency of local militants on the Wilsonian state. But the wartime mobilization also fostered contrary developments. The emergence of shop committees promoted what NWLB examiner Richard B. Gregg described as a "decentralizing tendency among the unions," leading some to predict a rank-and-file "split with the old union leaders." Federal regulation had also abetted the rise of mass organizations that challenged craft union leadership, promoting the development of what Selig Perlman and Philip Taft later called "war begotten machinery for concerted action." Too, the war helped stir local political organizing that called into question labor's reigning orthodoxies of voluntarism, the necessity of a division between trade union and party, and the value of the alliance between the AFL and the Democrats. In short, the experience of war had shaped a labor movement that itself could reach no easy agreement regarding how far industrial democracy should go.[9]

Those laborites for whom industrial democracy amounted to a radical vision were hopeful as the war ended that their dream might soon become a reality. "Like a plant that finds its normal way of growth blocked," wrote George P. West in his report on the AFL's 1918 convention, the labor movement was "sending its shoots towards the daylight here and there through developments within State and city bodies." Independent political initiatives sprang from local labor councils and city centrals from Pittsfield to Portland, Oregon, and from Bridgeport to Catasauqua, Pennsylvania. A New Jersey Federation of Labor convention saw delegates adopt a radical platform of economic reforms inspired by the British Labour Party's reconstruction program. Radicals were encouraged by the railway unions' lobbying for government ownership of the rails under the Plumb Plan, a program that promised "industrial democracy" on the nation's transit lifeline. And Basil Manly drafted "Labor's Fourteen Points" for the Chicago Federation of Labor, demanding the creation of a "League of Workers" to parallel the League of Nations, public works to ease unemployment, government ownership of transportation and communications, and amnesty for political prisoners. Lending urgency to such efforts was the strike wave of 1919. It saw four million workers walk off their jobs, many of them coupling political demands such as freedom for labor prisoner Tom Mooney to their economic ones.[10]

Many of these developments concerned Samuel Gompers and some of his colleagues on the AFL's Executive Council. They feared that their movement might abandon its traditional stance of voluntarism and craft-based economic organization for a socialist-oriented program that masqueraded as nothing more than industrial democracy. On September 8, 1919, the day before Boston's unionized police walked off their jobs and as steelworkers were girding themselves for their own huge strike, Gompers's ally John P. Frey of the International Molders' Union drafted a letter that shed much light on the fears of the AFL's conservatives. "The menace to our movement, as I see it today," Frey informed Gompers, "is no longer from the outside but it comes from within our own ranks." Union leaders must "keep our movement from being captured by a new set of dreamers," Frey argued. Gompers needed little persuading on that score. Following the war, he strove to ensure that his own vision of the "new industrial democracy"—traditional trade union bargaining unfettered by government intrusion—would prevail.[11]

Even before the war ended, labor conservatives were growing protective of that vision. AFL leaders were especially concerned that wartime federal regulation of workplace representation had opened the door to baneful radical influences. Such concerns bubbled to the surface in September 1918 in a clash between Matthew Woll and the staffs of the NWLB and WLPB. The occasion for this battle was a recommendation delivered by NWLB staffer Charles P. Sweeney to the Council of National Defense. It called for a program to train the newly elected shop committee representatives in defense industries so that they might bargain on equal terms with management. Sweeney recommended that the CND adopt a British model: the Central Labour College, which was jointly administered by the South Wales Miners Federation and the National Union of Railwaymen. He proposed to send a delegation to England to study the college and to return to create an American version of it. Felix Frankfurter of the WLPB lent his enthusiastic support to Sweeney's plan.[12]

Woll, Gompers's partner on the CND, was positively alarmed by the suggestion. The socialist leanings of British trade unionists, Frankfurter's ties to the renegade Sidney Hillman of the ACWA, and the sympathy that NWLB staffers such as Sweeney tended to accord to labor progressives evidently led Woll to fear that any such federal program would serve as a schoolhouse for labor radicals bent on overthrowing the AFL's tried and true methods. Woll determined to stop the plan before it started. In a letter to CND members, Woll insisted that shop committees were "merely instruments of expediency during the war period." He warned that a training program for delegates might permanently entrench these temporary committees, deterring "orderly, well founded . . . trade union groups" from engaging in traditional collective bargaining. If implemented, Woll cautioned in language that indicated the depth of his paranoia, Sweeney's plan would do nothing less than "place the stamp of approval of our National Government on the socialistic theory of Karl Marx."[13]

AFL conservatives were relieved when the war's end killed Sweeney's initiative. But following the armistice, they still had their hands full in defending their voluntarist vision of industrial democracy amid a surge of demands from trade unionists for continued government regulation of the workplace under the rubric of "reconstruction." Such demands, inspired in part by the British Labour Party, succeeded in prodding the AFL's 1918 convention to authorize the appointment of the Committee on Reconstruction. Progressive unionists hoped that the committee would endorse a broad range of proposals, including a national unemployment program, a forty-four-hour workweek, a labor party, and government ownership of the railways. But President Gompers ensured that they would not get what they sought. He stacked the committee with his ideological kinsmen. John Frey, who believed that the enemy within was trade unionism's chief foe in 1919, chaired the committee. Gompers's trusted allies G. W. Perkins, of the Cigar Makers, and Matthew Woll served under him.

Progressives could not have been more disappointed with the final report of Frey's committee. Delivered to the 1919 AFL convention, it declared "Democracy in Industry" as the AFL's first priority, but it ignored most of the means that progressives hoped to employ to secure that end. It criticized the calls for a national public works program, ignored the issue of hours legislation, skirted the question of government ownership of the railroads, and termed independent labor political action "disastrous." As one scholar later noted, the 1919 convention that received this report saw "the first skirmish between radicals and conservatives" after the war. It was also the deciding skirmish. In a convention where sixty-five union leaders were authorized to cast 82 percent of the ballots, progressives could not match the strength of conservatives. Besides endorsing Frey's report, this convention handed progressives two other setbacks. It passed one resolution that struck at the heart of the "decentralizing tendency" in the union movement, forbidding city central unions from calling strikes or conducting strike votes. It also rejected a proposal that would have provided for the direct election of AFL officers by rank-and-file referendum. By the end of 1919, talk of creating "DEMOCRACY in the labor movement as well as in Politics and Industry" was muted for the foreseeable future.[14]

As conservatives reasserted control over the direction of the AFL, labor progressives could no longer rely on one instrumentality—shop committees—that had recently aided them in crafting an alternative to conservative policies. Following November 1918, shop committees were rendered useless by the collapse of the government agencies that had protected their integrity during the war. Progressive supporters of industrial unionism were among the first to realize the dangers inherent in shop committees that employers could freely constitute and dominate without government interference. And so it was they, not the most conservative AFL leaders, who first moved to attack the continued existence of shop committees following the war. Several Ohio delegates to the 1919 AFL convention, acting at the behest of a National Committee for Organizing Iron and Steel Workers that found itself increasingly bedeviled by the spread of company unions in 1919, asked the AFL to formalize its opposition to any method of representation aside from trade unions. This the AFL delegates gladly did. The convention's resolution against shop committees and company unions confirmed the disappointment of those who once hoped that shop committees would provide "an enormous stimulus to industrial unionism."[15]

As the instrumentalities that had once aided labor militants crumbled, the backlash against radicals and progressives began to spread into individual unions as well. This Thermidor produced a curious phenomenon in postwar intraunion politics: the reactionary impulses were often most pronounced in the progressive unions that had most benefited from the war. Unions such as the Machinists, the United Mine Workers, and the Amalgamated Clothing Workers had thrived under wartime federal regulation. Their organizations spread, their ranks bulged, their members enjoyed unprecedented access in Washington, and their leaders were most invested in preserving what they had gained in wartime. But these unions had also hosted rank-and-file activists who capitalized on the rising expectations of their coworkers to promote increased militancy. Not coincidently, it was the IAM's William Johnston, the UMW's John L. Lewis, and the ACWA's Sidney Hillman who "wielded disciplinary sanctions against rebellious members most frequently and most draconically," as David Montgomery has observed.[16]

This pattern was especially evident in the IAM, where socialist leader Johnston had fallen under attack by his left wing. By the time the war ended, Johnston's union was in the midst of a profound reshaping. His membership had virtually doubled in less than two years. IAM members had played a leading role in forming local labor parties in Pittsfield and Bridgeport, in initiating militant organizing drives in electrical and munitions industries, and in supporting seemingly radical initiatives such as the Seattle general strike. Sympathy for the IWW and the Canadian-born One Big Union (OBU) ran deeper in the IAM than in any other union. And the supporters of IAM agitator Carl Person continued "stirring up mischief," according to Johnston. Nor were IAM militants happy with the compromises Johnston had struck with business leaders on the NWLB. After the war they did not hesitate to damn the "regular autocrats in the Grand Lodge," as one member termed them. Faced with such roiling dissension within his union, Johnston decided to clamp down on his rivals in 1919.[17]

The defeat of the Electrical Manufacturing Industry Labor Federation in its 1918–19 strike against GE provided the opening for Johnston's counterattack. He lost no time in acting. Less than two weeks after the federation surrendered to GE in January 1919, Johnston outflanked its leaders and effectively destroyed their organization's independence. On January 26, 1919, the electrical federation met in Schenectady to plan its future in the wake of the GE debacle. Its leaders invited Frank Walsh to address them. Walsh could not attend. But William Johnston did come to Schenectady, apparently as an uninvited guest. Speaking to an overflow crowd of GE machinists at the Van Curler Auditorium, he lambasted electrical federation leaders for the conduct of the recent strike. "Johnston made it clear to the machinists," according to one press account, "that they were doing wrong in following the dictations of the officers of the Electrical Manufacturing Industry Labor Federation rather than the counsel of their own union officers."[18]

Schenectady machinists generally objected to Johnston's interference. But the union president held the high cards. The GE strike had bankrupted the electrical federation and had strained the treasuries of IAM locals. To preserve their organization, federation leaders needed Johnston's support. So when delegates met the next day, they let Johnston and other national officers sit in. With Johnston's encouragement, they changed their organization's name to the Joint Metal Trades Council—an act that symbolized the end of their attempt to create a distinct organization of electrical workers—and they agreed to seek an AFL charter and to work more closely with the internationals in the future. Not content with this victory, Johnston and the IAM General Executive Board then summoned several former electrical federation machinists to a Washington meeting that turned into a court martial of sorts. Union officers berated these members for conducting the GE strike without sanction, and the International repudiated the forty thousand dollars in debts incurred by IAM locals during the battle. Without funds and support from national union leaders, former electrical federation activists were no longer in any position to pursue an independent local strategy in their industry.[19]

Having dealt sternly with electrical industry militants, Johnston then turned his attention to the renegade Sam Lavit and his District 55 in Bridgeport. During the spring of 1919, District 55 organized a series of militant strikes against layoffs and the blacklisting of union members. In the course of those strikes, Lavit apparently began extending District 55 membership to workers outside the IAM's jurisdiction and aiding nonmembers with strike benefits. These actions openly violated union bylaws. Coupled with Lavit's continuing criticism of Johnston's leadership, these developments gave the union president ample room to settle the score with his Bridgeport rival. On August 7, 1919, Johnston suspended Lavit from the IAM, revoked the charter of Lavit's own Lodge 30, replacing it with a rival lodge, and dissolved the troublesome District 55. Bridgeport machinists were nearly unanimous in their defense of Lavit. But Johnston overrode their objections. Having suspended Lavit, he also tried to end publication of Lavit's newspaper, the *Bridgeport Labor Leader*. Amazingly, Lavit, the man who had become virtually synonymous with machinists' militancy during the war, had been read out of the labor movement by the fall of 1919.[20]

Johnston and other national IAM leaders continued their campaign against union insurgents in the following months. On October 30, 1919, secretary-treasurer E. C. Davison sent a circular to all lodges condemning the OBU and instructing union officers to "discourage and oppose any movement within our ranks that will tend to disrupt our Association." To encourage compliance, the union held a special four-day conference of business agents and organizers at the IAM's headquarters in December 1919. Johnston warned that convention against radicals who were determined to "set aside the work of years"; and the IAM president met this threat, whether real or perceived, with evident vigor. In the two years following the war, the IAM General Executive Board repeatedly voted to expel members suspected of advocating OBUism, IWWism, or communism.[21]

As dissidents were rooted out of the IAM, Sam Lavit struck off on his own, helping found a dual industrial union called the Amalgamated Metal Workers of America (AMWA). Three years after the armistice, Lavit and his allies were still trying to invoke the memory of the war in defense of a radical vision of industrial democracy. "We fought for France, England, and Belgium, now let us fight for America," read one AMWA leaflet. "Let us organize industrially, let us demand that the factories be reopened, that we may produce the many things necessary for the workers of America." But Lavit and other militants found themselves increasingly marginalized within a labor movement that was on the defensive. Although it grew to as many as twelve thousand members in 1920, the AMWA was laid low by the postwar depression, leaving Lavit—like so many other wartime militants—without a viable organization through which to defend his vision of democracy in industry.[22]

FROM INDUSTRIAL DEMOCRACY TO INDUSTRIAL RELATIONS

As the labor movement closed ranks following the war, a corps of labor experts emerged to articulate their own vision of democracy in industry. The most important of them were veterans of wartime labor agencies, adept at the use of democratic rhetoric and schooled in the new methods of securing consent in the workplace. Like Frederick W. Taylor's disciple, Morris L. Cooke, many of those experts left Washington in 1919 believing that American business "must not delay installing some system of industrial democracy in every factory and workshop in the land." Fanning out into employment offices, consulting firms, and the academy, they helped found a new profession: industrial relations.[23]

Many of the efficiency experts who had gone to Washington in 1917— including those who hoped to honor Robert Valentine's vision of workplace efficiency secured through the consent of workers—had been disappointed by wartime service. Throughout much of the war, they saw their influence curbed by frank partisans of trade unionism in agencies such as the Department of Labor. The one agency that sought to study systematically and to alleviate the problems of inefficiency, Felix Frankfurter's WLPB, accomplished little. Meanwhile the NWLB, which admitted comparatively few efficiency experts into the ranks of its staff, dominated the war labor apparatus. But the demobilization of labor agencies in 1919 created an opportunity for efficiency advocates. They suddenly emerged as a new kind of professional who promised to harmonize industrial democracy with sound business management and who sought to construct what William Henry Smyth called a "rationalized Industrial Democracy."[24]

The labor economists, efficiency engineers, and personnel managers who emerged from government service were generally convinced that the Great War had brought about nothing less than a watershed in workplace relations. "We cannot turn back if we would," asserted Royal Meeker, the commissioner of the Bureau of Labor Statistics. "We must march forward in the direction in which our faces are now set." Professionals such as Meeker made enthusiastic advocates of industrial democracy. Rare was the veteran of wartime service who did not cheer the passing of industrial autocracy. The time had come to effect the "representation of organized interests" in the workplace, William Leiserson argued. "Democracy is far better for all of us," concluded Henry L. Gantt. He believed that industrial democracy could release "the infinite energy of all the people for creative work" if businesspeople only asked experts like himself to show them how to bring this about.[25]

To be sure, these veterans had unique experience to share. Many of them had administered shop committee elections or had supervised collective bargaining. Others had investigated and mediated disputes or administered training programs for frontline supervisors. They were highly sought after amid the labor turmoil of 1919. Three NWLB examiners—William L. Stoddard, who had handled GE shop committees at Lynn and Pittsfield, and Willard G. Aborn and William L. Shafer, who had done the same at Bridgeport—wrote articles and books on the benefits of employee representation. Meyer Bloomfield left the Emergency Fleet Corporation to edit the nation's first industrial relations newsletter. Major Byrnes H. Gitchell, who had mediated labor disputes for the Department of War, departed for a job with the American Men's and Boys' Clothing Manufacturers Association. William Leiserson left the Labor Department to arbitrate disputes in the men's clothing industry in Rochester.[26]

Those who did not write for the popular press or serve as arbitrators or personnel consultants often entered the academy, where they hoped to train a new generation of conscientious employers and managers. NWLB staffer

Francis Bird departed for Dartmouth. His colleague William F. Ogburn headed to Columbia. Leon Marshall left the Fleet Corporation for the University of Chicago, and A. B. Wolfe left the SLAB for the University of Texas.

From their postwar positions of influence, these individuals helped define the field of industrial relations. Their message: the arrival of democracy in industry had brought an end to the irrational, arbitrary, and inefficient "foreman's empire." In the pages of the journal *Industrial Management*, a forum for such ideas after the war, one writer argued that the era of the "shop committee sounds the death knell of the hard-fisted, arbitrary, narrow-minded foreman." The passing of the foreman's day was not to be mourned as long as employers harnessed the benefits of workers' participation. Because industrial relations experts promised to show them how, employers increasingly turned to them, and their field boomed. Although only five hundred persons had attended a national conference of personnel managers in 1917, nearly three thousand did so three years later. And delegates to the founding convention of the Industrial Relations Association of America in 1920 listened attentively to descriptions of the innovations undertaken by the new technicians of industrial democracy.[27]

It is worth remembering that in its infant stages the profession of industrial relations was no more united in its vision of industrial democracy than the wartime labor movement had been. The tentativeness with which its practitioners talked of balancing the old ways and the new hinted at the ambiguity and disagreement that characterized their nascent field. Meeker thought that industry should aim for "a combination of democracy and autocracy." Gantt, meanwhile, contrasted unworkable "debating-society methods" of industrial democracy to effective shop governance based on "demonstrated facts." Neither man was clear about just how "democracy" would be brought to bear. But no issue helped sort out the views of industrial relations advocates more than did the question of union recognition.[28]

Immediately after the war there was no consensus among industrial relations professionals regarding unions. One faction hailed them as legitimate representatives of workers' interests and sought to cooperate with them to improve workplace efficiency. Morris L. Cooke, for example, enlisted Samuel Gompers as his coeditor for a 1920 volume titled *Labor, Management, and Production*. Lincoln Filene, meanwhile, hoped that "great progress" could be had on "this industrial efficiency problem" by working with the AFL. But another faction generally condemned unions as outmoded, inefficient, conflict-generating organizations that would only disrupt the construction of what Gantt called "the right kind of democracy."[29]

Which of these schools of thought would dominate the field of industrial relations was not immediately clear as the war ended. Wartime service had produced articulate proponents from each camp. Two such individuals were Otto S. Beyer and W. L. Mackenzie King. Both Beyer and King earned reputations as innovators in workplace representation during the war. Yet these men differed in their approach to trade unions. Beyer came to believe that unions were a necessary prerequisite for industrial democracy. King did not. While he defended the rights of union members against discrimination, King tended to view employee representation plans as fruitful cooperative efforts and unions as disruptively contentious organizations.

Beyer's wartime education began when he assumed the direction of the Arsenal Orders Branch of the U.S. Army's Ordnance Department. In that post, he became deeply interested in ways to streamline production in federal arsenals. A railway engineer before the war, he had already shown interest in methods that would combine efficiency and consent. His new post allowed him the freedom to experiment. The result was an inventive cooperative management program that Beyer introduced to the arsenals right after the war. In an effort to cut costs so as to keep arsenals competitive with private arms makers, Beyer involved workers in shop floor decision making. At the Rock Island, Illinois, arsenal where the program originated, workers were invited to help determine piece rates and were permitted to select their own foremen. The unionized arsenal employees responded enthusiastically. They saw Beyer's plan as an enormous improvement over the Taylorist methods that they had previously confronted. Following the start of Beyer's plan, one arsenal employee told the War Department that "the change of heart of the men towards the management is quite noticeable." Previously, arsenal workers "would be continually kicking and protesting," this correspondent reported, but "since the employees began to participate this feeling has completely disappeared."[30]

Beyer's intent was not to undercut the union, even though Basil Manly found that there was "less radicalism at the Arsenals" after the introduction of the plan "than there was before." Rather, unionists generally favored the plan because Beyer worked closely with them in its design and implementation. Enemies of trade unionism also noticed this cooperation. They termed Beyer's plan the "Rock Island Soviet." The resulting publicity earned Beyer the enmity of many career ordnance officers, politicians, and manufacturers. This ultimately was his undoing. By the summer of 1919, private contractors were demanding the abolition of the arsenals. Although Beyer enlisted the aid of some prominent defenders, including Justice Louis D. Brandeis, his program had attracted too much controversy. So in late 1919, Secretary of War Baker replaced Beyer with a career army officer and later disbanded the Arsenal Orders Branch.[31]

Undeterred, Beyer carried his advocacy of industrial democracy with a union face into civilian life, making the railroads his prime concern. Even before he left the army, Beyer helped organize a meeting of laborites and progressives at Washington's Cosmos Club on April 8, 1919, to discuss the future of the railroads. At that meeting, he offered a plan that promised "efficiency through democracy" on the rails. "Let it be fully realized that the term Democratic Control of Industry is fast becoming the rallying term for a new and significant industrial movement," Beyer told the Cosmos Club gathering. To realize democratic control, he called for government administration of the railways with strong union participation—a version of what he had created in the arsenals. Beyer's idea helped crystallize the movement for the Plumb Plan. Subsequently he worked with Bert Jewell of the AFL's Railway Employees Division, William Johnston of the IAM, and Warren Stone of the Brotherhood of Engineers for its passage in the Congress. Although the Plumb Plan was never enacted, Beyer did insert its faith in union-management cooperation into the labor-management cooperation plan he drafted for the B&O Railroad in 1922. By then Beyer had emerged as one of the most pro-union industrial relations consultants in the country. However, by then it was also clear that he was in a distinct minority among industrial relations practitioners.[32]

Much more popular became the views of W. L. Mackenzie King. Since he was first engaged by John D. Rockefeller Jr. to help fashion a representation plan at CFI in the aftermath of the Ludlow massacre, King had been a leading advocate of workplace representation. His 1918 book, *Industry and Humanity*, confirmed his place in the front ranks of its theorists; his wartime experience only enhanced his reputation. King spent a great deal of time in 1918 and 1919 in the United States, acting as a consultant for the Rockefeller interests, General Electric, and Bethlehem Steel, as they struggled to respond to wartime demands for democracy in the workplace. Frank Walsh's prewar foe did not directly oppose unionism. But he did defend the principle that employers should not have to bargain collectively with any entity apart from a committee of their own workers. And in doing that King helped provide the intellectual rationale behind company unionism.[33]

King entered the fray with two fundamental assumptions that would ultimately separate him from Beyer. He sought to replace what he considered "brute struggle" in the workplace with the ideal of "mutual service," and he believed government efforts to promote industrial democracy by aggressively intervening in the workplace were counterproductive. In his book on the subject, King outlined what he considered the essentials of proper representation in industry. Industrial governance, he maintained, should aim to provide representation to four parties: capital, labor, management, and the community. Out of "round table" deliberations between these parties, he argued, "the conflict of opposed interests will vanish before an understanding of common interests." Unions were not essential to this process. In fact the inference underlying King's work, as one scholar has pointed out, was that American unions would "eventually give way to more cooperative, less combative agencies."[34]

About the role of the state, King was much less ambiguous. Perhaps still smarting from his tangle with the USCIR, King had been critical of the intervention of the NWLB into workplace relations during wartime. Federal involvement, he believed, increased the chances that workers would choose conflict over cooperation, turning to strikes and trade unionism and exploiting government agencies to win otherwise unattainable demands. In a confidential memo to GE executives during the war, King outlined the dangers as he saw them. The NWLB and other agencies, he concluded, "enabled [workers] to adopt tactics which quickly brought about intervention from the outside." Thus federal intervention actually encouraged militancy. When "appeal to outside intervention is left open to employees, corporations must expect that advantage will sooner or later be taken of it," King explained. The only way to halt the cycle of labor militancy and government intervention was for companies to "render appeals for intervention improbable" by instituting their own forms of representation.[35]

King's vision quickly emerged as the dominant one within industrial relations circles. Even before 1919 had ended, representation plans that bore his stamp were in place or under development at CFI, Standard Oil, General Electric, and Bethlehem Steel. Eugene Grace personally thanked King for his assistance, noting that King's representation plan "proved most conducive to promoting cordial relations" with his employees. And the labor movement's bitter epithet, "Rockefeller unionism," provided an enduring monument to King's successful endeavors. Those who sympathized with Beyer's ideals fared less well. They had been briefly encouraged by the formation of the Federated American Engineering Societies (FAES) in 1920, whose first president, Herbert Hoover, attempted to foster continued collaboration between efficiency engineers and unions. Within two years of its founding, however, conservatives gained the upper hand in the FAES. By 1921 progressive engineers were forced to retreat to more hospitable environs in academia or in the clothing industry, where the ACWA survived and a group of progressive employers implemented efficiency methods with the union's cooperation. Banished to these small pockets of experimentation, progressive efficiency engineers could do little more than bide their time as the company union movement usurped much of their influence.[36]

As the Great War came to an end, America's leading employers understood that wartime developments had created what Howard Dickman later called a moral "duty to bargain." One of the first to accept the challenge was the man who had been vilified by prewar proponents of industrial democracy, John D. Rockefeller Jr. Only weeks after the armistice, Rockefeller began a campaign to influence his fellow employers. On December 5, 1918, Rockefeller addressed the Reconstruction Conference of the U.S. Chamber of Commerce in Atlantic City. In his speech, Rockefeller praised the work of the NWLB in the United States and of the Whitley committees in England. He suggested that the spirit of their reforms already had been embodied in the representation plans he had introduced at CFI and Standard Oil, and he invited employers to emulate him. "Surely it is not consistent for us as Americans," Rockefeller later explained, "to demand democracy in government and practice autocracy in industry." Rockefeller later paid for the distribution of over one million copies of this speech. He was soon inundated by requests from executives at the American Sash and Door Company, Willys-Overland, the Wisconsin Chamber of Commerce, the Baltimore Dry Docks and Shipbuilding Company, and many other companies seeking his advice on workplace representation.[37]

One of the first to follow Rockefeller's example was General Electric, a company that was still recovering from its bout of wartime labor militancy. The growth of the electrical federation had shocked GE officials. Following the lockout of the union in December 1918, corporate counsel Owen D. Young sought to understand what had gone wrong. In January 1919, he commissioned a private investigation. What he found disturbed him and led him to authorize a more thorough study. Young subsequently hired journalist Atherton Brownell to study GE employee relations in secret and to prepare a report and recommendations. Brownell's report sketched a dire picture of restive workers and reorganizing unions. One of its lone bright spots was the situation in Lynn, where Brownell found that shop committees had worked to diffuse conflict. He therefore recommended that the company establish shop committees in each GE plant "as a shock absorber to labor troubles." His recommendations were supported by GE's Lynn managers. Richard H. Rice, who succeeded Walter Fish as superintendent of the Lynn plant, became an enthusiastic proponent of his shop committees. "My advice to those who ask me about introducing the Works Council into their plant," Rice explained, "is that it is a very excellent thing to do." With Young's encouragement, other GE plants moved to replicate the Lynn success story.[38]

Later in 1919, Young joined John D. Rockefeller Jr., A. C. Bedford of Standard Oil, and executives from seven other large-scale enterprises in creating the secret Special Conference Committee, a group of corporate executives who advocated workplace representation after the war. Over the next two years, hundreds of colleagues followed their lead in fostering what one government official called "a deluge of shop committees and employee-representation plans." The New Jersey State Chamber of Commerce sponsored three conferences on "Democracy in Industry." At least sixteen Cleveland firms adopted employee representation plans. Nationally, over 700,000 workers had some kind of company-sponsored representation by 1921. Edward Filene, a lonely voice for such ideas before the war, now found many of his employer colleagues "quite evangelistic about industrial democracy." According to former NWLB member Frederic C. Hood, managers simply "got Shop Committee religion."[39]

To be sure, most employers embraced this version of industrial democracy only as an alternative to unionism and a method to stabilize workplace relations. Of the 225 shop representation plans in operation in 1919, fully 175 of them were among firms in the metal trades, where labor militancy had been endemic and trade unionism's growth robust. In such strike-prone industries, workplace representation was a way of "inoculating against Bolshevism," as one pamphlet put it. But if most managers adopted the religion of industrial democracy at the last minute, their conversion sounded convincing. J. R. McWane of Birmingham's American Cast Iron Pipe Company expressed relief that "the day of the 'big stick' in industry has passed and we have learned a better way." Antiunion idealogue Walter G. Merritt hoped that now employers would "go bravely forward with the democratic faith" to substitute "factory solidarity" for "class solidarity." And Leopold Demuth, a New York manufacturer, assured skeptics that the implementation of a representation plan at his business did not impair his authority at all. "On the contrary," he boasted, "that authority has been strengthened."[40]

Of course, many employers had little choice but to put on such a brave face. Workers had so successfully equated unionism with "an American feeling" during the war that managers had to do more than simply lock out unions and crush them after the war. They could not restore their legitimacy at the point of a bayonet. But they might regain it through employee representation. Thus one of the outstanding features of the postwar company union movement was the overt way in which employers attempted to lay claim to the ideal of industrial democracy. A publicist named John Leitch devised an elaborate bicameral shop committee model, complete with upper and lower houses, a constitution, and an executive branch—the plant manager—en-

THE GOODYEAR TIRE & RUBBER CO.

GRIEVANCES
MR ADAMS

"Don't Go Away Sore—Let's Talk It Over."

As this company poster makes clear, many employers understood the importance of establishing grievance procedures through their employee representation plans following the war, ca. 1921. (Hagley Museum and Library, Wilmington, Delaware)

dowed with veto power. He peddled this plan to corporate managers around the country as his "Industrial Democracy." Many companies that preferred their own models to Leitch's—such as the Dan River and Riverside Cotton Mills Company of Virginia—also called their company unions "Industrial Democracies." Others, meanwhile, adopted variations on the theme. A plan designed by Paul Litchfield of Goodyear Tire and Rubber was called the "Industrial Republic." Each of these plans bore testament to employers' vital interest in making industrial democracy their own after the war.[41]

But before democracy was to come to industry, virtually all employers felt that it must first be made safe. The chief problem with shop committees during the war had been the interference of the government investigators who protected the committees from managerial domination. A 1919 study by the National Industrial Conference Board pointed out that with "few exceptions" the most unfavorable experiences with representation were those in which the government had set up the committees. Once government meddling was eliminated, it was important that representation plans be initiated from the right quarter. Managers naturally agreed with Young's adviser Atherton Brownell that "the initiative for the machinery" of workplace representation should "come from the intellectual class, namely the company."[42]

As employers sought to take the initiative for representation away from workers, they also tightened control over its implementation. Management personnel invariably supervised postwar shop committee voting. And although the NWLB had usually demanded that elections be held off of company grounds, postwar elections were held on-site; those prospective industrial democrats who had not learned from firsthand experience were informed by helpful NICB reports that efforts "to hold elections away from the plant and outside of work hours have not met with success."[43]

To ensure that representation plans would function smoothly once created, employers narrowly defined the industrial rights they were granting in order to create what Litchfield of Goodyear called "a citizenship of the right type." The wartime shop committees of the NWLB did not restrict the right to vote for representatives on the basis of nationality, sex, or race. But postwar employers were not so democratic. Goodyear demanded that workers be at least eighteen years old, American citizens fluent in English, and employees for at least six months before they could qualify as "Industrians"— Goodyear's term for its company citizens. International Harvester and New York Telephone also required committee representatives to be U.S. citizens. American Multigraph set a quota for committee representatives so that men would outnumber women by four to one. The Bloedel Donovan Lumber Mills of Bellingham, Washington, among many others, explicitly excluded IWW members from company citizenship. Meanwhile, supervisors usually qualified as representatives of workers on the committees.[44]

Such "democracies" offered workers' representatives a severely limited sphere of power. Matters concerning the work process, piece rates, and classification, all of which were the subject of negotiation in NWLB shop committees, were regularly excluded from postwar shop committee agendas. Such items, as one NICB manual explained, "are clearly subjects to be reserved to the jurisdiction of management, except in so far as a Works Council may make suggestions or recommendations relating thereto." William L. Stoddard, the former NWLB examiner in Lynn who hired himself out as a consultant to employers after the war, advised that such issues be kept off the table. A properly administered shop committee, he argued, would make clear that plant affairs would be "controlled jointly or collectively up to a certain point only." The NICB suggested a new term to describe the kind of negotiations that were to occur under shop committee representation. It was to be "collective dealing" rather than collective bargaining.[45]

Clearly, postwar company unions offered a watered-down version of democracy in industry. Rather than seeking to empower workers, they were mostly intended to "transmit the personality and character of the management to the men most effectively," as one GE manager put it; they were instruments through which to "cultivate the interest of the rank and file in the problems of management." Indeed, most of their supporters agreed that postwar shop committees were useful primarily for one purpose. D. R. Kennedy, an adviser to several companies that instituted representation plans, put his finger on it. It made no difference whether a plant called its plan a shop committee or a works council, Kennedy argued. For by any name they all meant "the one big fundamental point—*the open shop*." For most managers, that, of course, was the attraction. Mary Van Kleeck learned as much when she studied the representation plan at Rockefeller's CFI. Following the war, she interviewed Dick Hart, who served as CFI's counsel when it set up its company union, and was shocked by Hart's blunt description of the philosophy of his company's president. "When I asked whether he had 'a yearning for democracy,'" Van Kleeck recalled, "Hart laughed and said that he was a thorough-going autocrat."[46]

Yet it is not enough to point out the limitations of postwar shop committees and the duplicity of some of their proponents. Those who would understand the legacy of World War I for American labor cannot afford to minimize how successful employers were in using their version of industrial democracy to regain legitimacy after the war. Although they carefully limited the extent to which they shared power with workers through committee representation, employers were forced to make significant concessions and to admit that workers had a right to a voice on the job.

The importance of this admission should not be overlooked. As more recent studies of such welfare capitalist pioneers as Goodyear and the Endicott-Johnson Company have shown, where workers possessed weak union traditions, shop committees provided opportunities for collective expression and served as a check on capricious management decisions. Enlightened employers understood, as one scholar put it, that "an alienated company union was no more useful than an AFL local" in their plants. Such employers were likely to tolerate more autonomy from their shop committees than AFL leaders were willing to admit. At GE, for example, shop committees served as an effective vehicle for workers' protests during a period of layoffs and wage reductions that occurred between 1920 and 1922. In Lynn and Schenectady, walkouts by machinists, molders, coremakers, and armature winders disrupted production. Workers claimed "they would rather quit than stand for what they considered an injustice," and through their committees they circulated petitions with "a great deal of agitation." Such talk led one company investigator to worry that the G.E. *Review*, a paper designed to trumpet the virtues of industrial democracy at the Pittsfield plant, was being "used by agitators," and officials in Schenectady even canceled a scheduled speech on shop representation for fear that it would only stir further unrest. In Lynn, meanwhile, shop committee representatives confessed privately that they were "still trade unionists at heart." Similarly, the Goodyear Industrial Assembly demanded wage increases in 1923 and went so far as to adjourn their meetings indefinitely until management took their demands seriously.[47]

It was because such company unions could occasionally serve as effective instruments for the expression of grievances that they helped retard unionization in the early twenties. This accounts for the ambivalence with which a good number of employers viewed workplace representation. Many managers came to find their shop committees uncomfortably independent—or at least autonomous enough to make them sympathetic to the conclusion drawn by of one their colleagues: "If we had a choice," that employer commented in an NICB survey, "we think that we would be glad to eliminate this committee."[48]

Nor can it be denied that employers' representation plans compared favorably to unions in the minds of a significant number of workers. If some workers felt unions were too exclusive, shop committees promised a broader industrial citizenship. Thus John Leitch boasted that his plan would work "with both male and female labor, with skilled and unskilled workers, with the illiterate and the intelligent, with those who couldn't speak English and those who could"—certainly a wider spectrum of workers than that sought out by the typical AFL craft union. If other workers saw unions as inhibiting the industrious, shop committees offered "equality of opportunity—not equality of power or equality of reward," as another company union proponent put it. And if still other workers saw unions as conflict-ridden organizations, shop committees promised to foster cooperation. At least one employer was willing to bet that the average worker sought only that. "There isn't any element in this country that is more jealous for the sacred principles involved in individual ownership" than the nation's workers, concluded H. R. Fitzgerald of the Dan River Cotton Company. All they wanted was "to be treated fairly." The quiescence of those workers who enjoyed the fruits of 1920s welfare capitalism lent more than a little credence to Fitzgerald's argument.[49]

At the very least, AFL unionists found the company unions frustrating rivals. Activists were obligated to attack their credibility continually in the years after the war. But the content of their attacks revealed how much unions themselves had fallen on the defensive and how successful employers were in usurping labor's central demand. At International Harvester, activists condemned employers for trying to "bunco their employees into thinking that they are getting a real taste of industrial democracy." John Golden of the UTW, meanwhile, lashed out at the "57 varieties" of "industrial democracy" that circulated after the war. There was "one plan and one plan only" that ensured real industrial democracy, he claimed, and that was "trade union collective bargaining."[50]

Those workers who had been most active in organizing during the war did not willingly surrender their claim to industrial democracy following the armistice. "The American labor movement will fight this Rockefeller plan of organization," announced Schenectady's GE activists, so that real "industrial democracy shall be applied." Yet the fact that unionists were forced to distinguish between industrial democracy and company unionism hinted at the success employers enjoyed in equating the two.[51]

That trade unionists were forced to make this distinction also illustrated how much things had changed since 1915. When Frank Walsh and Basil Manly had invoked "industrial democracy" in the final report of the USCIR, they did so in defense of trade unionism. Only a half decade later, thanks in large measure to the war's impact, workplace relations were significantly more democratic in many sectors of industry. Yet it was hardly the sort of democracy that Walsh and Manly had foreseen. Such employers as Walsh's erstwhile foe John D. Rockefeller Jr. appeared to have as much claim to industrial democracy as did trade unionists in the 1920s, leaving Americans no closer to answering the question that had perplexed Leon Marshall in 1918: What is industrial democracy? The great labor struggles that had unfolded since 1912 had irrevocably placed that question at the center of America's debate regarding the labor problem. But they had failed to provide a definitive answer to Marshall's question. That task would fall to a subsequent generation. And this made the legacy of labor's "great war" bitter indeed for those activists who had so recently believed that the "dream of industrial democracy is coming true."[52]

EPILOGUE.
THE ORIGINS OF
MODERN AMERICAN
LABOR RELATIONS

In a short time—perhaps within two years—the die
will be cast, and the form of the new world will be
fashioned beyond the power of living men and women
materially to change.
—*Allan L. Benson, 1919*

Organized labor's political reversal following the
Great War could scarcely have been more dramatic. In 1918, Washington in-
siders joked that Samuel Gompers had keys to the White House. Three years
later the jokes came at Gompers's expense. A Lafayette-Marne Day dinner
commemorating the Franco-American wartime alliance, held in Washington on September 6, 1921, aptly illustrated how much the tables had turned.
Gompers was a guest at that dinner. In a short speech to the assembled,
he praised the commitment of those who fought the war on the battlefields
of France and in the workshops of the United States. Gompers's speech
elicited some polite applause. He was then followed to the rostrum by another
honored guest, the war hero whom he called "our own wonderful Pershing."
But General John J. Pershing did not reciprocate Gompers's generous words.
Instead, when Pershing rose to speak, "rage fairly consumed him," one observer recalled. He "denied that organized labor had been loyal" during the
war, and "he poured upon the head" of Gompers "a torrent of passionate
contradiction" while organized labor's chief sat humiliated before a "tense and
antagonistic" audience. Afterward Pershing gloated over his dressing down

of "our distinguished old foreign reprobate." When Gompers "implied that American labor had won the war," Pershing explained, "I couldn't restrain myself." So much had changed in the four years since President Wilson himself had stood with Gompers to address an AFL convention.[1]

Nor was the news from the field any better for Gompers and his movement. The 1920s saw the continuing erosion of union ranks and brought no hope of organizing the mass production industries that had been targeted by trade unionists during the Great War. Certainly, organizing failures were not total. In 1923, long after the Red Scare had passed, the memory of union defeats of 1919 had dimmed, and a vigorous open-shop campaign had run its course, union membership was still nearly one million more than it had been in 1914. But, judged in the light of what might have been, the failure seemed immense. To many it appeared that, as one writer put it, the AFL had simply resembled "a grand hotel" in the Wilson era. Hundreds of thousands of workers "checked in, but also checked out, or were driven out." Among those most embittered by this turn of events were militants such as Sam Lavit, who had been so hopeful in that earlier era. Lavit had signed his letters "Yours for Industrial Democracy" during the war. But soon after the armistice he had come to believe that the promised "reconstruction" was simply "the watchword of reaction."[2]

Yet reaction was not the only legacy of that time when dreams of reconstruction had excited radicals. Surveying vestiges of English culture that date to the Great War—from pub closing hours instituted to keep workers sober, to wristwatches (originally a fad in the trenches) meant to keep them on time— Paul Fussell has argued that the "whole texture of British daily life could be said to commemorate the war still." It would not be stretching the point too far to make the same claim for the United States. The Great War left lasting imprints on American politics and culture. And, as with most of the nations that partook in that savage war, the developments that unfolded in the United States between 1914 and 1920 established patterns of industrial relations that would endure for much of the century.[3]

The era of the Great War left the United States a new vocabulary with which to debate the "labor question." The term "industrial democracy" had rarely appeared in American discussions before 1912. It seemed to be everywhere ten years later. Employers continued to "appropriate the unions' slogan" as a name for their company unions, as Irving Bernstein reminds us. But so too did progressives and laborites continue to articulate their vision with this term. The Intercollegiate Socialist Society rechristened itself the League for Industrial Democracy following the war. Glenn Plumb defended his plan for government ownership of the railroads in a book titled *Indus-*

trial Democracy. And in 1922 a group of religious leaders formed the Church League for Industrial Democracy, headed by Rev. Charles D. Williams, a veteran of Frank Walsh's CIR. The very ubiquity of the term memorialized how much the war had changed the American workplace. And when trade unionism again arose in mass production industries in the 1930s, it was "industrial democracy" that unionists promised to secure.[4]

The era of the Great War also saw the rise of new patterns of labor management in the United States. What Frank Walsh and Basil Manly had termed "industrial autocracy" in 1915 had not been overturned in the half decade that followed. But it had been deeply compromised. As E. S. Cowdrick of the Colorado Fuel and Iron Company saw it, the "spell of fear which once forced unquestioning obedience" in the workplace had been "broken" once and for all. In response, industrial relations experts and personnel managers attempted to construct a more just and rational workplace. They did so in the belief that it was "better to have a democracy in industry than a revolution in industry," as one Connecticut employer put it. But their very efforts set in motion a revolution of a different sort, encouraging workers' rising expectations and planting seeds that would germinate in the welfare capitalism of the 1920s, only to be ultimately harvested by the industrial unionism of the 1930s.[5]

Employee representation plans never spread widely through American industry during the decade following the war. It is likely that no more than 10 percent of all workers in manufacturing and mining enjoyed access to shop committee representation by the late 1920s. But where such programs were absent, other benefits of welfare capitalism did spread, including job ladders, profit sharing, and sickness and disability benefits. What was more, the Great War provided a schoolhouse for enlightened managers in such corporations as General Electric, where President Gerard Swope began to speak of "the citizenship theory of labor relations," and in the Taylor Society, where Henry P. Kendall and others kept alive the notion that efficiency could be served by workplace democracy. When the welfare capitalism of the 1920s collapsed in the Great Depression, individuals such as Kendall and Swope were among the first to recognize that the state would have to step in to rescue the order that they had sought to construct.[6]

The Great War left a lasting imprint on American politics as well. The crusade for industrial democracy was unable to sustain the tenuous coalition of trade unionists, progressives, Democrats, and radicals that it had brought together on the eve of the war. During the war that coalition had begun to unravel, and by 1919 it had been destroyed. But relationships forged during the era of the Great War continued to influence political developments. The alliance between the AFL and Wilson's Democratic Party would cool in the

1920s, only to be revived and placed on more durable footing by Franklin D. Roosevelt's New Deal. When that happened, the veterans of labor's Great War would play a key role in the process. Through the 1920s Basil Manly and Frank Walsh kept their ideals alive, Manly as coordinator for the 1924 La Follette campaign, and Walsh as New York's most prominent labor lawyer. In 1932 Walsh headed a committee of Progressives for Roosevelt, and Manly went on to serve as a member (and ultimately the chair) of the New Deal's Federal Power Commission. Meanwhile, other veterans of the earlier struggles spread throughout Franklin Roosevelt's administration, from Felix Frankfurter, who ran a virtual employment bureau for New Dealers, and Otto S. Beyer, who took a post on the National Mediation Board, to William Leiserson, who served on the National Labor Relations Board, and Leon C. Marshall, who joined the National Recovery Administration.

No less did the Great War lastingly shape American labor. Trade unionism emerged from the World War I era more oriented toward Washington, more bureaucratic, and more inimical to radicalism than before. But it also emerged with leaders—including Sidney Hillman and John L. Lewis—who had experienced firsthand what Steve Fraser has called "the institutional interior of the state apparatus." They felt comfortable in turning again to the state in the 1930s. And, when they founded the Congress of Industrial Organizations (CIO) to unionize mass production industries, they could rely on the skills of a number of individuals who had pioneered industrial organizing during World War I. Alfred Coulthand, one of the union militants blacklisted by GE after the war, helped organize the United Electrical Workers at Lynn GE. Horace Riviere, the French Canadian who called out textile weavers during the Rhode Island loomfixers' strike, led the Textile Workers Organizing Committee in New England. And J. A. Lipscomb, an organizer of the failed 1918 Birmingham steel strike, helped reorganize the Mine, Mill, and Smelter Workers in depression-era Alabama.[7]

It is more difficult, of course, to measure the impact of the events described in this book on rank-and-file workers. What lessons were drawn by the black steelworkers who attended Ulysses Hale's strike meetings in Alabama, by the one thousand GE workers organized by Laura Cannon in Fort Wayne, or by the immigrant weavers who responded to Horace Riviere's strike call in Rhode Island? One might reasonably speculate that those who had organized, if only briefly, those who imbibed the wartime fusion of the identities of citizen and worker, or those who learned to assert their rights to "democracy in industry" never again returned to their prewar conceptions of what they deserved in the workplace. Nor does it seem too much to claim that those workers who had won shop representation might have been lastingly changed by their experience. After the war, writer Carroll French thought that it was likely that shop committees "set forces at work whose ultimate consequences cannot be foreseen. Certainly, employees who have experienced representation through shop committees will never be satisfied with less. The chances are rather that they will desire more." The events of the 1930s would certainly bear out the truth of French's analysis.[8]

When John Bellingham appeared before the NWLB on behalf of the Electrical Manufacturing Industry Labor Federation in January 1919, he made a solemn prediction. "Keep your eye on what Schenectady and the allied plants are doing," he told NWLB officials, for "what Schenectady thinks today, the United States does tomorrow, so far as organized labor is concerned."[9] Bellingham was more prescient than he knew. In many ways, the roots of the New Deal labor order—from patterns of industrial organization to models of federal regulation—may be traced back to the struggle to democratize the workplace that took place in Schenectady and so many other settings during the First World War.

And it was only during the New Deal era that the nation would finally reach anything approaching a consensus regarding the meaning of industrial democracy. During those years the phrase that meant so many different things to so many different people during the Great War came to mean one thing. With radicalism contained under the rubric of the CIO and with employer-dominated shop committees prohibited from bargaining on behalf of workers by Section 8(a)2 of the Wagner Act, industrial democracy came to mean trade union collective bargaining under the supervision of a regulatory state. Although that definition made industrial democracy less "ecumenically satisfying" than it had been in the heady days of progressivism's full flower, this was a durable formula. Indeed, it lasted for nearly two generations.

In the late twentieth century, however, the form of industrial democracy that took shape under the New Deal has begun to decompose. Mass production industry is vanishing from the United States, and the regulatory state that can trace its roots back to the Progressive era no longer commands sufficient electoral support to protect it from its enemies. Changing political and economic conditions have placed unions on the defensive and put the labor question again on the national agenda—usually as a question of how American workers might better compete in a global economy. These new developments have in turn resurrected old problems, as a wide spectrum of business leaders, politicians, and management experts have sought to reopen questions that were seemingly settled during the 1930s. To those familiar with the events described in this book, recent developments might seem eerily familiar. After eighty years, Americans appear to be coming full circle to a world before there was a Soviet Union or a New Deal, when there was yet no consensus regarding the role of the state in society, when voluntarism was the dominant social philosophy.

Not surprisingly, as this new economic and political world takes shape, some Americans are advancing new ideas regarding the organization of the workplace. One measure of how far this rethinking has progressed is the extent to which more recent observers have begun to argue that traditional unions have outlived their historical purposes. In words that echo those of 1920s employee representation advocates, such thinkers contend that the global economy demands more flexible and "cooperative" forms of workplace representation that will boost productivity and harness the creativity of workers for the benefit of their enterprises.[10] This sort of thinking has attracted a powerful political following. Nothing better indicates this than the recent efforts that have been undertaken to revise Section 8(a)2 of the Wagner Act—efforts, which, if successful, would reopen the door to employer-initiated shop committees and perhaps even company unions.

The voices that have once again raised this long-dormant debate about the suitability of unions as workers' representatives demonstrate the degree to which we have returned to pre–New Deal conceptions of labor relations. And, like Americans following the Great War, no longer do we share any meaningful consensus on the most vital questions. Nor is there reason to believe that a new consensus will soon replace the one that has crumbled over the last generation. In 1993, President Bill Clinton's secretary of labor Robert Reich and his secretary of commerce Ron Brown appointed the Commission on the Future of Worker-Management Relations to try to suggest the basis for a new consensus. "A healthy society cannot long continue along the path" of "confrontational" labor relations, warned the chairman of that commission, former secretary of labor John T. Dunlop. His words faintly recalled the USCIR report of 1915. But like Frank Walsh's effort, Dunlop's commission produced no legislative remedy that would bridge divisions among enlightened businesspeople and antiunion employers, liberals and libertarians, managers and workers.[11]

So Americans seem to approach once again a crossroads in the development of their labor relations not all that different from the one that they approached during the era of the Great War. Yet our current problems are different in some significant ways. Indeed, those who believe that there can be no democracy in American industry that is not guaranteed by a strong labor movement may well occupy a *less* favorable position than did their forebears. There are at least two reasons for this. First, as this book suggests, the degree to which workers have been able to secure democracy in their workplaces has been linked for some time to the power and political orientation of the federal government. Clearly, the struggle for industrial democracy that stirred so many early in this century coincided with and drew strength from the rise of a strong regulatory state. That a conjuncture of forces is now undermining that model of government is beyond question. All those who share labor's cause have reason to fear the consequences of this development.

But there is another, perhaps more pressing cause for concern. This is simply that the one word that was most central to Progressive-era discussions of the labor problem is virtually absent from the discourse of present-day policymakers. That word is "democracy." Contemporary calls for the revision of the Wagner Act or the reinvention of workplace representation are replete with references to "the need for cooperation" between workers and employers, as the Dunlop Commission phrased it. But seldom do such discussions seriously assess the quality of democracy in the workplace. No doubt this would surprise Progressive-era reformers. In their time they came to understand the close connection between workplace democracy—even if they could not agree on its meaning—and the fate of democracy itself. Unfortunately, however, the Walsh Report's warning that political democracy can thrive "only where there is industrial democracy" finds little resonance today.[12] As we stand on the cusp of an economic transformation that promises changes at least as vast as those ushered in by industrialism, that fact should comfort no one.

NOTES

ABBREVIATIONS USED IN THE NOTES

AC   Anthony Capraro Papers, Immigration History Research Center, St. Paul, Minnesota

ACWA   *Amalgamated Clothing Workers of America Records,* University Publications of America

AFLEC   Minutes of the Executive Council of the AFL, George Meany Memorial Archives, Silver Spring, Maryland

AREP   Amos R. E. Pinchot Papers, Library of Congress, Washington, D.C.

CEP   Carl E. Person Papers, Walter Reuther Memorial Archive, Detroit, Michigan

CM   Charles McCarthy Papers, State Historical Society of Wisconsin, Madison, Wisconsin

CND   Records of the Council of National Defense, National Archives, Washington, D.C.

DJS   David J. Saposs Papers, State Historical Society of Wisconsin, Madison, Wisconsin

DOJ   Records of the Department of Justice, National Archives, Washington, D.C.

DOL   Records of the Department of Labor, National Archives, Washington, D.C.

DS   Doris Stevens Papers, Schlesinger Library, Radcliffe College, Cambridge, Massachusetts

FDR   Franklin D. Roosevelt, Assistant Secretary of the Navy Papers, Franklin D. Roosevelt Presidential Library, Hyde Park, New York

FF   Felix Frankfurter Papers, Library of Congress, Washington, D.C.

FJH   Florence Jaffray Harriman Papers, Library of Congress, Washington, D.C.

FM   Frank Morrison Letterbooks, George Meany Memorial Archives, Silver Spring, Maryland

FMCS   Records of the Federal Mediation and Conciliation Service, National Archives, Washington, D.C.

FPW   Frank P. Walsh Papers, New York Public Library, New York

FWT   Frederick W. Taylor Papers, Stevens Institute of Technology, Hoboken, New Jersey

HCH	Herbert C. Hoover Papers, Herbert C. Hoover Presidential Library, West Branch, Iowa
IAM	International Association of Machinists Library, Washington, D.C.
JB	John Brophy Papers, Mullen Library, Catholic University of America, Washington, D.C.
JD	Josephus Daniels Papers, Library of Congress, Washington, D.C.
JDR	John D. Rockefeller Jr. Papers, Rockefeller Archives Center, North Tarry-town, New York
JF/CFL	John Fitzpatrick Papers, Chicago Federation of Labor Records, Chicago Historical Society, Chicago, Illinois
JJP	John J. Pershing Papers, Library of Congress, Washington, D.C.
JM	*John Mitchell Papers*, Microfilming Corporation of America
JPF	John P. Frey Papers, Library of Congress, Washington, D.C.
JPT	Joseph P. Tumulty Papers, Library of Congress, Washington, D.C.
JRC	John R. Commons Papers, State Historical Society of Wisconsin, Madison, Wisconsin
LDB	Louis D. Brandeis Papers, Library of Congress, Washington, D.C.
LFP	Louis F. Post Papers, Library of Congress, Washington, D.C.
MASC	Records of the Manufacturers' Association of Southern Connecticut, Bridgeport Public Library, Bridgeport, Connecticut
MID	Records of the Military Intelligence Division of the War Department General and Special Staffs, National Archives, Washington, D.C.
MLC	Morris L. Cooke Papers, Franklin D. Roosevelt Presidential Library, Hyde Park, New York
MVK	Mary Van Kleeck Papers, Walter Reuther Memorial Archive, Detroit, Michigan
NCF	Records of the National Civic Federation, New York Public Library, New York
NCWC	National Catholic War Council Papers, Mullen Library, Catholic University of America, Washington, D.C.
NDB	Newton D. Baker Papers, Library of Congress, Washington, D.C.
NICB	Records of the National Industrial Conference Board, Hagley Museum and Library, Wilmington, Delaware
NWLB	Records of the National War Labor Board, National Archives, Washington, D.C.
ODY	Owen D. Young Papers, St. Lawrence University, Canton, New York
OMR	Records of the Offices of the Messrs. Rockefeller, Rockefeller Archives Center, North Tarrytown, New York
OSB	Otto S. Beyer Papers, Library of Congress, Washington, D.C.
PMC	*Records of the President's Mediation Commission, 1917–1919*, University Publications of America
RF	Rockefeller Foundation Papers, Rockefeller Archives Center, North Tarry-town, New York
RFI	Rockefeller Family Interests Records, Rockefeller Archives Center, North Tarrytown, New York
RML	Robert M. La Follette Sr. Papers, Library of Congress, Washington, D.C.

RWW Robert W. Woolley Papers, Library of Congress, Washington, D.C.

SGLB Samuel Gompers Letterbooks, Library of Congress, Washington, D.C.

SGWF War Files of President Samuel Gompers, George Meany Memorial Archives, Silver Spring, Maryland

TDP Thomas Duke Parke Diaries, Birmingham Public Library, Birmingham, Alabama

TR Theodore Roosevelt Papers, Library of Congress, Washington, D.C.

USCIR *Records of the U.S. Commission on Industrial Relations, 1912–1915*, University Publications of America

USFA Records of the Fuel Administration, National Archives, Washington, D.C.

USRA Records of the United States Railroad Administration, National Archives, Washington, D.C.

USSB Records of the United States Shipping Board, National Archives, Washington, D.C.

WBD William B. Dickson Papers, Pennsylvania State University, State College, Pennsylvania

WBW William B. Wilson Papers, Historical Society of Pennsylvania, Philadelphia, Pennsylvania

WHT William Howard Taft Papers, Library of Congress, Washington, D.C.

WJL W. Jett Lauck Papers, Alderman Library, University of Virginia, Charlottesville, Virginia

WLMK William Lyon Mackenzie King Papers, Canadian National Archives, Ottawa, Canada

WML William M. Leiserson Papers, State Historical Society of Wisconsin, Madison, Wisconsin

WW Woodrow Wilson Papers, Library of Congress, Washington, D.C.

INTRODUCTION

1. *Congressional Record*, 65th Cong., 2d sess., July 22, 1918, p. 9173.

2. Telegram to Woodrow Wilson, July 14, 1918, and Employees Brief, August 9, 1918, casefile 231, NWLB; Crowther, "The Fetish of Industrial Democracy," 23; L. C. Marshall to A. S. Johnson et al., July 25, 1918, series 350, box 37, file 53000-1, USSB.

3. Hobsbawm, *Labouring Men*, chap. 8. See also Dubofsky, "Workers' Movements in North America, 1873–1920," 38.

4. See Nelson, *Frederick W. Taylor*; Nelson, *A Mental Revolution*; Braverman, *Labor and Monopoly Capital*; Noble, *America by Design*; Montgomery, *Workers' Control in America*.

5. Evans, Rueschemeyer, and Skocpol, *Bringing the State Back In*; Thompson, *The Making of the English Working Class*, 12.

6. On the first school, see Link, *"The Higher Realism of Woodrow Wilson"*; Link, *Woodrow Wilson and the Progressive Era*; Leuchtenberg, "The New Deal and the Analogue of War"; Blum, *Woodrow Wilson and the Politics of Morality*; Davis, "Welfare, Reform, and World War I."

On the second school, see Skowronek, *Building a New American State*; Cuff, "Herbert Hoover, the Ideology of Voluntarism, and War Organization during the Great War"; Cuff,

"Organizing for the War"; Cuff, *The War Industries Board*; Hawley, *The Great War and the Search for a Modern Order*; Wiebe, *The Search for Order*; Kennedy, *Over Here*.

On the third school, see Sklar, "Woodrow Wilson and the Political Economy of Modern U.S. Liberalism"; Sklar, *The Corporate Reconstruction of American Capitalism*; Kolko, *The Triumph of Conservatism*; Weinstein, *The Corporate Ideal in the Liberal State*; Lustig, *Corporate Liberalism*. For a critique of this approach, see Block, "Beyond Corporate Liberalism."

7. At least two books do probe the working-class dimensions of progressive reform: see Buenker, *Urban Liberalism and Progressive Reform*, and Thelen, *The New Citizenship*. But neither sheds much light on Wilsonianism. On Wilson labor policies, see Cuff, *The War Industries Board*; Kennedy, *Over Here*; Conner, *The National War Labor Board*; Ramirez, *When Workers Fight*; Bustard, "The Human Factor"; Hurvitz, "The Meaning of Industrial Conflict in Some Ideologies of the Early 1920's"; Breen, "Administrative Politics and Labor Policy in the First World War"; Breen, "The Labor Market, the Reform Impetus, and the Great War"; Breen, "The Mobilization of Skilled Labor in World War I."

8. Skocpol, *Protecting Soldiers and Mothers*; Skocpol, "Political Response to Capitalist Crisis"; Block, "The Ruling Class Does Not Rule"; Block, *Revising State Theory*. For differing perspectives, see Poulantzas, *Political Power and Social Classes*, and Miliband, *Class Power and State Power*.

9. On labor and the law, see Atleson, *Values and Assumptions in American Labor Law*; Dubofsky, *The State and Labor in Modern America*; Ernst, "The Lawyers and the Labor Trust"; Fink, "Labor, Liberty, and the Law"; Forbath, *Law and the Shaping of the American Labor Movement*; Hattam, *Labor Visions and State Power*; O'Brien, "Business Unionism versus Responsible Unionism"; Ross, *A Muted Fury*; Tomlins, *Labor Law in America*; Tomlins, *The State and the Unions*.

10. Mink, *Old Labor and New Immigrants*; Greene, " 'The Strike at the Ballot Box' "; Greene, *Pure and Simple Politics*. See also Karson, *American Labor Unions and Politics*; Greenstone, *Labor in American Politics*; and Rogin, "The Political Functions of an Antipolitical Doctrine."

11. For an overview, see Brody, "The Old Labor History and the New"; Montgomery, "To Study the People"; Kazin, "Struggling with Class Struggle"; Kreuger, "American Labor Historiography"; and Fink, "American Labor History."

12. Examples of the "old" approach are Jones, "The Wilson Administration and Organized Labor"; Krivy, "American Organized Labor and the First World War"; Smith, "Organized Labor and the Government"; Grubbs, *The Struggle for Labor Loyalty*; Best, "President Wilson's Second Industrial Conference"; Hurvitz, "Ideology and Industrial Conflict"; Larson, *Labor and Foreign Policy*. The most insightful examples of community or craft studies include Frank, *Purchasing Power*; Arnesen, *Waterfront Workers of New Orleans*; Emmons, *The Butte Irish*; Goldberg, *A Tale of Three Cities*; Cooper, *Once a Cigar Maker*; Kazin, *The Barons of Labor*; Barrett, *Work and Community in the Jungle*; and Norwood, *Labor's Flaming Youth*. On the synthesis question, see Moody and Kessler-Harris, *Perspectives on American Labor History*. And for one ambitious attempt at a synthetic history of this period, see Dawley, *Struggles for Justice*.

13. Montgomery, *The Fall of the House of Labor*; Montgomery, *Workers' Control in America*.

14. Montgomery, *Workers' Control in America*, 98, 99.

15. Montgomery, *The Fall of the House of Labor*, 370, 7.

16. Zeitlin, " 'Rank and Filism' in British Labour History," 47; Tolliday and Zeitlin, eds., *Shop Floor Bargaining and the State*. The phrase "cockpit of social consciousness" is drawn from Kazin, "The Limits of the Workplace," 111. See also Kazin, *The Populist Persuasion*.

17. Jacoby, *Masters to Managers*, 4; Jacoby, *Employing Bureaucracy*; Gitelman, *Legacy of the Ludlow Massacre*; Nelson, "The Company Union Movement"; Nelson, *Managers and Workers*.

18. Gerstle, *Working-Class Americanism*; see also Cohen, *Making a New Deal*.

19. Montgomery's work itself has left open to question how widespread the demand for workers' control actually was. He cites no specific examples of the use of the workers' control slogan in the essay on "new unionism" that most scholars cite in reference to his argument. See Montgomery, *Workers' Control in America*, 99.

20. Gerstle, *Working-Class Americanism*. On the plasticity of the concept of industrial democracy, see Gilbert, *Designing the Industrial State*, 80–120; Brody, "Workplace Contractualism in Comparative Perspective"; Lichtenstein and Harris, "A Century of Industrial Democracy in America"; Derber, "Thoughts on the Historical Study of Industrial Democracy"; Derber, *The American Idea of Industrial Democracy*; Gudza, "Industrial Democracy"; Dickman, *Industrial Democracy in America*. On the search for a transcendent political language, see Salvatore, "Some Thoughts on Class and Citizenship," 216; Kazin, *The Populist Persuasion*. For the cigar makers' statement, see "Statement on Behalf of the Striking Cigar Makers from the Offterdinger Factory," casefile 1, box 19, NWLB.

21. Walsh quoted in *Bridgeport Labor Leader*, August 29, 1918.

22. For more on this, see the essays in Lichtenstein and Harris, *Industrial Democracy in America*.

CHAPTER ONE

1. United States Commission on Industrial Relations, *Final Report of the Commission on Industrial Relations*, 17–18.

2. "Investigation by Flashlight," *New Republic*, February 13, 1915, 35–36; *Masses*, quoted in Adams, *Age of Industrial Violence*, 220; *Seattle Union Record*, November 13, 1915; *Christian Socialist* (September 1915): 1.

3. *Iron Age*, August 26, 1915, 474; *New York Herald*, May 30, 1915; Chambers, *Paul U. Kellogg and "The Survey,"* 49–50; Fitch, "The Commons Report," 8; "Industrial Conflict," *New Republic*, August 28, 1915, 90–91; quotation from Commons, *Myself*, 167.

4. Kaufman, *Samuel Gompers and the Origins of the AFL*, chaps. 1–3; Rogin, "The Political Functions of an Antipolitical Doctrine"; Dubofsky, *The State and Labor in Modern America*, chap. 2; Greene, "The Strike at the Ballot Box" (Ph.D. diss.), 104–30.

5. Greenstone, *Labor in American Politics*, 30–31; Greene, "The Strike at the Ballot Box" (Ph.D. diss.), 288–307; Gompers, "Labor's Political Campaign," 803; William B. Wilson, "The Democratic Party and Labor," 9.

6. Wilson quote from Link et al., *The Papers of Woodrow Wilson*, 19:245; Jones, "The Wilson Administration and Organized Labor," 41; Boemeke, "The Wilson Administration, Organized Labor, and the Colorado Coal Strike," chap. 2; Smith, "Organized Labor and the Government in the Wilson Era."

7. Clements, *The Presidency of Woodrow Wilson*, 73–75; Gompers, "Labor's Political Program," 804–8; Dubofsky, "Abortive Reform," 202.

8. Grossman, *The Department of Labor*, 9–10; *New York Times*, March 9, 1913.

9. Pritchard, *William B. Wilson*; Babson, *William B. Wilson and the Department of Labor*; William B. Wilson, "The Democratic Party and Labor," 24; Clements, *The Presidency of Woodrow Wilson*, 76–78.

10. Post, "A Carpet-Bagger in South Carolina," 73; Clements, *The Presidency of Woodrow Wilson*, 77–78; "The Labor Department and Its Conciliators," *Machinists' Monthly Journal* 28 (April 1916): 344–45.

11. Bing, "The Work of the Wage-Adjustment Boards," 423; *Proceedings of the Thirty-Third Annual Convention of the American Federation of Labor*, 174–75; Boston Branch of the NMTA to President Woodrow Wilson, April 4, 1914, series 5, folder 74, WBW; Boemeke, "The Wilson Administration, Organized Labor, and the Colorado Coal Strike," 100–104.

12. Sarasohn, *The Party of Reform*, 184. Woodrow Wilson to Ben R. Tillman, March 21, 1913; quotation from Ben R. Tillman to Woodrow Wilson, March 24, 1913; and W. B. Wilson to Woodrow Wilson, May 13, 1913, all in series 4, casefile 19c, reel 172, WW.

13. Gompers, *American Labor and the War*, 35–36.

14. Hunter, *Labor in Politics*, 10; Keiser, "John Fitzpatrick and Progressive Unionism"; McKillen, "Chicago Workers and the Struggle to Democratize Diplomacy"; Maurer, *It Can Be Done*; Rodden, *The Fighting Machinists*, 47–49; Perlman, *The Machinists*, 39; Raddock, *Portrait of an American Labor Leader*.

15. Foner, *History of the Labor Movement in the United States*, vol. 5, *The AFL in the Progressive Era*, chap. 1; Adams, *Age of Industrial Violence*, 1–24; Fine, "Without Blare of Trumpets," chaps. 4–5; Steffens, "An Experiment in Good Will," 1436.

16. Chambers, *Paul U. Kellogg and "The Survey,"* 49; petition quoted in Rapport, "The United States Commission on Industrial Relations," 216.

17. Adams, *Age of Industrial Violence*, 60–72.

18. Rapport, "The United States Commission on Industrial Relations," 36–43.

19. William B. Wilson, "Memorandum for the President Relative to Nominations of Members for the Commission on Industrial Relations," April 22, 1913; Woodrow Wilson to Louis D. Brandeis, April 24, 1913; Brandeis to Wilson, May 19, 1913; all in series 4, casefile 158, reel 231, WW.

20. Harriman, *From Pinafores to Politics*, 131.

21. Louis D. Brandeis to Woodrow Wilson, May 26, 1913; Brandeis to W. G. McAdoo, May 22, 1913; Boyd Fisher to Woodrow Wilson, June 27, 1913; all in series 4, casefile 158, reel 231, WW.

22. Frank Walsh to Woodrow Wilson, June 20, 1913, series 4, casefile 158, reel 231, WW; Barton, "Frank P. Walsh," 24; Walsh to George Creel, September 3, 1913, and Joseph B. Shannon to Charles P. Higgins, September 4, 1913, both in box 33, FPW.

23. Barton, "Frank P. Walsh," 24; "Chairman Walsh," *Masses* 6 (September 1915): 10.

24. Ralph Sucher, "Draft Biographical Sketch of Frank P. Walsh," box 104, FPW; first quotation from Barton, "Frank P. Walsh," 24; Garwood, *Crossroads of America*, 195–97; Reddig, *Tom's Town*, 33–37, 53–58; second quotation from Walsh to David E. Lilienthal, January 10, 1921, box 10, FPW; last quotation from Barton, "Frank P. Walsh," 24.

25. First quotation from Walsh to David E. Lilienthal, January 10, 1921, box 10, FPW;

Creel, *Rebel at Large*, 43–54; journalist quoted is Boyd Fisher to Woodrow Wilson, June 27, 1913, series 4, casefile 158, reel 231, WW; Garwood, *Crossroads of America*, 198; Walsh quoted in Creel, "Why Industrial War," 6.

26. Frank P. Walsh, "Lawson and Liberty," 87; Walsh to John Fitzpatrick, February 11, 1921, box 10, FPW; Walsh to Doris Stevens, June 28, 1916, folder 35, and Walsh to Stevens, October 21, 1915, folder 33, DS. Walsh had a love affair with National Women's Party activist Doris Stevens during 1915–16 that is chronicled in correspondence contained in the Stevens papers.

27. First quotation from Walsh to Doris Stevens, November 14, 1915, folder 33, and Walsh to Stevens, May 7, 1916, folder 35, DS; historian quoted is Montgomery, *The Fall of the House of Labor*, 361; Shanley, "Mr. Frank Walsh's Career," 329–31; Walsh's view of his profession is in Walsh to Stevens, August 17, 1916, file 35, DS; Creel, "Why Industrial War," 6; Rapport, "The United States Commission on Industrial Relations," 84; Walsh's view of feminism is in Walsh to Stevens, December 29?, 1915, folder 30, DS; Meehan, "Frank P. Walsh and the American Labor Movement," 27; Walsh's view of political independence is in Walsh to Patrick Cook, December 4, 1916, box 4, FPW.

28. Frank Walsh to Doris Stevens, February 22, 1916, folder 30, DS; Sara Bard Field to Walsh, July 30, 1915, box 33, and Helen Marot to Walsh, June 1, 1917, box 4, FPW.

29. *New Republic*, August 28, 1915, 89; Walsh quote from untitled, undated opening charge to the USCIR, box 33, FPW; Commons, *Myself*, 165–66.

30. For background, see Adams, *Age of Industrial Violence*.

31. Walsh quoted in *New York Times*, February 16, 1914; Tumulty quotation from Link, *The Papers of Woodrow Wilson*, 50:379; Florence Harriman to Woodrow Wilson, February 18, 1914, box 11, FJH; Rapport, "The United States Commission on Industrial Relations," 109.

32. Walsh quotation from Frank P. Walsh to Charles McCarthy, July 15, 1914, reel 7, CM; Smith and Martin quoted in *Congressional Record*, 63d Cong., 2d sess., July 7, 1914, pp. 11681–83; L. O. Bricker to Walsh, July 14, 1914, Lewis K. Brown to Walsh, July 24, 1914, and Walsh to Brown, July 24, 1914, all in reel 7, CM; A. M. Daly, "Steel and Iron at Birmingham," August 1914, reel 12, *USCIR*. On the strike in Atlanta, see Fink, *The Fulton Bag and Cotton Mill Strike of 1914–1915*.

33. *New Republic*, August 28, 1915, 89; Lippmann, "Mr. Rockefeller on the Stand," 12–13. See also "Rockefeller Knew," *La Follette's Weekly Magazine* 7 (June 1915): 2.

34. Frank Walsh to William Marion Reedy, April 17, 1915, box 33, FPW.

35. John Werlick to Woodrow Wilson, June 20, 1915, series 4, casefile 158, reel 232, WW; "Walsh and Wilson," *Machinists' Monthly Journal* 28 (August 1915): 682; W. A. Bowen to Woodrow Wilson, May 4, 1915, series 4, casefile 158, reel 232, WW.

36. First quotation from Creel, "Why Industrial War," 6; Walsh's second quotation from "Testimony of W. L. M. King Given before the U.S. Commission on Industrial Relations," May 24–25, 1915, pp. 64–65, box 18, folder 131, record group 3, series 900, RF.

37. Rodgers, *The Work Ethic in Industrial America*, 58; Strum, *Brandeis*, 24; Forcey, *The Crossroads of Liberalism*; Forcey, "Walter Weyl and the Class War," 272; Lippmann, *Drift and Mastery*, 81; Walter Lippmann to Theodore Roosevelt, June 1, 1914, reel 185, TR. For splendid accounts of the origins of the industrial democracy discourse, see Montgomery, "Industrial Democracy or Democracy in Industry?" and Harris, "Industrial Democracy and Liberal Capitalism."

38. Gitelman, *Legacy of the Ludlow Massacre*, 17–20, 37–67; Perlman and Taft, *History of Labor in the United States*, 336–40; Esberey, *Knight of the Holy Spirit*, 75–83.

39. Walsh, "Perilous Philanthropy," 262, 264; *Proceedings of the Twenty-Fifth Consecutive and Second Biennial Convention of the United Mine Workers of America*, 1:531.

40. United States Commission on Industrial Relations, *Final Report and Testimony*, 8:7763–7897, 7794; "Testimony of W. L. M. King Given before the U.S. Commission on Industrial Relations," Washington, D.C., May 24–25, 1915, box 18, folder 131, record group 3, series 900, RF.

41. Charles McCarthy to Frank Walsh, October 17, 1914, USCIR file, box 42, WML; Walsh "Perilous Philanthropy," 262–64; Walsh to J. D. Rockefeller Jr., July 24, 1915, Industrial Relations Committee, subject file 35, AREP; Basil Manly to Walsh, June 19, 1915, box 33, FPW; United States Commission on Industrial Relations, *Final Report of the Commission on Industrial Relations*, 17–18; Commons, *Myself*, 167; Harriman, *From Pinafores to Politics*, 175.

42. Chambers, *Paul U. Kellogg and "The Survey*," 49–50; Fitch, "The Commons Report," 8; "Industrial Conflict," *New Republic*, August 28, 1915, 90–91; Hoke Smith to Jerome Jones, March 28, 1916, folder 7, box 24, AREP; Sandburg, "The Walsh Report," 198; Mrs. Lee Champion to Woodrow Wilson, June 1, 1915, series 4, casefile 158, reel 232, WW; Adams, *Age of Industrial Violence*, 219–20; Eugene V. Debs to Walsh, October 9, 1915, box 33, FPW.

43. "Industrial Conflict," *New Republic*, August 28, 1915, 90.

44. Walsh quoted in *Proceedings of the Twenty-Fifth Consecutive and Second Biennial Convention of the United Mine Workers of America*, 1:541.

45. Marot, *American Labor Unions*; Howe, *The Confessions of a Reformer*; Howe, *Why War?*; Marchand, *The American Peace Movement*, 245. Quotations from "Minutes of the Meeting of the Committee on Industrial Relations," Saturday, December 11, 1915, pp. 3–4, box 4, JF/CFL; Walsh to Helen Marot, August 26, 1915, box 33, and Barton to Walsh, November 17, 1915, box 34, FPW.

46. Basil Manly to Walsh, August 24, 1915, box 33, and Walsh to Manly, November 22, 1915, box 34, FPW; first quotation from "A Follow-up Committee on Industrial Relations," *Survey*, November 13, 1915, 155–56; Adams, *Age of Industrial Violence*, 220; inaugural statement from untitled memo, [1915], Industrial Relations Committee, subject file 35, AREP.

47. "A Follow-up Committee on Industrial Relations," *Survey*, November 13, 1915, 156; Frank Walsh to Basil Manly, November 22, 1915, box 34, FPW; union assessment quoted in "Organization to Urge Industrial Reforms," *Machinists' Monthly Journal* 27 (November 1915): 1072; "The Industrial Committee," *Masses* 7 (January 1916): 8; Frank P. Walsh to City Central Presidents, December 29, 1915, AREP; "Americanized by the Unions," *Rochester [N.Y.] Labor Herald*, December 31, 1915; San Francisco opinion quoted in *San Francisco Labor Clarion*, January 28, 1916; critical opinion from *Iron Trade Review*, January 27, 1916, 214–15.

48. Dante Barton to Amos Pinchot, March 28, 1916, folder 7, box 24, AREP; Nestor, *Women's Labor Leader*, 162; "Strange Bedfellows: Sociologists and Saloonists," *Iron Trade Review*, January 27, 1916, 215; Pittsburgh spokesperson quoted in Barton, "The Pittsburgh Strikes," 715. For background on these strikes, see Brody, *Steelworkers in America*, 181–82; and Montgomery, *The Fall of the House of Labor*, 324–27.

49. Vincent St. John to Walsh, October 8, 1915, box 2, and St. John to Walsh, Febru-

ary 7, 1916, box 3, FPW; Walsh quotation on Haywood in Walsh, "My Impressions of the Witnesses and Their Testimony," 6; Hapgood, *The Spirit of Labor*; Kazin, *The Barons of Labor*, 73–74; United States Commission on Industrial Relations, *Final Report and Testimony*, 11:10699; Johannsen quotation from Johannsen to Walsh, n.d. [December 17, 1915], box 2, FPW.

50. *Seattle Union Record*, December 4, 1915; "Walsh, A Great Tribune," *American Federationist* 22 (July 1915): 514–15; Gompers to Theodore Johnson, May 24, 1917, reel 222, SGLB; John B. Lennon to Dante Barton, December 5, 1916, box 34, FPW; "Minutes of the Meeting of the Committee," December 15, 1915, AREP; Frank P. Walsh to City Central Presidents, December 29, 1915, Industrial Relations Committee, subject file 35, AREP; Helen Marot to Amos Pinchot, November 15, 1915, box 22, AREP; "Minutes of the Second Meeting of the Committee on Industrial Relations," March 9, 1916, folder 7, box 24, AREP; Dante Barton to Walsh, March 25, 1916, box 34, FPW.

51. Smith, "Organized Labor and Government," 266–68; Clements, *The Presidency of Woodrow Wilson*, 80–81. A fascinating account of the role that Wilson's foreign policy played in drawing together the progressive "coalition of 1916" is contained in Knock, *To End All Wars*, chap. 6.

52. *New York Times*, September 1, 4, 1916.

53. Quotation on the Adamson Act from *New York Call*, September 3, 1916; quotation to friend from Walsh to Doris Stevens, August 17, 1916, file 35, DS.

54. Dante Barton to John Fitzpatrick, April 17, 1919, box 4, JF/CFL; Walsh to Amos Pinchot, June 1, 1916, and Dante Barton to Amos Pinchot, June 1, 1916, both in box 26, AREP; Republican criticism from *Republican Campaign Book*, 372–73; "Democrats Are Asked to Abolish All Profit," *New York Call*, June 15, 1916; Walsh testimony quoted form untitled statement [by Frank P. Walsh before the Democratic Platform Committee], June 14, 1916, box 5, JF/CFL; "Wilson and Labor," Miscellaneous Campaign Literature file, box 35, RWW.

55. "Democrats Are Asked to Abolish All Profit," *New York Call*, June 15, 1916; James A. Reed to Joseph Tumulty, September 9, 1915, series 4, casefile 158, reel 232, WW.

56. Sarasohn, *The Party of Reform*, chap. 7.

57. Meeting described in Frank Walsh to Doris Stevens, August 17, 1916, file 35, DS; Woodrow Wilson to Walsh, November 23, 1916, box 34, Walsh to Manly, June 27, 1916, box 3, and Manly to Walsh, June 8, 1916, box 34, all in FPW.

58. Manly to Howe, June 22, 1916, box 3, FPW; Democratic operative's quotation from Paul McCaskill to Walsh, September 27, 1916, box 3, FPW; Walsh to Manly, June 22, 1916, box 34, FPW; Dante Barton, "The Wilson Volunteers in New York State," [1916], folder 6, box 24, AREP.

59. Dante Barton to Amos Pinchot, November 2, 1916, and George P. West to Amos Pinchot, April 19, 1916, both in box 26, AREP; Walsh quotation regarding Wilson from *Schenectady Gazette*, October 18, 1916; *Cleveland Citizen*, October 28, 1916; *Schenectady Citizen*, October 20, 1916.

60. Sarasohn, *The Party of Reform*, 208.

61. Walsh to Stephen Wise, November 12, 1918, box 4; Stephen Wise to Walsh, November 15, 1918, box 4; Barton to Walsh, November 10, 1916, box 34; all in FPW.

CHAPTER TWO

1. Hopkins, "Democracy and Industry," 59–60.

2. Carlton, *The Industrial Situation*, 146–48; Ward, *The Labor Movement*, 183, 194; Brandeis quoted in United States Commission on Industrial Relations, *Final Report and Testimony*, 8:7664; and Walling, *Progressivism — and After*, 122–23. Abner E. Woodruff's series, "The Evolution of Industrial Democracy," appeared in *Solidarity* between November 4 and December 9, 1916; quotation from *Solidarity*, June 5, 1915, 2.

3. Laughlin, "Business and Democracy," 89, 93; Hopkins, "Democracy and Industry," 63.

4. *New York Times*, July 25, 1918; Feldman, *Army, Industry, and Labor in Germany*; *Monthly Labor Review* 8 (June 1919): 308; National Industrial Conference Board, *Strikes in American Industry in Wartime*, 3–5; Lombardi, *Labor's Voice in the Cabinet*, 199; National Industrial Conference Board, *Strikes in American Industry in Wartime*, 13.

5. Wilson quoted in Krivy, "American Organized Labor and the First World War," 270–71.

6. Warne, *Workers at War*, 152–56; Watkins, *Labor Problems*, 92; Krivy, "American Organized Labor and the First World War," 72–73; Douglas, *Real Wages in the United States*, 204–5; National Industrial Conference Board, *Wartime Changes in Wages*; quotation from *Bridgeport Labor Leader*, January 10, 1918.

7. Kennedy, *Over Here*, 260; Tumulty, "Suggestion of a Statement," [1917], misc. file, box 48, JPT.

8. Watkins, *Labor Problems*, chap. 3; Bing, "The Nerve Center of War Production," 345–47; Potter, "War Boom Towns," 346–52; National Industrial Conference Board, *Strikes in American Industry in Wartime*, 6–9.

9. The role that military service or the threat of induction into the military played in shaping workers' consciousness in the World War I years remains a largely unexplored topic. But in his 1992 dissertation, Gerald Shenk does examine the impact of the draft on the labor market. See " 'Work or Fight,' " especially 151–52. Bridgeport, Connecticut, munitions workers were among those who felt most victimized by employer-dominated local draft boards. See William F. Hoffman to William B. Wilson, March 18, 1918, casefile 33-1116, FMCS.

10. Lombardi, *Labor's Voice in the Cabinet*, 176–79, 183–84; Jones, "The Wilson Administration and Organized Labor," 324–30; Bustard, "The Human Factor," 59–64; Watkins, *Labor Problems*, 41–42; Krivy, "American Organized Labor and the First World War," 58–59; and Wagner loyalty oath, casefile 4, box 1, NWLB.

11. Foner, *History of the Labor Movement in the United States*, vol. 7, *Labor and World War I*, 270–74; Dubofsky, *We Shall Be All*, 385–91. For a different interpretation of the Wilson administration's role in Bisbee, see Huginnie, " 'Strikitos,' " 320–38.

12. Stephenson Kent to Newton D. Baker, November 10, 1917, in Link, *The Papers of Woodrow Wilson*, 44:564–65.

13. Dubofsky, *We Shall Be All*, 383; *Kansas City Star*, August 6, 7, 9, 10, 11, 13, 16, 1917.

14. Watkins, *Labor Problems*, chap. 3.

15. "Transcript of Proceedings," August 23, 1918, p. 1155, and August 23, 1918, p. 1133, casefile 231, NWLB.

16. "Transcript of Proceedings," August 19, 1918, p. 889, casefile 231, NWLB; H. H. Edge to John J. Casey, December 5, 1918, casefile 33-819, FMCS; J. F. Anderson to William B. Wilson, October 19, 1917, and J. J. Casey, "Preliminary Report of Conciliator," November 20, 1917, both in casefile 33-817, FMCS.

17. Testimony of Elizabeth Gillespie, "Transcript of Proceedings," August 23, 1918, p. 1193, casefile 231, NWLB.

18. "Transcript of Proceedings," August 13, 1918, p. 427, casefile 231, NWLB.

19. National Industrial Conference Board, *Problems of Industrial Readjustment in the United States*, 13–14, 18, 26.

20. *St. Louis Globe-Democrat*, July 14, 15, 16, 17, 18, 1917; Gibbs, "The Lead Belt Riot and World War One."

21. IBEW organizer Charles Keaveny quoted in "Transcript of Proceedings," August 19, 1918, p. 836, casefile 231, NWLB; "Report on Labor Conditions near Jacksonville," February 16, 1918, series 290, box 12, USSB; *Journal of Electrical Workers and Operators* 12 (December 1917): 244. On the "habits of solidarity," see Hobsbawm, *Labouring Men*, 144.

22. Greenwald, *Women, War, and Work*, 120–23; casefiles 33-567 and 33-2576, FMCS; "Report of the Examiner on Administration of Award," August 21, 1918, casefile 40, NWLB.

23. *Proceedings of the Thirty-Sixth Annual Convention of the American Federation of Labor*, 223; Rudwick, *Riot at East St. Louis*, 27–28, 142–56; *Erie Union Labor Journal*, June 8, 1917; *Schenectady Gazette*, June 18–27, 1917; *Machinists' Monthly Journal* (August 1917): 681; "IAM General Executive Board Minutes," May 28–June 28, 1917, IAM.

24. *Congressional Record*, 65th Cong., 2d sess., February 25, 1918, pp. 2594, 2597.

25. Haber, *Efficiency and Uplift*, chap. 3; Jacoby, *Employing Bureaucracy*, chap. 4; Braverman, *Labor and Monopoly Capital*; Noble, *America by Design*; quotation from Nelson, *Frederick W. Taylor*, 193.

26. Wilson quoted in Special Committee of the House of Representatives, *Hearings to Investigate the Taylor and Other Systems of Shop Management*, 1466; Aitken, *Scientific Management in Action*; legislation quoted in Nadworny, *Scientific Management and the Unions*, 82–83.

27. Commons, *Myself*, 178; assessment of Valentine from C. Bertrand Thompson to Frederick W. Taylor, December 19, 1914, file 52G, and Taylor to Carl G. Barth, December 30, 1914, file 113D, FWT; defense of Taylorism quoted in Special Committee of the House of Representatives, *Hearings to Investigate the Taylor and Other Systems of Shop Management*, 1462; Hoxie, *Scientific Management and Labor*, 106–7, 112.

28. Lorwin, *The Women's Garment Workers*, chaps. 22–28; Brandeis quoted in Strum, *Louis D. Brandeis*, 178.

29. Strum, *Brandeis*, 32; Strum, *Louis D. Brandeis*, 159–66; United States Commission on Industrial Relations, *Final Report and Testimony*, 1:991–1011. Quotations from Brandeis, *Business—A Profession*, 54; Brandeis, "Efficiency by Consent," 108–9; and "Brandeis on the Labor Problem: How Far Have We Come on the Road to Industrial Democracy?" *La Follette's Weekly Magazine*, May 24, 1913, 5.

30. Parrish, *Felix Frankfurter*, 51–52; Steel, *Walter Lippmann*, 120.

31. R. G. Valentine, "Audits of Industrial Relations," n.d. [1915], Industrial Relations Committee, subject file 35, AREP; Robert G. Valentine to Franklin D. Roosevelt, July 17, 1913, Commission on Industrial Relations Papers, box 20, DOL.

32. Valentine, "The Progressive Relation between Efficiency and Consent," 7–11.

33. Valentine and Tead, "Work and Pay," 241–58; clipping, January 8, 1917, Valentine file, reel 119, FF.

34. "Discussion of H. S. Person, 'The Manager, the Workman, and the Social Scientist,'" *Bulletin of the Taylor Society* 3 (December 1917): 6–7; Meiksins, "The 'Revolt of the Engineers' Reconsidered"; Drury, "Democracy as a Factor in Industrial Efficiency," 25; Cooke, "Who Is Boss in Your Shop?" 5.

35. Burritt, *Profit Sharing*, chap. 4; Kendall, *The Kendall Company*, 12–13; Walsh quotation from Frank P. Walsh to John D. Rockefeller Jr., July 24, 1915, Industrial Relations Committee, subject file, AREP; Rockefeller quotation from J. D. Rockefeller Jr. to E. H. Weitzel, March 3, 1916, box 13, folder 107, RFI; Foner, *History of the Labor Movement in the United States*, vol. 6, *On the Eve of America's Entry into World War I*, chap. 4; Gitelman, *Legacy of the Ludlow Massacre*; King, *Industry and Humanity*, 241.

36. Hopkins, "Democracy and Industry," 63, 66; Drury, "Democracy as a Factor in Industrial Efficiency," 16.

37. Gompers, "Labor's Participation in Government," 105.

38. Wolman, *The Growth of American Trade Unions*, 85; Lorwin, *The American Federation of Labor*, 124–26; Perlman quotation from Commons et al., *History of Labour in the United States*, 2:524.

39. Dubofsky, *We Shall Be All*, 319–46; Fraser, *Labor Will Rule*, chaps. 3–4.

40. Dubofsky, *When Workers Organize*; Keiser, "John Fitzpatrick and Progressive Unionism"; Montgomery, *Workers' Control in America*, chap. 3; Maurer, *It Can Be Done*.

41. Gompers, "Labor History in the Making," 24.

42. Gompers, "Economic Organization and the Eight-Hour Day," 46; Gompers, "Labor History in the Making," 19.

43. Gompers, "Labor History in the Making," 32–33.

44. Ibid., 19.

45. Gompers quoted in Larson, *Labor and Foreign Policy*, 21; Gompers, *American Labor and the War*, 18; *Proceedings of the Thirty-Fourth Annual Convention of the American Federation of Labor*, 280–81, 473; *Proceedings of the Thirty-Sixth Annual Convention of the American Federation of Labor*, 383; *Birmingham Labor Advocate*, February 26, 1916; American Federation of Labor, *American Federation of Labor*, 66.

46. Gompers, "American Labor's Position in Peace or War"; Larson, *Labor and Foreign Policy*, 85; Krivy, "American Organized Labor and the First World War," 30; Daniel Tobin to Samuel Gompers, March 30, 1917, and "Circular," n.d. [March 1917], subject file 2, reel 1, SGWF.

47. Gompers quoted in Karson, *American Labor Unions and Politics*, 100; "Resolution Adopted at Meeting of Executive Committee," April 15, 1917, entry 10A-A1, box 323, Resolutions file, CND; Daniel Tobin to Gompers, April 12, 1917, and Herbert M. Merrill to Gompers, April 9, 1917, subject file 2, reel 1, SGWF; "Minutes of Executive Committee Meeting," April 30, 1917, p. 4, entry 10A, box 2, file 352, CND.

48. W. B. Wilson to Frank Farrington, August 17, 1918, casefile 33-620, FMCS (thanks to Carl Weinberg for calling my attention to this); National Industrial Conference Board, *Strikes in American Industry in Wartime*, 6–9, 19–20.

49. Rodden, *The Fighting Machinists*, 47–49; historian's quotation from Perlman, *The Machinists*, 39; Johnston quoted in Special Committee of the House of Representatives,

Hearings to Investigate the Taylor and Other Systems of Shop Management, 419; *Machinists' Monthly Journal* 26 (June 1914): 545.

50. Person Defense League, *Corporate Greed and Lawlessness*; United States Commission on Industrial Relations, *Final Report and Testimony*, 10:9699–10066; Perlman, *The Machinists*, 40–42; Person quotation from Person, *The Lizard's Trail*, 418, 462; remaining quotations from L. B. Dorgan to John Louis, November 3, 1916, and C. P. Gibson to "Sir and Brother," November 6, 1916, both in box 3, CEP.

51. Bucki, "The Pursuit of Political Power," 29–34; Bucki, "Dilution and Craft Tradition"; *New York Call*, July 27, 1915.

52. Gompers, *Seventy Years of Life and Labor*, 2:344; *New York Call*, July 20, 21, 22, 23, 1915.

53. First quotation from R. M. McWade to W. B. Wilson, August 1, 1917, casefile 33-567, FMCS; second quotation from Edmund Leigh to "Chief," June 28, 1918, casefile 33-1116, FMCS; "IAM General Executive Board Minutes," October 13–23, 1919, IAM; Montgomery, *Workers' Control in America*, 129, 133; Isaac Russell to W. Jett Lauck, September 3, 1918, casefile 132, box 20, NWLB; Bing, *Wartime Strikes*, 73.

54. George J. Bowen to Robert M. McWade, April 30, 1917, file 33-347, FMCS; "IAM General Executive Board Minutes," May 28–June 28, 1917, IAM; *Bridgeport Labor Leader*, March 28, April 4, 25, 1918; "To the Employers of Machinists in Bridgeport and Vicinity," n.d., file 33-817, FMCS.

55. McCartin, "Labor's Great War," 192–204.

56. Schatz, *The Electrical Workers*, 28–52; Fred Thompson, *The IWW*, 28–29.

57. Atherton Brownell, "Report of an Investigation into Industrial Conditions in the Several Plants of the General Electric Company," p. 20, found in box marked "GE Labor Policy," ODY; Bellingham's quotations from *Schenectady Citizen*, February 11, 1916, January 12, July 20, and August 10, 1917; C. B. Ambrose, "In re American Union against Militarism," July 28, 1917, box 2490, file 10101-53, MID.

58. Kennedy, *Over Here*, 262; *Textile Worker* 5 (February 1918): 3–4; *International Socialist Review* 12 (June 1917): 731–32; Taft, *The AFL in the Time of Gompers*, 362; Bustard, "The Human Factor," chap. 4; Bing, *Wartime Strikes*, 141–42; quotation from Wehle, "War Labor Policies and Their Outcome in Peace," 322.

59. Quoted in Watkins, *Labor Problems*, 41.

CHAPTER THREE

1. Ellis W. Hawley, "The Great War and Organizational Innovation: The American Case" (unpublished paper in possession of the author), 1.

2. *Auto Worker* 1 (May 1919): 3–4.

3. Quoted in Westbrook, *John Dewey*, 204.

4. *American Federationist* 25 (March 1918): 213; Krivy, "American Organized Labor and the First World War," 33–35; Josephson, *Sidney Hillman*, 160–62.

5. Howe, *Why War?*; Marchand, *The American Peace Movement*, 249, 305.

6. Frank Walsh to Rev. Daniel S. McCorkle, December 26, 1917, box 5, FPW; "From the Committee on Industrial Relations for Immediate Release," n.d. [February 1917], box 5, JF/CFL; Amos Pinchot to Walsh, March 27, 1917, box 4, and Basil Manly to Walsh, August 24, 191[5], box 33, FPW.

7. Frank P. Walsh, *Address before the City Club of Chicago, February* 20, 1915 (n.p., n.d.), 6 (pamphlet in the collection of the Library of Congress); Walsh to Johannsen, April 12, 1917, box 4, FPW; Louis P. Lochner to Walsh, May 18, June 14, and June 15, 1917, box 4, FPW; Marchand, *The American Peace Movement*, 305; Walsh to Scott Nearing, January 30, 1918, box 5, FPW; Nearing to Walsh, September 6, 1917, box 5, FPW.

8. Weinstein, *Decline of Socialism*, 126–31; Radosh, *American Labor and United States Foreign Policy*, chap. 1.

9. Grubbs, *Struggle for Labor Loyalty*, 40–45; Krivy, "American Organized Labor and the First World War," 45; Maurer, *It Can Be Done*, 228; Commons quoted in Vaughn, *Holding Fast the Inner Lines*, 24, 55–57.

10. Lorwin, *The American Federation of Labor*, 151; Grubbs, *Struggle for Labor Loyalty*, 57–64.

11. Dubofsky, *We Shall Be All*, 353–58. Quotation is from p. 357.

12. Ibid., 376–422.

13. See Bourne, *War and the Intellectuals*. For further background, see Larson, *Labor and Foreign Policy*; Radosh, *American Labor and United States Foreign Policy*; and Hendrickson, "The Pro-War Socialists."

14. Barton to Walsh, April 24, 1917, box 34, FPW.

15. Walsh to Johannsen, December 27, 1916, box 4, FPW; Helen Marot to Amos Pinchot, September 1, 1916, box 26, AREP.

16. Johannsen quoted in *Proceedings of the Twelfth Consolidated Convention of the International Brotherhood of Boiler Makers*, 42; Walsh to Bill Haywood, May 1, 1917, Walsh to Harry Weinberger, July 12, 1917, and Walsh to Albert S. Burleson, July 24, 1917, all in box 4, FPW.

17. W. P. Harvey to Walsh, June 12, 1917, box 4, FPW; Harold Callender, "From the National Labor Defense Council," *San Francisco Organized Labor*, September 1, 1917; Walsh to Rev. Daniel S. McCorkle, December 26, 1917, box 5, FPW.

18. Helen Marot to Walsh, June 1, 1917, box 4, FPW; Gompers to Theodore Johnson, May 24, 1917, reel 222, SGLB.

19. Johannsen to Walsh, September 4, 1917, box 5, Helen Marot to Walsh, June 1, 1917, box 4, and Walsh to Jack Reed, June 4, 1917, box 4, all in FPW.

20. W. P. Harvey to Walsh, June 20, 1917, box 4; Johannsen to Walsh, September 4, 1917, box 5; copy of Johannsen to Gompers, October 25, 1917, box 5; Johannsen to Walsh, November 20, 1917, box 5; all in FPW.

21. The committee included AFL secretary Frank Morrison; head of the AFL Metal Trades Department, James O'Connell; James Lord of the AFL's Mining Department; Warren S. Stone of the Brotherhood of Locomotive Engineers; William B. Wilson; Ralph Easley of the National Civic Federation (NCF); NCF official V. Everitt Macy; A. Parker Nevin of the NAM; Lee Frankel of Metropolitan Life Insurance; and Louis B. Schram of the National Brewers' Association. For background, see Kennedy, *Over Here*, 114–15.

22. Quoted in Bustard, "The Human Factor," 39.

23. Quotation from Wehle, "The Adjustment of Labor Disputes," 126; Raddock, *Portrait of an American Labor Leader*, 92–94.

24. Krivy, "American Organized Labor and the First World War," 181–82; Dubofsky, *The State and Labor in Modern America*, 66–67.

25. Wehle, "The Adjustment of Labor Disputes," 123–28; *Proceedings of the Twelfth Consolidated Convention of the International Brotherhood of Boiler Makers*, 12.

26. Wehle, "The Adjustment of Labor Disputes," 129; Bing, *Wartime Strikes*, 95–98; Bing, "The Work of the Wage-Adjustment Boards," 436–37; Colin Davis, "Bitter Storm."

27. Follett, *The New State*, 4; Dewey quoted in Westbrook, *John Dewey*, 202. On the emergence of the "new American state" during this period, see Skowronek, *Building a New American State*.

28. Cuff, *The War Industries Board*; Cuff, "We Band of Brothers," 141.

29. Burgess, "Organized Production and Unorganized Labor," 141; quotation from Christie, *Morris Llewellyn Cooke*, 34–35; Jacoby, *Employing Bureaucracy*, 144; Schiesl, *The Politics of Efficiency*, 163–65; Alford, *Henry Laurence Gantt*, chaps. 14–15; Alford, "An Industrial Achievement of the War," 97–100; Dennison, *Henry S. Dennison*, 15–16.

30. Strum, *Brandeis*, 26; Cramer, *Newton D. Baker*, 133; Beaver, *Newton D. Baker and the War Effort*, 52; Steel, *Walter Lippmann*, 120–23; Davis, *Spearheads for Reform*, 50–52. See also Urofsky and Levy, "Half Brother, Half Son."

31. Parrish, *Felix Frankfurter*, chap. 5; Gerber, *The Limits of Liberalism*, 151–53; Frankfurter to Gompers, April 20, 1917, reel 36, FF.

32. Jones, "The Wilson Administration and Organized Labor," 346; Parrish, *Felix Frankfurter*, 87–97; Kennedy, *Over Here*, 263.

33. Frankfurter to Marion Denman, October 9, 1917, FF; "Report of the President's Mediation Commission," January 9, 1918, pp. 18, 20–21, reel 3, *PMC*.

34. Cooke quotation from Cooke, "Who Is Boss in Your Shop?" 3; Layton, *The Revolt of the Engineers*, 154–78; Gantt quoted in Charles W. Wood, "Startling New Plan for 'Industrial Democracy' Backed by New York Business Men and Engineers," *New York World*, June 30, 1918, 1E; Follett, *The New State*, 3; Graebner, *The Engineering of Consent*, chap. 2. Donald Stabile aptly terms the philosophy that emerged from this period "efficiency with a human face"; see Stabile, *Prophets of Order*, 96.

35. Burgess, "Organized Production and Unorganized Labor," 141; Wehle, "War Labor Policies and Their Outcome in Peace," 334, 336.

36. Jones, "The Wilson Administration and Organized Labor," 332; Wilson quoted in Committee on Public Information, *War, Labor, and Peace*, 7–14.

37. *Survey*, February 23, 1918, 575–76; *Proceedings of the Twelfth Consolidated Convention of the International Brotherhood of Boiler Makers*, 12.

38. Oscar Nelson to W. B. Wilson, February 2, 1918, file 33-950, FMCS.

39. Fay, *Labor in Politics*, 17, 21; Gary quoted in Brody, *Steelworkers in America*, 204.

40. Writing in the 1930s, Lewis Lorwin first posed the critique of AFL collaboration with the wartime Wilson administration. Participation in the war labor program, Lorwin argued, converted union leaders into "business agents on a scale never before dreamed of" and encouraged them to "put aside their roles of organizers and strike leaders to become conciliators and mediators." A decade later John Steuben agreed that the federation's stance "practically meant the transformation of the AFL from an independent trade union center to a government department which assumed the duty of preventing strikes and if necessary breaking them." Most recently, Simeon Larson has contended that the AFL's cooperation with the government was nothing more than "an instrument to ingratiate organized labor with the ruling powers in industry and government." Such scholars

have generally argued that the war led to the triumph of conservatism within labor's ranks. See Lorwin, *The American Federation of Labor*, 172, 170; Steuben, *Labor in Wartime*, 67; Larson, *Labor and Foreign Policy*, 91.

41. Curtis N. Mitchell to William Hale Brown, November 21, 1917, reel 3, PMC.

42. Frankfurter to Baker, September 4, 1917, reel 1, NDB; Frankfurter to Marion Denman, October 1, 1917, FF.

43. Memorandum Submitted by the Amalgamated Clothing Workers of America, [July 5, 1917], War Department file, part 1, reel 3, ACWA; Fraser, *Labor Will Rule*, 118–19.

44. Barrett, *Work and Community in the Jungle*, 191–200; Johanningsmeier, *Forging American Communism*, 94–98.

45. *Chicago Tribune*, February 15, 16, 19, 21, 27, and 28, 1918; Walsh quoted in *Chicago Daily News*, March 7, 1918; Johanningsmeier, *Forging American Communism*, 99–105; Fitzpatrick quoted in Chenery, "Packington Steps Forward," 37.

46. *Butcher Workman* (March 1918): 4; *Butcher Workman* (June 1918): 1.

47. Lilburn S. Trigg to Walsh, March 3, 1918, box 5, FPW.

48. Bustard, "The Human Factor," vii–viii; film dialogue quoted in W. B. Wilson to H. A. Garfield, December 18, 1918, entry 1, box 19, USFA; agent quotation from Edmund Leigh to Stanley King, July 3, 1918, box 3638, file 10634-114-8, MID; Gompers to W. B. Wilson, August 30, 1917, reel 225, SGLB.

49. *Congressional Record*, 65th Cong., 2d sess., April 10, 1918, pp. 4906, 2592, 2602; Bruere, "Copper Camp Patriotism," 202.

50. "Memorandum," n.d. [1917], Interdepartmental Correspondence/Labor file, box 9, FDR; Freidel, *Franklin D. Roosevelt*, 329–31; Cuff, "The Politics of Labor Administration," 546–69.

51. Quotation from Post, "Living a Long Life Over Again: A Memory Voyage across the Latter Half of the Nineteenth Century and the First Quarter of the Twentieth," typescript, pp. 385–86, LFP; Frankfurter to E. M. House, January 9, 1918, reel 41, FF; Bustard, "The Human Factor," chap. 7; Fitch, "Peace at Home," 189–91; Conner, *The National War Labor Board*, 25–27.

52. On Worden, see Sidney Fine, *"Without Blare of Trumpets,"* 65–66.

53. Pringle, *Life and Times of William Howard Taft*, 1:126–38; Taft quoted in *Machinists' Monthly Journal* 27 (July 1915): 587; Walsh quoted in the *Schenectady Gazette*, October 20, 1916.

54. Pringle, *Life and Times of William Howard Taft*, 2:916; Taft to Nellie Taft, March 28, 1918, reel 27, Taft to Luther A. Brewer, October 8, 1918, reel 552, Taft to Nellie Taft, July 26, 1918, reel 27, and February 13, 1919, reel 27, all in WHT.

55. Taft to Nellie Taft, March 30, 1918, reel 27, WHT; Basil Manly, "Memorandum: Some Features of a National Industrial Judiciary," November 20, 1919, box 43, Pre-Commerce subject file, HCH; Pringle, *Life and Times of William Howard Taft*, 2:920.

56. Poulantzas, *Political Power and Social Classes*; Ralph Miliband, "Poulantzas and the Capitalist State," 83.

57. Taft to Nellie Taft, March 29 and March 30, 1918, reel 27, WHT.

58. Lauck, *Report of the Secretary of the National War Labor Board*, 121–23.

59. Drew to Magnus W. Alexander, July 9, 1918, "Committee on Labor Policies, 1917–1919" file, series 5, NICB.

60. Taft to Nellie Taft, March 30, 1918, reel 27, WHT; Walsh quoted in Conner, *The National War Labor Board*, 33.

61. Kennedy, *Over Here*, 266; Conner, *The National War Labor Board*, 30.

62. Taft to Nellie Taft, May 2, 1918, reel 27, WHT.

63. Taft to Walsh, September 27, 1918, reel 551, and Taft to Frederick N. Judson and William Harman Black, October 8, 1918, reel 551, both in WHT.

64. Edmund Leigh to Stanley King, July 3, 1918, box 3638, file 10634-114-8; A. T. Bagley, "In re: People's Council," August 10, 1917, box 2490, file 10101-46; Officer in Charge to Director of Naval Intelligence, March 18, 1918, box 2774, file 10110-546-53; Anton Johannsen file, n.d. [1918], box 2790, file 10110-923; untitled report, New York City, September 17, 1918, box 2790, file 10110-923-1; A. E. Stevenson to Nicholas Biddle, November 20, 1918, box 3762, file 10902-13; affidavits from reporters, box 2718, file 10110-76; all in MID. Col. M. Churchill to Walsh, July 2, 1918, box 6, FPW. Rose's activities reported in *Cincinnati Enquirer*, October 29, 1917.

65. Conner, *The National War Labor Board*, chap. 3.

66. Taft to Nellie Taft, May 25, 1918, reel 27, WHT.

67. Taft to Nellie Taft, June 1, 1918, reel 27, WHT; "Minutes of the Thirteenth Meeting of the Executive Committee," June 7, 1918, series 2, NICB.

68. Walter S. Drew, "Observations on Bridgeport and Smith and Wesson Cases," September 23, 1918, "Committee on Labor Policies, 1917–1919" file, series 5, NICB.

69. Taft quoted in Pringle, *Life and Times of William Howard Taft*, 2:919; employer H. F. Perkins quoted in Lombardi, *Labor's Voice in the Cabinet*, 256.

70. Walsh to J. I. Sheppard, July 8, 1918, box 6, FPW.

CHAPTER FOUR

1. *Monthly Labor Review* 8 (June 1919): 308; Lauck, *Report of the Secretary of the National War Labor Board*, 7, 11; quotation from Moderwell, "The National War Labor Board," 48.

2. Wolman, *The Growth of American Trade Unions*, 33–36; Dubofsky, *Industrialism and the American Worker*, 123; Perlman, *Democracy in the International Association of Machinists*, 4.

3. "Transcript of Proceedings," December 3, 1918, pp. 163–65, casefile 619, NWLB.

4. Conference Committee Report, n.d. [1918], series 24, box 84, National Labor Adjustment Agencies Conference Committee Folder, NWLB; "Confidential Memo respecting Employees Committee of General Electric," August 5, 1918, file 196, C26858–68, WLMK.

5. "Findings in re Machinists, et al. v. Frick Company, et al.," casefile 40, NWLB; Conner, *The National War Labor Board*, 50–61. A fine overview of the war's impact on the structure of internal labor markets is provided in Jacoby, *Employing Bureaucracy*, chap. 5.

6. Casefile 642, NWLB; "Findings in re Employees v. Worthington Pump and Machinery," casefile 14, NWLB.

7. "Confidential Memorandum respecting Employees' Committees," August 5, 1918, file 196, C26858–68, WLMK; "Bulletin of the Manufacturers' Association," July 8, 1918, box 1, MASC.

8. *Berkshire Evening Eagle*, May 6, 1918; "Transcript of Proceedings," June 22, 1918,

casefile 127, NWLB; "Findings in re Employees v. General Electric," June 28, 1918, casefile 19, NWLB; "Findings of Section in re Employees v. Smith and Wesson Arms Company, Springfield, Mass.," casefile 273, NWLB; on discrimination see casefile 97, on reinstatement see casefile 328, on blacklisting see casefile 154, on strike activity see casefile 748, and on the use of the draft see casefile 22, all in NWLB; Conner, *The National War Labor Board*, 117–25; Lauck, *Report of the Secretary of the National War Labor Board*, 53–56.

9. Clements, *The Presidency of Woodrow Wilson*, 85; minimum wage decisions are found in casefiles 19, 21, 35, 95, 127, 132, 163, 195, 216, 317, 337, 416, 454, 472, 521, 542, 594, 913, 937, and 978, and job classification decisions are found in casefiles 40, 46, 129, 163, 297, 320, 371, 570, 571, and 674, all in NWLB; Moderwell, "The National War Labor Board," 48; Lauck quoted in Senate Committee on Education and Labor, *Hearing before the Committee*, 7.

10. Sample of 165 decisions drawn from entry 112, boxes 1–20, USRA.

11. "Minutes of Meeting Held in Philadelphia," December 13, 1918, p. 13, entry 86, box 2, casefile 12, USRA.

12. "Confidential Memorandum respecting Employees' Committees," August 5, 1918, pp. 4–5, 10, file 196, C26858-68, WLMK.

13. Gregg, "The National War Labor Board," 61.

14. Curtis N. Mitchell to William Hale Brown, November 21, 1917, reel 3, *PMC*; committee member Martin Murphy quoted in Barrett, *Work and Community in the Jungle*, 201; Montgomery, "New Tendencies in Union Struggles and Strategies," 107.

15. W. L. Stoddard, "Report on Committee Elections," January 23, 1919, casefile 231, and "Transcript of Proceedings," casefile 231, August 14, 1918, p. 507, NWLB. It should be noted that my reading of this evidence contradicts Jeffrey Haydu's argument that shop elections tended to "dilute" union "influence on shop committees because craft unionists were usually not strong enough to control departmentwide elections." See Haydu, *Between Craft and Class*, 192.

16. G. B. McCormack to Rembrandt Peale, February 22, 1918, entry 19, box 1355; A. L. Light to J. P. White, November 9, 1918, entry 19, box 1344; Arthur Appleyard to U.S. Fuel Administration, February 5, 1918, entry 19, box 1340; John P. White to John B. Welsh, June 19, 1918, and James A. Gordon to John P. White, June 18, 1918, both in entry 19, box 1341; all in USFA.

17. T. E. Carroll to Henry R. Seager, June 27, 1918, box 10, entry 290, USSB; E. E. Belcher to J. W. Bridwell, March 16, 1918, entry 86, casefile 1, box 1, USRA; Harry E. Downing to C. Piez, September 12, 1918, box 13, entry 350, USSB.

18. W. L. Stoddard, "Lynn Works, Representation of Employees," n.d., casefile 231, NWLB.

19. The NWLB docket contained a total of 1,125 cases. The IAM brought 154 of them (13.7 percent of the total); the Amalgamated Association of Street and Electrical Railway Employees brought 150 (13.3 percent); the Iron Molders Union brought 103 (9.2 percent); the Carpenters brought 58 (5.2 percent); the Electrical Workers brought 44 (3.9 percent); the Laborers brought 21 (1.9 percent); federal labor unions brought 20 (1.8 percent); and central labor unions brought 7 (0.6 percent).

20. On "spark plug" unionists, see Charles Tilly and Edward Shorter, *Strikes in France, 1880–1968*; on Lynn voting, see D. C. Lash, "Summary of Election Returns," December 13, 1918, casefile 231, NWLB.

21. "Report of Robert M. Buck," January 30, 1919, p. 8, casefile 130, NWLB; quotation from Daniel H. Cox to Emmet L. Adams, May 10, 1918, box 16, entry 350, USSB.

22. "Transcript of Proceedings," September 24, 1918, pp. 12–13, casefile 231, NWLB; quotation of anonymous worker in Stoddard, *The Shop Committee*, 88; Hugh McCabe to Basil Manly, March 24, 1919, "Shop Committee File," entry 15, box 53, NWLB.

23. Isaac Russell to W. Jett Lauck, October 16, 1918, casefile 22, NWLB; Morrison to W. H. Johnston, December 4, 1918, vol. 505, FM.

24. "Transcript of Proceedings," August 29, 1918, casefile 158, NWLB; anonymous quote from National Industrial Conference Board, *Experience with Works Councils in the United States*, 22. Reports of coal operator interference in Van Bittner to James B. Neale, September 9, 1918, entry 19, box 1340, USFA; undated memo [1918], entry 1, box 18, White file, USFA; and J. R. Kennamer to J. P. White, February 25, 1918, entry 19, box 1355, USFA; and quotation in Van Bittner to James B. Neale, September 9, 1918, entry 19, box 1340, USFA.

25. Owen D. Young to E. W. Rice Jr., August 8, 1918, box marked "G.E. Labor Policy," ODY; "Minutes of Special Executive Board Meeting," September 13, 1918, box 1, MASC; "Minutes of the Twenty-Sixth Meeting of the National Industrial Conference Board," October 10, 1918, pp. 6–7, series 3, NICB.

26. "Rebuttal Brief Submitted by Employees, Exhibit A," casefile 231, NWLB.

27. "Transcript of Proceedings," casefile 231, p. 775, NWLB; McCartin, "An American Feeling." For a suggestive interpretation of the ways in which labor embraced "Americanism" during the war, see Kazin, *The Populist Persuasion*, 69–74.

28. On "Prussian," see "Record of Proceedings of Mass Meeting of Employees," May 2, 1918, casefile 18, NWLB; on Bridgeport, see *Bridgeport Labor Leader*, November 21, 1918; on TCI, see *Birmingham Labor Advocate*, March 2, 1918; on "hunnism," see Frank Fisher to Herbert Hoover, September 9, 1918, entry 19, box 1342, USFA; on Utica, see D. B. Lucy to Attorney General, November 6, 1919, classified subjects files, box 3370, file 16-137, DOJ; on the Illinois Central, see "Statement of Harry A. Marsalis," January 7, 1919, entry 86, box 5, USRA; on "de-kaisering," see *Pennsylvania Labor Herald*, November 22, 1918.

29. *Bethlehem Booster*, June 15, 1918, 2–3; *Lynn Telegram*, April 2, 14, June 16, 19, 20, 1917; *Bethlehem Globe*, April 4, 7, 12, June 6, 1917; "Interview with Annie Trina," AC.

30. "Report of the Discharge of Mrs. C. W. Brooks from the Magazine Department," October 9, 1918, casefile 217, NWLB.

31. Newark quote from an advertisement in the *Newark Star-Eagle*, June 24, 1918, in casefile 720, NWLB; Akron leaflet in casefile 172, NWLB; *Bridgeport Labor Leader*, August 22, 1918; Bethlehem episode described in "Transcript of Proceedings," January 15, 1919, casefile 22, NWLB.

32. Resolutions Committee, UMW Local 517, to U.S. Fuel Administration, [1918], entry 19, box 1340, USFA; "Supplemental Brief of Employees, Exhibit A," casefile 231, NWLB.

33. "Memorandum for Mr. Marshall in re Federal Shipbuilding Company," May 28, 1918, series 350, box 8, file 18024-1, USSB.

34. "Memorandum for Professor W. Z. Ripley," December 13, 1918, War Department file, part 1, reel 3, ACWA; W. B. Wilson to Woodrow Wilson, July 30, 1918, series 13, Department of Labor files, folder 112, WBW; Wilson quotation in Jones, "The Wilson Administration and Organized Labor," 376–77.

35. J. R. Blackburn to the U.S. Fuel Administration, September 4, 1918, and Charles A. Bygate to James B. Neale, September 9, 1918, both in entry 19, box 1348, USFA; "Tran-

script of Proceedings," September 3, 1918, p. 47, casefile 233, NWLB; Watkins, *Labor Problems*, 106; Fay, *Labor in Politics*, 36.

36. Peterson and Fite, *Opponents of War*; Murphy, *World War I and the Origin of Civil Liberties*; Hough, *The Web*; Brooks, *Labor's Challenge to the Social Order*, 278.

37. "Interview with Fred Teluchik," March 31, 1919, and "Statement concerning Wood Mill of the American Woolen Company given by Rose and Grace Santora," April 29, 1919, both in AC; American Fuel Co., Salt Lake, Utah, to U.S. Fuel Administration, October 3, 1918, entry 19, box 1340, USFA.

38. "Transcript of Proceedings," June 22, 1918, morning session, p. 36, and June 22, 1918, afternoon session, p. 12, casefile 127, NWLB.

39. "Report of Robert M. Buck," January 30, 1919, casefile 130, NWLB; "Memorandum on Shop Committee System, General Electric Company, Pittsfield, Mass.," February 7, 1919, casefile 19, NWLB; Marie L. Obenauer to E. B. Woods, October 11, 1918, and Elizabeth Christman to Woods, October 11, casefile 132, box 20, NWLB.

40. Orleck, *Common Sense and a Little Fire*, 6; casefile 132, NWLB; Stevens, *Jailed for Freedom*, 271–72.

41. Curry quoted in *Bridgeport Labor Leader*, September 5, 1918.

42. Florence E. Clark to Miss Crosson, April 12, 1919, box 19, folder 193c; "Complaints and Adjustments, Harrisburg Series, #25," February 19, 1919, box 18, folder 187g; Cora Knisely to Miss Clark, May 11, 1919, box 18, folder 187h; Report 379, [1919], box 17, folder 182; all in entry 97, USRA.

43. "Proceedings of the Conference of Trade Union Women," October 4–5, 1918, entry 24, box 84, NWLB; Walsh to Woodrow Wilson, October 30, 1918, box 6, FPW; Obenauer to Lauck, "Memorandum concerning Awards Affecting Women," September 9, 1918, entry 13, Obenauer file, NWLB; Conner, *The National War Labor Board*, 146–48.

44. On Cannon, see "Brief of Fort Wayne General Electric Workers," January 8, 1919, casefile 1011, NWLB; on Parmer, see casefile 14, NWLB. On other women activists, see "Brief for Women Workers in the Case of Employees v. the Colt's Patent Fire Arms Co.," n.d., casefile 217; Mildred Rankin to Lauck, October 15, 1918, casefile 217; and John T. O'Brien to E. B. Woods, November 28, 1918, casefile 95; all in NWLB.

45. Anna Crosson to Miss Clark, April 4, 1919, entry 97, box 19, folder 193c, USRA; Mrs. Raymond Robbins, quoted in Alan Davis, "Welfare, Reform, and World War I," 525–26.

46. Walsh to W. Jett Lauck, memorandum, August 30, 1918, box 6, FPW; Gudza, "Social Experiment," 8; Grossman, *The Department of Labor*; Lombardi, *Labor's Voice in the Cabinet*.

47. Swing, *"Good Evening!"* 11; Lewis, *In Their Own Interests*, 53; Miller and Blitch to Capt. W. R. Bowler, May 9, 1918, series 290, box 10, Carroll file, USSB; Sidney J. Catts to W. B. Wilson, April 7, 1919, and Catts to Wilson, April 22, 1919, file 8/102D, both in box 19, DOL.

48. "Transcript of Proceedings," March 28, 1918, pp. 117, 120, entry 372, box 4, USSB.

49. Docket JY-620, entry 112, box 7, USRA. For a similar case, see docket AG-731, entry 112, box 8, USRA.

50. A. A. Walker to William G. McAdoo, September 12, 1918, entry 86, box 8, casefile 194, USRA.

51. W. Celles to Mr. Taft and Mr. Walsh, September 11, 1918, casefile 98, box 46, file 1, folder 2, NWLB; Taft to Walsh, October 20, 1918, reel 199, WHT.

52. Elex Anderson to W. G. McAdoo, July 31, 1918, entry 86, box 5, casefile 95; entry 86, box 7, casefile 160; E. R. Johnson to W. S. Carter, August 6, 1918, entry 86, box 6, casefile 120-A; Nelson Quarles and Ed Mallice to G. W. W. Hanger, December 5, 1918, and Quarles and Mallice to Hanger, December 19, 1918, entry 86, box 9, casefile 238; John H. Dailey et al. to J. J. Forrester, September 14, 1919, entry 86, box 35, casefile 878; all in USRA.

53. Unsigned letter to President Wilson, September 6, 1918, casefile 98, box 46, file 1, folder 2, NWLB; I. Ross to V. E. Macy, September 13, 1918, box 14, entry 290, USSB.

54. Dewey quoted in Shapiro, "The Great War and Reform," 332.

55. "Record of Proceedings of Mass Meeting of Employees," May 2, 1918, casefile 18, NWLB.

56. Galloway quoted in "Transcript of Proceedings," August 14, 1918, afternoon session, p. 24, and Fitzpatrick quoted in "Transcript of Proceedings," August 14, 1918, morning session, p. 25, both in casefile 130, NWLB; on telephone workers, see Ethel Smith, "Government Control and Industrial Rights," *Life and Labor* (April 1919): 86; on cigar makers, see "Statement on Behalf of the Striking Cigar Makers from the Offterdinger Factory," casefile 1, box 19, NWLB.

CHAPTER FIVE

1. Todd, "The National War Labor Board and the Labor Movement," 54–57.

2. Gompers, *Labor and the Employer*, 30.

3. Golden quoted in "Transcript of Proceedings," March 19, 1919, p. 21, casefile 1123, NWLB; Mills, *The New Men of Power*, 9.

4. Quotations from "Executive Session Minutes," June 28, 1918, pp. 17–22, NWLB; McCartin, "Using the 'Gun Act,' " 519–28.

5. J. F. Anderson to W. B. Wilson, December 17, 1918, casefile 1011, NWLB.

6. "Transcript of Proceedings," December 18, 1918, p. 28, casefile 495, NWLB; Johnston quoted in "Executive Session Minutes," February 13, 1919, afternoon session, p. 8, NWLB.

7. Straw, "The Collapse of Biracial Unionism"; Letwin, "Interracial Unionism," 550–54; William Johnson to John P. White, June 5, 1918, box 1343, and operator's quotation from W. W. Curtis to Harry Garfield, November 26, 1917, box 1354, both entry 19, USFA.

8. *Birmingham Labor Advocate*, June 9, 23, 1917; *Birmingham Age-Herald*, June 4, 1917; J. R. Kennamer to W. R. Fairley, June 8, 1917, and Woodrow Wilson to William B. Wilson, August 13, 1917, both in file 33-618, FMCS; Dubofsky and Van Tine, *John L. Lewis*, 29–30; Fairley to John Mitchell, August 10 and August 29, 1917, reel 35, *JM*.

9. General correspondence, file 33-618, FMCS.

10. Woodrow Wilson to William B. Wilson, August 13, 1917, file 33-618, FMCS; Bing, *Wartime Strikes*, 95–98; general correspondence, file 33-618, FMCS.

11. *Birmingham Age-Herald*, August 31, September 7, 8, 1917; *Birmingham Labor Advocate*, December 29, 1917; W. R. Fairley to W. B. Wilson, August 29, 1917, and Hywell Davies to William B. Wilson, September 7, 1917, file 33-618, FMCS; *Proceedings of the Twenty-Sixth Convention of the United Mine Workers of America*, 447.

12. Howatt and supporter quoted in *Proceedings of the Twenty-Sixth Convention of the United Mine Workers*, 49, 386, 396; quotation of Kansas miner in William McFadden to J. P. White, March 14, 1918, entry 19, box 1345, USFA; Indiana miner quoted in *Proceed-

ings of the 1918 Convention of District 11, United Mine Workers of America, 212–24 (found in box 1357, entry 19, USFA).

13. W. W. Curtis to Harry Garfield, November 26, 1917, box 1354, and W. D. Duncan to Harry Garfield, October 19, 1918, box 1341, both in entry 19, USFA; Brophy Diary, May 15, 16, 1917, May 8, May 31, and October 2, 1918, and Brophy to Officers and Members of District 2, August 20, 1917, in Brophy scrapbooks, all in JB.

14. Union leader's quotation from W. D. Duncan to Harry Garfield, October 19, 1918, box 1341; quotation of operator from W. W. Curtis to Harry Garfield, November 26, 1917, box 1354; evidence of miners' devices to circumvent the penalty clause found in Fred Blumskall to U.S. Fuel Administration, September 5, 1918, box 1340; E. R. Short to Harry Garfield, November 14, 1917, box 1354; Charles A. Bygate to James B. Neale, September 9, 1918, box 1348; David Cameron to Rembrandt Peale, July 20, 1918, box 1340; all in entry 19, USFA.

15. Ransey to F. S. Peabody, June 14, 1917, file 33-618, FMCS; *Birmingham Labor Advocate*, July 7, 1917.

16. Kennamer quoted in *Birmingham Age-Herald*, August 2, 1917; industrial autocracy quotation from *Birmingham Labor Advocate*, September 29, 1917; quotation of operator from C. A. Moffett to Franklin K. Lane, June 6, 1917, and James L. Davidson to F. S. Peabody, June 8, 1918, file 33-618, FMCS.

17. W. T. Kraft to John P. White, September 21, 1918, entry 19, box 1340, USFA.

18. Quotation from "Transcript of Proceedings," August 9, 1918, p. 72, casefile 231, NWLB. See also "Statement of Employees," May 18, 1918, casefile 19, NWLB; *Berkshire Evening Eagle*, April 11, 16, 1918.

19. "Report of Conciliators Skeffington and Casey to Director of Conciliation Kerwin," May 13, 1918, and "Brief of the Schenectady Metal Trades Council," casefile 20-127, NWLB; *Berkshire Evening Eagle*, May 6, 1918.

20. "Transcript of Proceedings," casefile 127, NWLB.

21. "Findings in re Employees v. General Electric Company," casefile 127, NWLB; *Schenectady Citizen*, October 4, 1918.

22. W. Jett Lauck to Adam Wilkinson, June 15, 1918, casefile 19, and "Executive Session Minutes," June 28, 1918, afternoon session, pp. 9–11, both in NWLB; Conner *The National War Labor Board*, 117–25.

23. *Lynn Telegram*, April 15, 24, 1918; "Employees Brief," August 9, 1918, casefile 231, NWLB. Quotation from "Brief Submitted by the Lynn Works, General Electric Company," September 10, 1918, Exhibit I, casefile 231, NWLB.

24. "Employees Brief," August 9, 1918, p. 47, casefile 231, NWLB; *Lynn Telegram*, July 15, 16, 1918; *Lynn Telegram-News*, July 22, 28, 29, 30, 1918; *Lynn Daily-Evening Item*, July 15, 1918; S. S. Ringer to Woodrow Wilson, July 18, 1918, casefile 231, NWLB; Bellingham quoted in *New York Times*, July 16, 1918. Lynn workers also benefited from the support of the United Shoe Workers of America. See Cumbler, *Working-Class Community in Industrial America*, 56–64.

25. "Brief Submitted by the Lynn Works, General Electric Company," September 10, 1918, p. 3, casefile 231, NWLB; "Report of Conciliator Skeffington to Hugh L. Kerwin," September 21, 1918, casefile 231, NWLB; strike leaders quoted from "Employees Brief," August 9, 1918, p. 55, casefile 231, NWLB.

26. E. B. Woods, "Memo on Lynn General Elections," casefile 231, NWLB; Peterson

quoted in *Journal of Electrical Workers and Operators* 18 (October 1918): 135; Fort Wayne worker quoted by Atherton Brownell, "Special Report," p. 57, box marked "GE Labor Policy," ODY; Erie described in *Journal of Electrical Workers and Operators* 18 (December 1918): 237.

27. Frank Morrison to David L. Kevlin, September 16, 1918, vol. 503, FM; John R. Alpine to David Kevlin, September 23, 1918, SGLB; quotation from *Journal of Electrical Workers and Operators* 18 (December 1918): 237.

28. "Transcript of Proceedings," August 14, 1918, pp. 511–14, casefile 231, NWLB.

29. Taft to Walsh, October 20, 1918, reel 199, WHT.

30. "Brief Submitted by the Lynn Works, General Electric Company," September 10, 1918, pp. 19–20, casefile 231, NWLB; "Transcript of Proceedings," August 14, 1918, p. 516, casefile 231, NWLB; W. L. Stoddard to E. B. Woods, December 6, 1918, Data Relative to Shop Committees, casefile 231, NWLB.

31. *Erie Digest*, November 27, 28, 1918; *Schenectady Citizen*, December 6, 1918. Although the elected leadership of the federation was dominated by the members of the SMTC, its board members were evenly distributed and included R. A. Jones of Schenectady, Stanley Ringer of Lynn, W. Koenig of Fort Wayne, and A. C. Kennedy of Erie.

32. *Erie Dispatch*, November 25, 26, 1918; quotations from the "Brownell Report," pp. 19, 56, box marked "GE Labor Policy," ODY.

33. Quotation from *Schenectady Citizen*, December 6, 1918; *Erie Dispatch*, November 27, 1918; *Schenectady Gazette*, November 27, 1918; Frank Morrison to David L. Kevlin, September 16, 1918, vol. 503, FM; John R. Alpine to Kevlin, September 23, 1918, SGLB.

34. Walsh quoted in "Executive Session Minutes," October 22, 1918, p. 6, and see "Transcript of Proceedings," December 18, 1918, p. 28, both in casefile 495, NWLB.

35. "Preliminary Hearing," August 5, 1918, p. 26, casefile 231, NWLB; Taft to Walsh, October 18, 1918, and Taft to Walsh, October 20, 1918, reel 199, WHT; "Executive Session Minutes," October 24, 1918, afternoon session, pp. 53–58, NWLB. Johnston acquiesced even as the board received reports that organized workers were being harassed at Lynn. On this point, see Walter Pyne to W. Jett Lauck, October 22, 1918, casefile 231, NWLB.

36. *Erie Dispatch*, November 28, 1918.

37. *Schenectady Gazette*, November 8, 1918; *Berkshire Evening Eagle*, November 25, 29, December 2, 4, 1918; quotations from Eaton, "The Pittsfield Rebellion," 245–46. Kevlin's campaign against incumbent William C. Moulton specifically targeted women, because he helped deliver many of them raises at GE.

38. H. F. Perkins to E. B. Woods, November 28, 1918, casefile 19, and "Memorandum for Mr. Manly," December 5, 1918, casefile 127, NWLB.

39. *Bridgeport Labor Leader*, January 31, February 14, 21, April 25, 1918. For background, see Bucki, "The Pursuit of Political Power," 29–34.

40. Quotation from Lavit to H. L. Kerwin, February 8, 1918, casefile 33-1116, FMCS; Liberty strike reported in casefile 33-1026, FMCS; *Bridgeport Labor Leader*, April 4, 18, May 9, 16, 1918; "Memorandum in Bridgeport, Conn. Matter," May 4, 1918, casefile 132, box 19, NWLB.

41. "Statement by the Management of the New Brunswick Plant of the Wright-Martin Aircraft Corporation," casefile 132, box 20; "Memorandum of Decision on Bridgeport Rates by the Labor Adjustment Board of Army Ordnance," June 7, 1918, casefile 132, box 19; "Mr. Wallace Speaking for the Remington Company before the NWLB," n.d., casefile

132, box 19; "Executive Session Minutes," June 27, 1918, morning session, p. 52; Sam Lavit to Fred Hewitt, June 15, 1918, casefile 132, box 19; all in NWLB. Conner, *The National War Labor Board*, 53–61.

42. "Executive Session Minutes," June 27, 1918, morning and afternoon sessions, NWLB; *Bridgeport Labor Leader*, July 3, 1918.

43. *Bridgeport Telegram*, April 16, 1918; "Transcripts of Proceedings," July 1, 2, 5, 6, 17, 1918, casefile 132, box 22, and "Wage Investigation, Bridgeport, Connecticut, July 1918," casefile 132, box 19, NWLB; *Bridgeport Labor Leader*, August 8, 1918; and "Report and Recommendations of William H. Johnston in the Controversy of Employees in the Bridgeport Case," n.d.; "Proposed Finding Submitted by the Employers in the Case of the Employees v. the Employers in the City of Bridgeport, Conn.," n.d.; and Isaac Russell, "Recommendation for Award," August 4, 1918; all in casefile 132, box 19, NWLB. Frederick Judson was a Missouri Democrat who served as state chairman of the Taft-led League to Enforce Peace. See Judson, *The Labor Decisions of Judge Taft*.

44. "Executive Session Minutes," August 13, 1918, afternoon session, NWLB.

45. "Executive Session Minutes," August 15, 1918, afternoon session, and August 16, 1918, morning session, pp. 1–6, NWLB; *Bridgeport Labor Leader*, August 8, 22, 1918; *Bridgeport Telegram*, August 15, 16, 1918; May 29, 1919; machinist quoted in Isaac Russell to W. Jett Lauck, August 20, 1918, casefile 132, box 20, NWLB; Walsh and employer quoted in *Bridgeport Telegram*, August 23, 1918.

46. "Findings in re the Machinists of Bridgeport v. Employers," casefile 132, NWLB; Osborne to Eidlitz, August 20, 1918, casefile 132, box 20, NWLB; quotations from Isaac Russell to W. Jett Lauck, August 29, 1918, entry 13, Russell file, casefile 132, NWLB; William Harvey to Lauck, August 30, casefile 132, box 20, NWLB.

47. "Executive Session Minutes," August 27, 1918, morning session, pp. 1–12, NWLB; Rev. George M. Brown quoted in *Bridgeport Telegram*, September 2, 1918; Smith and Wesson quoted in *Iron Age*, September 5, 1918; Johnston quoted in *Bridgeport Telegram*, September 3, 1918.

48. *Iron Age*, September 5, 1918, 584; W. P. Harvey to Lauck, September 2, 1918, Loyall Osborne to W. Jett Lauck, September 3, 1918, and Otto Eidlitz to Lauck, September 4, 1918, all in casefile 132, box 20, NWLB.

49. Observer quoted in Isaac Russell to W. Jett Lauck, September 15, 1918, entry 13, Russell file, and Russell to Lauck, September 3, 1918, both in casefile 132, box 20, NWLB; statement quoted in *Bridgeport Labor Leader*, September 5, 1918, and *Bridgeport Telegram*, September 7, 12, 1918. Telegram quoted is Lavit to Woodrow Wilson, September 6, 1918, casefile 132, box 20, NWLB.

50. Isaac Russell to W. Jett Lauck, September 9, 1918, and Lauck to Loyall Osborne, September 4, 1918, casefile 132, box 20, NWLB; A. B. Bielaki to J. B. Colpoys, September 7, 1918, file 33-1819, FMCS; Johnston to Lavit, September 10, 1918, casefile 132, box 20, NWLB; and machinists quoted in Russell to Lauck, September 11, 1918, casefile 132, box 20, NWLB.

51. Russell to Lauck, August 29, September 4, 11, 1918, casefile 132, box 20, NWLB; Walsh to Taft, August 30, 1918, box 6, FPW; Taft and Walsh to W. B. Wilson, September 10, 1918, file 33-1116, FMCS; Conner, *The National War Labor Board*, 133–34.

52. Woodrow Wilson to District 55, September 13, 1918, casefile 132, box 20, NWLB; Tumulty to "Dear Governor," n.d. [September 1918], series 4, casefile 4341, reel 366, WW;

Lavit to Woodrow Wilson, September 16, 1918, file 33-819, FMCS; Isaac Russell to Tumulty, September 17, 1918, series 4, casefile 4341, reel 366, WW.

53. *Bridgeport Telegram*, September 5, 1918; E. B. Woods, "Conduct of Election—Bridgeport, Connecticut, September 4, 1918 and Following," casefile 132, box 20, NWLB; Isaac Russell to W. Jett Lauck, September 7, 1918, casefile 132, box 20, NWLB; Isaac Russell to J. P. Tumulty, September 22, 1918, series 4, casefile 4341, reel 366, WW.

54. Charlotte E. Rowe to Taft, September 9, 1918, entry 19, NWLB; Rose's account in Rose to W. P. Harvey, September 11, 1918, Harvey to W. Jett Lauck, October 4, 1918, and "Preliminary Report of B. F. Copeland," n.d., all in casefile 217, NWLB; quotation from Hugh McCabe to Basil Manly, March 24, 1919, "Shop Committees" file, entry 15, box 53, NWLB.

55. *Bridgeport Telegram*, August 3, 20, 1918; *Bridgeport Labor Leader*, August 8, 1918; NWLB examiner's quotation and Rankin quotations from Rankin to Walsh, October 9, 1918, casefile 132, box 20, NWLB; Marie Obenauer to W. Jett Lauck, "Memorandum concerning Awards Affecting Women," September 9, 1918, entry 13, Obenauer file, NWLB; Curry quoted in *Bridgeport Labor Leader*, September 5, 1918.

56. Rankin to Frank Walsh, October 9, 1918, casefile 132, box 20, NWLB; Ver Vane quoted in Ver Vane to Walsh, October 3, 1918, casefile 132, box 20, NWLB; *Bridgeport Telegram*, September 25, 1918; *Bridgeport Labor Leader*, October 31, 1918.

57. *Bridgeport Labor Leader*, October 3, 1918; *Bridgeport Telegram*, September 18, 19, 26, 1918.

58. *Bridgeport Telegram*, September 25, 26, 1918; *Bridgeport Labor Leader*, October 3, 1918; "Minutes of Meeting of Local Board of Mediation and Conciliation Held at Bridgeport, November 4, 1918," casefile 132, box 20, NWLB; *Bridgeport Telegram*, November 16, 21, 1918. My interpretation of the local board differs from Jeffrey Haydu's. He argues that it "operated against local union influence" and "guaranteed the impotence of individual shop committees." His interpretation holds true only for the period after the armistice. See Haydu, *Between Craft and Class*, 193.

59. *Bridgeport Telegram*, September 17, November 6, 1918; Lavit to Frank Walsh, October 14, 1918, box 6, FPW.

60. *Bridgeport Labor Leader*, January 17, March 28, April 4, 25, 1918.

61. "Minutes of Meeting of Local Board of Mediation and Conciliation Held at Bridgeport, CT," November 8, 18, 1918, box 20, and "Minutes of Meeting of Local Board of Mediation and Conciliation, March 31, 1919," box 21, both in casefile 132, NWLB; *Bridgeport Herald*, March 20, 1919; *Bridgeport Evening Post*, March 22, 1919; "Minutes of Meeting of Local Board of Mediation and Conciliation, March 31, 1919," casefile 132, box 21, NWLB; W. L. Shafer, "Memorandum of Investigation of Committee Plan of the Automatic Machine Co.," March 20, 1919, casefile 132, box 21, NWLB; "Certain Data in re Shop Committees at Bridgeport," casefile 132, box 21, NWLB; Alpheus Winter to E. B. Woods, January 2, 1919, casefile 132, box 21, NWLB.

CHAPTER SIX

1. *New York Call*, August 31, 1918.

2. Carl V. Harris, *Political Power in Birmingham*, 19–20, 115–16; McKiven, *Iron and Steel*, chaps. 6, 9.

3. Taft and Fink, *Organizing Dixie*, 3–42; McKiven, *Iron and Steel*, 122–23; Raymond Swing, "Examiner's Report," June 20, 1918, casefile 2, NWLB. See also Spero and Harris, *The Black Worker*, 248–49; Norrell, "Caste in Steel," 671–72; Northrup, "The Negro and Unionism," 30; Foner, *Organized Labor and the Black Worker*, 120–28.

4. A. M. Daly, "Steel and Iron at Birmingham," August 1914, reel 12, *USCIR*.

5. *Birmingham Ledger*, February 20, 21, 1918; *Birmingham News*, February 22, 1918; Frank Morrison to John Williams, February 26, 1918, vol. 500, FM; Morrison to B. W. King, March 1, 1918, vol. 500, FM; Morrison to Thomas H. Flynn, March 26, 1918, vol. 501, FM; Raymond Swing, "Examiner's Report," June 20, 1918, casefile 2, NWLB; W. Fairley to John Mitchell, March 12, 1918, reel 36, *JM*.

6. Gompers to William B. Wilson, March 30, 1918, vol. 501, FM; *Machinists' Monthly Journal* 30 (April 1918): 374–75.

7. Lipscomb quoted in *Proceedings of the Seventh Annual Convention of the Alabama State Federation of Labor*, 29. My interpretation of this strike differs from that of Henry M. McKiven in several respects, the most important being that I believe that black workers demonstrated a considerable amount of interest in the AFL during the strike. McKiven does not. I base my interpretation on two sources not consulted by McKiven: records of the NWLB, which had an examiner on the scene, and the letterbooks of Frank Morrison, who coordinated AFL support for the walkout. See McKiven, *Iron and Steel*, 105–11.

8. Spero and Harris, *The Black Worker*, 248; Raymond Swing, "Examiner's Report," June 20, 1918, casefile 2, NWLB; Frank Morrison to Thomas H. Flynn, April 9, 1918, and Morrison to Flynn, May 3, 1918, vol. 501, FM.

9. "Minutes of the Executive Council Meeting of February 12, 1918, Afternoon Session," pp. 20–23, and "Minutes of the Executive Council Meeting of February 16, 1918, Morning Session," pp. 47–48, AFLEC; Frank Morrison to B. W. King, April 11, 1918, Morrison to E. N. Nockels, April 11, 1918, and Morrison to Nockels, April 25, 1918, all in vol. 501, FM.

10. Frank Morrison to B. W. King, April 10, 1918, vol. 501, FM; B. W. King to Frank Morrison, April 10, 1918, casefile 2, NWLB.

11. "Transcript of Proceedings," May 9, 1918, casefile 2, NWLB.

12. Quotations from B. M. Squires to W. B. Wilson, June 22, 1918, casefile 33-1061, and Mrs. G. H. Mathis to Louis Post, September 3, 1917, file 33-618, FMCS; Klan leaflet quoted in *Birmingham Age-Herald*, May 7, 1918; *Birmingham Ledger*, May 7, 1918; *Birmingham News*, May 7, 1918.

13. Frank Morrison to U. W. Hale, May 24, 1918, and Morrison to Hale, June 4, 1918, both in vol. 502, FM; Raymond Swing, "Examiner's Report," June 20, 1918, casefile 2, NWLB.

14. W. R. Crowell, G. H. House, and W. A. Quillan to J. W. McQueen, April 9, 1918; "Case Digest"; "Transcript of Proceedings," May 25, 1918; Charles A. Bell to W. J. Lauck, October 26, 1918; Lauck to Bell, December 6, 1918; H. P. Freeman to M. A. Flynn, February 12, 1919; all in casefile 12, NWLB. Telegrams initiating the case are in "Executive Session Minutes," May 11, 1918, morning session, pp. 3–5, NWLB. *Cleveland Citizen*, August 24, 1918.

15. *Birmingham Labor Advocate*, June 1, 1918; Fortney Johnston to C. E. Michael, June 22, 1918, and Raymond Swing, "Examiner's Report," June 20, 1918, casefile 2, NWLB.

16. Trotter, *Coal, Class, and Color*, 165; *Workmen's Chronicle*, March 9, April 13, 1918; *Birmingham Reporter*, May 25, June 8, 1918.

17. Raymond Swing, "Examiner's Report," June 20, 1918, casefile 2, NWLB; "Tar and Feathers Applied to Negro," clipping, casefile 33-1061, FMCS; Taft and Fink, *Organizing Dixie*, 49–50; Spero and Harris, *The Black Worker*, 248; W. B. Bankhead to W. B. Wilson, June 14, 1918, casefile 12, NWLB; *Birmingham Labor Advocate*, June 15, 1918.

18. Fortney Johnston to C. E. Michael, June 22, 1918, and J. Gaslin to Fortney Johnston, June 7, 1918, both in casefile 2, NWLB; Taft to Walsh, October 18, 1918, and Taft to Walsh, October 20, 1918, both reel 199, WHT.

19. "Executive Session Minutes," July 8, 1918, afternoon session, pp. 29–33; Olander quoted in "Executive Session Minutes," July 9, 1918, afternoon session, pp. 29–33; and Walsh quoted in "Executive Session Minutes," July 11, 1918, morning session, pp. 3–4; all in NWLB.

20. Frank Morrison to Edward Crough, July 20, 1918, vol. 502, FM; *Birmingham Age-Herald*, September 22, 1918; reports of subsequent Klan intimidation found in the *Birmingham Ledger*, July 10, 1918; *New York Times*, September 1, 1918; Snell, "The Ku Klux Klan in Jefferson County," 14–16; Edwin Newdick, "Bitter and Dangerous Alignment — Employers Foster Race Prejudice," entry 1, box 19, file 8/102D, DOL; Olander quoted in "Executive Session Minutes," July 9, 1918, afternoon session, pp. 31–33, NWLB.

21. Details of the strike reported in memorandum, October 2, 1917, Labor Department subject file, box 528, JD; *Pittsburgh Post*, September 18, 19, 22, 24, 25, 26, 29, 30, October 1, 4, 1917; *New York Call*, September 24, 1917; Mary Senior's interview with James Conn, Pittsburgh Interviews, box 26, folder 6, DJS.

22. Mary Senior interviews with Mr. Ling and J. W. Hendricks, Bethlehem Interviews, box 26, folder 7, DJS; *Bethlehem Globe*, August 13, 1917; B. M. Nienburg, "Report on the Administration of the Clause Affecting Women in the Award of Bethlehem and Saucon Plants of the Bethlehem Steel Company," August 31, 1918, casefile 22, NWLB.

23. "Memorandum," June 7, 1918, casefile 22, NWLB; "Investigation of the Bethlehem Steel Controversy," June 19, 1918, casefile 22, NWLB.

24. "Investigation of the Bethlehem Steel Company Controversy," June 18, 1918, casefile 22, NWLB.

25. Casefile 33-1227, FMCS; "Investigation of the Bethlehem Steel Controversy," June 19, 1918, casefile 22, NWLB.

26. W. P. Harvey, "Memorandum for Mr. Walsh," June 20, 1918, Harvey file, entry 13, NWLB.

27. "Executive Session Minutes," June 27, 1918, morning session, pp. 12–16; July 12, 1918, morning session, pp. 7–13; July 24, 1918, morning session, pp. 3–4; and July 30, 1918, morning session, pp. 13–48; all in NWLB.

28. Williams to Lauck, July 5, 1918, casefile 22; "Executive Session Minutes," June 27, 1918, morning session, pp. 12–16, NWLB.

29. "Executive Session Minutes," July 31, 1918, afternoon session, pp. 17–33, and August 1, 1918, morning session, p. 10, both in NWLB; "Finding in re Machinists, Electrical Workers, et al. v. Bethlehem Steel Company," July 31, 1918, casefile 132, NWLB.

30. Records of these organizing drives may be found in casefiles 129, 170, 198, 232, 401, 418, 419, 420, and 472, and records of AAISTW progress, in casefiles 134, 416, 913, NWLB.

31. Johanningsmeier, *Forging American Communism*, 114–16; Foster, *The Great Steel Strike*, 17; *Proceedings of the Thirty-Eighth Annual Convention of the American Federation*

of Labor, 163, 207; W. Z. Foster to John Fitzpatrick, June 22, 1918, box 7, JF/CFL; Foster to Walsh, July 6, 1918, box 6, FPW.

32. For a report on the NWLB, see *Amalgamated Journal*, May 31, 1918; for the quotation, see *Amalgamated Journal*, October 24, 1918.

33. Foster, *The Great Steel Strike*, 25; casefiles 102 and 134, NWLB.

34. "Executive Session Minutes," September 11, 1918, afternoon session, pp. 1–16, WJL; Jones to W. Jett Lauck, September 10, 1918, casefile 22, NWLB.

35. "Executive Session Minutes," September 11, 1918, afternoon session, pp. 1–16, WJL.

36. Urofsky, *Big Steel and the Wilson Administration*, 92, 291; quotations from Matthew Woll and Thomas Rickert are in "Executive Session Minutes," September 13, 1918, afternoon session, pp. 60–61, WJL; Joint Chairmen to Secretary of War, September 17, 1918, casefile 22, NWLB; Benedict Crowell to Grace, September 21, 1918, casefile 22, NWLB.

37. Selekman, *Employes' Representation in Steel Works*, 78–79; Foster, *The Great Steel Strike*, 27.

38. Casefile 129, NWLB; Eggert, *Steelmasters and Labor Reform*, 105, 116–18; McCleester quoted in "Detailed Survey of Plan of Representation of the Midvale Steel and Ordnance Company," pp. 11–12, Midvale folder 5, box 7, WBD.

39. Quotations from Agnes Johnson to Elizabeth Christman, November 10, 1918, and Isaac Russell to W. Jett Lauck, October 16, 1918, both in casefile 22, NWLB. Election petitions are in entry 23, boxes 74–75; election results are in Henderson to Woods, October 28, 1918; W. Jett Lauck to Major General C. C. Williams, October 17, 1918; and "Transcript of Proceedings," January 15, 1919; all in casefile 22, NWLB.

40. Foster, *The Great Steel Strike*, 17; Brody, *Labor in Crisis*, 69–70.

41. Brooks, "The United Textile Workers," 116–20; Fones-Wolf, "Religion and Trade Union Politics," 41; Kelly, *Nine Lives for Labor*, 65–88.

42. Brooks, "The United Textile Workers," 54, 75–79; *Textile Worker* 4 (February 1916): 31.

43. *Textile Worker* 6 (March 1919): 473; Brooks, "The United Textile Workers," 301; *Atlanta Constitution*, August 15, 19, 20, 21, 1918; Mitchell, *Textile Unionism*, 39–40; Hall et al., *Like a Family*, 185–86; casefile 549, NWLB.

44. "Executive Session Minutes," May 21, 1918, p. 10, WJL; *Textile Worker* 6 (July 1918): 101–4.

45. *Providence Evening Bulletin*, July 1, 2, 1918; *Manchester Union*, July 1, 3, 4, 6, 8, 1918.

46. W. Jett Lauck to William Harvey, July 4, 1918; Lauck to John Golden, July 4, 1918; Isaac Russell to Lauck, July 4, 1918; Harvey to Lauck, July 3, 1918; Harvey to Lauck, July 4, 1918; "Henry B. Endicott Award," July 5, 1918; all in casefile 145, NWLB. Lyman, *Henry B. Endicott*, 48; *Manchester Union*, July 6, 8, 1918.

47. *Providence Evening Bulletin*, July 3, 6, 1918; quotation from *Fibre and Fabric*, August 31, 1918, a clipping of which is in casefile 275, NWLB.

48. *Providence Evening Bulletin*, July 1, 2, 1918.

49. UTW official quoted in "Written Statement [by employees] to Be Presented into the Record at the Opening Hearing before the NWLB in Providence, R.I.," n.d. [October 11, 1918], casefile 275, NWLB; quotation from "Interview with Annie Trina," AC; for mention of UTW efforts among weavers, see *Providence Evening Bulletin*, July 2, 17, 1918; McMahon quoted in *Textile Worker* 5 (February 1918): 10.

50. *Providence Evening Bulletin*, July 16, 18, 21, 22, 23, 24, 26, 29, August 7, 1918; *Providence News*, August 14, 1918; *Textile Worker* 6 (July 1918): 101–4; "Written Statement [by employees] to Be Presented into the Record at the Opening Hearing before the NWLB in Providence, R.I.," n.d. [October 11, 1918], casefile 275, NWLB; Golden to W. Jett Lauck, July 31, 1918, casefile 275, NWLB. For background on Riviere, see Kelly, *Nine Lives for Labor*, 90–98.

51. *Providence Evening Bulletin*, July 8, 16, August 2, 19, 1918; Buhle, "Italian-American Radicals and Labor in Rhode Island," 141; Golden to W. Jett Lauck, July 31, 1918, casefile 275, NWLB.

52. *Providence Evening Bulletin*, October 12, 1918; Examiners to Richard Comstock, n.d., and "Written Statement [by employees] to Be Presented into the Record at the Opening Hearing before the NWLB in Providence, R.I.," n.d. [October 11, 1918], casefile 275, NWLB; Thomas McMahon to W. Jett Lauck, October 26, 1918, casefile 275, NWLB; "Transcript of Proceedings," December 17, 1918, casefile 275, NWLB; "Executive Session Minutes," November 12, 1918, morning session, pp. 24–25, NWLB.

53. H. K. Skeffington to H. L. Kerwin, October 30, 1918, casefile 827, NWLB.

54. John R. Dennis to W. Jett Lauck, November 26, 1918, casefile 827, NWLB; quotation from "Original Complaint," casefile 827, NWLB; and on UTW losses, see "Transcript of Proceedings," January 10, 1919, p. 99, casefile 827, NWLB.

55. Wood, "Great Co-operative Machine That Grew Out of the War," 8.

CHAPTER SEVEN

1. *Schenectady Gazette*, November 8, 1918; *Amalgamated Journal*, November 14, 1918.

2. Daniels quoted in *Textile Worker* 6 (December 1918): 326–27; Tead, "Labor and Reconstruction," 534.

3. Carlton, *Organized Labor in American Industry*, 288; *Railway Carmen's Journal* 23 (March 1919): 148, as quoted in Colin J. Davis, "The Nation's Railroad Shopmen and World War I: The Dilemma of Growth" (paper presented at the Symposium on Labor in World War I, George Meany Memorial Archives, 1989).

4. Hobson, *Democracy after the War*, 180.

5. Walsh to V. A. Olander, December 4, 1918, box 7, FPW; McKillen, "Chicago Workers and the Struggle to Democratize Diplomacy," 69, 102.

6. "Executive Session Minutes," November 20, 1918, morning session, pp. 42–63, NWLB.

7. Conner, *The National War Labor Board*, 158; Walsh to V. A. Olander, December 4, 1918, box 7, FPW.

8. Conner, *The National War Labor Board*, chap. 10.

9. "Memo on the Bethlehem Situation, November 17, 1918, Urgent"; "Ruling No. 2: In the Matter of Layoffs of Members of Shop Committees," November 22, 1918; Gregg to E. B. Woods, November 26, 29, December 6, 20, 1918; "Statement regarding the Administration of the Bethlehem Award," December 21, 1918; all in casefile 22, NWLB; *Pennsylvania Labor Herald*, December 28, 1918.

10. Gregg to Woods, November 28, 1918, casefile 22; "Executive Session Minutes," December 6, 1918, pp. 56–60; Grace to Taft and Manly, December 12, 1918, casefile 22;

colleague quoted is Fred Hewitt in "Executive Session Minutes," December 19, 1918, afternoon session, p. 41; "Transcript of Proceedings," January 15, 1919, pp. 4–14, casefile 22; all in NWLB.

11. "Executive Session Minutes," January 18, 1919, morning session, pp. 1–6; February 4, 1919, afternoon session, pp. 15–56; March 4, 1919, afternoon session, pp. 64–74; quotation from David Williams to W. Jett Lauck, March 3, 1919, casefile 22; David Williams to Thomas S. Butler, June 17, 1919, "Miscellaneous" file, entry 19; all in NWLB.

12. Casefile 420; "Transcript of Proceedings," November 20–21, 1918, casefile 418; both in NWLB.

13. Taft quoted in "Executive Session Minutes," April 8, 1919, morning session, p. 28, NWLB; on progress in auto organizing, see casefile 158, NWLB; anonymous automakers are quoted in J. T. O'Brien to E. B. Woods, January 6, 1919, casefile 95, NWLB.

14. Conner, *The National War Labor Board*, 163–66.

15. Ibid., 167–72; *Nation*, March 22, 1919, 414.

16. *Schenectady Gazette*, December 13, 17, 1918.

17. The General Executive Board of the IAM never discussed the strike, and after the fact, the union officially opposed it. See "IAM General Executive Board Minutes," January 28–February 2, 1919, IAM; "Executive Session Minutes," December 18, 1918, morning session, p. 4, NWLB; *Lynn Telegram-News*, December 17, 19, 21, 22, 23, 24, 27, 29, 30, 1918, January 14, 1919. According to H. J. Skeffington of the Department of Labor, the Lynn workers believed that a "sympathetic strike would forfeit them the protection and the award of the War Labor Board." See Skeffington to Kerwin, December 23, 1918, and Skeffington to Kerwin, "Final Report," January 11, 1919, casefile 33-2931, FMCS. A letter from W. Jett Lauck to Charles Keaveny in Lynn confirmed this perception. See Lauck to Keaveny, December 21, 1918, casefile 231, NWLB.

18. *Schenectady Gazette*, December 23, 24, 25, 1918.

19. *Schenectady Gazette*, January 4, 6, 1919; casefile 170-115, FMCS; leaflet in *Schenectady Labor Bulletin*, December 28, 1918, exhibit A, casefile 1011, NWLB; "Minutes of the NWLB Executive Board Meeting," January 8, 1919, casefile 19, NWLB; and foreman quoted in David Kevlin to W. Jett Lauck, January 31, 1919, and G. R. Smith to Assistant Secretary of Labor, February 15, 1919, casefile 19, NWLB.

20. I. K. Russell to Walsh, January 9, 1919, box 7, FPW.

21. Brooks, "The United Textile Workers," 234–36; Buhle, "Italian-American Radicals and Labor in Rhode Island," 124–30; Goldberg, *A Tale of Three Cities*, 27–30, 38–39; Swing, "The Blame for Lawrence," 652.

22. "Executive Session Minutes," February 4, 1919, afternoon session, pp. 10–15, NWLB.

23. "Executive Session Minutes," February 11, 1919, afternoon session, pp. 91–92, NWLB.

24. "Transcript of Proceedings," February 13, 1919, pp. 33–34, casefile 1123, NWLB; and Golden quoted in "Transcript of Proceedings," March 13, 1919, p. 146, casefile 112, NWLB; "Executive Session Minutes," February 13, 1919, afternoon session, pp. 1–18, NWLB.

25. *Paterson Evening News*, April 10, 1919.

26. "Statement Issued Today by Secretary of Labor Wilson," October 30, 1918, series 4, casefile 19, reel 171, WW; Walsh quoted in *Democratic Manual, 1918* (Washington, D.C., 1918), box 27, and NWLB praised by the Democratic Party in "Progress of Labor

under Wilson Administration and Democratic Congress," pamphlet, n.d. [1918], Democratic National Party Publicity, box 27, both in RWW.

27. Manufacturers of Worcester, Massachusetts, "The Voter and His Employees" (pamphlet dated September 19, 1918), series 7, folder 109, Department of Labor files, WBW.

28. Burner, *The Politics of Provincialism*, 34, 36–38; Kennedy, *Over Here*, 244; Blum, *Woodrow Wilson and the Politics of Morality*, 152–56; Sarasohn, *The Party of Reform*, 238. While the Democratic vote declined in most Pennsylvania cities in 1918, this did not occur in centers of organizing such as Allentown, Bethlehem, Johnstown, Reading, and Wilkes-Barre. See Makarewicz, "The Impact of World War I on Pennsylvania Politics," 12.

29. Barr quoted in *Iron Age*, November 14, 1918, 1208; Manly quoted in *Iron Age*, June 19, 1919, 1656; Diary of Thomas Duke Parke, November 9, 1918, TDP.

30. *New Orleans Times-Picayune*, April 3, 1919.

31. Sidney J. Catts to W. B. Wilson, April 7, 1919, and Catts to Wilson, April 22, 1919, entry 1, box 19, file 8/102D, DOL; Samuel M. Wolfe to A. Mitchell Palmer, April 18, 1919, A. Mitchell Palmer file, box 46, JPT.

32. *New York Tribune*, April 21, 1919; Thomas L. Blanton to Woodrow Wilson, February 12, 1920, series 4, casefile 350, reel 256, WW; Blanton quoted in *Congressional Record*, 66th Cong., 2d sess., February 3, 1920, p. 2395.

33. Blanton quoted in *Congressional Record*, 66 Cong., 1st sess., May 29, 1919, pp. 420–24, and 66th Cong., 2d sess., May 11, 1920, p. 6879; Carlos Bee quoted in *Congressional Record*, 66th Cong., 2d sess., May 11, 1920, p. 6879.

34. Quotation in *Proceedings of the Twenty-Fourth Annual Convention of the National Association of Manufacturers*, 342.

35. Fay, *Labor in Politics*, 233; House Committee on Appropriations, *House Committee on Appropriations: Third Deficiency Appropriation Bill*, 421, 444; Zieger, *Republicans and Labor*, 9.

36. Harrison quoted in *Proceedings of the Eighth Annual Convention of the Alabama State Federation of Labor*, 11; Cleveland and Schafer, *Democracy in Reconstruction*; Wildman, *Reconstructing America*; Ryan, *Social Reconstruction*; Tead, "Labor and Reconstruction"; *Report of the Proceedings of the Thirty-Ninth Annual Convention of the American Federation of Labor*, 70–80; Clements, *The Presidency of Woodrow Wilson*, 206–7; Gerard Swope, "Memorandum on Readjustment Problem," November 6, 1918, reel 60, LDB; "After the War Industrial Reconstruction Commission," March 16, 1918, box 99, NCF; Laidler, "Washington and the Coming Reconstruction," 11.

37. Lippmann, "Memorandum on Reconstruction," December 19, 1917, reel 60, LDB; "After the War—Reaction or Reconstruction?" *New Republic*, January 19, 1918, 331–33; Clements, *The Presidency of Woodrow Wilson*, 205–6; Frankfurter, "Memorandum for Secretary Wilson on Labor Representation in Reconstruction," November 11, 1918, reel 4, NDB; W. B. Wilson to Frankfurter, November 12, 1918, War Department file, reel 20, FF.

38. *Amalgamated Journal*, November 14, 1918; Victor Olander to H. L. Kerwin, March 27, 1919, file 13/150, box 3, entry 4, DOL; Walsh to Olander, December 4, 1918, and "Memorandum on the Present Status of the NWLB" [anonymous, but probably by Basil Manly], February 24, 1919, box 7, FPW; National Catholic War Council, *Social Reconstruction*, 13; Pringle, *Life and Times of William Howard Taft*, 2:920–21; Taft quoted in *Washington Post*, April 14, 1919.

39. *American Industries* 19 (June 1919): 16, as quoted in Conner, *The National War Labor Board*, 181.

40. On Gompers's suspicion of Frankfurter, see Mrs. Gertrude Beeks Easley to Matthew Woll, October 29, 1918, entry 10A, box A4, file 334, CND; "Memorandum to the Secretary of Labor from Mr. Frankfurter," September 6, 1918, Eight-Hour Day file, reel 120, FF. The campaign against Frankfurter was apparently begun by Matthew Woll. See Woll to John Fitzpatrick, November 16, 1918, box 7, JF/CFL. The mobilization of the AFL against Frankfurter is evident in the following correspondence: John H. Walker to Frankfurter, December 13, 1918, reel 66, FF; Frankfurter to John Fitzpatrick, December 10, 1918, Ed Nockels to Frankfurter, December 23, 1918, Frankfurter to Fitzpatrick, December 28, 1918, and Frankfurter to Fitzpatrick, January 4, 1919, all in reel 33, FF; Walsh to Ed Nockels, January 6, 1919, box 7, FPW; W. H. Taft to Nellie Taft, September 21, 1918, reel 27, WHT. On Wilson's decision, see Clements, *The Presidency of Woodrow Wilson*, 206.

41. West, "Progress of American Labor," 755; Tumulty to Woodrow Wilson, June 4, 1919, and "Suggestions of Mr. Tumulty," n.d. [June 4, 1919], box 50, JPT.

42. *Congressional Record*, 66th Cong., 1st sess., 1919, pp. 40–42; Fay, *Labor in Politics*, 145; West, "Will Labor Lead?" 600.

43. Samuel Harden Church, "The Criminal Leadership of Labor," speech dated November 11, 1919, Labor folder, box 32, RWW; Tumulty to Woodrow Wilson, June 15, 1918, box 48, JPT; Tumulty to Wilson, August 22, 1919, box 50, JPT.

44. D'Arista, *Federal Reserve Structure*, 31–32. For Basil Manly's views of postwar spending, see *Reconstruction* 1 (April 1919): 99–100. On W. B. Wilson's postwar public works planning, see Clements, *The Presidency of Woodrow Wilson*, 207. The president rejected such plans.

45. Jones, "The Wilson Administration and Organized Labor," 425–45; W. B. Wilson to Woodrow Wilson, December 12, 1919, Chronological file, WBW.

46. Manly, "America Is Passing the Danger Point," 161–64; Lauck to Woodrow Wilson, August 5, 1919, box 37, WJL.

47. Lorwin, *The American Federation of Labor*, 177–79; Hurvitz, "Ideology and Industrial Conflict."

48. *National Industrial Conference, Stenographic Transcript*, 768–70.

49. On W. B. Wilson's views of the first conference, see Wilson to James Duncan, April 22, 1920, Chronological file, WBW.

50. Basil Manly, "Memorandum: Some Features of a National Industrial Judiciary," November 20, 1919, box 43, Pre-Commerce subject file, HCH.

51. Owen Young quoted in "The Open and Closed Shop," unsigned, undated typescript memorandum, "Industrial Conference" file, ODY; for Gompers's suspicions of Stanley King and other conferees, see Gompers to William B. Wilson, February 20, 1920, copy in box 43, Pre-Commerce subject file, HCH; *Report of Industrial Conference Called by the President*, 9, 31.

52. *Report of Industrial Conference Called by the President*, 8; Horace B. Drury, "The Tribunal Plan of the President's Industrial Conference: A Classification of Criticisms," February 19, 1920, box 45, Pre-Commerce subject file, HCH; Chenery, "The Proposed Industrial Plan," 424–32.

53. Section title from Yeats's poem "The Second Coming," in W. B. Yeats, *the Poems*,

ed. Daniel Albright (London: J. M. Dent and Sons, 1990), 235. Lauck quoted in Senate Committee on Labor and Education, *Hearing before the Committee*, p. 7.

54. Walsh to Frank E. Wolfe, December 30, 1918, box 7, and Walsh to Basil Manly, December 30, 1918, box 7, FPW.

55. Walsh to John Shillady, February 25, 1919, and Walsh to Anna Louise Strong, February 25, 1919, both in box 7, FPW; Walsh quoted in *Pennsylvania Labor Herald*, October 4, 1919; Johnston to Walsh, February 24, 1919, box 7, FPW.

56. Walsh to Taft, November 27, 1918, reel 201, WHT; Walsh to Johannsen, December 30, 1918, box 7, FPW.

57. "Transcript of Proceedings," March 13, 1919, p. 38, casefile 491, NWLB; *Washington Post*, March 14, 1919; Basil Manly to Walsh, March 19, 1919, box 8, FPW; Rose Moriarty to Basil Manly, March 20, 1919, and Manly to Moriarty, March 24, 1919, both in casefile 491, NWLB.

58. Walsh to George Creel, May 22, 1916, box 3, FPW; Walsh to William E. Lyons, March 19, 1919, box 8, FPW. Military intelligence agents kept tabs on Walsh's activity on behalf of a free Ireland; see casefile 9771-183, box 2192, MID.

59. Walsh, "Windows Alight in Connaught," 225–27; *Times* (London), May 14, 1919; Creel, *Rebel at Large*, 220; Tillman, *Anglo-American Relations*, 199–200; Manning, *Frank P. Walsh and the Irish Question*, 56; McCartan, *With De Valera in America*, 17–18; Woodrow Wilson to Tumulty, June 9, 1919, box 79, JPT; Walsh Diary, June 11, 1919, box 29, FPW.

60. Walsh, "Wilson Administration's Turn against Labor," 4–6; "Frank P. Walsh Again Sharply Criticizes Wilson Administration's Terrorism," *Reconstruction* 1 (March 1920): 107–9.

61. Walsh to Dudley Field Malone, August 21, 1920, box 9, FPW; Walsh to P. H. Callahan, March 9, 1919, and Walsh to Fitzpatrick, March 12, 1919, box 8, FPW.

62. Craig, *After Wilson*, 16–17; "Interview of Mr. Frank P. Walsh," typescript, June 22, 1920, box 34, FPW.

63. Quote is from Tyson, "Labor Swallows the Forty-Eighters," 588; Malone, "The Birth of the Third Party," 467–68; Pinchot quote in Pinchot to James Maurer, March 20, 1920, box 41, AREP; on efforts to recruit La Follette, see Basil Manly, "Conference at Madison, Wisconsin, July 25–27," n.d. [1920], box B86, RML.

64. Pinchot to Arthur Wray, December 14, 1920, box 40, AREP. For the best summary of the labor issue in the 1920 election, see Zieger, *Republicans and Labor*, chap. 2.

65. Howe, *The Confessions of a Reformer*, 282; Weyl quoted in Forcey, *The Crossroads of Liberalism*, 296; Walsh to Aylward, July 6, 1921, box 10, FPW.

CHAPTER EIGHT

1. Clark, *Common Sense in Labor Management*, 18.

2. *Journal of Electrical Workers and Operators* 18 (October 1918): 135; "Transcript of Proceedings," August 22, 1918, p. 1075, casefile 231, NWLB; *Reconstruction* 1 (April 1919): 97.

3. Matthew Woll, "The Policy of Organized Labor," in Powell, *Social Unrest*, 581; *Auto Worker* 1 (July 1919): 1.

4. Wehle, "War Labor Policies and Their Outcome in Peace," 336; Crowther, *Common*

Sense and Labour, 6–7; Norrell, *James Bowron*, 233; Cowdrick, "What Are We Going to Do with the Boss?" 195.

5. Tead, "Labor and Reconstruction," 541–42; "Employees' Participation in Management and Profits," n.d. [1919], box 32, folder 20, NCWC; Ryan, *Social Reconstruction*, 161–81; Ryan, *Industrial Democracy*; Husslein, *Democratic Industry*; Batten, *The New World Order*; Lauck, *Political and Industrial Democracy*, 27–30; Best, "President Wilson's Second Industrial Conference," 515; "Platform of the Party of Industrial Democracy for the Campaign of 1920," box 119, FPW.

6. Lauck quoted in Senate Committee on Education and Labor, *Hearing before the Committee*, 9; Richmond quoted in *Schenectady Works News*, December 12, 1919, 18–20.

7. *Auto Worker* 1 (July 1919): 1; Drew quoted in Fine, *"Without Blare of Trumpets,"* 204; Crowther, "The Fetish of Industrial Democracy," 23.

8. Brandes, *American Welfare Capitalism*, 27.

9. Gregg, "The National War Labor Board," 61; *Iron Age*, June 26, 1919, 1727; Perlman and Taft, *History of Labor in the United States*, 437. For background, see Kopald, *Rebellion in the Labor Unions*.

10. West, "Progress of American Labor," 753; McKillen, "Chicago Workers and the Struggle to Democratize Diplomacy," chap. 2; *Amalgamated Journal*, December 19, 1918; Plumb and Roylance, *Industrial Democracy*; Lorwin, *The American Federation of Labor*, 174.

11. John P. Frey to Samuel Gompers, September 8, 1919, box 10, JPF; Gompers, *Labor and the Employer*, 305.

12. Charles P. Sweeney, "Labor's Need for Educational Equipment to Effectively Exercise the Newly Secured Right of Collective Bargaining," n.d. [September 1918], and Felix Frankfurter to Grosvenor Clarkson, September 11, 1918, SGWF.

13. Matthew Woll to Grosvenor Clarkson, October 24, 1918, subject file no. 2, SGWF.

14. Frey Scrapbooks, container 23, JPF; *Proceedings of the Thirty-Ninth Annual Convention of the American Federation of Labor*, 70–80, 203–4, 446–49; Lorwin, *The American Federation of Labor*, 174–75, 191–93; Perlman and Taft, *History of Labor in the United States*, 411; Maud Swartz, "In Convention with the American Federation of Labor," *Life and Labor* (August 1919): 204; Montgomery, "New Tendencies in Union Struggles and Strategies," 99.

15. *Proceedings of the Thirty-Ninth Annual Convention of the American Federation of Labor*, 249–50, 302–3.

16. Montgomery, "New Tendencies in Union Struggles and Strategies," 97.

17. Perlman, *Democracy in the International Association of Machinists*, 4; W. H. Johnston to J. J. Collins, March 5, 1919, box 3, and Nicholas Horn to Alex Kohen, April 9, 1919, box 3, both in CEP.

18. McCartin, "Labor's Great War," 227–35; *Schenectady Gazette*, January 25, 27, 28, 1919 (quotation from January 28, 1919).

19. *Schenectady Gazette*, January 28, 29, 1919; "IAM General Executive Board Minutes," January 28–February 2, 1919, IAM.

20. *Bridgeport Labor Leader*, August 7, 14, October 30, 1919; "IAM General Executive Board Minutes," October 13–23, 1919, January 28–March 8, 1920, IAM.

21. Bercuson, *Fools and Wise Men*; *Pennsylvania Labor Herald*, November 15 (Davison quotation), 22, December 6 (Johnston quotation), 1919; Perlman, *Democracy in the Inter-*

national Association of Machinists, 50; "IAM General Executive Board Minutes," April 22–25, 1919, October 13–23, 1919, January 28–March 8, 1920, September 7–October 6, 1920, December 15–20, 1920, February 21–March 3, 1921, IAM.

22. Amalgamated Metal Workers of America leaflet, May 1921, box 2839, file 10110-2265, MID; Savage, *Industrial Unionism in America*, 284–88.

23. Cooke, *An All-American Basis for Industry*, 5.

24. Smyth, " 'Technocracy,' " 212.

25. Meeker, "Industrial Democracy," 19; Leiserson, *Employment Management, Employee Representation, and Industrial Democracy*, 5; Alford, *Henry Laurence Gantt*, 259–61.

26. Stoddard, "Toward an Era of Democratic Control," 253–54; Stoddard, "A Little Shop Committee System," 284–85; Stoddard, *The Shop Committee*; Aborn and Shafer, "Representative Shop Committees," 29–32; Leiserson, *Employment Management, Employee Representation, and Industrial Democracy*.

27. Nelson, *Managers and Workers*, 148–62; Jacoby, *Employing Bureaucracy*, chap. 5; MacNamara, "Shop Committees and the Foreman," 102; *Proceedings of the Annual Convention of the Industrial Relations Association of America* (n.p., 1920), 365–80.

28. Meeker, "Industrial Democracy," 19; Alford, *Henry Laurence Gantt*, 259–61.

29. Cooke, Gompers, and Miller, *Labor, Management, and Production*; Filene to Cooke, June 13, 1919, box 8, MLC; Alford, *Henry Laurence Gantt*, 196.

30. "Status of Arsenal Orders Branch," n.d., and "The Development of Production Committees in Harness Shops of Rock Island Arsenal, Ordnance Department, U.S. Army," n.d., both in War Department file, reel 120, FF.

31. Basil Manly, "Industrial Democracy in the Arsenals," December 4, 1919, War Department file, reel 120, FF; Glenn Stuart Lunden, "The 'B' in the B&O Plan: Otto Beyer and the Development of Union-Management Cooperation on the Baltimore and Ohio Railroad in the 1920s" (Senior thesis, Wesleyan University, 1983), 11–14.

32. Otto S. Beyer, "Efficiency through Democracy in the Railway Industry of America," typescript, April 8, 1919, box 114, OSB.

33. J. W. Powell to W. L. M. King, September 22, 1919, and Richard H. Rice to King, September 29, 1919, both in box 71, file 550, Friends and Services, OMR.

34. King, *Industry and Humanity*, 89, 263; Gitelman, *Legacy of the Ludlow Massacre*, 260.

35. "Confidential Memorandum respecting Employees' Committees in the Works of General Electric Company at Pittsfield, Mass. and Schenectady, NY," August 5, 1918, pp. 4–5, 10, file 196, WLMK.

36. E. G. Grace to King, September 26, 1919, box 71, file 550, Friends and Services, OMR; Bruce E. Kaufman, *Origins and Evolution of the Field of Industrial Relations*, chap. 2; Zieger, "Herbert Hoover, the Wage-Earner, and the 'New Economic System,' " 88–91; Fraser, *Labor Will Rule*, 128–29.

37. Dickman, *Industrial Democracy in America*, 242; John D. Rockefeller Jr., "Representation in Industry," December 5, 1918, box 2, folder 77, J. D. Rockefeller Jr. Personal Papers, OMR; "Remarks of John D. Rockefeller Jr. at the National Industrial Conference, Oct. 16, 1919, Washington, DC," box 2, folder 80, Personal Papers, Speeches file, JDR; correspondence, Colorado Fuel and Iron Co., box 13, folder 107, RFI; Gitelman, *Legacy of the Ludlow Massacre*, 268–69.

38. Case and Case, *Owen D. Young*, 193–95; Atherton Brownell, "Report of an Investigation into Industrial Conditions in the Several Plants of the General Electric Company, Together with Recommendations for a Plan to Improve Them," n.d. [1919], pp. 66–67, and R. H. Rice to E. W. Rice Jr., May 16, 1920, in box marked "GE Labor Policy," ODY.

39. Case and Case, *Owen D. Young*, 196; William Leiserson is the government official quoted in Best, "President Wilson's Second Industrial Conference," 513; National Industrial Conference Board, *Works Councils in the United States*, 2, 11; Employee Representation file, part 2, box 82, WJL; Cleveland Chamber of Commerce, *Employee Representation in Industry*; Nelson, "The Company Union Movement," 338; Rodgers, *The Work Ethic in Industrial America*, 59; Dunn, *The Americanization of Labor*, 128–29; Filene, *The Way Out*, 129; Hood, *The Employment Relation*, 24.

40. Nelson, "The Company Union Movement," 344; *Inoculating against Bolshevism*; ACIPCO, 75; Merritt, *Factory Solidarity or Class Solidarity?* 24; Leopold Demuth, "Two Years of Industrial Democracy at the Plant of Wm. Demuth & Co." leaflet, n.d. [ca. 1921], reel 10, JRC.

41. Bernstein, *The Lean Years*, 170; Leitch, *Man to Man*, 140; Hall et al., *Like a Family*, 217; Litchfield, *The Industrial Republic*.

42. National Industrial Conference Board, *Works Councils in the United States*, 107–8, 112; Atherton Brownell, "Report of an Investigation into Industrial Conditions in the Several Plants of the General Electric Company, Together with Recommendations for a Plan to Improve Them," n.d. [1919], p. 6, in box marked "GE Labor Policy," ODY.

43. National Industrial Conference Board, *A Works Council Manual*, 13; Stoddard, *The Shop Committee*, 66–67.

44. Litchfield, *The Industrial Republic*, 33; *Industrial Representation Plan of the Goodyear Tire and Rubber Company*, 8; *Harvester Industrial Council* (n.p., March 10, 1919); *Plan of Representation* (New York: New York Telephone Company, December 1920); *Multigraph Industrial Democracy*, pamphlet, n.d. [1919], reel 10, JRC; Bloedel Donovan Lumber Mills, *Shop Committee Plans and Standard Practice Rules* (Bellingham, Wash.: Bloedel Mills, n.d. [1923]). Unless otherwise noted, these pamphlets are in the collection of the Hagley Museum and Library, Wilmington, Del.

45. National Industrial Conference Board, *A Works Council Manual*, 2–3; Stoddard, *The Shop Committee*, 22; *Iron Age*, September 11, 1919, 728; Wolfe, *Works Committees and Joint Industrial Councils*, 71–72; National Industrial Conference Board, *Works Councils in the United States*, 2.

46. R. H. Rice to E. W. Rice, May 16, 1920, in box marked "G.E. Labor Policy," ODY; "Outline of the Industrial Representation Plan of the Colorado Fuel and Iron Company and the Partnership Plan of the Dutchess Bleachery, Wappingers Falls, NY," n.d. [1921], folder 19-10, series 2, subseries B, MVK; Kennedy quoted in Douglas, "Shop Committees," 93–94; Mary Van Kleeck to John M. Glen, February 27, 1921, folder 19-9, series 2, subseries B, MVK.

47. Zahavi, *Workers, Managers, and Welfare Capitalism*, chap. 4; Nelson, *American Rubber Workers*, 102–10 (quotation regarding alienated shop committees on p. 105). GE labor organizing is discussed in J. W. Elwood to Owen D. Young, May 11, 12, 13, 19, 1920; E. Z. Steever to Young, June 10, 1920; Steever to Young, September 18, 1922; S. M. Crocker to G. E. Emmons, June 17, 1922; Young to William H. Johnston, January 4, 1922; Sherman T. Rogers to Victor Starzenski, January 17, 1922; all in box marked "GE Labor

Policy," ODY. See also *Journal of Electrical Workers and Operators* 20 (May 1921): 648. Lynn unionists are quoted in Bruere, "West Lynn," 23.

48. National Industrial Conference Board, *Works Councils in the United States*, 84.

49. "How John Leitch Handles Labor," Industrial Conference file, box 44, Pre-Commerce subject file, HCH; Leeds, "Democratic Organization," 13; Fitzgerald quoted in *Summary of the Southern Industrial Conference*, 19–20.

50. *New Majority*, March 22, 1919; Golden quoted in *Textile Worker* 7 (October 1919): 308–9. See also *Textile Worker* 7 (December 1919): 404. ˙

51. *Schenectady Gazette*, December 23, 1918.

52. *Minneapolis Labor Review*, September 20, 1918.

EPILOGUE

1. For Gompers's description of Pershing, see *Textile Worker* 6 (December 1918): 338. The account of the Lafayette-Marne dinner is from Levinson, *Labor on the March*, 43, and Pershing is quoted in John J. Pershing to May Pershing, September 11, 1921, JJP (my thanks to Gene Smith for bringing this citation to my attention).

2. Troy, *Trade Union Membership*, 1; "grand hotel" quotation from Steuben, *Labor in Wartime*, 150; Lavit's correspondence quoted from Lavit to Frank Walsh, October 14, 1918, box 6, FPW; Lavit quoted in *Bridgeport Labor Leader*, March 27, 1919.

3. Fussell, *The Great War and Modern Memory*, 315.

4. Bernstein, *The Lean Years*, 170; League for Industrial Democracy, *Twenty Years of Social Pioneering*; Plumb and Roylance, *Industrial Democracy*; *Chicago Tribune*, March 29, 1922; Golden and Ruttenberg, *The Dynamics of Industrial Democracy*; Gerstle, *Working-Class Americanism*, 182–87.

5. Cowdrick, "What Are We Going to Do with the Boss?" 195; Coldwell, "Collective Bargaining: A Democracy of Industry," December 6, 1918, Chronological file 198, folder 21, WBW.

6. Swope quoted in Brody, *Workers in Industrial America*, 59. During the New Deal era, Swope helped shape the National Recovery Administration, and Kendall advised Francis Perkins's Labor Department.

7. Fraser, "Dress Rehearsal for the New Deal," 221; Cumbler, *Working-Class Community in Industrial America*, 68; Kelly, *Nine Lives for Labor*, 95–98; Kelley, *Hammer and Hoe*, 66.

8. French, *The Shop Committee*, 105.

9. "Transcript of Proceedings," casefile 20-127, January 8, 1919, 5 P.M. session, NWLB.

10. For a provocative example of such thinking, see Heckscher, *The New Unionism*.

11. Commission on the Future of Worker-Management Relations, *Fact Finding Report*, 26.

12. Commission on the Future of Worker-Management Relations, *Final Report and Recommendations*, 2; United States Commission on Industrial Relations, *Final Report of the Commission on Industrial Relations*, 18.

BIBLIOGRAPHY

MANUSCRIPT AND ARCHIVAL SOURCES

Birmingham, Alabama
Birmingham Public Library
   Thomas Duke Parke Diaries
   Sloss-Sheffield Company Records
   Philip Taft Research Notes Collection on Alabama Labor
   George B. Ward Scrapbooks

Bridgeport, Connecticut
Bridgeport Public Library
   Manufacturers' Association of Southern Connecticut Records

Cambridge, Massachusetts
Schlesinger Library, Radcliffe College
   Doris Stevens Papers

Canton, New York
St. Lawrence University
   Owen D. Young Papers

Charlottesville, Virginia
Alderman Library, University of Virginia
   W. Jett Lauck Papers

Chicago, Illinois
Chicago Historical Society
   Chicago Federation of Labor Records/John Fitzpatrick Papers

Detroit, Michigan
Walter Reuther Memorial Archive, Wayne State University
   Lester Cappon Papers
   Carl E. Person Papers
   Mary Van Kleeck Papers

Hoboken, New Jersey
Stevens Institute of Technology
    Frederick W. Taylor Papers

Hyde Park, New York
Franklin D. Roosevelt Presidential Library
    Morris L. Cooke Papers
    Franklin D. Roosevelt Papers

Madison, Wisconsin
State Historical Society of Wisconsin
    John R. Commons Papers
    William M. Leiserson Papers
    Charles McCarthy Papers
    David J. Saposs Papers

New York, New York
New York Public Library
    National Civic Federation Records
    Frank P. Walsh Papers

North Tarrytown, New York
Rockefeller Archives Center
    John D. Rockefeller Jr. Papers
    Rockefeller Family Interests Records, Offices of the Messrs. Rockefeller
    Rockefeller Foundation Papers, Administration, Programs and Policy

Ottawa, Canada
Canadian National Archives
    William Lyon Mackenzie King Papers, Manuscript Group 26

Philadelphia, Pennsylvania
Historical Society of Pennsylvania
    William B. Wilson Papers

St. Paul, Minnesota
Immigration History Research Center
    Anthony Capraro Papers

Silver Spring, Maryland
George Meany Memorial Archives
    American Federation of Labor Executive Council Minutes
    Frank Morrison Letterbooks
    War Files of President Gompers

State College, Pennsylvania
Pennsylvania State University
   William B. Dickson Papers

Washington, D.C.
Catholic University of America, Mullen Library
   John Brophy Papers
   National Catholic War Council Papers
Library of Congress, Manuscripts Division
   Newton D. Baker Papers
   Ray Stannard Baker Papers
   Otto S. Beyer Papers
   Louis D. Brandeis Papers
   Albert S. Burleson Papers
   Josephus Daniels Papers
   Felix Frankfurter Papers
   John P. Frey Papers
   Samuel Gompers Letterbooks
   Florence Jaffray Harriman Papers
   Oliver Wendell Holmes Jr. Papers
   Robert M. La Follette Sr. Papers
   Robert Lansing Papers
   John J. Pershing Papers
   Amos R. E. Pinchot Papers
   Louis F. Post Papers
   Theodore Roosevelt Papers
   Raymond Gram Swing Papers
   William Howard Taft Papers
   Joseph P. Tumulty Papers
   Woodrow Wilson Papers
   Robert W. Woolley Papers
National Archives
   Records of the Council of National Defense, Record Group 62
   Records of the Federal Mediation and Conciliation Service, Record Group 280
   Records of the Fuel Administration, Record Group 67
   Records of the Justice Department, Record Group 60
   Records of the Labor Department, Record Group 174
   Records of the National War Labor Board, Record Group 2
   Records of the United States Railroad Administration, Record Group 14
   Records of the United States Shipping Board, Record Group 32
   Records of the War Department General and Special Staffs (Military Intelligence
      Division), Record Group 165
   Records of the War Industries Board, Record Group 61
   Records of the War Labor Policies Board, Record Group 1

West Branch, Iowa
Herbert C. Hoover Presidential Library
  Herbert C. Hoover Papers

Wilmington, Delaware
Hagley Museum and Library
  Bethlehem Steel Company Papers
  National Industrial Conference Board Records

PUBLISHED MANUSCRIPT COLLECTIONS

Amalgamated Clothing Workers of America Records. Frederick, Md.: University Publica-
  tions of America, 1989. Microfilm.
American Federation of Labor Records: The Samuel Gompers Era. Frederick, Md.: Uni-
  versity Publications of America, 1985. Microfilm.
John Mitchell Papers. Glen Rock, N.J.: Microfilming Corporation of America, 1974.
  Microfilm.
Link, Arthur S., ed. *The Papers of Woodrow Wilson*. 64 vols. Princeton: Princeton Univer-
  sity Press, 1964–94.
Records of the President's Mediation Commission, 1917–1919. Frederick, Md.: University
  Publications of America, 1985. Microfilm.
Records of the U.S. Commission on Industrial Relations, 1912–1915. Frederick, Md.:
  University Publications of America, 1985. Microfilm.

NEWSPAPERS

Atlanta Constitution, 1918
Berkshire Evening Eagle, 1916–19
Bethlehem Globe/Globe-Times, 1917–20
Birmingham Age-Herald, 1917–19
Birmingham Ledger, 1918
Birmingham News, 1918
Birmingham Reporter, 1918
[Birmingham] Workmen's Chronicle, 1918
Bridgeport Telegram, 1917–19
Chicago Daily News, 1918
Chicago Tribune, 1918, 1922
Cleveland Citizen, 1916–18
Erie Dispatch, 1918–19
Kansas City Star, 1917
Lynn Daily-Evening Item, 1918
Lynn Telegram/Telegram-News, 1917–19
Manchester Union, 1918–19
New Orleans Times-Picayune, 1919
New York Times, 1913–19
Paterson Evening News, 1919

Pittsburgh Post, 1916–17
Providence Evening Bulletin, 1918
Schenectady Citizen, 1916–19
Schenectady Gazette, 1916–18
St. Louis Globe-Democrat, 1917–18
Washington Post, 1919

CONTEMPORARY JOURNALS

Christian Socialist, 1915
Iron Age, 1915–20
La Follette's Weekly Magazine, 1913–15
The Masses, 1915
Monthly Labor Review, 1917–19
The Nation, 1914–19
The New Republic, 1915–19
Reconstruction, 1919–20
The Survey, 1915–19

TRADE UNION AND RELATED PERIODICALS AND NEWSPAPERS

Amalgamated Journal, 1917–20
American Federationist, 1912–20
The Auto Worker, 1919
Birmingham Labor Advocate, 1916–20
Bridgeport Labor Leader, 1917–20
Butcher Workman, 1917–18
Erie Union Labor Journal, 1916–20
Journal of Electrical Workers and Operators, 1916–21
Machinists' Monthly Journal, 1916–20
Minneapolis Labor Review, 1916–20
The New Majority, 1919
New York Call, 1915–18
Pennsylvania Labor Herald, 1918–20
Schenectady Citizen, 1916–19
Seattle Union Record, 1915–17
Solidarity, 1915–16
The Spark Plug, 1917
St. Louis Labor, 1916–20
The Textile Worker, 1916–20

CONVENTION PROCEEDINGS

Proceedings of the Seventh Annual Convention of the Alabama State Federation of Labor.
    Tuscaloosa, Ala., 1918.

Proceedings of the Eighth Annual Convention of the Alabama State Federation of Labor.
Mobile, Ala., 1919.
Proceedings of the Thirty-Third Annual Convention of the American Federation of Labor.
Washington, D.C., 1913.
Proceedings of the Thirty-Fourth Annual Convention of the American Federation of Labor.
Washington, D.C., 1914.
Proceedings of the Thirty-Sixth Annual Convention of the American Federation of Labor.
Washington, D.C., 1916.
Proceedings of the Thirty-Eighth Annual Convention of the American Federation of Labor.
Washington, D.C., 1918.
Proceedings of the Thirty-Ninth Annual Convention of the American Federation of Labor.
Washington, D.C., 1919.
Proceedings of the Annual Convention of the Industrial Relations Association of America.
N.p., 1920.
*Proceedings of the Twelfth Consolidated Convention of the International Brotherhood of
Boiler Makers, Iron Ship Builders, and Helpers of America.* Kansas City, Mo., 1917.
*Proceedings of the Twenty-Fourth Annual Convention of the National Association of
Manufacturers.* New York, 1919.
*Proceedings of the Twenty-Fifth Consecutive and Second Biennial Convention of the
United Mine Workers of America.* 2 vols. Indianapolis, 1916.

GOVERNMENT DOCUMENTS

Army Ordnance Industrial Section. *Handbook of Information concerning Government
Boards and Department Sections Dealing with Labor.* Washington, D.C.: Government
Printing Office, 1918.
Commission on the Future of Worker-Management Relations. *Fact Finding Report:
Commission on the Future of Worker-Management Relations, May 1994.* Washington,
D.C.: U.S. Departments of Labor and Commerce, 1994.
———. *Final Report and Recommendations.* Washington, D.C.: U.S. Departments of
Labor and Commerce, 1994.
Committee on Public Information. *War, Labor, and Peace.* Washington, D.C.: Committee on Public Information, 1918.
House Committee on Appropriations. *House Committee on Appropriations: Third Deficiency Appropriation Bill, 1919.* 65th Cong., 3d sess., vol. 185. Washington, D.C.:
Government Printing Office, 1919.
Lauck, W. Jett. *Report of the Secretary of the National War Labor Board to the Secretary
of Labor for the Twelve Months Ending May 31, 1919.* Washington, D.C.: Government
Printing Office, 1920.
Leiserson, William M. *Employment Management, Employee Representation, and Industrial Democracy.* Washington, D.C.: Government Printing Office, 1919.
National Industrial Conference, Stenographic Transcript. Washington, D.C.: Galt and
Williams, 1919.
Report of Industrial Conference Called by the President. New York: M. B. Brown, 1920.
Report of the Secretary of the National War Labor Board to the Secretary of Labor for the

Twelve Months Ending May 31, 1919. Washington, D.C.: Government Printing Office, 1919.

Senate Committee on Education and Labor. *Hearing before the Committee on Education and Labor, United States Senate, on the Report of the Industrial Conference.* Washington, D.C.: Government Printing Office, 1920.

Special Committee of the House of Representatives. *Hearings to Investigate the Taylor and Other Systems of Shop Management.* 3 vols. Washington, D.C.: Government Printing Office, 1912.

United States Commission on Industrial Relations. *Final Report and Testimony Submitted to the Congress by the Commission on Industrial Relations.* 11 vols. Washington, D.C.: Government Printing Office, 1916.

————. *Final Report of the Commission on Industrial Relations.* Washington, D.C.: Government Printing Office, 1916.

Walsh, Francis Patrick. *Aims and Purposes of the National War Labor Board.* Bulletin of the NWLB. Washington, D.C.: Government Printing Office, 1918.

BOOKS

ACIPCO: A Story of Modern Industrial Relations. Birmingham, Ala.: American Cast Iron Pipe Company, 1920.

Adams, Graham, Jr. *Age of Industrial Violence, 1910–15: The Activities and Findings of the United States Commission on Industrial Relations.* New York: Columbia University Press, 1966.

Aitken, Hugh G. J. *Scientific Management in Action: Taylorism at Watertown Arsenal.* Princeton: Princeton University Press, 1985.

Alford, Leon P. *Henry Laurence Gantt: Leader in Industry.* New York: Harper and Brothers, 1934.

American Federation of Labor. *American Federation of Labor: History, Encyclopedia, Reference Book.* Washington, D.C.: n.p., 1919.

Arnesen, Eric. *Waterfront Workers of New Orleans: Race, Class, and Politics, 1863–1923.* New York: Oxford University Press, 1991.

Atleson, James B. *Values and Assumptions in American Labor Law.* Amherst: University of Massachusetts Press, 1983.

Babson, Roger W. *William B. Wilson and the Department of Labor.* New York: Brentano's, 1919.

Baker, Ray Stannard. *Woodrow Wilson: Life and Letters.* 8 vols. Garden City, N.Y.: Doubleday, 1927–39.

Barrett, James R. *Work and Community in the Jungle: Chicago's Packinghouse Workers, 1894–1922.* Urbana: University of Illinois Press, 1987.

Batten, Samuel Zane. *The New World Order.* Philadelphia: American Baptist Publication Society, 1919.

Beaver, Daniel R. *Newton D. Baker and the War Effort, 1917–19.* Lincoln: University of Nebraska Press, 1966.

Bercuson, David J. *Fools and Wise Men: The Rise and Fall of the One Big Union.* Toronto: McGraw-Hill, 1978.

Bernstein, Irving. *The Lean Years: A History of the American Worker, 1920–1933*. Boston: Houghton Mifflin, 1960.

Bing, Alexander M. *Wartime Strikes and Their Adjustment*. New York: E. P. Dutton, 1921.

Block, Fred. *Revising State Theory: Essays in Politics and Postindustrialism*. Philadelphia: Temple University Press, 1987.

Blum, John Morton. *Woodrow Wilson and the Politics of Morality*. Boston: Little, Brown, 1956.

Bodnar, John. *Immigration and Industrialization: Ethnicity in an American Mill Town*. Pittsburgh: University of Pittsburgh Press, 1977.

Bourne, Randolph. *War and the Intellectuals*. Edited by Carl Resek. New York: Harper Torchbooks, 1964.

Brandes, Stuart D. *American Welfare Capitalism, 1880–1940*. Chicago: University of Chicago Press, 1976.

Brandeis, Louis D. *Business—A Profession*. Boston: Hale, Cushman and Flint, 1933.

Braverman, Harry. *Labor and Monopoly Capital: The Degradation of Work in the Twentieth Century*. New York: Monthly Review, 1975.

Breen, William J. *Uncle Sam at Home: Civilian Mobilization, Wartime Federalism, and the Council of National Defense, 1917–1919*. Contributions in American Studies, no. 70. Westport, Conn.: Greenwood, 1984.

Brody, David. *Labor in Crisis: The Steel Strike of 1919*. New York: Harper and Row, 1965.
———. *Steelworkers in America: The Non-Union Era*. Cambridge: Harvard University Press, 1960.
———. *Workers in Industrial America: Essays on the Twentieth-Century Struggle*. New York: Oxford University Press, 1980.

Brooks, John Graham. *Labor's Challenge to the Social Order: Democracy Its Own Critic and Educator*. New York: Kennikat, 1920.

Buenker, John D. *Urban Liberalism and Progressive Reform*. New York: Scribner's Sons, 1973.

Burner, David. *The Politics of Provincialism: The Democratic Party in Transition, 1918–32*. Westport, Conn.: Greenwood, 1967.

Burowoy, Michael. *Manufacturing Consent: Changes in the Labor Process under Monopoly Capitalism*. Chicago: University of Chicago Press, 1979.

Burritt, Arthur W. *Profit Sharing: Its Principles and Practice*. New York: Harper and Brothers, 1918.

Carlton, Frank Tracy. *The Industrial Situation: Its Effect upon the Home, the School, the Wage Earner, and the Employer*. New York: Fleming H. Revell, 1914.
———. *Organized Labor in American Industry*. New York: D. Appleton, 1920.

Case, Josephine Young, and Everett Needham Case. *Owen D. Young and American Enterprise: A Biography*. Boston: David R. Godine, 1982.

Chambers, Clark A. *Paul U. Kellogg and "The Survey": Voices for Social Welfare and Social Justice*. Minneapolis: University of Minnesota Press, 1971.

Christie, Jean. *Morris Llewellyn Cooke: Progressive Engineer*. New York: Garland Publishing, 1983.

Clark, Neil M. *Common Sense in Labor Management*. New York: Harper and Brothers, 1919.

Clements, Kendrick A. *The Presidency of Woodrow Wilson*. Lawrence: University Press of Kansas, 1992.

Cleveland Chamber of Commerce. *Employee Representation in Industry: Some Plans in Operation in Cleveland*. Cleveland: n.p., 1923.

Cleveland, Frederick A., and Joseph Schafer, eds. *Democracy in Reconstruction*. Boston: Houghton Mifflin, 1919.

Cohen, Lizabeth. *Making a New Deal: Industrial Workers in Chicago, 1919–39*. New York: Cambridge University Press, 1990.

Commons, John R. *Myself*. New York: Macmillan, 1934.

Commons, John R., et al. *History of Labour in the United States*. 4 vols. New York: Macmillan, 1918–34.

Conner, Valerie Jean. *The National War Labor Board: Stability, Social Justice, and the Voluntary State in World War I*. Chapel Hill: University of North Carolina Press, 1983.

Cooke, Morris L., Samuel Gompers, and Fred J. Miller, eds. *Labor, Management, and Production*. Philadelphia: American Academy of Political and Social Science, 1920.

Cooper, Patricia. *Once a Cigar Maker: Men, Women, and Work Culture in American Cigar Factories, 1900–1919*. Urbana: University of Illinois Press, 1987.

Craig, Douglas B. *After Wilson: The Struggle for the Democratic Party, 1920–1934*. Chapel Hill: University of North Carolina Press, 1992.

Cramer, C. H. *Newton D. Baker: A Biography*. New York: World Publishing, 1961.

Creel, George. *Rebel at Large: Recollections of Fifty Crowded Years*. New York: G. P. Putnam's Sons, 1947.

Crowther, Samuel. *Common Sense and Labour*. New York: Doubleday, Page, 1920.

Cuff, Robert D. *The War Industries Board: Business-Government Relations during World War I*. Baltimore: Johns Hopkins University Press, 1973.

Cumbler, John T. *Working-Class Community in Industrial America: Work, Leisure, and Struggle in Two Industrial Cities, 1880–1930*. Westport, Conn.: Greenwood, 1979.

D'Arista, Jane W. *Federal Reserve Structure and the Development of Monetary Policy: 1915–1935*. Washington, D.C.: Government Printing Office, 1971.

Davis, Allen F. *Spearheads for Reform: The Social Settlements and the Progressive Movement, 1890–1914*. New York: Oxford University Press, 1967.

Dawley, Alan. *Struggles for Justice: Social Responsibility and the Liberal State*. Cambridge: Harvard University Press, 1991.

Dennison, James T. *Henry S. Dennison: New England Industrialist Who Served America*. New York: Newcomen Society of North America, 1955.

Derber, Milton. *The American Idea of Industrial Democracy, 1865–1965*. Urbana: University of Illinois Press, 1970.

Dickman, Howard. *Industrial Democracy in America: Ideological Origins of National Labor Relations Policy*. La Salle, Ill.: Open Court, 1987.

Douglas, Paul H. *Real Wages in the United States, 1890–1926*. New York: Houghton Mifflin, 1930.

Dubofsky, Melvyn. *Industrialism and the American Worker, 1865–1920*. Arlington Heights, Ill.: Harlan Davidson, 1975.

———. *The State and Labor in Modern America*. Chapel Hill: University of North Carolina Press, 1994.

———. *We Shall Be All: A History of the Industrial Workers of the World.* 2d ed. Urbana: University of Illinois Press, 1988.

———. *When Workers Organize: New York City in the Progressive Era.* Amherst: University of Massachusetts Press, 1968.

Dubofsky, Melvyn, and Warren Van Tine. *John L. Lewis: A Biography.* Abridged ed. Urbana: University of Illinois Press, 1986.

Dunn, Robert W. *The Americanization of Labor: The Employers' Offensive against the Trade Unions.* New York: International Publishers, 1927.

Eggert, Gerald. *Steelmasters and Labor Reform, 1886–1923.* Pittsburgh: University of Pittsburgh Press, 1981.

Emmons, David M. *The Butte Irish: Class and Ethnicity in an American Mining Town, 1875–1925.* Urbana: University of Illinois Press, 1988.

Esberey, Joy E. *Knight of the Holy Spirit: A Study of William Lyon Mackenzie King.* Toronto: University of Toronto Press, 1980.

Evans, Peter B., Dietrich Rueschemeyer, and Theda Skocpol, eds. *Bringing the State Back In.* New York: Cambridge University Press, 1985.

Fay, Charles Norman. *Labor in Politics or Class versus Country: Considerations for American Voters.* [Cambridge, Mass.]: privately printed, 1921.

Feldman, Gerald D. *Army, Industry, and Labor in Germany, 1914–1918.* Princeton: Princeton University Press, 1966.

Filene, Edward A. *The Way Out.* Garden City, N.Y.: Doubleday, Page, 1924.

Fine, Sidney. *"Without Blare of Trumpets": Walter Drew, the National Erectors' Association, and the Open Shop Movement, 1903–57.* Ann Arbor: University of Michigan Press, 1995.

Fink, Gary M. *The Fulton Bag and Cotton Mill Strike of 1914–1915: Espionage, Labor Conflict, and New South Industrial Relations.* Ithaca: ILR Press, 1993.

———. *Labor's Search for Political Order: The Political Behavior of the Missouri Labor Movement, 1890–1940.* Columbia: University of Missouri Press, 1973.

Follett, Mary Parker. *The New State: Group Organization, the Solution of Popular Government.* New York: Longmans, Green, 1918.

Foner, Philip S. *History of the Labor Movement in the United States.* Vol. 5, *The AFL in the Progressive Era, 1910–1915.* New York: International Publishers, 1980.

———. *History of the Labor Movement in the United States.* Vol. 6, *On the Eve of America's Entry into World War I, 1915–16.* New York: International Publishers, 1982.

———. *History of the Labor Movement in the United States.* Vol. 7, *Labor and World War I, 1914–1918.* New York: International Publishers, 1987.

———. *Organized Labor and the Black Worker, 1619–1981.* New York: International Publishers, 1981.

Forbath, William E. *Law and the Shaping of the American Labor Movement.* Cambridge: Harvard University Press, 1991.

Forcey, Charles B. *The Crossroads of Liberalism: Croly, Weyl, Lippmann, and the Progressive Era, 1900–25.* New York: Oxford University Press, 1961.

Foster, William Z. *The Great Steel Strike and Its Lessons.* New York: Heubsch, 1920.

Frank, Dana. *Purchasing Power: Consumer Organizing, Gender, and the Seattle Labor Movement, 1919–1929.* New York: Cambridge University Press, 1994.

Fraser, Steve. *Labor Will Rule: Sidney Hillman and the Rise of American Labor.* New York: Free Press, 1991.

Freidel, Frank. *Franklin D. Roosevelt: The Apprenticeship.* Boston: Little, Brown, 1952.

French, Carroll E. *The Shop Committee in the United States.* Baltimore: Johns Hopkins University Press, 1923.

Fussell, Paul. *The Great War and Modern Memory.* New York: Oxford University Press, 1975.

Garwood, Darrell. *Crossroads of America: The Story of Kansas City.* New York: W. W. Norton, 1948.

Genovese, Eugene D. *Roll, Jordan, Roll: The World the Slaves Made.* New York: Pantheon, 1974.

Gerber, Larry G. *The Limits of Liberalism: Josephus Daniels, Henry Stimson, Bernard Baruch, Donald Richberg, Felix Frankfurter, and the Development of the Modern American Political Economy.* New York: New York University Press, 1983.

Gerstle, Gary. *Working-Class Americanism: The Politics of Labor in a Textile City, 1914–1960.* New York: Cambridge University Press, 1989.

Gilbert, James. *Designing the Industrial State: The Intellectual Pursuit of Collectivism in America, 1880–1940.* Chicago: Quadrangle Books, 1972.

Gitelman, Howard M. *Legacy of the Ludlow Massacre: A Chapter in American Industrial Relations.* Philadelphia: University of Pennsylvania Press, 1988.

Goldberg, David. *A Tale of Three Cities: Labor Organization and Protest in Paterson, Passaic, and Lawrence, 1916–1921.* New Brunswick: Rutgers University Press, 1989.

Golden, Clinton S., and Harold Ruttenberg. *The Dynamics of Industrial Democracy.* 1942. Reprint, New York: Da Capo, 1973.

Gompers, Samuel. *American Labor and the War.* New York: George H. Doran, 1919.

———. *Labor and the Employer.* New York: E. P. Dutton, 1920.

———. *Seventy Years of Life and Labor.* 2 vols. New York: E. P. Dutton, 1925.

Graebner, William. *The Engineering of Consent: Democracy and Authority in Twentieth-Century America.* Madison: University of Wisconsin Press, 1987.

Greene, Julie. *Pure and Simple Politics: The American Federation of Labor, 1881–1917.* New York: Cambridge University Press, 1997.

Greenstone, J. David. *Labor in American Politics.* Chicago: University of Chicago Press, 1977.

Greenwald, Maurine Wiener. *Women, War, and Work: The Impact of World War I on Women Workers in the United States.* Westport, Conn.: Greenwood, 1980.

Grossman, Jonathan. *The Department of Labor.* New York: Praeger, 1973.

Grubbs, Frank L. *The Struggle for Labor Loyalty: Gompers, the AFL, and the Pacifists.* Durham: Duke University Press, 1968.

Haber, Samuel. *Efficiency and Uplift: Scientific Management in the Progressive Era, 1890–1920.* Chicago: University of Chicago Press, 1964.

Hall, Jacquelyn Dowd, James Leloudis, Robert Korstad, Mary Murphy, Lu Ann Jones, and Christopher B. Daly. *Like a Family: The Making of a Southern Cotton Mill World.* Chapel Hill: University of North Carolina Press, 1987.

Hapgood, Hutchins. *The Spirit of Labor.* New York, 1907.

Harriman, Florence Jaffray. *From Pinafores to Politics.* New York: Henry Holt, 1923.

Harris, Carl V. *Political Power in Birmingham, 1871–1921*. Knoxville: University of Tennessee Press, 1977.

Harris, Howell John. *The Right to Manage: The Industrial Relations Policies of American Business in the 1940s*. Madison: University of Wisconsin Press, 1982.

Hattam, Victoria C. *Labor Visions and State Power: The Origins of Business Unionism in the United States*. Princeton: Princeton University Press, 1993.

Hawley, Ellis W. *The Great War and the Search for a Modern Order: A History of the American People and Their Institutions*. New York: St. Martin's, 1992.

Haydu, Jeffrey. *Between Craft and Class: Skilled Workers and Factory Politics in the United States and Britain, 1890–1922*. Berkeley: University of California Press, 1988.

Heckscher, Charles C. *The New Unionism: Employee Involvement in the Changing Corporation*. New York: Basic, 1988.

Hobsbawm, Eric J. *Labouring Men: Studies in the History of Labour*. Garden City, N.Y.: Doubleday, 1964.

Hobson, John A. *Democracy after the War*. New York: Macmillan, 1917.

Hood, Frederic C. *The Employment Relation*. Boston: Associated Industries of Massachusetts, 1919.

Hough, Emerson. *The Web: The Authorized History of the American Protective League*. Chicago: Reilly and Lee, 1919.

Howe, Frederic C. *The Confessions of a Reformer*. New York: Scribner's Sons, 1925.

———. *Why War?* New York: Scribner's Sons, 1916.

Hoxie, Robert Franklin. *Scientific Management and Labor*. 1915. Reprint, New York: Augustus M. Kelley, 1966.

Hunter, Robert. *Labor in Politics*. Chicago: Socialist Party, 1915.

Husslein, Joseph, S.J. *Democratic Industry: A Practical Study in Social History*. New York: P. J. Kennedy and Sons, 1919.

Industrial Representation Plan of the Goodyear Tire and Rubber Company. Akron: Goodyear Tire and Rubber Company, 1919.

Inoculating against Bolshevism. N.p., [1919].

Jacoby, Sanford M. *Employing Bureaucracy: Managers, Unions, and the Transformation of Work in American Industry, 1900–45*. New York: Columbia University Press, 1985.

———, ed. *Masters to Managers: Historical and Comparative Perspectives on American Employers*. New York: Columbia University Press, 1991.

Johanningsmeier, Edward P. *Forging American Communism: The Life of William Z. Foster*. Princeton: Princeton University Press, 1994.

Josephson, Matthew. *Sidney Hillman: Statesman of American Labor*. Garden City, N.Y.: Doubleday, 1952.

Judson, Frederick. *The Labor Decisions of Judge Taft*. Cleveland: n.p., 1907.

Karson, Marc. *American Labor Unions and Politics, 1900–1918*. Carbondale: Southern Illinois University Press, 1958.

Kaufman, Bruce E. *The Origins and Evolution of the Field of Industrial Relations in the United States*. Ithaca: ILR Press, 1993.

Kaufman, Stuart B. *Challenge and Change: The History of the Tobacco Workers International Union*. Kensington, Md.: Bakery, Confectionery, and Tobacco Workers International Union, 1986.

———. *Samuel Gompers and the Origins of the AFL*. Westport, Conn.: Greenwood, 1973.

Kazin, Michael. *The Barons of Labor: The San Francisco Building Trades and Union Power in the Progressive Era*. Urbana: University of Illinois Press, 1987.

———. *The Populist Persuasion: An American History*. New York: Basic, 1995.

Kelley, Robin D. G. *Hammer and Hoe: Alabama Communists during the Great Depression*. Chapel Hill: University of North Carolina Press, 1990.

Kelly, Richard. *Nine Lives for Labor*. New York: Praeger, 1956.

Kendall, Henry P. *The Kendall Company: Fifty Years of Yankee Enterprise*. New York: Newcomen Society of North America, 1953.

Kennedy, David M. *Over Here: The First World War and American Society*. New York: Oxford University Press, 1980.

King, W. L. Mackenzie. *Industry and Humanity*. 1918. Reprint, Toronto: University of Toronto Press, 1973.

Knock, Thomas J. *To End All Wars: Woodrow Wilson and the Quest for a New World Order*. New York: Oxford University Press, 1992.

Kolko, Gabriel. *The Triumph of Conservatism: A Reinterpretation of American History, 1900–1916*. New York: Free Press, 1963.

Kopald, Sylvia. *Rebellion in the Labor Unions*. New York: Boni and Liveright, 1924.

Larson, Simeon. *Labor and Foreign Policy: Gompers, the AFL, and the First World War, 1914–1918*. Rutherford, N.J.: Fairleigh Dickinson Press, 1974.

Lasch, Christopher. *The New Radicalism in America, 1889–1963: The Intellectual as a Social Type*. New York: Alfred A. Knopf, 1965.

Lauck, W. Jett, *Political and Industrial Democracy, 1776–1926*. New York: Funk and Wagnalls, 1926.

Layton, Edwin T., Jr. *The Revolt of the Engineers: Social Responsibility and the American Engineering Profession*. Cleveland: Case Western Reserve University Press, 1971.

League for Industrial Democracy. *Twenty Years of Social Pioneering: The League for Industrial Democracy Celebrates Its Twentieth Anniversary*. New York: League for Industrial Democracy, 1926.

Leitch, John. *Man to Man: The Story of Industrial Democracy*. New York, 1919.

Levinson, Edward. *Labor on the March*. New York: Harper and Brothers, 1956.

Lewis, Earl. *In Their Own Interests: Race, Class, and Power in Twentieth-Century Norfolk, Virginia*. Berkeley: University of California Press, 1991.

Lichtenstein, Nelson, and Howell John Harris, eds. *Industrial Democracy in America: The Ambiguous Promise*. New York: Cambridge University Press, 1993.

Link, Arthur S. *"The Higher Realism of Woodrow Wilson" and Other Essays*. Nashville: Vanderbilt University Press, 1971.

———. *Woodrow Wilson and the Progressive Era, 1910–17*. New York: Harper and Brothers, 1954.

Lippmann, Walter. *Drift and Mastery: An Attempt to Diagnose the Current Unrest*. New York: Mitchell Kennerly, 1914.

Litchfield, Paul. *The Industrial Republic: Reflections of an Industrial Lieutenant*. Cleveland: Corday and Gross, 1946.

Lombardi, John. *Labor's Voice in the Cabinet: The History of the Department of Labor from Its Origin to 1921*. New York: Columbia University Press, 1942.

Lorwin, Lewis L. *The American Federation of Labor: History, Policies, and Prospects.* Washington, D.C.: Brookings Institution, 1933.

———. *The Women's Garment Workers.* New York: Heubsch, 1924.

Lustig, R. Jeffrey. *Corporate Liberalism: The Origins of Modern American Political Theory, 1890–1920.* Berkeley: University of California Press, 1982.

Lyman, George H. *Henry B. Endicott: A Brief Memoir of His Life and Services to the State and Nation.* Boston: n.p., 1921.

McCartan, Patrick. *With De Valera in America.* New York: Brentano, 1939.

McKiven, Henry M., Jr. *Iron and Steel: Class, Race, and Community in Birmingham, Alabama, 1875–1920.* Chapel Hill: University of North Carolina Press, 1995.

Manning, Julie. *Frank P. Walsh and the Irish Question: An American Proposal.* Washington, D.C.: Georgetown University Press, 1989.

Marchand, C. Roland. *The American Peace Movement and Social Reform, 1898–1918.* Princeton: Princeton University Press, 1973.

Marot, Helen. *American Labor Unions.* New York: Henry Holt and Company, 1914.

Maurer, James Hudson. *It Can Be Done.* New York: Rand School Press, 1938.

Merritt, Walter G. *Factory Solidarity or Class Solidarity?* New York: n.p., [1919].

Miliband, Ralph. *Class Power and State Power.* New York: Verso, 1983.

Mills, C. Wright. *The New Men of Power.* New York: Harcourt Brace, 1948.

Mink, Gwendolyn. *Old Labor and New Immigrants in American Political Development: Union, Party, and State, 1875–1920.* Ithaca: Cornell University Press, 1986.

Mitchell, George S. *Textile Unionism in the South.* Chapel Hill: University of North Carolina Press, 1931.

Montgomery, David. *The Fall of the House of Labor: The Workplace, the State, and American Labor Activism, 1865–1925.* New York: Cambridge University Press, 1987.

———. *Workers' Control in America: Studies in the History of Work, Technology, and Labor Struggles.* New York: Cambridge University Press, 1979.

Moody, J. Carroll, and Alice Kessler-Harris, eds. *Perspectives on American Labor History: The Problem of Synthesis.* DeKalb: Northern Illinois University Press, 1989.

Murphy, Paul L. *World War I and the Origin of Civil Liberties in the United States.* New York: Norton, 1979.

Nadworny, Milton. *Scientific Management and the Unions: A Historical Analysis, 1900–1932.* Cambridge: Harvard University Press, 1955.

National Catholic War Council. *Social Reconstruction: A General Review of the Problems and Survey of Remedies.* Washington, D.C.: National Catholic War Council, 1919.

National Industrial Conference Board. *Experience with Works Councils in the United States.* Research Report no. 50. New York: National Industrial Conference Board, 1922.

———. *Problems of Industrial Readjustment in the United States.* Research Report no. 15. Boston: National Industrial Conference Board, 1919.

———. *Strikes in American Industry in Wartime: April 6 to October 6, 1917.* Research Report no. 3. Boston: National Industrial Conference Board, 1918.

———. *Wartime Changes in Wages.* Research Report no. 20. Boston: National Industrial Conference Board, 1919.

———. *A Works Council Manual.* Supplemental Research Report no. 21. Boston: National Industrial Conference Board, 1920.

―――. *Works Councils in the United States.* Research Report no. 21. Boston: National Industrial Conference Board, 1919.

Nelson, Daniel. *American Rubber Workers and Organized Labor, 1900–1941.* Princeton: Princeton University Press, 1988.

―――. *Frederick W. Taylor and the Rise of Scientific Management.* Madison: University of Wisconsin Press, 1980.

―――. *Managers and Workers: Origins of the New Factory System in the United States, 1880–1920.* Madison: University of Wisconsin Press, 1975.

―――, ed. *A Mental Revolution: Scientific Management since Taylor.* Columbus: Ohio State University Press, 1992.

Nestor, Agnes. *Women's Labor Leader: An Autobiography.* Rockford, Ill.: Bellevue Books, 1954.

Noble, David F. *America by Design: Science, Technology, and the Rise of Corporate Capitalism.* New York: Alfred A. Knopf, 1977.

Norrell, Robert J. *James Bowron: The Autobiography of a New South Industrialist.* Chapel Hill: University of North Carolina Press, 1991.

Norwood, Stephen H. *Labor's Flaming Youth: Telephone Operators and Worker Militancy, 1878–1923.* Urbana: University of Illinois Press, 1989.

Orleck, Annelise. *Common Sense and a Little Fire: Women and Working-Class Politics in the United States, 1900–1965.* Chapel Hill: University of North Carolina Press, 1995.

Parrish, Michael E. *Felix Frankfurter and His Times.* New York: Free Press, 1982.

Perlman, Mark. *Democracy in the International Association of Machinists.* New York: John Wiley and Sons, 1962.

―――. *The Machinists: A New Study in American Trade Unionism.* Cambridge: Harvard University Press, 1961.

Perlman, Selig, and Philip Taft. *History of Labor in the United States: Labor Movements, 1896–1932.* New York: Macmillan, 1934.

Person, Carl E. *The Lizard's Trail: A Story of the Illinois Central and Harriman Lines Strike of 1911 to 1915 Inclusive.* Chicago: Lake Publishing, 1918.

Person Defense League. *Corporate Greed and Lawlessness.* Chicago: Person Defense League of Cook County, Illinois, 1915.

Peterson, H. D., and Gilbert Fite. *Opponents of War, 1917–1918.* Seattle: University of Washington Press, 1968.

Plumb, Glenn E., and William G. Roylance. *Industrial Democracy: A Plan for Its Achievement.* New York: B. W. Heubsch, 1923.

Poulantzas, Nicos. *Political Power and Social Classes.* London: New Left Books, 1973.

Powell, Lyman P., ed. *The Social Unrest: Capital, Labor, and the Public in Turmoil.* New York: Review of Reviews, 1919.

Pringle, Henry F. *The Life and Times of William Howard Taft.* 2 vols. New York: Farrar and Rhinehart, 1939.

Pritchard, Paul W. *William B. Wilson: The Evolution of a Central Pennsylvania Mine Union Leader.* Philadelphia: University of Pennsylvania Press, 1944.

Raddock, Maxwell C. *Portrait of an American Labor Leader: William L. Hutcheson.* New York: American Institute of Social Science, 1955.

Radosh, Ronald. *American Labor and United States Foreign Policy.* New York: Random House, 1969.

Ramirez, Bruno. *When Workers Fight: The Politics of Industrial Relations in the Progressive Era, 1896–1916*. Westport, Conn.: Greenwood, 1978.

Reddig, William M. *Tom's Town: Kansas City and the Pendergast Legend*. Philadelphia: J. B. Lippincott, 1947.

Republican Campaign Book. N.p.: Republican National Committee, 1916.

Rodden, Robert G. *The Fighting Machinists: A Century of Struggle*. Washington, D.C.: Kelly Press, 1984.

Rodgers, Daniel T. *The Work Ethic in Industrial America, 1850–1920*. Chicago: University of Chicago Press, 1978.

Ross, William. *A Muted Fury: Populists, Progressives, and Labor Unions Confront the Courts, 1890–1937*. Princeton: Princeton University Press, 1994.

Rudwick, Elliott. *Riot at East St. Louis, July 2, 1917*. Carbondale: Southern Illinois University Press, 1964.

Ryan, Fr. John A. *Industrial Democracy from a Catholic Viewpoint*. Washington, D.C.: Rossi-Bryn, 1925.

———. *Social Reconstruction*. New York: Macmillan, 1920.

Sarasohn, David. *The Party of Reform: Democrats in the Progressive Era*. Jackson: University of Mississippi Press, 1989.

Savage, Marion Dutton. *Industrial Unionism in America*. 1922. Reprint, New York: Arno, 1971.

Schaffer, Ronald. *America in the Great War: The Rise of the War Welfare State*. New York: Oxford University Press, 1991.

Schatz, Ronald. *The Electrical Workers: A History of Labor at General Electric and Westinghouse, 1923–60*. Urbana: University of Illinois Press, 1983.

Schiesl, Martin J. *The Politics of Efficiency: Municipal Administration and Reform in America, 1800–1920*. Berkeley: University of California Press, 1977.

Selekman, Ben M. *Employes' Representation in Steel Works: A Study of the Industrial Representation Plan of the Minnequa Steel Works of the Colorado Fuel and Iron Company*. New York: Russell Sage Foundation, 1924.

Sklar, Martin J. *The Corporate Reconstruction of American Capitalism, 1890–1916: The Market, the Law, and Politics*. New York: Cambridge University Press, 1988.

Skocpol, Theda. *Protecting Soldiers and Mothers: Political Origins of Social Policy in the United States*. Cambridge: Harvard University Press, 1992.

Skowronek, Stephen. *Building a New American State: The Expansion of National Administrative Capacities, 1877–1920*. New York: Cambridge University Press, 1982.

Spero, Sterling D., and Abram L. Harris. *The Black Worker: The Negro and the Labor Movement*. 1931. Reprint, New York: Atheneum, 1974.

Stabile, Donald. *Prophets of Order: The Rise of the New Class and Socialism in America*. Boston: South End, 1984.

Steel, Ronald. *Walter Lippmann and the American Century*. New York: Vintage, 1981.

Steuben, John. *Labor in Wartime*. New York: International Publishers, 1940.

Stevens, Doris. *Jailed for Freedom*. New York: Boni and Liveright, 1920.

Stoddard, William Leavitt. *The Shop Committee: A Handbook for the Employer and Employee*. New York: Macmillan, 1919.

Strum, Phillipa. *Brandeis: Beyond Progressivism*. Lawrence: University of Kansas Press, 1993.

————. *Louis D. Brandeis: Justice for the People*. Cambridge: Harvard University Press, 1984.

Summary of the Southern Industrial Conference on Human Relationships in Industry. Blue Ridge, N.C.: Industrial Department, YMCA, 1920.

Swing, Raymond Gram. *"Good Evening!": A Professional Memoir by Raymond Swing*. New York: Harcourt, Brace, and World, 1964.

Taft, Philip. *The AFL in the Time of Gompers*. New York: Harper and Row, 1957.

Taft, Philip, and Gary Fink. *Organizing Dixie: Alabama Workers in the Industrial Era*. Westport, Conn.: Greenwood, 1981.

Thelen, David. *The New Citizenship: The Origins of Progressivism in Wisconsin*. Columbia: University of Missouri Press, 1972.

Thompson, E. P. *The Making of the English Working Class*. New York: Pantheon, 1964.

————. *Whigs and Hunters: The Origin of the Black Act*. New York: Pantheon, 1975.

Thompson, Fred. *The IWW: Its First Fifty Years*. Chicago: Industrial Workers of the World, 1955.

Tillman, Seth P. *Anglo-American Relations at the Paris Peace Conference of 1919*. Princeton: Princeton University Press, 1961.

Tilly, Charles, and Edward Shorter. *Strikes in France, 1880–1968*. New York: Cambridge University Press, 1972.

Tolliday, Steven, and Jonathan Zeitlin, eds. *Shop Floor Bargaining and the State: Historical and Comparative Perspectives*. New York: Cambridge University Press, 1985.

Tomlins, Christopher. *Labor Law in America: Historical and Critical Essays*. Baltimore: Johns Hopkins University Press, 1992.

————. *The State and the Unions: Labor Relations, Law, and the Organized Labor Movement in America, 1880–1960*. New York: Cambridge University Press, 1985.

Trachtenberg, Alexander, ed. *American Socialists and the War*. New York: Rand School, 1917.

Trotter, Joe William, Jr. *Coal, Class, and Color: Blacks in Southern West Virginia, 1915–23*. Urbana: University of Illinois Press, 1990.

Troy, Leo. *Trade Union Membership, 1897–1962*. New York: Columbia University Press, 1965.

Urofsky, Melvyn I. *Big Steel and the Wilson Administration: A Study in Business-Government Relations*. Columbus: Ohio State University Press, 1969.

Urofsky, Melvyn, and David W. Levy, eds. *"Half Brother, Half Son": The Letters of Louis D. Brandeis to Felix Frankfurter*. Norman: University of Oklahoma Press, 1991.

Vaughn, Steven. *Holding Fast the Inner Lines: Democracy, Nationalism, and the Committee on Public Information*. Chapel Hill: University of North Carolina Press, 1980.

Walling, William English. *American Labor and American Democracy*. 2 vols. New York: Harper, 1926.

————. *Progressivism—and After*. New York: Macmillan, 1914.

Ward, Harry F. *The Labor Movement from the Standpoint of Religious Values*. New York: Sturgis and Walton, 1917.

Warne, Frank J. *The Workers at War*. New York: Century, 1920.

Watkins, Gordon S. *Labor Problems and Labor Administration in the United States during the War*. Urbana: University of Illinois Press, 1920.

Weinstein, James. *The Corporate Ideal in the Liberal State, 1900–1918*. Boston: Beacon, 1968.

———. *The Decline of Socialism in America*. New York: Monthly Review Press, 1967.

Westbrook, Robert B. *John Dewey and American Democracy*. Ithaca: Cornell University Press, 1991.

Wiebe, Robert. *The Search for Order, 1877–1920*. New York: Hill and Wang, 1967.

Wildman, Edward, ed. *Reconstructing America: The Next Big Job*. Boston: Page, 1919.

Wolfe, A. B. *Works Committees and Joint Industrial Councils*. Philadelphia: U.S. Shipping Board, Emergency Fleet Corporation, Industrial Relations Division, 1919.

Wolman, Leo. *The Growth of American Trade Unions, 1880–1923*. 1924. Reprint, New York: Arno, 1975.

Zahavi, Gerald. *Workers, Managers, and Welfare Capitalism: The Shoeworkers and Tanners of Endicott Johnson, 1890–1950*. Urbana: University of Illinois Press, 1988.

Zieger, Robert H. *Rebuilding the Pulp and Paper Workers Union, 1933–41*. Knoxville: University of Tennessee Press, 1984.

———. *Republicans and Labor, 1919–1929*. Lexington: University of Kentucky Press, 1969.

ARTICLES, ESSAYS, AND PAMPHLETS

Aborn, Willard G., and William L. Shafer. "Representative Shop Committees: America's Industrial Roundtable." *Industrial Management* 58 (July 1919): 29–32.

Alford, Leon P. "An Industrial Achievement of the War." *Industrial Management* 55 (February 1918): 97–100.

Arnesen, Eric. "Crusades against Crisis: A View from the United States on the 'Rank-and-File' Critique and Other Catalogues of Labor History's Alleged Ills." *International Review of Social History* 35, 1 (1990): 106–27.

———. "Following the Color Line of Labor: Black Workers and the Labor Movement before 1930." *Radical History Review* 55 (Winter 1993): 53–87.

Barton, Dante. "Frank P. Walsh." *Harper's Weekly*, September 27, 1913, 24.

———. "The Pittsburgh Strikes." *International Socialist Review* 16 (June 1916): 715.

Best, Gary Dean. "President Wilson's Second Industrial Conference." *Labor History* 16 (Fall 1985): 505–20.

Bing, Alexander M. "The Nerve Center of War Production." *Survey Graphic*, June 22, 1918, 345–47.

———. "The Work of the Wage-Adjustment Boards." *Journal of Political Economy* 27 (June 1919): 421–56.

Block, Fred. "Beyond Corporate Liberalism." *Social Problems* 24 (February 1977): 352–60.

———. "The Ruling Class Does Not Rule: Notes on the Marxist Theory of the State." *Socialist Revolution* 32 (March–April 1977): 6–28.

Brandeis, Louis D. "Efficiency by Consent." *Industrial Management* 55 (February 1918): 108–9.

Breen, William J. "Administrative Politics and Labor Policy in the First World War: The U.S. Employment Service and the Seattle Labor Market Experiment." *Business History Review* 61 (Winter 1987): 583–605.

—————. "The Labor Market, the Reform Impetus, and the Great War: The Reorganization of the City-State Employment Exchanges in Ohio, 1914–1918." *Labor History* 29 (Fall 1988): 475–97.

—————. "The Mobilization of Skilled Labor in World War I: 'Voluntarism,' the U.S. Public Service Reserve, and the Department of Labor, 1917–1918." *Labor History* 32 (Spring 1991): 253–72.

Brody, David. "The Old Labor History and the New." *Labor History* 20 (Winter 1979): 111–26.

—————. "Workers and Work in America: The New Labor History." In *Ordinary People and Everyday Life*, edited by James B. Gardner and George R. Adams. Nashville: University of Kentucky Press, 1983.

—————. "Workplace Contractualism in Comparative Perspective." In *Industrial Democracy in America: The Ambiguous Promise*, edited by Nelson Lichtenstein and Howell John Harris. New York: Cambridge University Press, 1993.

Bruere, Robert W. "Copper Camp Patriotism." *Nation*, February 21, 1918, 202–3.

—————. "West Lynn." *Survey*, April 1, 1926, 21–27, 49.

Bucki, Cecelia. "Dilution and Craft Tradition: Bridgeport, Connecticut Munitions Workers, 1915–1919." *Social Science History* 4 (Winter 1980): 105–24.

Buhle, Paul. "Italian-American Radicals and Labor in Rhode Island." *Radical History Review* 17 (Spring 1978): 121–52.

Burgess, Kathy. "Organized Production and Unorganized Labor: Management Strategy and Labor Activism at the Link-Belt Company, 1900–1940." In *A Mental Revolution: Scientific Management since Taylor*, edited by Daniel Nelson. Columbus: Ohio State University Press, 1992.

Chenery, William L. "Packington Steps Forward." *Survey*, April 13, 1918, 35–38.

—————. "The Proposed Industrial Plan: A Symposium of Criticism." *Survey*, January 17, 1920, 424–32.

Cheney, E. P. "The Trend toward Industrial Democracy." *Annals of the American Academy of Political and Social Science* 90 (July 1920): 1–9.

Cooke, Morris L. *An All-American Basis for Industry*. Philadelphia: n.p., [1919].

—————. "Who Is Boss in Your Shop? Individual vs. Group Leadership, and Their Relation to Consent and the Ideals of Democracy." *Bulletin of the Taylor Society* 3 (August 1917): 3–10.

Cowdrick, E. S. "What Are We Going to Do with the Boss?" *Industrial Management* 60 (September 1920): 194–96.

Creel, George. "Why Industrial War." *Collier's*, October 18, 1913, 5–6, 31–33.

Cronin, James E. "The 'Rank and File' and the Social History of the Working Class." *International Review of Social History* 34 (1989): 78–88.

Crowther, Samuel. "The Fetish of Industrial Democracy." *World's Work* 39 (November 1919): 23–27.

Cuff, Robert D. "Herbert Hoover, the Ideology of Voluntarism, and War Organization during the Great War." *Journal of American History* 64 (September 1977): 358–72.

—————. "Organizing for the War: Canada and the U.S. during World War I." In *Historical Papers*, 141–53. Ottawa: Canadian Historical Association, 1969.

—————. "The Politics of Labor Administration during World War I." *Labor History* 21 (Fall 1980): 546–69.

———. "We Band of Brothers: Woodrow Wilson's War Managers." *Canadian Review of American Studies* 5 (Fall 1974): 135–48.

Davis, Alan F. "The Flowering of Progressivism." In *The Impact of World War I*, edited by Arthur S. Link. New York: Harper and Row, 1969.

———. "Welfare, Reform, and World War I." *American Quarterly* 19 (Fall 1967): 516–33.

Derber, Milton. "Thoughts on the Historical Study of Industrial Democracy." *Labor History* 14 (Fall 1973): 599–611.

Douglas, Paul H. "Shop Committees: Substitutes for, or Supplement to, Trade-Unions?" *Journal of Political Economy* 29 (February 1921): 89–107.

Drury, Horace B. "Democracy as a Factor in Industrial Efficiency." *Annals of the American Academy of Political and Social Science* 65 (May 1916): 15–26.

Dubofsky, Melvyn. "Abortive Reform: The Wilson Administration and Organized Labor, 1913–1920." In *Work, Community, and Power: The Experience of Labor in Europe and America, 1900–1925*, edited by James E. Cronin and Carmen Sirianni. Philadelphia: Temple University Press, 1983.

———. "Workers' Movements in North America, 1873–1920." In *Labor in the World Social Structure: Based on the First USSR Colloquium on World Labor and Social Change, 1980*, edited by Immanuel Wallerstein, pp. 22–43. Beverly Hills: Sage, 1983.

Eaton, Walter Pritchard. "The Pittsfield Rebellion." *New Republic*, December 28, 1918, 245–46.

Fink, Leon. "American Labor History." In *The New American History*, edited by Eric Foner. Philadelphia: Temple University Press, 1990.

———. "Labor, Liberty, and the Law: Trades Unionism and the Problem of the American Constitutional Order." *Journal of American History* 74 (December 1987): 904–25.

Fitch, John A. "The Commons Report." *Survey*, January 1, 1916, 8.

———. "Peace at Home: The Double Danger of Strikes and Coercion." *Survey*, May 26, 1917, 189–91.

Forcey, Charles B. "Walter Weyl and the Class War." In *American Radicals*, edited by Harvey Goldberg. New York: Monthly Review Press, 1957.

Frank, Dana. "Housewives, Socialists, and the Politics of Food." *Feminist Studies* 11 (Summer 1985): 255–86.

Fraser, Steve. "Dress Rehearsal for the New Deal: Shop-Floor Insurgents, Political Elites, and Industrial Democracy in the Amalgamated Clothing Workers." In *Working-Class America: Essays on Labor, Community, and American Society*, edited by Michael H. Frisch and Daniel J. Walkowitz. Urbana: University of Illinois Press, 1983.

Frieburger, William. "War Prosperity and Hunger: The New York Food Riots of 1917." *Labor History* 25 (Spring 1984): 217–39.

Fones-Wolf, Ken. "Religion and Trade Union Politics in the United States, 1880–1920." *International Labor and Working-Class History* 34 (Fall 1988): 39–55.

Gibbs, Christopher C. "The Lead Belt Riot and World War One." *Missouri Historical Review* 71 (July 1977): 396–418.

Gompers, Samuel. "American Labor's Position in Peace or War." *American Federationist* 24 (April 1917): 269–81.

———. "Economic Organization and the Eight-Hour Day." *American Federationist* 22 (January 1915): 43–46.

————. "Labor History in the Making—The 1915 AF of L Convention." *American Federationist* 23 (January 1916): 17–38.

————. "Labor's Participation in Government." *American Federationist* 23 (February 1916): 105–10.

————. "Labor's Political Campaign: Its Causes and Progress—Labor's Duty." *American Federationist* 19 (October 1912): 801–4.

————. "Labor's Political Program." *American Federationist* 19 (October 1912): 804–8.

Greene, Julie. "'The Strike at the Ballot Box': The American Federation of Labor's Entrance into Election Politics, 1906–1909." *Labor History* 32 (Spring 1991): 165–92.

Gregg, Richard B. "The National War Labor Board." *Harvard Law Review* 33 (November 1919): 38–69.

Gudza, Henry P. "Industrial Democracy: Made in the U.S.A." *Monthly Labor Review* 107 (May 1984): 26–33.

————. "Social Experiment in the Labor Department: The Division of Negro Economics." *Public Historian* 4 (Fall 1982): 7–37.

Harris, Howell John. "Industrial Democracy and Liberal Capitalism." In *Industrial Democracy in America: The Ambiguous Legacy*, edited by Nelson Lichtenstein and Howell John Harris. New York: Cambridge University Press, 1993.

Hendrickson, Kenneth E. "The Pro-War Socialists, the Social Democratic League, and the Ill-Fated Drive for Industrial Democracy in America." *Labor History* 11 (Summer 1970): 304–22.

Hopkins, Ernest M. "Democracy and Industry." *Annals of the American Academy of Political and Social Science* 65 (May 1916): 57–67.

Hurvitz, Haggai. "Ideology and Industrial Conflict: President Wilson's First Industrial Conference of October, 1919." *Labor History* 18 (Fall 1977): 509–24.

Jensen, Richard. "The Causes and Cures of Unemployment in the Great Depression." *Journal of Interdisciplinary History* 19 (Spring 1989): 553–83.

Kazin, Michael. "The Limits of the Workplace." *Labor History* 30 (Winter 1989): 110–13.

————. "Struggling with Class Struggle: Marxism and the Search for a Synthesis of U.S. Labor History." *Labor History* 28 (Fall 1987): 497–514.

Kreuger, Thomas A. "American Labor Historiography, Old and New: A Review Essay." *Journal of Social History* 4 (Spring 1971): 277–85.

Laidler, Harry W. "Washington and the Coming Reconstruction." *Intercollegiate Socialist* 7 (December–January 1918–19): 8–11.

Laughlin, J. Laurence. "Business and Democracy." *Atlantic Monthly* 116 (July 1915): 89–98.

Leeds, Morris E. "Democratic Organization in the Leeds and Northrup Company, Inc." *Annals of the American Academy of Political and Social Science* 90 (July 1920): 13–17.

Letwin, Daniel. "Interracial Unionism, Gender, and 'Social Equality' in the Alabama Coal Fields, 1878–1908." *Journal of Southern History* 61 (August 1995): 519–54.

Leuchtenberg, William E. "The New Deal and the Analogue of War." In *Change and Continuity in Twentieth-Century America*, edited by John Braeman et al. Columbus: Ohio State University Press, 1968.

————. "The Pertinence of Political History: Reflections on the Significance of the State in America." *Journal of American History* 73 (December 1986): 585–600.

Lichtenstein, Nelson, and Howell John Harris. "A Century of Industrial Democracy in

America." In *Industrial Democracy in America: The Ambiguous Promise*, edited by Nelson Lichtenstein and Howell John Harris. New York: Cambridge University Press, 1993.

Lippmann, Walter. "Mr. Rockefeller on the Stand." *New Republic*, January 30, 1915, 12–13.

McCartin, Joseph A. "An American Feeling: Workers, Managers, and the Struggle over Industrial Democracy during the World War I Era." In *Industrial Democracy in America: The Ambiguous Promise*, edited by Nelson Lichtenstein and Howell John Harris. New York: Cambridge University Press, 1993.

———. "Using the 'Gun Act': Federal Regulation and the Politics of the Strike Threat during World War I." *Labor History* 33 (Fall 1992): 519–28.

MacNamara, M. J. "Shop Committees and the Foreman." *Industrial Management* 60 (August 1920): 102–3.

Malone, Dudley Field. "The Birth of the Third Party." *Freedman*, July 28, 1920, 467–68.

Manly, Basil. "America Is Passing the Danger Point." *Reconstruction* 1 (June 1919): 161–64.

Meeker, Royal. "Industrial Democracy." *Annals of the American Academy of Political and Social Science* 90 (July 1920): 18–21.

Meiksins, Peter. "The 'Revolt of the Engineers' Reconsidered." *Technology and Culture* 29 (April 1988): 219–46.

Miliband, Ralph. "Poulantzas and the Capitalist State." *New Left Review* 82 (1973): 83–92.

Moderwell, Hiram K. "The National War Labor Board." In *The American Labor Yearbook, 1919–1920*, edited by Alexander Trachtenberg. New York: Rand School, 1920.

Montgomery, David. "Industrial Democracy or Democracy in Industry?: The Theory and Practice of the Labor Movement, 1870–1925." In *Industrial Democracy in America: The Ambiguous Legacy*, edited by Nelson Lichtenstein and Howell John Harris. New York: Cambridge University Press, 1993.

———. "New Tendencies in Union Struggles and Strategies in Europe and the United States, 1916–1922." In *Work, Community, and Power: The Experience of Labor in Europe and America, 1900–1925*, edited by James E. Cronin and Carmen Sirianni. Philadelphia: Temple University Press, 1983.

———. "To Study the People." *Labor History* 21 (Fall 1980): 485–512.

Nelson, Daniel. "The Company Union Movement, 1900–1937: A Re-examination." *Business History Review* 56 (Autumn 1982): 335–57.

Norrell, Robert J. "Caste in Steel: Jim Crow Careers in Birmingham, Alabama." *Journal of American History* 73 (December 1986): 671–72.

Northrup, Herbert R. "The Negro and Unionism in the Birmingham, Alabama Iron and Steel Industry." *Southern Economic Journal* 10 (July 1943): 27–40.

O'Brien, Ruth. "Business Unionism versus Responsible Unionism: Common Law Confusion, the American State, and the Formation of Pre–New Deal Labor Policy." *Law and Social Inquiry* 18 (Spring 1993): 255–96.

Post, Louis F. "A Carpet-Bagger in South Carolina." *Journal of Negro History* 10 (January 1925): 10–79.

Potter, Zenas. "War Boom Towns I—Bridgeport." *Survey Graphic*, December 4, 1915, 346–52.

Price, Richard. "'What's in a Name?': Workplace History and 'Rank and Filism.'" *International Review of Social History* 34, 1 (1989): 62–77.

Reid, Alistair. "Dilution, Trade Unionism, and the State in Britain during the First World War." In *Shop Floor Bargaining and the State: Historical and Comparative Perspectives*, edited by Steven Tolliday and Jonathan Zeitlin. New York: Cambridge University Press, 1985.

Richberg, Donald. "Democratization of Industry." *New Republic*, May 12, 1917, 49–51.

Rogin, Michael. "The Political Functions of an Antipolitical Doctrine." *Industrial and Labor Relations Review* 14 (July 1962): 521–35.

Salvatore, Nick. "Some Thoughts on Class and Citizenship in America in the Late Nineteenth Century." In *In the Shadow of the Statue of Liberty: Immigrants, Workers, and Citizens in the American Republic, 1880–1920*, edited by Marianne Debouzy. Urbana: University of Illinois Press, 1992.

Sandburg, Carl. "The Walsh Report." *International Socialist Review* 16 (October 1915): 198–201.

Shanley, Timothy D. "Mr. Frank Walsh's Career." *America*, July 5, 1918, 329–31.

Shapiro, Stanley. "The Great War and Reform: Liberals and Labor, 1917–19." *Labor History* 12 (Summer 1971): 323–44.

Sklar, Martin J. "Woodrow Wilson and the Political Economy of Modern U.S. Liberalism." In *A New History of Leviathan: Essays on the Rise of the American Corporate State*, edited by Ronald Radosh and Murray N. Rothbard. New York: Dutton, 1972.

Skocpol, Theda. "Political Response to Capitalist Crisis: Neomarxist Theories of the State and the Case of the New Deal." *Politics and Society* 10, 2 (1980): 155–201.

Smith, John S. "Organized Labor and the Government in the Wilson Era." *Labor History* 3 (Fall 1962): 265–86.

Smyth, William Henry. "'Technocracy': Ways and Means to Gain Industrial Democracy." *Industrial Management* 57 (March 1919): 208–12.

Steffens, Lincoln. "An Experiment in Good Will." *Survey*, December 31, 1911, 1434–36.

Stoddard, William L. "A Little Shop Committee System." *Survey*, May 17, 1919, 284–85.

———. "Toward an Era of Democratic Control." *Survey*, May 10, 1919, 253–54.

Straw, Richard A. "The Collapse of Biracial Unionism: The Alabama Coal Strike of 1908." *Alabama Historical Quarterly* 37 (Spring 1975): 92–114.

Swing, Raymond. "The Blame for Lawrence." *Nation*, April 26, 1919.

Tead, Ordway. "Labor and Reconstruction." *Yale Law Review* 7 (April 1918): 529–42.

Todd, Laurence. "The National War Labor Board and the Labor Movement." In *The American Labor Yearbook, 1919–1920*, edited by Alexander Trachtenberg. New York: Rand School, 1920.

Tyson, Francis. "Labor Swallows the Forty-Eighters." *Survey*, August 2, 1920, 587–88.

Valentine, Robert G. "The Progressive Relation between Efficiency and Consent." *Bulletin of the Taylor Society* 2 (January 1916): 7–11.

Valentine, Robert G., and Ordway Tead. "Work and Pay: A Suggestion for Representative Government in Industry." *Quarterly Journal of Economics* 31 (February 1917): 241–58.

Walsh, Frank P. "Lawson and Liberty." *International Socialist Review* 16 (August 1915): 87.

———. "My Impressions of the Witnesses and Their Testimony." *Solidarity*, July 31, 1915, 6.

———. "Perilous Philanthropy." *Independent*, August 23, 1915, 262–64.

———. "Wilson Administration's Turn against Labor." *Reconstruction* 2 (January 1920): 4–6.

———. "Windows Alight in Connaught." *America*, June 7, 1919, 225–27.

Wehle, Louis B. "The Adjustment of Labor Disputes Incident to Production for War in the United States." *Quarterly Journal of Economics* 32 (November 1917): 122–41.

———. "War Labor Policies and Their Outcome in Peace." *Quarterly Journal of Economics* 33 (February 1919): 321–43.

West, George P. "The Progress of American Labor." *Nation*, June 29, 1918, 753–55.

———. "Will Labor Lead?" *Nation*, April 19, 1919, 600–601.

Wilson, William B. *The Democratic Party and Labor*. Address to the Democratic Women's Luncheon Club of Philadelphia, 1924, and published as pamphlet (in Library of Congress).

Wood, Charles H. "Great Co-operative Machine That Grew Out of the War—Shall It Be Junked?" *Reconstruction* 1 (January 1919): 8.

Zeitlin, Jonathan. "'Rank and Filism' and Labour History: A Rejoinder to Price and Cronin." *International Review of Social History* 34, 1 (1989): 89–102.

———. "'Rank and Filism' in British Labour History: A Critique." *International Review of Social History* 34, 1 (1989): 42–61.

———. "Shop Floor Bargaining and the State: A Contradictory Relationship." In *Shop Floor Bargaining and the State: Historical and Comparative Perspectives*, edited by Steven Tolliday and Jonathan Zeitlin. New York: Cambridge University Press, 1985.

Zieger, Robert H. "Herbert Hoover, the Wage-Earner, and the 'New Economic System,' 1919–29." In *Herbert Hoover as Secretary of Commerce: Studies in New Era Thought and Practice*, edited by Ellis W. Hawley. Iowa City: University of Iowa Press, 1974.

DISSERTATIONS AND THESES

Boemeke, Manfred F. "The Wilson Administration, Organized Labor, and the Colorado Coal Strike, 1913–1914." Ph.D. diss., Princeton University, 1983.

Brooks, Thomas R. R. "The United Textile Workers of America." Ph.D. diss., Yale University, 1934.

Bucki, Cecelia Frances. "The Pursuit of Political Power: Class, Ethnicity, and Municipal Politics in Interwar Bridgeport, 1915–36." Ph.D. diss., University of Pittsburgh, 1991.

Bustard, Bruce I. "The Human Factor: Labor Administration and Industrial Manpower Mobilization during World War I." Ph.D. diss., University of Iowa, 1984.

Davis, Colin J. "Bitter Storm: The 1922 Railroad Shopmen's Strike." Ph.D. diss., State University of New York at Binghamton, 1988.

Ernst, Daniel. "The Lawyers and the Labor Trust: A History of the American Anti-Boycott Association, 1902–1919." Ph.D. diss., Princeton University, 1989.

Greene, Julie M. "The Strike at the Ballot Box: Politics and Partisanship in the American Federation of Labor, 1881–1916." Ph.D. diss., Yale University, 1990.

Huginnie, Andrea Yvette. "'Strikitos': Race, Class, and Work in the Arizona Copper Industry, 1880–1920." Ph.D. diss., Yale University, 1991.

Hurvitz, Haggai. "The Meaning of Industrial Conflict in Some Ideologies of the Early 1920's: The AFL, Organized Employers, and Herbert Hoover." Ph.D. diss., Columbia University, 1971.

Jones, Dallas Lee. "The Wilson Administration and Organized Labor, 1912–1919." Ph.D. diss., Cornell University, 1954.

Keiser, John Howard. "John Fitzpatrick and Progressive Unionism, 1915–1925." Ph.D. diss., Northwestern University, 1965.

Krivy, Leonard P. "American Organized Labor and the First World War, 1917–1918: A History of Labor Problems and the Development of a Government War Labor Program." Ph.D. diss., New York University, 1954.

McCartin, Joseph A. "Labor's Great War: Workers, Unions, and the State, 1916–20." Ph.D. diss., State University of New York at Binghamton, 1990.

McKillen, Elizabeth. "Chicago Workers and the Struggle to Democratize Diplomacy: 1914–24." Ph.D. diss., Northwestern University, 1988.

Makarewicz, Joseph T. "The Impact of World War I on Pennsylvania Politics with Emphasis on the Election of 1920." Ph.D. diss., University of Pittsburgh, 1972.

Meehan, Sr. Maria Eucharia. "Frank P. Walsh and the American Labor Movement." Ph.D. diss., New York University, 1962.

Rapport, Leonard. "The United States Commission on Industrial Relations: An Episode of the Progressive Era." Master's thesis, George Washington University, 1957.

Shenk, Gerald Edwin. " 'Work or Fight': Selective Service and Manhood in the Progressive Era." Ph.D. diss., University of California, San Diego, 1992.

Snell, William Robert. "The Ku Klux Klan in Jefferson County, Alabama, 1916–1930." Master's thesis, Samford University, 1967.

INDEX

Commission on Industrial Relations. *See* United States Commission on Industrial Relations

Commission on the Future of Worker-Management Relations, 226–27

Committee of Forty-Eight, 197, 198

Committee on Industrial Relations, 30–37, 56, 70; and World War I, 66–67

Committee on Public Information, 67, 84, 194

Commons, John R., 5, 13, 26, 29, 51, 67

Company unionism, 9, 28, 53–54, 164, 212–13, 214–20, 223; workers' responses to, 218–20

Conboy, Sara, 166

Congress, U.S., 81, 127, 194; and war labor agencies, 84–85, 186–87; Sixty-sixth, 184, 189

Congress of Industrial Organizations, 224, 225

Conner, Valerie Jean, 5, 177

Cooke, Morris L., 53, 76, 78, 208, 210

Corley, Robert, 95, 118

Coulthand, Alfred, 224

Council of National Defense, 57–58, 76, 85, 124, 188, 204; Advisory Committee on Labor of, 73, 242 (n. 21)

Cowdrick, E. S., 200, 223

Cox, James M., 197

Crawford, George G., 150

Creel, George, 26, 27, 67

Croly, Herbert, 27

Crosson, Anna, 114

Crough, Edward, 151, 155

Crough, Margaret, 45

Crowder, Enoch, 85

Crowther, Samuel, 200, 201

Cuff, Robert D., 5

Curry, Elizabeth, 112, 142, 143

Dailey, John, 117

Daly, A. M., 149

Daniels, Josephus, 74, 84, 174

Darrow, Clarence, 70

Davison, E. C., 208

Debs, Eugene V., 14, 29

De Guilo, Clara, 113

Delano, Frederick A., 19

Democratic Party: and Labor, 3, 16–17, 223–24; southern wing, 16–17, 25–26, 184–86; and Frank Walsh, 21, 25–26, 35–37, 194, 196–98

Demuth, Leopold, 215

Dennison, Henry S., 53, 76

Densmore, John, 16, 75

Deselets, Phil, 144–45

Deskilling. *See* Dilution

Dewey, John, 75, 118

Dickman, Howard, 214

Dickson, William B., 164

Dilution, 46–48, 58, 59, 96–97, 137

District 55, IAM: background of, 61–62; 1917–18 strikes of, 136–38, 139–42; reliance on government, 146; dissolution of, 207–8. *See* Lavit, Samuel

Division of Negro Economics, 75, 115

Dodge, John, 81

Doyle, J. Edwin, 45

Draft, military, 41, 85, 238 (n. 9)

Drew, Walter, 89, 201

Drury, Horace B., 53, 54

Dual unionism, 55, 133–34, 182

Dubofsky, Melvyn, 5

Duncan, W. D., 126

Dunlop, John T., 226

Dunlop Commission, 226–27

Dunne, Edward F., 196

Easley, Ralph, 73

Eastern Steel Company, 161, 178

Efficiency engineering. *See* Scientific management; Taylor, Frederick Winslow; Taylor Society

Eidlitz, Otto, 138; award in Bridgeport case, 139, 140, 142, 144, 145, 147

Eight-Hour Workday Conference, 182, 183

Elections (*see also* Labor politics):
—congressional: of 1918, 144–45, 184–85
—local: 62, 135–36
—presidential: of 1912, 14–15; of 1916, 34–37; of 1920, 197–98

Haydu, Jeffrey, 253 (n. 58)

Hayes, Frank J., 86, 125

Haynes, George E., 115. *See also* Division of Negro Economics

Haywood, Bill, 12, 29, 32–33, 68, 71

Henderson, Amos, 107

Hewitt, Fred, 141

Hillman, Sidney, 55, 66, 81, 82, 188, 204, 206, 224

Hitchman Coal and Coke Co. v. Mitchell et al., 84, 97

Hobsbawm, Eric, 2

Hobson, John A., 174

Holmes, Oliver Wendell, 52

Hood, Frederic C., 215

Hoover, Herbert C., 193, 201, 213

Hopkins, Ernest M., 38, 39, 49, 76–77

Hours of labor: and NWLB principles, 88; strikes over, 128, 150, 153, 182–83; in steel, 164. *See also* Adamson Act

House, Edward, 196

Howatt, Alex, 33, 125

Howe, Frederick, 30, 31, 198

Hoxie, Robert, 51, 52, 113

Hughes, Charles Evans, 34, 36

Hughes, William, 19

Hunkins, Hazel, 91, 112, 142

Hunter, Robert, 18, 67

Hutcheson, Bill, 18, 55, 57, 73–74, 86

Immigrant workers, 46; and industrial citizenship, 108–11, 165; at GE, 129, 130, 181; in steel, 156, 157, 165; in textiles, 166–67, 168, 169–70

Industrial conferences (of 1919): first conference, 191–93; second conference, 193–94

Industrial democracy, 1–2, 4, 7, 8–10, 38–40; ambiguous meaning of, 7, 119, 201; and USCIR final report, 12–14; early advocates of, 27; and Frank Walsh, 28–29, 194, 220, 223; and 1916 election, 34–37; and scientific management, 51–54; conflict within labor movement concerning, 58, 119, 202–3, 205; and wartime patriotism, 105–7; and middle-

class black leaders, 154; endorsed by Woodrow Wilson, 189; and postwar industrial conferences, 191; and 1920 election, 198; postwar discussions of, 199–202, 208–9; and postwar industrial relations, 208–13, 222–23; postwar co-optation by employers, 215–20; and Wagner Act, 225, 226, 227; and Dunlop Commission, 227

Industrial Democracy, Party of, 210

Industrial Management, 210

Industrial relations, 10, 11, 26, 51, 91, 222, 223. *See also* Industrial democracy: and postwar industrial relations

Industrial Relations Association of America, 210

Industrial unionism, 148–49, 166–67, 171–72. *See also* Electrical Manufacturing Industry Labor Federation; National Committee for Organizing Iron and Steel Workers; Stockyards Labor Council

Industrial Workers of the World, 3, 6, 12, 39, 55, 65, 206, 208, 217; government repression of, 68–70, 174

Inflation, 40–41

International Association of Machinists: and women workers, 48–49, 143–44; and rank-and-file dissidents, 59–60, 140–41; and wartime labor militancy, 59–63, 95, 122–23; at GE, 130; postwar conflicts within, 206–8. *See also* District 55, IAM; Johnston, William H.; Lavit, Samuel

International Brotherhood of Electrical Workers, 130, 131

International Harvester, 219–20

International Ladies' Garment Workers' Union, 55

International Longshoremen's Association, 63

International Photo-Engravers' Union, 183, 200

International Union of Mine, Mill, and Smelter Workers, 46, 151–55, 224

Interracial unionism, 117–18, 123, 127–28,

Litchfield, Paul, 216, 217
Little, Frank, 68
Living wage, 83, 88, 111
Lloyd, Henry Demarest, 27
Lloyd, W. J., 100
London Times, 196
Loree, Leonor F., 86
Los Angeles Times, 13, 18, 33, 94
Ludlow massacre, 24, 28
Lunn, George R., 62

McAdoo, William G., 20, 75, 116, 117, 179, 197
McCabe, Hugh, 143
McCarthy, Charles, 26, 29
McCleester, Paul, 164
McCumber, Porter J., 49, 84
McKiven, Henry, 254 (n. 7)
McMahon, Thomas, 169
McNamara, James, 18
McNamara, John J., 18
McWane, J. R., 215
Macy, V. Everit, 180, 191
Manly, Basil, 26, 87, 184, 195, 197, 203, 220, 224; and USCIR final report, 12, 29, 223; and CIR, 30, 32, 36; and NWLB, 91, 176–77; and postwar industrial conferences, 191, 193
Manufacturers' Association of Southern Connecticut, 97, 103
Marot, Helen, 27, 30, 31, 70, 72
Marsh, G. P., 78
Marshall, Leon C., 1, 4, 8, 76, 85, 210, 220, 224
Martin, Thomas S., 26
Masses, 13, 21, 31, 32
Mass unionism, 148–49, 166–67, 171–72
Maurer, James H., 55, 68
Meeker, Royal, 209
Merritt, Walter G., 138, 215
Michael, C. Edwin, 86
Midvale Steel Company, 161, 164, 178
Minimum wage rates, 111
Mink, Gwendolyn, 5
Mitchell, John, 124
Mixon, M. H., 154

Montgomery, David, 6–7, 206, 233 (n. 19)
Mooney, Tom, 71, 80, 133, 203
Morrison, Frank, 67, 73, 102; and Birmingham steel strike, 151–52, 156
Moton, R. R., 151
Munitions manufacturing. *See* Lake Torpedo; Remington Arms; Union Metallic Cartridge

Nation, 180
National Adjustment Commission, 75
National Association of Manufacturers, 19, 81, 177, 186, 188
National Civic Federation, 59
National Committee for Organizing Iron and Steel Workers, 148; origins of, 160–61; lack of support by craft unions, 162; slow growth of, 162, 166; and 1919 steel strike, 196; and postwar opposition to shop committees, 205
National Enameling and Stamping Company, 178
National Erectors' Association, 89
National Founders Association, 184
National Industrial Conference Board, 86, 103, 216, 217, 219
National Labor Defense Council, 70–73
National Lumber Manufacturers' Association, 185
National Metal Trades Association, 59
National War Labor Board, 65; principles of, 88; formation of, 89–90; as a voluntary agency, 90; staff, 90–91, 182; and Western Union, 92, 179; impact on labor militancy, 94–96, 213; shop committees of, 99–104, 217; and women workers, 111, 113–14; and black workers, 115, 116–18; and General Electric, 128–32, 134, 136, 180–81; employer resistance to, 134, 145, 168–70, 171, 175–76, 184; and Bridgeport munitions workers, 137–45; and Birmingham steel strike, 152–56; and Bethlehem Steel workers, 158–60, 162–66, 177–78; and Rhode Island textile workers, 168, 170–71; postwar paralysis of, 176–83; and silk workers, 182–83;

political attacks on, 184, 186; denied funding to finish its work, 187

National Woman's Party, 91, 143

National Women's Trade Union League, 27, 30, 112, 114

Nealey, William, 180, 181

Nearing, Scott, 67

Neill, Charles P., 17

Nestor, Agnes, 30

New Deal, 4, 11, 224, 225

Newdick, Edwin, 156

New Majority, 197

New Republic, 12, 24, 26, 27, 29, 30, 136, 188

New York Call, 35, 147

New York Herald, 13

New York Tribune, 185

Nockels, Ed, 55, 72, 83, 151

Obenauer, Marie L., 91, 113

O'Connell, Edwin, 61

O'Connell, James, 19, 30, 31, 59, 74, 152

O'Connor, T. V., 63

Ogburn, William F., 210

Olander, Victor, 86, 122, 155, 156, 175

Older, Fremont, 70

One Big Union, 206, 208

Ordnance Department, U.S. Army, 76, 159

Osborne, Loyall A., 86, 122, 138

Palmer, A. Mitchell, 191

Parmer, Mabel, 114

Patriotism: wartime, 104–5; link to union-ism, 104–6

Penalty clause, 125–26

Pennsylvania Labor Herald, 177

People's Council of America for Democracy and Peace, 67, 68

Perkins, G. W., 205

Perlman, Selig, 26, 202

Pershing, John J., 221–22

Person, Carl E., 60, 206

Peterson, John F., 100, 131, 132, 134, 199

Piece rates, 44–45, 129, 158

Piez, Charles E., 76, 79, 116

Pinchot, Amos, 30, 31, 66, 67, 197

Pittsfield Metal Trades Council, 129

Plumb, Glen, 222

Plumb Plan, 203, 212

Pollack Steel, 162

Post, Louis F., 16, 85

President's Industrial Conferences, 191–94

President's Mediation Commission, 77–80, 82–83, 99

Progressives, 4, 5, 10, 13, 14, 19, 27, 28, 30, 35, 37, 52, 65, 66, 67, 70, 76, 189, 197–98, 224

Propaganda: wartime, 10, 104

Protocol of Peace, 51–52

Purdum, William, 133

Radicals, 13, 24, 28, 30, 31, 32, 33, 36, 58–62, 81–82, 119, 121, 133, 183, 186, 203. *See also* Industrial Workers of the World

Railroad brotherhoods, 34

Railroad Labor Board, 187

Rameau, P. Colfax, 154

Rand School, 120

Rankin, Mildred, 112, 115, 142, 143

Ransey, Erskine, 127

Reconstruction, 187–91, 204–5, 222

Reconstruction, 172, 187, 196

Redbaiting, 158, 183, 186

Reed, James A., 17, 20, 35

Reed, John, 70, 72

Reed, Verner Z., 78

Reese, W. Murray, 154

Reich, Robert, 226

Remington Arms, 45, 61, 104, 137

Republican Party, 14, 19, 25, 34, 36, 84; and Sixty-sixth Congress, 184, 189

Rice, H. H., 159

Rice, Richard H., 214

Richmond, Charles A., 201, 202

Rickert, Thomas, 86, 167, 182

Right to organize, 28, 29, 65, 79, 84, 88, 92, 95, 97, 98, 106, 117, 122, 157, 166, 167, 191–93

Ripley, William Z., 82, 107

Riviere, Horace, 169–70, 224
Robbins, Margaret Drier, 114
Rockefeller, John D, Jr., 26, 28–29, 191, 220; and company unionism, 28, 54, 212, 214–15
Rogers, William C., 137
Roosevelt, Franklin D., 52, 85, 224
Roosevelt, Theodore, 14
Rose, Vernon, 91, 142, 143
Rosenwald, Julius, 193
Ross, I., 118
Russell, Charles Edward, 67
Russell, Isaac, 142
Russian Revolution, 186
Ryan, John A., 201
Ryan, Michael J., 196

St. John, Vincent, 24, 32
Sandburg, Carl, 29, 70, 71
Santora, Grace, 108
Santora, Rose, 108
Savage, Tom, 122, 159
Schenectady Citizen, 36
Schenectady Metal Trades Council, 62–63, 128–29, 133
Scientific management, 3, 10, 50–53, 59, 211. *See also* Taylor, Frederick Winslow; Taylor Society
Scollin, Patrick, 142, 144
Scott, Emmet J., 151
Seamen's Act, 3, 34
Seattle general strike, 195, 201
Seattle Union Record, 13, 33
Shafer, William L., 209
Shannon, Joe, 21
Sherman, John Y., 85
Shipbuilding Labor Adjustment Board, 74, 80, 101, 115, 187
Shop committees: wartime origins of, 78–80; and collective bargaining, 78–80, 99, 176; spread of, 99; impact on unions, 99–104, 202; employer resistance to, 100–101, 103–4, 130–31, 145; union control of, 100–102; and labor militancy, 102–4; and women workers, 112, 143; at GE, 129, 130–31; in muni-

tions plants, 140, 142–44; and industrial unionism, 147–48; in steel mills, 159–60, 163, 164–66; labor's opposition to, 204, 205; transformed into company unions, 205, 214–15, 218–19; lasting influence of, 225
Silk manufacturing, 182–83
Sinclair, Upton, 67
Sklar, Martin J., 4
Skocpol, Theda, 5
Skowronek, Stephen, 4
Slichter, Sumner, 26
Smith, Hoke, 17, 25–26, 29
Smith and Wesson Company, 1, 97, 138, 141, 162, 163, 178
Smyth, William Henry, 209
"Social equality," 123, 127
Socialist Labor Party, 61
Socialist Party, 3, 65, 67
Southern Democrats, 16–17, 25–26, 184–86
Spangler, J. L., 78
Spargo, John, 67
Special Conference Committee, 215
Standard Oil, 54, 213, 214
Starr, James, 183
Steffens, Lincoln, 18, 70
Stevens, Doris, 22, 235 (n. 26)
Stimson, Henry L., 201
Stockyards Labor Council, 82, 131, 146
Stoddard, William L., 133, 209
Stokes, Rose Pastor, 67
Stone, Warren, 212
Stone, William J., 21
Strikes: wartime, 1–2, 39, 42, 63, 94; munitions, 60–61, 137–38, 139–41, 207; coal mining, 124; electrical manufacturing, 128, 130–32; sit-down, 132; steel, 150–56, 161, 196; iron ore mining, 153, 155; textile, 167–70, 182; New York harbor, 179–80
Strong, Benjamin, 190
Sullivan, Olive, 91
Supreme Court, U.S., 84, 97
Survey, 18, 29, 80, 86
Sweeney, Charles P., 204

Swing, Raymond, 91, 115, 152, 153, 154, 155, 156, 162
Swope, Gerard, 187, 223

Taft, Philip, 202
Taft, William H., 14, 15, 191; and USCIR, 15, 19; and WLCB, 86–88; and Frank Walsh, 87–88; and NWLB staff, 91; and Western Union case, 92–93; and black workers, 116–17, 155; and electrical workers, 122, 129; and Bridgeport case, 138, 141; and Alabama ore miners, 153; and postwar NWLB, 176, 177–79; proposes postwar collective bargaining, 188; and Felix Frankfurter, 189
Taylor, Frederick Winslow, 3, 50, 59, 76, 208
Taylor, James A., 145
Taylorism. *See* Scientific management
Taylor Society, 50, 223
Tead, Ordway, 52
Teluchik, Fred, 108
Tennessee Coal and Iron Company, 104, 149
Textile manufacturing, 166–71
Thompson, E. P., 4
Tighe, Michael, 161, 172
Tillman, Ben, 17
Tobin, Daniel, 58
Todd, Laurence, 120, 136, 146
Tomlins, Christopher, 5
Trotter, Joe W., Jr., 154
Tumulty, Joseph, 25, 35, 41, 141, 189, 190, 196

Underwood Tariff, 25
Union Metallic Cartridge, 143
Union recognition: demands for, 43, 58, 153. *See also* Right to organize
United Garment Workers, 55, 82, 167
United Mine Workers, 100, 103, 106, 123–28, 152, 196, 206
United States Commission on Industrial Relations, 9, 190; final report of, 12–14, 29, 226–27; origins of, 18–19; investigations of, 24–30; and scientific manage-

ment, 51; and Birmingham steelworkers, 149
United States Employment Service, 75, 187
United States Fuel Administration, 75, 99, 100–101
United States Housing Corporation, 75
United States Railroad Administration, 75, 98, 179–80; and black workers, 116–17
United States Shipping Board, 118
United States Steel, 149, 150, 164
United Textile Workers, 63, 166–71, 182–83

Valentine, Robert G., 51, 52–53, 76, 208
Van Dervoort, William H., 86
Van Kleeck, Mary, 113, 218
Van Lear, Thomas, 68
Ver Vane, Elsie, 143–44
Violence: antiunion, 42, 154–55

Wagner Act, 225
Walker, John H., 78
Wallace, Paul, 147–48, 186
Walling, William English, 39, 67
Walsh, Frank P.: and industrial democracy, 8, 28–29, 194, 220, 223; and USCIR final report, 12–14, 29, 226–27; and Woodrow Wilson, 19–20, 35–36, 195–97; named USCIR head, 20–21; background of, 21–24; and black workers, 22, 115; and Doris Stevens, 22, 235 (n. 26); and USCIR hearings, 25–27; and CIR, 30–37; and Samuel Gompers, 33; support for World War I, 66–68; and AALD, 68, 194; and NLDC, 70–73; and Chicago stockyards, 83; and WLCB, 86–88; and William H. Taft, 87–88; and NWLB staff, 90–91; and Western Union case, 92–93; and women workers, 113, 195; and Pittsfield decision, 122; and General Electric, 129; and NWLB employer members, 134, 175; and Bridgeport case, 138, 139, 141; and steelworkers, 149, 152, 155–56, 159, 161; and Alabama ore miners, 153; and tex-